Tim,

Great memor
of the Oak a
it contains

Regards,
Dave

STAND AND BE COUNTED

First published 2013

ISBN 978-0-9576187-0-1

Published by Blackhall Publishing, Berwick upon Tweed

Sales Contact: Sales@blackhallpublishing.co.uk

Printed by Martins the Printers, Berwick upon Tweed
www.martins-the-printers.com

STAND AND BE COUNTED

THE STORY OF

DAVID WAKEFIELD

"The only thing necessary for the triumph of evil is for good men to do nothing."
Edmund Burke (philosopher)

CHAPTERS

THANKS TO

Gloria Oatridge – for some early typing

Ken Greig - for reading and providing feedback

Joy Cogle - for reading and providing feedback

Billy Wilson - for encouragement

Janice Hodgson - for editing and proof-reading

Kyle Dickson - for creating the book cover

Yvonne Davies – for insisting I read the book before publishing

Foreword

You will read what motivated me to write these memoires of my fifty seven years and possibly wonder why it doesn't contain many more funny stories. One of my oldest and dearest friends asked that question when he reviewed this book. "You should put more in" Steve said, "You have loads of them".

Well I haven't added anything; it would have been too long. I shall maybe write a collection of funny stories later in life. For the time being a 137,000 word condensed account of my life seems plenty.

Most names have been changed to protect the innocent and guilty!

David Wakefield
January 2013

PART ONE

Introduction

So there I stood, poised with brick in hand, bank branch office window before me, to commit criminal damage at a moment that was possibly to be the lowest point in my life. I was in despair.

I had tried, unsuccessfully, to get myself arrested for most of that Saturday evening in February 2005. Surely this would do the trick! I had trudged into Coventry and through its centre for fully 5 miles, from pub to pub, mobile in hand. I, had had a few drinks on my travels, but I was clear of mind; I was on a mission. I was simply attention seeking.

I had made a succession of 999 calls protesting the disgraceful treatment administered to me, my family and my wife by the NHS, primarily the staff of Solihull Hospital. I told my story to bar staff and shop keepers and asked them to call the police and report my behaviour. For the first time in my life I was demonstrating! I had been radicalised!

I hadn't any particular loathing for the victim bank. My loathing is shared equally amongst them all, and it was years before the banking crisis that was to create so many problems for me. I even felt a little amused, that this bank, possibly the most often damaged in town, should have the misfortune of yet again being on the receiving end.

The brick hit the window with some considerable force but failed to penetrate. I can testify to the significant quality of the toughened glass used by this bank but could never recommend you join them.

I turned to the gobsmacked onlookers (it was quite a busy street) and crossed the road to the chip shop. I walked in nonchalantly; Mr Cool Calm and Collected. "Please don't be alarmed. I'm not going to cause any trouble." there was stunned silence and a simple nod of acknowledgement from behind the counter. "Did you see me do that?" I asked. Another nod of acknowledgement. "Good" I said. "I won't be buying any chips today but would you be kind enough to telephone the police and tell them that Dave Wakefield has just smashed it?"

I explained why I'd smashed the window, and with a nod of approval I'm sure that yet another call was made to the police control room. Indeed, if man can live on sympathy alone I had secured a long life that day. Unfortunately sympathy is of little use to anyone. The story that I told unfolds in a later chapter amid a series of major disasters that plagued me after my return to 'Old Blighty' in 2003, following nearly 50 years of a life blessed with rich and varied experiences that I will treasure to my dying day.

That the years that followed were disastrous is simply life itself. All experiences pleasant and unpleasant can make you a wiser and better person. You are the person created by the sum total of your experiences in life. Fortunately I have become well balanced as a result of my experiences, others are not so lucky.

I explained to the shopkeeper that my wife had been suddenly and inexplicably discharged from the secure ward of Solihull hospital on the Thursday before, having been compulsorily admitted 3 weeks earlier, and was quite clearly in as bad a state as when she went in.

The shop keeper had promised to call the police, as had several barmaids in several pubs earlier that day. I'm still not sure just how desperately keen I was on being arrested. I wanted publicity and attention. An appearance in magistrates' court would help. On the other hand I was ashamed, and didn't want to go quite that far. I had already embarrassed myself by crying on the shoulder of a good friend in the middle of a crowded bar.

What I was really doing was venting my anger and airing my fears. Not for the first time, nobody was listening to me. My wife was mentally ill, being ill treated, and it seemed those upon whom we place our trust, and rely upon, were happy to see me and my family suffer the same fate. My faith in those I needed to help me had been destroyed.

The outcome of this dark tale is told later. There was worse to come. It wasn't the worst day of my life after all! My return to Britain in 2003, after over 5 years living in the Far East pursuing a dynamic professional career, had been a culture shock. The country had, in my view, become a far worse place than it had been in the mid-nineties. There was so much evidence of greed, selfishness and moral bankruptcy. The events surrounding my wife's mental illness were just a part of a series of cruel events that had an overwhelmingly traumatic effect on me.

I was such a strong person. In many ways I still am. It is therefore difficult to understand how a well balanced professional man, with fully 18 letters after his name, a Rotarian, a mediator, holder of the Duke of Edinburgh Gold Award, a certificate for bravery, a man of good character and repute, a peaceful, friendly, jovial and law-abiding citizen, can fall apart the way I did that February night? But I did, and although I can never say I was lucky to have had the experience, I am a better person for having had it. I look on it as a beneficial experience, one that helps me to understand others and see life from yet another perspective. Those perspectives are reflected in the interesting years bound into the pages of this book.

Chapter One
Defining Years

I was born when I was around about ten and will probably die before I'm forty as a result of worry, a blow to the head or fits of laughter. Either way, it will be with a smile on my face; after all, it's important to keep up appearances. I have been called 'Smiler' throughout my life, by relative strangers and friends alike; not so much a nickname as an occasional address in reference to my demeanour.

My parents moved to Allesley Park, Coventry, from across the city where they had lived with my grandparents for five years. My Mum and Dad told me that when they moved in they literally had just a couple of orange boxes to sit on. Getting a mortgage was not easy and a substantial amount had to be saved first. I spent the first eighteen years of my life living in this suburban house with my parents.

I lived with my sister, Linda, five years my senior and our dog, Minka a Labrador cross, who was a gentle faithful dog and ever present in my life until his death from old age when I was about seventeen. Minka would go everywhere with me. Minka lived until fifteen years of age and for those years enjoyed a full life producing two litters of pups to the delight of family and friends. Other pets came and went during the fifteen years of Minka's life; hamsters, mice, gerbils, love birds, stick insects, budgies, guinea pigs, goldfish and tortoises they all passed through our front door only to disappear under skirting boards, bury themselves in the garden, fly off or die. I'll leave you to match the animal with the fate. I made money out of selling stick insects. It was possibly my first entrepreneurial venture. They were a lucrative line for exchange or sale at school and I bred them well- it wasn't difficult. Steve Parker, my friend and neighbour, was terrified of tortoises and wouldn't come in the garden if they were out of their pen. I still rib him about that.

The children in the area were quite a close knit bunch of kids but were relatively naive as we were quite privileged living on a good quality housing estate. We were not living in ghettos in the worst part of the city. We were probably sheltered from the harsh realities of living in inner city slums. Those that moved in to our locality must have been reasonably successful, stable and financially responsible to have afforded to live in their own homes on a new development. Mortgages were not easy to obtain without a deposit saved over a year or two. The population was financially more responsible in those days, but more importantly so were the banks. The people that moved on to the estate were working class people that would represent the new emerging middle classes; teachers, bus drivers engineers and council workers. Coventry workers were the best paid in the country in the 1960's and even better paid than many Londoners. The fire brigade strike started because Coventry firemen were earning more than their London colleagues!

Being born a baby boomer (between 1945 and 1965) was a lucky touch of fate. I was born into a decade when children still played outside, walked the fields and climbed trees. I was a teenager in the 1960's, a decade of liberation, fine music, the birth of free speech and women.

As a child I did what 1960's kids did; egg collecting, train spotting, car number plate recognition, playing marbles, games of war, going to the circus each Easter, the fairground, the carnival and the 'works' pantomime. I spent time helping the train signalman in the Canley Hill signal box; saw the last journey of the Flying Scotsman with assembled crowds on bridges and embankments. I walked the fields and played games.

Schools were being revolutionised with comprehensive schools coming into being. Finding a job after school was easy, you could do just about anything you wanted, and good remuneration was provided for in the workplace; if you fancied another job there were plenty available. You could just walk into another job the same day – particularly in Coventry – the boom city and the place to be in the 1960's and early 1970's. Factories (yes, we once had them) were thriving and the city had an abundance of them. I was a mid-term baby boomer, born in a boom town; the Detroit of Britain.

I was given free cod liver oil, milk and orange juice when I went to school. I was born into a post war era when people of Britain expected and demanded that 'to the victors the spoils' (even my favourite comic was called 'The Victor').

The country couldn't afford it but they made it their business to deliver it. The Yanks demanded to be paid for their contribution to the war effort and that threatened to derail our country but the Cold War meant that they needed our country as a forward base so they lent us some more money to fund our appetite for the good times. Our NHS was created on the money that was borrowed. We finished paying them back in the mid 1990's. The bad management of this country has continued ever since.

In the 1950's the primary school playground activities were great fun and it being the decade after the Second World War, war games were common place although I am sure they weren't playing them in Germany. At playtime we would walk around the playground shouting, "Who wants a game of war? Who wants a game of war?" All the

6

children that wanted to be in my army followed me around behind me whilst a challenger, an opponent, would be chanting the same appeal, and he would gather a rival army. The opposing forces would meet on the playground or playing field and would simply charge at each other, on mass and on the command, each of us making our own version of gunfire noises and presenting our own dramatic versions of being shot and killed. It was pure theatre.

The opposing forces would meet amidst the sound of machine gun fire from the mouth. There might be an order to retreat for dramatic effect. The entire episode was an art form. Everyone was living the experience of some film hero or dramatic event. It was undoubtedly a celebration of our victory over 'the Hun' and we were all dreaming. We were the victors and we were glamorising the realities of war because the country was doing the same through television and film. We were glorying in our triumph and I'm not sure that is countenanced these days.

These games of war extended into evenings and weekends at home, in the streets, in the fields and the alleyways (sounds like a Churchill speech doesn't it) but on those occasions we were armed with either a piece of wood DIY fashioned into a 'Tommy' gun or a ready made toy gun. We battled from morning to night. The dramatic simulated deaths were impressive but for those of us who liked to win, any suggestion that "you're dead" would produce the response, "no I'm just wounded" or "no it's just a flesh wound". We had great fun and when 'The Man from U.N.C.L.E. became popular on TV (as a result of the Cold War) we soon became spies instead of soldiers.

'Collecting' was also a popular kiddie pursuit, car registration numbers, and train numbers for free, or picture cards purchased with a packet of bubble gum or a packet of cigarettes or cigars. A set would comprise thirty or more cards. My favourite was the American Civil War cards that only now I understand are major collectors' items. They were educational as well as being suitably graphic, gruesome and well made. They were really interesting. In the playground we would swap cards in order to get the full set quickly. The playground was full of marble games, small chucks being hollowed out all over the place. Marbles and ball bearings were swapped and won. Conker games were every boy's pastime in the autumn. It's sad that they are banned in playgrounds now because of health and safety nonsense. What has happened to the Country?

My generation of baby boomers were lucky enough to live through a period when, as a youngster, outdoor activities like climbing trees, catching fish, and wandering off unsupervised were normal. I was a birds egg collector; a hobby that was quite common at the time, but is obviously, and quite rightly, unacceptable now.

In the formative years, my infant and junior school days, much of my leisure time had been spent in the 'entry', the access road to garages at the back of the houses, and the field beyond. I remember I would return home from school and be the first home on many an occasions. My sister would follow shortly afterwards from Barkers Butts. Minka, the dog, would have been waiting in the kitchen. We would go across the fields or in the entry. Minka lived to a pretty good age because of all the exercise he got.

Beyond the fields was Allesley Village and on the approach to the village were some orchards from where we would 'scrump' apples. Derek Blakemore still complains about the occasion when he was up the apple tree when the owner (the vicar) arrived and we all ran off and left him up the tree. Alan and I don't quite remember it that way. We simply didn't hang about. No point in us all getting caught was there!

I also recall the day that I was playing with other kids around the foot of a giant oak tree next to a deep hollow that we called 'the dip'. We tied rope from the tree branch and swung across the 'dip'. It was a popular meeting place for kids around the area. One of the older kids, Mick M I think, was climbing the tree with an air rifle. The gun was loaded and accidentally discharged a pellet into my leg. I ran off back home, crying and I remember the police being called out. I hope Mick didn't get in too much trouble for that.

As kids, and by that I mean to the age of maybe 13, we played football and cricket in the entry. Steve Parker, my friend from next door, was a brilliant footballer and just about everything involving a ball. He had trials for Tottenham for soccer, and he played for the county at tennis, cricket and football. The little short arse was even a 100 metres runner at county level. He was particularly gifted.

As it happens I wasn't particularly confident on the sports field and I never played enough to improve. I was good with an air rifle and darts, and not bad at table tennis. My Dad hung a dart board on the garden wall, made a table tennis table, and purchased me a match quality air rifle from a friend at work. At twelve years of age I was a very good marksman.

There were no drugs and the perception was that there was little threat from child molesters, although judging by the number of Priests that are now recognised as having messed about with kids, it is just as likely that it was simply not discussed. It was a taboo subject. Anyway, in hindsight, it feels as though they were relatively safe years. In the 1950's and early 1960's I would walk down to the brook (stream) or the pond in the cow fields and catch newts, tiny frogs or tadpoles. We would collect birds' eggs, something that I would never do now, but that was commonplace. There was a 'connect' with nature even though I lived in the city.

I would be taken to the pub garden on a dry summer's day, or if it was raining sit with a bottle of pop and crisps in the car while my parents were in the pub. I would collect empty bottles and make money by handing them in at the pub 'outdoor' or off-licence, getting something like three pence a bottle. Most pubs had an 'outdoor'.

With all the problems we have these days with litter and the problems of recycling it, it would be very 'green' and responsible to reintroduce 'deposits' on bottles and cans. The big companies can hand back 20 or 30 pence on each empty can and bottle presented to them and dispose of them themselves. Good idea?

Occasionally, but not too often because I felt guilty, I would collect the bottles from the bottle crates stacked at the side of the pub, and take them back into the pub to claim the money on the bottle. Uncharacteristically naughty and obviously dishonest, but it was a trick that a friend taught me. I thought it cheeky and a little dishonest but didn't see it as theft; it was simply viewed as lucrative fun. The only thing I ever contemplated stealing was a toy soldier from the counter of the local shop. I was terrified I would be seen, and never actually lifted it off the counter.

According to my Mum (and her friends said it as well) I was a kind, well behaved little boy, always polite, well turned out and shy in the presence of adults. That's the way most kids were at my school in those days. When adults were talking we were 'seen and not heard' - generally well disciplined kids. According to the school report books my mum kept, I was a well behaved kid, well thought of by teachers and other kids alike.

1964 was a lucky year for me, a defining year. I failed my eleven plus exams but got a place in a comprehensive school by the skin of my teeth. Don't let anyone tell you that the eleven plus examination was good for children. Better streaming takes place the way the Germans do it; aptitude based at fourteen years of age I believe. This is good for the child and good for the nation.

I was offered a place at the new Woodlands Comprehensive School by good fortune, otherwise I would have joined some equally able friends at Barkers Butts Secondary School and without any realistic chance of taking 'O' Levels, and destined to take CSE Examinations having already been branded a failure at just eleven years of age. These days, the 'O' Level and the CSE examinations are of course merged.

9

I remember my parents taking me to one side one night and explaining that I had not passed my eleven plus but that an opportunity had arisen and asked if I wanted to go to Woodlands Comprehensive School, an all boys' school. It was a serious discussion. I had apparently been a narrow failure and I was told that I would have to work hard if I was to make a choice to go to this school. I was excited by the prospect. The impression I got was that my parents would be making sacrifices in sending me to this school. Woodlands had a strict uniform code and for a growing lad this meant an annual expense. My friends, Richard Lyons, Barry Bennett, and others who had failed the eleven plus, did not get this opportunity.

When I reflect on my achievements at Woodlands compared with say Richard Lyons, my achievements were colossal. Richard was an equally intelligent and capable boy and achieved high CSE results at Barkers, but had no real chance of sitting an 'O' Level, let alone passing one. I left school with five 'O' Levels and two CSE top grades. I quickly realised that 'streaming' of this kind, at that early stage of life was wrong. It was a handicap to development.

Woodlands School in Coventry was one of the first comprehensive schools in the entire country. It was also regarded as one of the best in the country. The pupils were required to adhere to a strict uniform code and were always smartly turned out. Good discipline was a pre-requisite to remaining in the school.

The school comprised children from the immediate vicinity and children in the locality who had passed their eleven plus beyond that immediate locality. I lived about three miles, and a combined walk and bus ride away. The mix of pupils ensured a level of equality of a socialist kind. Woodlands School had a reputation for producing good sportsman including some of international renown, including my old friend Dave Moorcroft of world record holder fame in the 5000 metres. England rugby players, Grewcock and Neil Back and more recently Tom Wood, were also educated there. Woodlands School provided opportunities for all, and most of the kids took that opportunity to some extent or another. There will have been relative failures, but no system is perfect. Parents were proud of Woodlands School and the kids were proud to say they attended it.

The school had a strict headmaster, Mr. Thompson, and it operated a house system. I was in McLaughlin house and the housemaster was a Mr. Burdett. I have very fond memories of Mr. Burdett. He was a hard, yet warm natured man who treated his children as a family in the true spirit of the house system.

10

That first journey to school was terrifying. I was so very apprehensive and felt very new and out of place as I got out of my Dad's car on that first day, sporting a brand new uniform, cap and satchel containing brand new sports gear, swimming trunks and sandwiches. My Mum wanted to make sure I had everything! I remember my Mum being proud and nervous as she waved goodbye at the door. I hated the fuss and I hated looking 'new' and conspicuous.

I was particularly good at chess and would play Mr. Burdett perhaps a couple of times a month in the centre of the house room. At no time did the other kids take the piss or call me a creep. Such was the attitude of the kids and the respect that Mr. Burdett had.

I eventually captained the school chess team from the third form onward, and at that stage I was probably one of the best, if not the best, young player in the city. But my interest tailed off and although I retained the captaincy others were playing more, and getting better. I was starting to lose. I stopped playing when I left school.

I had a real, albeit reluctant, appetite for studying. This is what Woodlands School and my parents did to me. I knew that I wanted to achieve and I believe that I achieved to the best of my ability at that point in time. I did not want to let my parents down, and this was my driving force, although it placed great pressure on me. Years later, when in Hong Kong, I understood why I was reading of young Chinese committing suicide around examination time each school year.

I can't really say that I enjoyed my schooling that much, because one of the weaknesses of Woodlands was that if you did not show a sporting bent, then the sports department, in particular Mr Jack P, a P.E. teacher with a particular interest in rugby, would have no interest in you whatever. Unless, that is, you were able to demonstrate natural ability that would fit you into the school team. It may have placed the school in the limelight as it won competition after competition and it may have produced international rugby players, but it stank of a closed shop, elitist, public school style attitude. There was no interest in helping those that needed guidance and confidence. We never had a single lesson concerning the rules of the game. This was perhaps the only, yet significant, weakness I saw in the school. I wanted desperately to participate and compete in sport. I wanted to maximize my potential. The school was never going to do this. I never told anyone of my concern.

I was disappointed because my father would have been proud of a rugby playing son. I wanted to be sporty, and I particularly wanted to play rugby; it was the family sport. My Dad and my uncle were keen rugby players (Uncle Eric was international standard and

11

played for Coventry before becoming chairman and President). Both were rugby fans. Not playing rugby is one of the biggest disappointments in my life. As I have already stated, I blame Jack P to some extent for that, god rest his soul (I understand that he eventually hung himself).

Jack, for whatever reason, didn't attempt to teach anyone the rules of rugby and although I showed lots of willing on the rugby pitch, I never really got to grips with the forward pass rule. I was never told it! And therefore every time I received the ball and passed it the game was held up. Had I played rugby I believe I would have made a decent player.

As it happened, I did get a chance to play for the school reserve football team although the same principle applied there, not much coaching. I did find a niche in areas where others were not much interested. I played hockey. I played hockey with Steve Baker, who was the number two in the chess team. He excelled at the game of hockey and played for Warwickshire and I think for England at one time. I became quite accomplished and on the hockey pitch I grew in confidence and became a good player.

I also showed a tiny interest in cross country running. Unlike some others, I did not stop in Tile Hill Woods to meet the girls from the neighbouring school, or hide and smoke a fag until the second lap. I actually played the game and ran.

I was quite 'arty'. I am not sure to what extent my artistic talents were hereditary but my Granddad Horton would sit me on his knee for what seemed like hours. He would sketch anything from an apple to an ornament. Through the eyes of an infant he seemed very good. I sketched a lot before I entered my teens.

As it happened my artistic bent was never developed and, like chess and darts, I lost interest or perhaps didn't have the time. In fact I was developing a habit of becoming bored with things. I was disinclined to get involved in any specific interest in any depth.

My brother-in-law taught at Woodlands School for many years from shortly after my departure, and he eventually left having seen a decline in standards following the departure of, the headmaster, Mr. Thompson. The place was apparently never quite the same again.

It was during my school years that I learnt how naive I was, and how sheltered my upbringing had been. There were some rough and tough lads at Woodlands. I had no idea what 'fuck' meant and I had never had sex or heard of 'fingering'. I doubt any of those that teased me did either, but I was still uncomfortable and embarrassed.

I have said in the past that my father never really took any interest in me, and he was certainly not the man to give a sex education; in point of fact he was simply typical of his generation. If he had tried to give me a sex education I'd have been very embarrassed anyway. God forbid that my Mum even thought of trying.

My mother was mainly responsible for bringing me up, and she took charge of all those important parental duties that are discharged in the formative years. Her work was fairly comprehensive and effective. It stood me in good stead for adulthood, but she never approached the taboo subject of sex. I don't think this was unusual in those days. They taught biology at Woodlands; that was the sum total of my sex education. No surprise then that I found myself sitting in the 'Paris' cinema watching Swedish porn films!

As you will know, it is at about eleven or twelve years of age that you decide you want to be your own person and become an argumentative obnoxious adolescent teenage arsehole – but only toward your parents. That said I listened to my parents. I just didn't want them to know it. I wanted to demonstrate to my parents that I had my own mind and I would make it up; nobody else! On the quiet, I would usually follow their advice even if they never knew it. As parents we tend to think our children never listen to us, but they usually do.

Even now I can still be a little naïve, certainly stubborn, but the sheltered life I had led was lost in my teens. Losing the shelter is a tricky business rather like merging with motorway traffic from the slip road, it can be problematic. I certainly felt lonely and vulnerable at times. A typically insecure teenager I guess.

Peer pressure was immense and difficult to resist. I used a filter system and tried to distinguish the good direction from the bad but developed a knack for avoiding conflict with those that I disapproved of or disliked. I learnt that enemies find you quickly enough, and therefore there is no need to go out of your way to seek them out and make them. Kill people with kindness.

If the hand of friendship was extended I never rejected it. I embraced those I disliked, distrusted and disapproved of. My father once told me to keep my enemies close to me. It was a fantastic piece of advice and possibly the best I have ever received. And do you know doing things that way helps you find some good in everyone.

13

One of the people who had a significant influence on my life was Alan Bainbridge our next door neighbour. Alan had a great interest in music and history and his wonderful wife Norma, was a lively, fun loving extrovert with an acting bent. At thirteen or fourteen I would babysit for their two sons, Martin and Carl. That sounds ridiculous now, given that they were just a few years younger than me, but just a few years difference in age, in your early years is very significant. I still regard Martin and Carl as great friends although I seldom see them.

Through Alan, I developed an interest in history and most importantly an appreciation of all kinds of music, albeit, yet again to no great depth. Alan was good with children, a warm hearted man who eventually went on to fulfil his ambition and become a teacher. He lost his wife but at nearly 80 years of age, and looking sixty, he has clearly moved on, and is still active watching with a passion, Warwickshire cricket and Coventry City Football Club. The Bainbridge's are a wonderful family.

My interest in Coventry City Football Club started as the result of a promise made by a friend of the family, Jim Dobbin, who was well connected to Coventry City Football Club in the early 1960's. He was a tailor and made their kit.

He told me that the Coventry goalkeeper, Bob Wesson, would come round and have tea with me at my home. I never forget my disappointment that the promise was never kept. But Jim did take me to my first game and as I recall it was a game between City and Colchester that City won 1-0 to win promotion from the third division to the second division under Jimmy Hill. I remember Jimmy Hill leading the 'sky blue song' in front of adoring fans massed on the pitch. We had won the Third Division Championship.

One of Jim's sons was mentally handicapped, he retained the mind of a ten year old through until his death aged about fifty. I enjoyed Drew's company. He had a brilliant brain and a cracking memory; his love was trains and Coventry City Football Club, and went to all games sitting in a special seat on the touchline. I miss Drew, we were good friends.

It must have been around that time that my friend Richard Lyons and I took my 'trolley' to the City team captain's house in the brand new neighbouring street. He, George Curtis, came out of the garden from the side of the house and autographed the trolley. I was tickled pink! I simply couldn't imagine the captain of a big football club, and Coventry were at the time, ever doing anything like that these days. They certainly wouldn't be living on Pangfield Park in an average three bed roomed house in a Coventry suburb!

14

The first time that I went alone to watch a game was when I got on a bus to cross the city and see the City beat Wolves 3-1 to pretty well clinch promotion to the First Division in 1967. I remember queuing at the turnstiles with Derek and Alan Blakemore (the twins); from 11.00am for a 3.00pm kick off. We got into the ground early, with sandwiches and rattles at the ready. We were right at the front, and eventually ended up at the side of the pitch amongst around 54,000 fans. There were fans watching from the floodlight towers, the roof of the stands and the boundary walls. It was chocker. That was a memorable day.

The following year Coventry was in the First Division, now the Premier League, and playing the likes of Manchester United and Liverpool, week in and week out. It was 1967. I would attend home games with my friends and became a regular. That first year I travelled to many away grounds with Mr and Mrs Patrice; neighbours. One of the most memorable of those early excursions was to Old Trafford, the football Mecca, where Coventry were thumped 4-0 on a cold Wednesday night. The result didn't matter. It was a fabulous atmosphere and the clubs first taste of the very best in British football.

There were other memorable away trips but mid way through the following season the Patrice's decided they would stop going to the away games. It was the year that football hooliganism really started. Wearing club colours became dangerous, and the friendly family fun days were over. It was 1968 and, perhaps coincidentally, the year of Enoch Powell's 'Rivers of Blood' speech. The skin head had arrived on the scene.

I continued to attend matches home and away, becoming a season ticket holder at home and travelling away by coach or train until I passed my driving test at seventeen, the year after I left school. I was on coaches that returned without a window left; stoned. I have lain, spread-eagled on the floor, as the bricks passed through. I have sat on a train as fans ripped the carriages apart and been on a 'soccer special', which sat on the railway track in 'no mans 'land', between Coventry and Wolverhampton, for several hours, waiting, while the train was boarded by police. No great surprise to see good peaceful fans terrorised into staying at home!

The irony is that I stood amongst the chanting fans because it was exciting. How I avoided being involved in a fight I will never know.

The only occasion I was attacked was when I was walking away from the City ground back to the town centre bus. A West Ham fan hit me on the head from behind with a bugle! I just kept walking and ignored him. He tried to push me into an alley but I

15

wouldn't be pushed. He cleared off. The hooligan culture was described by Desmond Morris, the naturalist, as tribal. Not everyone in the tribe is a hooligan, but there was a danger of being found guilty by association. I was lucky I suppose.

During my childhood years I found nothing that I could take a deep and prolonged interest in. It's part of my character. To this day I generally know a little about everything, and enjoy just about everything, but not to any great depth. I might be called a 'jack of all trades - master of none'. I get bored and move on to the next subject. I knew then that I needed a rich and varied lifestyle, and a rich and varied work activity.

I hadn't had to work during my school years as long as I performed at school and did my homework. My pocket money was generous. If my Dad encouraged me to do any work I always used the old chestnut, effective with my mother that work would get in the way of my progress at school. The decision to leave school changed things.

At sixteen I left school with some good 'O' Levels for my considerable effort. I was pleased for myself and my parents. They were proud of me. That summer I found some work before starting my chosen career.

My first job was at my Dad's Aunt's Wimpy Bar in the centre of Coventry. Aunt Gladys and Derek owned two franchised shops in Coventry and one in Nuneaton. I worked through most of the summer, firstly washing up, but graduated to waiting at tables, taking orders from the take-away counter, and then the actual business of cooking stuff. It was hard work but great fun.

To tell you the truth I was really quite good behind the griddle. Orders came in by the dozen and each meal had to be prepared quickly, properly and despatched to the table. It was the first time I had really understood and coped with multi-tasking. I must therefore question whether or not 'multi tasking' really is the preserve of women. I think it's a fallacy. After all, top chefs and arguably the best waiters are largely men.

After I had been working at the Wimpy for a few weeks, I got my friend Barry Bennett a job and we worked through into the early autumn. We had some great laughs at the Wimpy Bar and worked hard.

One day we had an interesting visit from plain clothed police officers. All the staff had to put their hands under an ultra violet light and low and behold it appeared that Scotty, the Restaurant Manager, had been putting his fingers in the till. Bye, bye Scotty – off to the 'fairy dell'.

One thing I remember about that experience was how frightened I was about putting my hands under the ultra-violet light. It's amazing how, even though you know darned well that you are not a thief, you feel quite guilty and worried. It crosses your mind that you could have touched something that was subsequently stolen, and "Bobs Your Uncle" you come under suspicion.

I needed the work at the Wimpy Bar not simply because I wanted the money but because, quite frankly, I had never had to work before, and I needed to get up to speed with the realities of it.

Aunt Gladys and her husband Derek went on to abandon the Wimpy franchise and patented their own franchise, Mr Big, an American Company that had failed to protect their brand in the UK. Within no time at all they had built up a network of around twenty five shops nationwide and did little more than provide customers with the tools to open and maintain their shops. Retirement in Tenerife followed. Sherry, their lovely daughter, married and moved to the States.

During my childhood I hated physical fighting, but stood up for myself if need arose. Incidents of fighting taught me the futility and mindlessness of the pursuit. I resented not having had sporting opportunities. I needed to have the sporting opportunities denied to me at school, and develop some of my physical potential. I knew I could excel at something.

So what did I do? I joined the Police Cadets in September at the ripe old age of sixteen. I think I wanted to be 'an attitude changer', rather than an 'enforcer'.

Chapter Two
The Police Cadets

I'm glad that I left school at sixteen because I was sick to the back teeth of studying and revising. University was an option but that meant staying on to sit 'A' Levels; I'd had enough. I decided to leave. I was apprehensive but I was ready to see if I could survive beyond the security of the family and the academic world. But what would I do? I hadn't a clue.

I attempted to become a commercial artist at Massey Ferguson but my application was half hearted and guided by the Careers Officer, who was unimaginative, and on reflection ill trained and inexperienced. I wasn't the right guy to have been put forward, but in any case I didn't get the job – thank God I was rejected. I considered the Fire Service, but they only recruited from the age of eighteen.

I decided I wanted to become a Police Cadet, about the biggest challenge a guy like me could take on. I do recall my father, whilst openly supporting whatever I wanted to do, having doubt written all over his face. After all I was 5' 7½", no great physical specimen of a man, any physical presence or skill, and frankly I was naive. I had led a sheltered life up until then although I remain thankful for that. I was well brought up.

The police accepted me on the assumption that by the time I got to be eighteen I would be 5' 8" which was the minimum height requirement at the time. That never happened. But what did happen between the ages of sixteen and eighteen was the making of me. I grew in stature and confidence. I discovered myself. I was an adventurer and I was to be trained as a cause for good. It was the exciting and rewarding life I wanted. I had fallen on my feet. I became more confident, physically stronger, fitter and worldlier. I was mixing with a bunch of fundamentally decent guys. The Police Cadets offered opportunities for academic advancement, and a gateway to becoming a constable at eighteen years of age. Over the next two years I was expected to further my education at the college where the training school was based. Coincidentally this college was a stones' throw away from my old school.

During those two years I bagged another six 'O' Levels' to go with the five from school. They were all in the framework of an H.N.C but I no longer had the enthusiasm or taste for academic study so my achievement was below my capability. I chose to sit subjects that helped me to have a balanced understanding of life such as The British

Constitution, Economics, Social Economics and Sociology. I re-took my Mathematics 'O' Level. I had failed it at school despite working extremely hard to pass it. I passed without even studying; the examination board was different; AEB rather than Joint Matriculation.

The variety of activity and training available courtesy of HM Constabulary was rich; I was actively and regularly engaged in First Aid training, swimming and life-saving, orienteering, canoeing, football, hockey, general P.E, and more, including the twice weekly run. I wanted to participate in everything, that was on offer; compulsorily or voluntarily. For the first time in my life I was really enjoying myself day in and day out and could truly regard myself as being very fit.

Marching on the drill square was part of the key to becoming a disciplined young man. None of us particularly enjoyed the drill square, but it taught us discipline. We marched regularly.

As part of the character building and boxing team selection process, we all had to be paired off for a good old scrap in the ring. It was of course only possible for me to meet against a bigger lad and my first opportunity was to meet Paddy Dowswell. I won to the amazement of everybody and came out like a 'windmill' to beat him before the three minutes were up. I made the next selection stage, and met Greg Hopkins. He was to become a talented boxer, but I packed one firmly on his nose, allegedly before the bell rang. I think it was, but I was charged up. As the laughter subsided the scrap was restarted. My early onslaught shook him up but wasn't enough. He went on to outbox me, but nevertheless I got through the three minutes on my feet, without loss of face or self-respect. That was all that counted. I was developing pride in myself and the respect of others.

Because of my intense dislike of fighting it was great to have the opportunity to prove my courage in a controlled environment. Greg went on to box for the police team and I was not to box again until Police Training School at Ryton-on-Dunsmore, but that's a story for later. Nothing I seem to do is without incident.

For such a short legged little guy I was surprised to find that I had squeezed myself into the Cross Country team, more because of my stamina than pace. We ran about four and half miles, twice a week, on the roads around the college. I seem to recall recording a best of about twenty seven minutes on those runs.

An old school friend of mine, Dave Moorcroft, of Olympic and World Record fame at 5,000 metres would often run with us. He was like a Gazelle. The running pack had

19

probably covered about ten paces by the time David was at the top of the college drive about fifty yards away. The gulf between him and the pack was massive.

When I ran for the team in the National Cross Country Championships at Cosford (the RAF base) I yet again amazed everybody, providing my best ever running performance; one of resilience and stamina. I finished 60th out a field of 180, at a time when Dave Moorcroft finished second. That thirteen mile cross country performance was probably another one of my proudest achievements at that time.

I played soccer. What I lacked in skill I made up for in determination and hard running. On one occasion I was substitute, but got the opportunity to get on the football field for the opposition; The Warwickshire Agricultural College, when they were a couple of men short and I scored both goals in their 8–2 defeat by my own team! What was particularly satisfying was the diving header past "Teeber" (Steve Poole), who was our goalkeeper. 'Why couldn't I play like that every week?' was the question asked by the lads. I think the answer is quite simple and it had been my problem throughout my school days; there were too many mouthy members of the team, and it affected my confidence. Some people seem to create their own confidence by damaging that of others. A good leader will build up a team member's confidence, not knock it. Quite apart from that, I seldom used to get the ball despite running into good positions. They had little confidence in me to do anything useful with it! It's a vicious circle.

We were being trained with a view to putting together a Gymnastics Display Team to appear at Olympia in London. I knew I simply knew, that I was not cut out for gymnastics (or was that just my lack of confidence?). Tragedy struck during a training session. We were expected to stride jump over a 6' high box on which Dave Greening was crouched. I guess that's about an 8' jump.

I found myself at the very front of the queue as those in front of me peeled off and appeared at the back of the queue. In true Dave Wakefield fashion I decided that I would hold my eventual position at the front. I became the first contender. Oh dear!

I did no more than catch my leg on the back of Dave Greening falling headlong over the box and breaking my left lower arm(radius and ulna), which saw me out of action physically for several (eight) months with pins holding together both bones. I was devastated because for a year I was restricted to non violent, non contact sport. My progress on the fitness ladder was curtailed. There were nonetheless silver linings.

My spare time was spent completing my Duke of Edinburgh's Gold Award, another accomplishment of which I am immensely proud. There are few people in the country that reach the gold level of the award scheme. If I had my way the scheme would become part of a compulsory education that either took the place of National Service or supplemented the existing educational curriculum as a character builder. Katy, my daughter, was educated in Indonesia, and completed the International Baccalaureate. She will testify to the value of having had to pass a seventh 'community service' course, in addition to the six (A level equivalent) subjects that formed the basis of the International Baccalaureate. To my mind it is essential that youngsters learn to understand people of other ethnic backgrounds, the aged, the sick, the disabled and the underprivileged. The Duke of Edinburgh Award Scheme provides all of that.

To complete the award I worked regular hours in an Old Peoples' Home, helped to run a Cub Pack, worked with Reform School Children, completed a 100 mile canoe test down the River Severn from Welshpool to Worcester in a day and a half, worked in a hospital and completed an Orienteering Test, after significant weekend training walks in Llanrearder, Wales.

It was a most satisfying experience to enter Buckingham Palace with my mother. It was something of a payback, and to see the look of pride on her face as the Duke of Edinburgh presented me with the Award was something special. She would have dined out on 'her invitation' to the Palace for months afterward.

As a staunch Royalist, it was one of the proudest moments in my life to receive my Gold Duke of Edinburgh's Award from 'the man himself'. An even greater prize was the look on my Mum's face as she accompanied me through 'The Grand Gate' into the Palace yard, up the staircase and into the 'Supper Room'. It was priceless. She felt so proud and privileged.

I still have the official invitation. It was accompanied by a separate admission pass. It reads: 'The Equerry-in-Waiting to The Duke of Edinburgh is desired by His Royal Highness to invite David Wakefield to attend the presentation of awards..........at Buckingham Palace on the afternoon of Wednesday 20th December 1972'. No time was given; it was on the admission pass, 2.15pm. It was a fabulous experience and a rare one at that.

We went to the palace with Paul Stachursky and his mother. Apart from Paul Scott Lee the year before, we were the only ones in the Force to receive the award I believe. To date I understand there are only 1,700 recipients of the Gold Standard Duke of Edinburgh's Award in the World, and it has run for fifty years.

Republicans should think hard about what alternatives we have to a proven well established system that separates our head of state from our Parliament, and is the envy of the world. Who would command enough respect to become President? What would the benefits be? The Royal Family actually earn this country money through tourism; this nonsense argument that they are an expense is garbage. Every president has a budget, and in any case a president under our system would be no less symbolic than a monarch. These people are short sighted, and fail to recognise the role of a sovereign and the tradition and pride that is engendered by her presence. I hold old fashioned 'lefty' education responsible – through the media and through the educational system. Anyway, I yet again digress.

There were, however, disappointments during my cadetship. There are always disappointments in life. One of the great disappointments of these years, one that festered with me, haunted me, for some years afterward, was my failure to complete the Ten Tors (arduous) Expedition on Dartmoor. It wasn't entirely my fault, but that is never consolation.

I was a member of a four man team that included (Sir) Paul Scott-Lee, (the former Chief Constable of West Midlands), my good friend Ian Brierley, and Greg Hopkins. We had to walk through marshland, heath and over hills, with back packs of some thirty pound in weight, over a distance of around fifty five miles between Ten Tors (hills) within a very strict timescale of a day and a half. A gunshot sounded the start and the finish as I remember.

Pete Estick, mentor, training sergeant, and friend, invited me to be in the team. I had reservations. I asked him if he thought I was fit enough as I had broken my arm about six months earlier, and been out of full action for several months. I was not yet fully fit. He turned the question around, and I said I'd give it a try.

Paul Scott-Lee was the Team Leader but unfortunately he made a costly navigational error on the first day, and as I recall we had walked some ten miles off our course, meaning that the following day we had to make up the lost distance and time. This might not have been beyond us if we'd walked into the night, but Greg and I were totally knackered and needed a rest. We set up camp in fading light next to a stream.

I had been exhausted, but after a good meal, sleep, hearty breakfast and a change of socks, I felt ready and able as we upped camp early the following morning. We set off to cross the stream. I fell in! My boots and socks had been nice and dry and now they were soaked. My morale swiftly plummeted. I felt my spirit erode at a rapid rate of knots.

It wasn't the done thing to offer or make excuses, and it doesn't sit right as I make them now, but I know now that I was suffering from exposure. I was ready to throw in the towel, and, for whatever reason, Greg Hopkins was ready to as well. Half the team were ready to give in.

Greg and I dropped out a few miles after leaving our camp site. I have utmost respect for Ian and Paul. They completed the remaining ten miles- ironically the distance that the navigational error had cost us - even though they knew that they could not receive a medal unless the entire team crossed the line.

I was at the finishing line when they appeared, running, over the hill. Despite their valiant effort they were still too late! They did not finish in the allotted time. Did that make me feel better? I had mixed feelings. I was ashamed. I had tasted failure before but not like this. I had given in and this was a first and I felt I had let the team down. This haunted me for years. It is only upon analysis that I have been able to find some consolation; some piece of mind. Even if I had continued with Greg we would never have finished in time to win our medals!

There were no celebratory drinks after the event even though our 'second team' had successfully completed the less arduous course. Pete Estick drove our bus back to Coventry and home. It was a quiet and miserable journey. I still occasionally ask myself why I couldn't push myself a little further, a little harder. Other times I know damn well that I must have given all that I could have given under the circumstances. Nevertheless, there was a team spirit and for years I felt partly responsible and blamed myself.

I explained this to Paul when I last saw him – over lunch in Northampton in the 1990's. He must have nurtured his own bad feelings about that fateful expedition.

I am now cleansed of my guilt feeling but the disciplined services are all about team work and support for one another. That bond, developed during training and exercise, creates a wonderful feeling of camaraderie, togetherness, and in most cases friendship. That is why I had felt guilt.

We all had great fun and great nights out in those days. We worked hard but also played hard. We were low paid; £6 per week as I recall, but it's not often you can get paid for having a ball! I still have fond memories of friendships that I forged in these days and reminisce with fondness the good times I had. I am still in regular contact with many of those guys.

To the training staff, my character builders, in particular Inspector Ray Dyde and Sergeant Pete Estick, I owe an eternal and special gratitude. I even offer thanks to Dave Farmer - he was supervising the gymnastics when I bust my arm, and he should have caught me as I fell. Legal action could have been taken but would not even have been contemplated. You don't do that.

Another great experience, and a lot of fun, was the initiative tests. We had two as I recall. On one occasion I was teamed up with Paul Stachursky ('Stack') and we came second.

The test was one of initiative and resourcefulness over a three day period on limited funds. It was a 'pairs' exercise. I kept a copy of one of the test sheets. The tasks were unusual and challenging and I can't see that they could be completed in this day and age. The test started at 10am on a Wednesday to midnight on the Friday.

We were given £1 (yes £1) each. No tasks could be carried out in Warwickshire, Birmingham, the Metropolitan area of London, or Blackpool. I don't know why Blackpool! We could not use our own transport; we had to use public transport, hitch or whatever. We did have our warrant cards.

The test comprised three sections. We had to complete one from each of the two groups in Section A, a minimum of six tasks from Section B and ten from Section C.

Points were awarded on the following basis;
Section A   20 points for each complete visit.
Section B   20 points for each task in each section completed in full.

Some kind of proof of having completed a task had to be produced. Oh and we didn't have a camera and there were no mobile phones in those days!

There was no preparation time. The tasks were as follows:

24

SECTION A
Visit the birth place, not just the town, of one person from each group.

GROUP 1
William Wordsworth
Amy Johnson
Captain James Cook
Guy Fawkes
William Booth

GROUP 2
Sir Walter Raleigh
Aneurin Bevan
Horatio Viscount Nelson
Wat Tyler
Sir Christopher Wren

SECTION B
Visit at least six of the following:

1. A racing stable and see a horse that took part in the 1972 Grand National.
2. A working windmill.
3. breatthysw (anagram) castle.
4. A shipyard employing more than 3,000 people.
5. A zoo where dolphins are kept.
6. An atomic power station.
7. Gladstone Park.
8. A railway engine shed.
9. A military museum.
10. A mink farm.
11. A swing bridge
12. A Tartan Athletic Track.

SECTION C
Obtain or do a minimum of ten of the following:

1. A library ticket for a County Borough Library.
2. Ride on a hovercraft.
3. A ticket for a journey on a private railway, signed by the driver.
4. The signature of a lifeboat coxswain.
5. An appointment card for a chiropodist.
6. Ride on a chair lift.
7. Sing in a male voice choir.
8. A race card for a horse race meeting held on 1st June 1972.
9. Autograph of an international sportsman.
10. Signature of Captain or First Officer of a seagoing liner.
11. A photograph of yourself in or near a spitfire or hurricane aeroplane.
12. A flight in an aeroplane.
13. Ride on an elephant.
14. A pawn ticket.
15. A bellis perennis.
16. Proof of having ridden in a pre 1920's automobile.
17. Ride on a penny-farthing bicycle.
18. Signature of a National Park warden.
19. A free sample from a matchbox factory.
20. Proof of having had a sauna bath.

How do you think you'd have tackled this? What would you do? Where would you go? How would you get there? Interesting isn't it.

I think that Paul Scott Lee was cadet of the year in my first year. I'd be surprised if I was wrong. Paul was a truly exceptional man, not the cleverest but certainly the most focused and driven man I have ever met. He believed he was going to be a chief constable. He knew it.

When we met over lunch near Northampton in the early 1990's he was already on his way to becoming an Assistant Chief Constable and told me his ambition was to become Chief Constable of West Midlands Police. That is exactly what he became.

Sir Paul Scott Lee is a really great guy and I am proud to have known him, and to have been his friend. It has been a privilege to have known and followed the career of someone like Paul. What made Paul so successful?

He exuded so much confidence and belief in his own destiny and reached the pinnacle of his career. He was determined and gritty. I have never known anyone quite like Paul, and observed with interest, from teenager to retirement, the career of a person who rose to become Chief Constable of the second biggest force in the country. His drive, belief and focus were almost tangible; unsettling. Not many people get to know someone like that. I remember Pete Estick, my training sergeant, telling me, "Paul's ambition is to become Chief Constable. And you know? He will".

It is also a privilege to have been a good friend of Dave Moorcroft and his wife Linda. In a different way, Dave was equally successful in the field of athletics, and it was great to have run with (after) a World record holder, and to follow his career from a teenager. Dave had a mix of natural talent and dedication and I guess those are the ingredients of a top sportsman.

The following year another great guy, Paul Quinney became cadet of the year pushing me (it was rumoured), into second place. Paul thoroughly deserved it. Big Paul has always been overweight at eighteen stone. He could never lose it, but at twenty two stone now, at fifty six years of age, just four stone more, he hasn't done badly over the years. It was Paul's determination that secured my respect.

Paul might have appeared big and 'shapely' but he was strong, and had underlying fitness. He was a gentle giant of a man and great fun. Paul has now retired from the police, his last job being identity parade duty officer with another old friend and pillow fight sparring partner from Ryton-on-Dunsmore training school days, Brent Kirton.

Paul Quinney has earned my utmost respect. He is a great example to anyone who feels handicapped by weight. If Paul could have achieved academically, he would have been a great leader, but he was never a 'swot', and could not be promoted without passing examinations. He retired after thirty years as a constable. I single Paul out for mention because I know he will appreciate it.

The years I spent in the Police Cadets could not have been better spent. They have been amongst the best years of my life. They made a man of me. They offered me further education and an array of sporting opportunities. When I think of those opportunities I ask myself where else I could have done all that I had done. I have mentioned many

27

activities but in addition I was taught judo and (sword) fencing and climbing in addition to the orienteering.

I turned down the opportunity, to crew the Winston Churchill sailing ship and take VSO (Voluntary Service Overseas). I didn't take these two opportunities because a better option arose that I have dedicated the next chapter to.

Running a Cub Scout pack, working with young offenders, the old, handicapped and underprivileged taught me understanding. I learnt to unselfishly work with, and alongside others, as a team – a true team. Not an illusion of teamwork, as presented by commercial companies to manipulate their staff. These employees invariably end up competing against each other in an unhealthy manner. I learnt to trust those around me. I earned respect and received it. Those around me earned my respect and trust.

My years in the Police Cadets did not isolate me from the real world. The idea was not to condition young men to become 'robo-cops'. With my short hair, I spent most free weekends with my 'civvy street' mates. I drank underage like the rest, at the Jules Verne pub, where we all met. We drank copious amounts of alcohol, partied, without getting violent or spoiling the evening for others. I mixed with decent guys, from different backgrounds and with different interests.

Incidentally, working in a hospital presented opportunities to attend great nursing and doctor parties. These characters were great practical jokers, and very much shared the black humour, that these vocations inevitably trigger. I had a lot of fun with nurses during my years of policing!

I was popular with the student community at college, and, somewhat bizarrely, became President of the Tile Hill College Students Union and attended the NUS (National Union of Students) Conference in Margate. I shared a room with a Warwick University guy. I remember with some disgust lying motionless in my bed, pretending to be asleep as he 'spanked the monkey' – gross!

I regularly went to see live music at the Lanchester Polytechnic College in the city centre, with my old friend Steve Drakeford; a printer. Steve died of a heart attack when he was just 43. Steve and I saw just about every big name entertainer of the late 1960's and early 1970's; some amazing concerts and performances.

The Lanchester Polytechnic, now Coventry University, was one of the top 'underground' venues in the Country and I spent many a Friday and Saturday night in the

Student Union building listening to great new sounds in a hall that held about 1,000 people. I must have cut a strange figure in those days, a short haired Police Cadet in a room full of long haired lads and hippy beaded girls, heads swinging to lively music; some drugged to the eyeballs. But I never had one intimidating glance. These people were peaceful and generally law abiding citizens; a thoroughly good bunch.

The annual Lanchester Arts Festival was amongst the best in the country, and included a number of 'firsts'. Monty Python gave their first ever stage performance at the festival in 1971. During the festival I saw Chuck Berry give his first performance of 'My Ding-a Ling at The Locarno Ballroom (it was recorded live on Chuck berry London sessions album). Immediately afterwards, in the same hall, I watched Pink Floyd.

The Rolling Stones, David Bowie, The Moody Blues and the Sensational Alex Harvey Band played at the Coventry theatre, all as part of the festival.

Week in week out I was watching the likes of Jack Bruce, Osibisa, Tyrannosaurus Rex, Yes, Ralph McTell, Strawbs, Atomic Rooster, Blodwyn Pig, Jethro Tull, Groundhogs, Fairport Convention, The Bonzo Dog Do Da Band, Curved Air, Mott the Hoople, Roxy Music, ELO, Wizzard, Gentle Giant, Caravan, Lindisfarne, Stone The Crows, Suzi Quattro, Steeleye Span, Cockney Rebel, Elton John, The Who, Arthur Brown and many others.

There were other local venues. I watched Coliseum at the University of Warwick. At the Chesford Grange I remember seeing Uriah Heep and Hawkwind. None of the venues were quite like that gymnasium hall in the student Union building at 'The Lanch'.

I remember one terrific concert that Steve Drakeford and I attended. It was in 1972 I think; at the Oval Cricket Ground. The billing included: Quintessence, America, Rod Stewart and the Faces, Mud, Emerson, Lake and Palmer, and The Who. Wooow!

I watched the 'The City', home and away, with Paul Hubbard and other friends. I watched Coventry Bees Speedway, with Steve Drakeford and Pete Wilford. Before I learnt to drive, we would travel to away speedway fixtures in Pete's three wheeled Reliant!

They were great times, and entertainment was reasonably priced and accessible to all. These days, prices are proportionately sky high and value for money is poor. Cinemas for example; generally you paid for two movies and get a full programme of entertainment.

29

During my teenage years I became a fit and proud man! I was a well rounded and balanced individual, and this of course meant that I was normal and occasionally naughty. Some of our nights out were wild, but always full of fun.

There is one particular story that simply has to be told even if my novice-like writing fails to capture the moment. Please bear with me and try to picture the scene.

A Fancy Dress Party was planned at the Warwick Hotel in Warwick. I decided to invite my good mate Rich Lynes and we both decided to take a girlfriend. I thought that we could go as 'undertakers' and Pete Wilford made up some cards bearing the name 'U. Shute and I. Berry'. It needed to be good!

Norma Bainbridge arranged for us to borrow a five foot long coffin from the Criterion Theatre where she performed. The girls would dress as vampires. It suited the girl I was with. She had black hair, had very good looks, and would have looked great as the one in The Munsters (not Uncle Fester). We wore top hats and appropriate and convincing tailed suits.

We set off from my house with the coffin safely strapped to the roof rack on my car, picked the girls up and headed off down the Warwick By-pass. We had some very strange looks. We navigated into Warwick and into a large car park at the rear of the ballrooms. There was a car park attendant and I stopped alongside him to ask if we were in the right place. "Is this the fancy dress ball" I asked.

He leaned in to the car and said, "Yes mate. You can park over there" and pointed to a vacant lot.

He watched us take the coffin off the roof, and pointed to the double doors. At that point I looked down at my girlfriend and had an idea.
"How tall are you?"

"5 feet 2 inches" she replied.

"You can get in. We'll carry you in. You'll need to lean your head forward a little, and hold the top on, but it'll work."

She agreed, and we rested the coffin on the bonnet, she climbed in, and we lifted each end on the shoulder, Richards's girlfriend holding the side. I was at the front and took the few steps to the front doors, through them, and left through a second set of doors.

Immediately I struggled through I saw the magnitude of the mistake. In the darkened room there were maybe a couple of hundred people and a, wait for it, catwalk!

I stopped, and tried to push backward, but Rich hadn't seen the dozens of faces peering in our direction, and the music was making communication difficult. Richard couldn't in any case back up. Eventually, with an increasingly nervous passenger emerging from the coffin, we had no choice but to enter the room and turn around inside to roars of laughter from the fashion show audience. I almost dropped the coffin through fits of laughter.

I didn't say anything to the car park attendant, there seemed little point, and simply asked him where the Warwick Hotel was, just round the corner as it turned out, and walked round to it. We didn't try another spectacular entry!

There are other good stories to tell, but I'll leave them for another time.

At eighteen years of age I had come of age. My father and mother were proud of me and I was proud of myself. Recently Paul Quinney told me that they were the best days of his life and I can fully understand why he feels that way. How sad that opportunities of the kind that I had, for kids these days, are so few. How my country has changed.

In the months approaching my admission to police training school I was offered a unique and rare opportunity by my employers. They gave me leave to join the Commonwealth Expedition. The patron was my old friend the Duke of Edinburgh!

The expedition leader was one Lieutenant Colonel Lionel Gregory. In summer 1972, I joined a band of doctors, students, nurses, soldiers and guys from others backgrounds and set off overland along the Asian Highway to Singapore. It was an adventure and feat of endurance of a lifetime! The experience was a lesson in understanding and appreciating other peoples of the world; their customs and their religions.

I intend telling the story of my incredible journey through Europe and Asia but pause, and change the mood, to dedicate a short paragraph to my friend and neighbour; Danny Parker.

Danny Parker

No autobiography of mine would be complete without mention of our family's next door neighbour, Danny Parker.

31

Danny was a gentleman, a scholar, a gardener and a drinker! He was accomplished in every respect. He was a well educated and well spoken man that enchanted me and others with a range of views and stories that were sometimes peppered with bad language. Danny was Steve and Christine's Dad.

Danny had been in the RAF during the war and spent all his working life at Courtaulds working in the research laboratory, although he nearly became a Catholic priest. He had by all accounts completed some of the 'training' but at any rate he didn't do it.

During my childhood, and beyond, Danny was one of my favourite adults; a real character and a wonderful man. He was always good towards me and made me laugh. He never talked down to me and seemed more like a friend. The entire neighbourhood was fond of Danny; a kind and gentle man.

Danny was known in all the pubs and clubs our side of the city centre if not the entire city. He was a pub character; and the pub was his second home. He was also a keen gambler. Danny was known to 'bless' his first pint of the day by placing it on the floor in front of the bar, kneeing beside it, saying a few words in Latin whilst crossing his chest in priest-like fashion. He would then pick it off the floor and drink it.

Danny educated me. He taught me to garden and taught me how to play poker. He taught me how to bet. He taught me, through observation, about the effects of alcohol on the body and soul, and about the joys of 'walking a lot'. If not walking, Danny favoured his motorbike for travel, and Jean, his wife, would cycle everywhere. Danny walked across the fields, to The Rainbow pub in Allesley Village, his favourite walk.

Everyone has an amusing story to tell about Danny, and he had an amusing story to tell. Danny loved his Saturday and Sunday lunchtime pint and would invariably arrive home 'late' in the afternoon, have his lunch and go to bed for a nap. His socks were always thrown from the back window into the yard, sometimes preceded by vocal complaint from wife Jean, or belated complaint as she picked them up off the ground. It was an amusing and comforting feature of a typical summer's weekend.

Danny wasn't always late home because he was in the pub playing dominos or cards. Sometimes Danny could be seen resting, smoking his pipe on a grass bank or sleeping in a tree somewhere between The Rainbow and home, and he was always prepared to stop and chat with anyone passing by. He was a very affable chap, and I loved to chat with him over the garden fence as he tended his vegetable garden that he had separated from Jeans

32

'flower' garden with what he called 'the great wall'. He had built it to clearly define areas of responsibility and territory. For Danny his plot was for him, and not for Jean. Flowers were not welcome. Flowers were right 'pansies'.

Danny loved his vegetable plot and gave me all sorts of instruction and gardening tips. He would collect mole hills from the 'cow fields' and use the soil on his plot. He produced a string of 'pearls of gardening wisdom' between intermittent puffs of his pipe. He was enthusiastic about talking, and I was enthusiastic about listening and I found Danny fascinating.

My parents were always very fond of Danny and Jean. They were exceptionally good neighbours. They had some hilarious encounters with Danny. They would tell of the day that he returned home from the pub one Christmas Day late on in his life. My parents were sitting in the picture window of Bill and Marjorie's house opposite.

Alan and Norma Bainbridge, Bill, Marjorie and my parents were sharing a Christmas lunchtime drink. Danny was seen arriving at the front gate of his house, somewhat inebriated, and before he opened the gate decided to have a pee against the wall. As he was doing so he spotted the assembly of drinkers in the window opposite and, always the gentleman, Danny swopped his grip from right to left in order that he could offer a polite wave to them. They all waved back and smiled, but were soon screaming with laughter. Danny zipped up, approached his front door before turning again to light his pipe and offer another wave.

On another Christmas morning I went around to the Parkers house to wish them a happy Christmas. My brother in law, Ollie, went with me on this occasion. Ollie was not very familiar with the Danny style of hospitality. A drink was thrust before us and we were encouraged to join in a game of something or other - it might have been cards.

Anyway, the whiskey came by the tumbler full and Ollie and I left a about an hour and a half, and a quarter of a bottle of whiskey apiece later, somewhat worse for wear. Ollie never forgets that Christmas Day; pissed before the clock even struck mid day. We struggled through a heavy meal, to avoid offending my Mum. We were both pretty much plastered and acted like complete clowns through the meal, and both got told off by the womenfolk.

On one of the rare occasions that Danny came in to our house for a drink, he was pie eyed upon departure. My Mum, who we appropriately nicknamed 'Mrs Bouquet' and Dad, saw him off from the front door. He proceeded to sing the praise of my Dad and

33

Mum as 'lovely people' and 'damn fine neighbours'. He commented in particular about what a lucky man my Dad was to have such a good wife, and what fine tits she had! He asked to feel one, and before there was any chance to reply he grabbed my Mum's right tit and remarked again how gorgeous they were.

My parents, giggling, waved him off down the pathway. Danny paused at the gate, lit his pipe, turned, smiled, waved goodbye and casually and somewhat solemnly strode off five or six paces to his own gate, smiled, waved again and returned to his own abode.

Steve was often sent to 'recover' Danny from the pub so that he could be escorted home for lunch. He would usually come back alone, but on occasions he was successful. Sometimes I would accompany him and wait for Danny. If it was raining and the pub was not too full we would sit inside but usually we would sit outside the pub, having been plied with pop and crisps, waiting for Danny to emerge. A walk back with Danny was always eventful and we were never certain that he would not stop for a sleep and send us on home.

When in entertaining pub form, Danny would tell stories of his RAF days and extend his arms out wide to imitate a bomber aircraft and hum the tune to 'The Dambusters' as he trotted around the room simulating an attack. It was usually this kind of innocent and inoffensive behaviour that prompted a demand, 'go home Danny'.

When thrown from the premises Danny usually bounced back a few days later, throwing his hat through a partially open door onto the floor beneath the feet of the landlord, as a gesture of good will and apology. Danny was usually forgiven.

Danny, as I remarked, always treated me like a grown up and always joined in on a game of Monopoly or Risk, but would favour a game of cards. I loved visiting Steve's house, loved the laughter that Danny provoked, and was fascinated at the battle Jean waged to keep him under control. It was a losing battle.

Steve was sometimes embarrassed by him, but generally he laughed too. Steve always regretted his Dad not taking an interest in his considerable sporting skills but is, I'm sure, proud of his Dad's character and popularity. Danny was a real character, a pub character the likes of which we see little of these days. He had no qualms about telling racist jokes or being controversial. He seemed to relish it. He was extremely clever and well read, well spoken and gentlemanly toward women; yet coarse and funny in a working class mischievous way.

When Danny was made redundant by Courtaulds at fifty five years of age he was devastated, bitter and hurt. He never worked again except to earn his beer money by using his motor cycle for courier services. He enjoyed that.

Danny died of a heart attack at the age of seventy whilst on holiday in Crete. For all the trouble and embarrassment he caused Jean she missed him dearly. Ten years on, Jean still rode here pedal cycle around the city; as fit as a fiddle, and an example to us all up until her recent death.

Danny began to drink a lot after his redundancy and I recall sharing Steve's concern. Danny would share one or two of his little secrets with me; like the whiskey hidden above the loft hatch! I think he was drinking up to a bottle and a half a day at one time.

I remember convincing him to go to AA. I arranged the appointment and we went in to town. He went in for the appointment and I waited outside. He reappeared about half hour later absolutely delighted with himself.

He had debated and convinced the councillor, that there was no reason whatsoever why he should stop drinking. He had explained all the benefits and she had been unable to give a convincing reason for him to stop! He led me in to the Cathedral where he was 'a little rude' to the cleric, and we left. That was the only time that I was ever embarrassed by Danny. His problem had become a real problem for him.

I could forgive Danny for that. He was a good man. At the reception following my father's funeral in 2009, Steve, Alan, Martin and Carl Bainbridge reminisced; exchanging stories and inevitably Danny became the subject. Oh we did laugh. Alan was in that sitting room watching Danny pee at the gate and retold the story.

Steve likes a drink and a gamble but hasn't been the healthiest of guys in recent years because of his awful eating habits, and takes care of himself; or rather his fine wife takes care of him. It is his sister, Christine that best represents the Danny I loved, likes a little too much booze, like me. The Parkers are a great family.

The fields between Torbay Road and the Rainbow pub in Allesley Village are no longer. Houses are immediately behind the old family home, and access to the village is via a pathway at the top of the hill to Allesley Hall, a short municipal golf course, a beautiful park with a children's play area. A pedestrian bridge spans the village by-pass and leads to the fine 16th Century coaching house that is the Rainbow, and the memories that it holds for me.

In front of the Allesley Hall, overlooking the park, with the village church beyond (the by-pass is cleverly concealed) sits a bench beneath a cluster of trees. On the bench there is a plaque that reads quite simply 'In loving memory of Danny Parker 1928 – 1998. REST A WHILE'. When I return to Coventry I go to that bench and I do exactly that.

Chapter Three
The Commonwealth Expedition

The Commonwealth Expedition was sponsored by The Duke of Edinburgh and led by Colonel Lionel Gregory. I had the honour of being on the expedition in 1972.

The objective was to travel overland and if possible through Bangladesh, recently partitioned from Pakistan, and Burma, in a state of near Civil War, then Malaysia and on into Singapore. En route we were to engage the local populations of villages, towns and cities to create understanding and good will on behalf of the peoples of the Commonwealth, putting on various forms of entertainment as the catalyst

On a previous expedition Royal Fleet Auxiliary ships, Sir Lancelot and Sir Galahad had secured passage around Burma, but that was not an option this time, so there was every chance the expedition would come to an abrupt halt on the Indian sub-continent. Getting through Pakistan, a country that had just received a thrashing from their Indian neighbours would be an obstacle in itself. They had left the Commonwealth following their defeat.

The expedition was represented by a multi national association of friends that were to bridge the barriers of religion, colour, creed, age and wealth that lie at the root of all conflict. We were British, Canadian and Singaporean in the main.

There were about 100 of us travelling in bus and Volkswagen dormer mobiles. We travelled an average of 300 miles a day through Belgium, Germany, Austria, Yugoslavia, Greece, Turkey, Iran, Afghanistan and through the Khyber Pass to Pakistan and in to India. The Pakistani Government agreed to open its land borders with India as a special case, but we didn't get into Bangladesh or Burma and different groups peeled off into the Himalayas and down to Sri Lanka. We then turned round and came back through the South Pakistan desert. Sounds simple doesn't it?

Getting through these countries, with all the political troubles between neighbouring countries, was not easy. Turkey was not flavour of the month with either Iran or of course Greece. Turkey had health problems – a serious nationwide cholera outbreak making border crossings awkward – and Turkey was not the friendliest of neighbours and not particularly friendly in the villages. We were stoned in just about every village we passed through – and I don't mean on hashish!

Lionel Gregory likened the spirit and camaraderie that was needed to endure the tough conditions, to those more commonly found in wartime.

Prior to our departure there was significant publicity on BBC '24 Hours' and on radio. The publicity was not all favourable, "Some don't like the idea of a purely Commonwealth venture nowadays". On a previous expedition there was a headline making crash in Yugoslavia, and the conditions were pretty gruelling, but The Duke of Edinburgh was a staunch supporter, and he appeared on the programme and didn't regard our new found membership to the EEC as any reason why we should disregard the Commonwealth, or abandon other friendships.

The expedition was felt to have reached its objective of stopping along route to put on cultural displays, organised meetings and put on concerts. A previous expeditionary was interviewed and put it quite succinctly: "You meet people in a way that you can't...as a tourist......and this warmth I have never had a chance to experience.....it's something that lasts".

Another veteran, who went on to become assistant Editor of Penthouse magazine, held a view akin to my own - that we were somewhat amateurish and the legacy was a little short of goodwill. However it remains my view that any interaction between young people and most of us were seventeen to twenty five, and peoples that had perhaps never seen a foreigner before, was good.

The Colonel likened the expedition to an ascent of Everest in terms of physical endurance. I have not climbed Everest and I don't think the Colonel had. I thought it a gross exaggeration, but where I can agree with him is that it was a very demanding endurance exercise. Once we had crossed the Bosporus, and in to Asia, the hazards were enormously increased.

Lionel Gregory once said "there is no adventure without risk", but that it was quite another thing "to take the risk and adventure". He was so right.

The logistics of the journey was the business of Col. Gregory. It was his territory obviously, but we all played a part in supplying, navigating, cooking setting up tents and scavenging (shopping). There were two drivers to each vehicle.

We trained at Denbury Camp off Dartmoor which was once a military camp and about to become a prison. The local pub, The Union, became a second home. I was principally a radio operator. A record of a few songs that were sung on the trip was made. I wasn't on it, but the song titles do bring back some fond memories – Baba Noma, Tiha Noci (Serbian) and Rasa Sayang (Singaporean).

My recollections of that great journey are limited in detail, and fragmented. I have not been able to find my diary and have had to make reference to 'The Colonels' book, 'With a Song and Not a Sword'. His story is mainly his, and not altogether mine, but reading his book did spark some memories.

We left Denbury in mid August and travelled virtually non-stop some 1,000 + miles to Zagreb in Yugoslavia. The Bishop of Wells offered a service before we left (his daughter, a doctor, was on the expedition as I recall). I showed some polite interest in the service but said my own private prayer.

After a 28 hour journey we took a break. The road from Zagreb to Belgrade was wicked and very dangerous; narrow, bumpy and full of oncoming Karakas lorry drivers – it would get a lot worse. We stopped for some time in Salzburg, some time in Zagreb, but the first real refreshing rest we had was in Kavalla, northern Greece. A ferry runs from Kavalla to the Aegean Sea island of Thasos. We camped on the beach, swam, and ate wonderful seafood .and got our first taste of 'the screaming ab dabs'. Otherwise the chill time in Kavalla was memorable

We travelled on to Istanbul, the point where east is said to meet the west, and crossed the Bosporus into Asia. A few days in Istanbul sightseeing prepared us for the culture shocks that we were to experience in the months to come, but could never have done so fully. It really got rough then. Istanbul is a cool place, but the poor road between it and the Turkish capital, Ankara, was frightening. Two hundred and seventy eight miles of road on which some 25 people a day were injured! Beyond Ankara - a village dotted wilderness. Worse was to come.

There wasn't much reason to appreciate others so far. Turkey was beautiful but the interior was primitive, harsh and wild; its people aggressive. The roads through the three mountain passes we negotiated were fraught with danger of landslip, oncoming kamikaze drivers and roads so narrow that passing was impossible. With shear drops and unverged roads reversing, when confronted with stubborn motorists, was terrifying and standoffs became a battle of wills. We had a couple of collisions on this, the most dangerous stretch of road that I think I have ever encountered.

Jetsetters may well claim that the world is smaller, and that they are experiencing it, but that is not correct. The remote regions of most countries, including our own if you think about it, are seldom seen or experienced by the tourist.

The old 'silk' route probably became the 'drug route' and an encounter with some guys travelling the hippy coach – an old Robin Hood bus from Nottingham – from Amsterdam through to India was testimony to that claim. Why these guys were smoking dope in a country that had capital punishment for possession was beyond me!

It dawned on me at this point that our expedition might not be so far away from the charabanc trip that 'The Colonel' feared some would label it. The difference was probably the make-up of the guys; army, police, doctors, nurses and oh, students.

In Turkey we encountered a bit of an uncomfortable hitch. We carried staple foods and 35 gallons of water. The water was OK but our vital supply of powdered egg was contaminated by diesel leaking from a can. We smelt awful for weeks – we couldn't afford to waste the egg!

Turkey was dramatic in its beauty and exciting, but dodging sheep, cattle, ponies and other animals crossing the road was uncomfortable. One of our vehicles hit a young boy. He was shaken rather than injured. A baying crowd gathered and the number plate was torn off – a common practice in Turkey. Police and private investigators arrived.

The investigator asked why the vehicle was in the gully – it is illegal. Because the driver dodged the boy. No it was out of control insisted the official. The Colonel asked why he drew that conclusion and he quoted the mother of the victim and a witness. The Colonel, sensing an impasse brilliantly declared that if that was what the official thought, and witnesses thought otherwise, then no man could investigate the matter – only Allah. The investigator, contented with the answer, settled matters by calming the crowd, and then asked for a lift to the next town!

Samsun on The Black Sea was a gas – swimming on water that rendered a person unsinkable was weird. The shortest route to Iran was via the Karabayir Pass, a treacherous route, but the Turkish Ambassador had offered no alternative if we were not to take the better, but longer, southern Turkish route – and of course we didn't.

We camped in the valley of Refahiye next to a clear mountain stream – bliss. One of the guys played Bach on his fiddle to a herd of cows! We had finished one of the most difficult parts of the journey and spirits were high. We had a great evening by the camp fire with a Yo Ho Ho and a bottle of rum!

The Iranian frontier was just 300 miles away and we were to camp in Maku just inside Iran and in the shadow of Mount Ararat – where I hoped to see Noah's Ark. A busy road to the border passed through Sakaltutan, Erzurum and Tahir. The road was good. Kevin Sparks was driving. We collided with an oncoming lorry just a few miles from the border. It took the side away and the driver kept going!

At the border the Turks were real baskets! They were as obnoxious and awkward as they could have been and it took a few hours to get permission to enter Iran even though our visas were watertight. When you are tired it is difficult to maintain manners and patience but we did.

The reception to greet us at Maku was stunning – the town turned out- the Mayor, the Assistant Governor and the Police Chief, in all his regalia. They came to greet us at our camp. It was like a scene from 'The Mouse That Roared'! It was a perfect example of Iranian courtesy and hospitality and one that cannot be surpassed by any reception I have received in any country. However, as 'The Colonel' quite rightly pointed out, although it was all genuine enough, at the root of it lay curiosity and excitement, aroused by seeing woman from Britain! Garlands and speeches through an interpreter followed. It was very humbling.

The curiosity turned a little extreme at night and armed police were posted around the camp – we had to escort the girls to the loo where hopeful admirers congregated. It was a dampener on an otherwise excellent impression, and a blemish that many a traveller will have experienced in countries where western woman are perceived as loose. Who is to blame for that?

We were shown the magnificent palace of the Sadar of Maku. Set in beautiful orchards and gardens with the snow capped Mount Ararat as a backdrop, it was stunningly beautiful on a cool sunny brightly blue skied day. I remember that day with amazing warmth.

The carpets and furniture was priceless and in perfect condition. The Persians measure wealth through the quality of the carpet; it's a symbol of status. How is it now under the Ayatollah I wonder?

41

Our next stop was Tabriz about 150 miles east. We camped next to the Shahgoli Pool with a stunning piece of architecture – a restaurant in the centre approached along a pathway lined with lights.

The Governor of Tabriz presented us with melons (yes, melons) and Iranian hospitality continued as crowds gathered. Boy scouts turned up to entertain 'the troops'. The press turned up and so did the TV. I sloped off with Charles Krajewski, coincidentally another cadet given leave of absence. The people spoke little English, but their warmth was equally apparent on the streets of Tabriz. I was falling in love with Iranians.

We visited the bazaar, one of the biggest and most important in the Middle East. Alcoves, arcades, and Saras (old store houses) adorned the streets, and goods and food stuff too numerous to mention were sold to the thousands that walked the streets. It was a vibrant and friendly experience.

That night I was forced to join in the choir to entertain dignitaries including the American Consular General. I say forced, but I was uncomfortable entertaining on stage thank you! I felt guilty about not joining in but I cringed at the thought.

We travelled 400 miles to Tehran where we camped out in the Manzarieh Gardens on the side of a mountain overlooking the city. There was stunning weather to accompany the stunning views. The Iranians were so kind.

We played soccer against a local club team and were two up at half time. Fitness and the heat cost us seven second half goals, but the game was played in great spirit.The team photo, taken afterwards, sadly does not include the opposition and cannot testify to the fact.

Tehran was fascinating and the streets were full with nothing other than Hillman Hunter motor cars! I haven't met many people that have been to Iran, for obvious reasons, so it was great to hear from my mates acquaintance, an ex stolen vehicle trafficker, who will remain nameless, who could 'talk up' the people and the place as I could.

'X' had been in a cell in Tehran during the revolution and overthrow of the Shah. The policemen were so excited by the tanks passing through the street that they invited him onto the street to watch. He did a runner!

We had now travelled 4,000 miles, and arrived in the first country that really showed a hospitality that complimented the beauty of the place; a complete experience. I remember the perfectly comfortable dry heat of the evenings, clear skies, moon moths and glow worms dancing in the darkness.

One night we barbequed two goats over a charcoal fire; had a few beers, a smoke and a joke. Everyone was happy here. It was warm in so many ways.

The next stage was a long desert run to Kabul in Afghanistan with a night at Mashed on route. We consumed a small quantity of Dukh on the journey. It is a yogurt and soda with lots of salt, and is excellent for the tummy and for countering dehydration.

We set off through the Elburz Mountains and a system of tunnels, on high quality mountain roads that meandered through the valleys toward the Great Salt Desert and the Caspian Sea. The publicity for our trip was so powerful and effective that at Shah Passand a great banner had been tied across the road greeting us. We weren't getting out of Iran easily! It wasn't scheduled, but we had to stop. It would have been rude and discourteous not to.

Mashed overnight, and then on to Fariman, where the local over exuberance was subject to police control. We crossed the Afghan border and into total darkness, setting up camp near Herat under a moonlit sky. We had had a long desert journey of some 300 miles which was without unfortunate incident and we were all very tired.

The journey from Kandahar across the wondrous desert plateau leaves you totally detached from the rest of the world. It has been likened to sailing through the darkness in a calm sea. The stillness and quiet is so eerie.

The Afghan people were simple and easy to please, and honourable behaviour was rewarded by hospitable people. But it was a wild place that seemed not to have changed for centuries, and in my view should not change. This is the mistake that the western world has engaged in, and has done for centuries – trying to teach decent people to be 'civilised' according to our values and not theirs. It was a land of bandits, but also decent ordinary people. The Koran was the law and the authority of the Hakim beyond question.

That Afghanistan is the focus of so much world attention this Century is little fault of their own. It is as a result of outside interference because Afghans have little history of expansionism or excursions beyond their borders. They are tribal.

43

In 1842, the British Indian Army invaded Afghanistan because they feared that the Russians, with whom we were at war, would try to outflank them and attack India. They were stuffed. They occupied the place with 5,000 troops and after the officers were systematically picked off to destabilise the ranks, they limped back through the Khyber Pass being picked off en route. One survived. The greatest military power in the world was soundly beaten.

The Indians took note, and recognised that the British were not unbeatable. This is widely regarded as the reason for the Indian uprising. The British tried again to control Afghanistan around 1879 and again failed.

Afghanistan is a wild rugged land of rocks and dust, mountains and valleys. For those of you that have ventured up to the volcano on Tenerife you will have a feel for it.

The Russians tried to tame the Afghans, and the Americans supplied their Taliban enemies with the missiles to kill them. Ironically their own weapons are now turned on them.

Afghanistan is an insignificant tribal country that the rest of the world has no business interfering with. Radicalisation of many Afghans has stemmed from outside incursions. There is no place for democracy in Afghanistan; only mutual trust, respect and tolerance, so that the different peoples of the country can co-exist in peace.

On the road to Kabul we came across a small covered wagon drawn by a mule. It was being led by two young men from Minnesota, USA. On the side of the wagon was written 'Walking around the Earth for UNICEF'. We chatted on the road side for some time. I took a photo. Nearly two months later, when returning to UK, we stopped in Quetta, in Pakistan, before entering the South Pakistan desert. A newspaper article told of their death at the hand of bandits close to the Kabul Gorge. They were armed, but ultimately defenceless. What a sorry wasteful loss of life.

We camped at the Qargha Dam, about ten miles outside Kabul, and stopped in the grounds of a building intended to be a hotel but one that never materialised. It was a failed project. An artful watchman tried to charge us for using the toilets, but the manager clipped his wings. The first shoes lost to theft occurred here; the Colonel and his partner had them nicked while they slept! I was to lose mine in a similar way in Delhi. We drank a healthy amount of local wine with a superb meal cooked by the Afghan hosts. A trip around Kabul was testimony to the basic living of these tribal peoples.

44

Kabul is located in a fertile valley at an altitude of some 6,000 feet and is dominated by two high hills either side of the city. Kabul was captured by the Arabs in 656 AD and they introduced Islam to the people. The bazaars were even more extraordinary than in Tabriz. The Four Arcades bazaar was burned by the Brits in the first Anglo-Afghan war but was still one of the most colourful I have ever seen; Afghan shirts, turbans, silks and cloths of every imaginable colour.

The noon gun, on the fortifications overlooking the city, would sound at noon each day. Sadly, the sound of a gun is less pleasing to the Afghan these days. The Kabul University, on the Kandahar Road near the old city, will be a less pleasant place these days. The only pleasant thing about Kabul these days would be the weather. Dry throughout the year, 90 degrees by day, with cool nights; winter temperate of 30 to 45 degrees with occasional snow.

Passage through the valleys and the Kabul Gorge was spectacular; the Kabul Gorge more so than the Kyber Pass. The Kabul Gorge is only about fifteen miles out of Kabul.

We arrived at the border post on the Kyber-Tor Kham – just an hour before sunset. To travel through after dark was very dangerous because of bandits so we hoped not to be held up. We were delayed at Customs and harassed by money touts offering double rate, but playing the black market on this trip was frowned upon by the Colonel.

The Indians travelling with us were allowed in to Pakistan, but for us it was touch and go. We travelled through the Kyber Pass, an amazing experience that captured my imagination of battles between British soldiers and tribesmen – mention of the film Carry on up the Kyber spoils it. Mud forts along route, some silhouetted in the setting sun, added to the dramatic feel to the occasion, and the badges of the famous regiments that fought here were seen on the crags. The Kyber Rifles – in bright green and white – wow!

A derelict town, Landikotal, and the total absence of any people, created a ghostly, frightening feel of desolation and danger.

We passed through Peshawar, gateway to the Swat Valley, a dangerous region for the Americans at the moment. We were warned not to approach Rawalpindi by night because there had been cases of highway robbery, murder and lots of shooting. After stopping for some local roadside food at a dhabas (eating place) – chapatti's, vegetables and dhal soup – oh and a cup of milky tea, we did just that!

Rawalpindi is strategically placed in the North West of Pakistan near the Khyber Pass. It was a British garrison town, and later an interim capital of Pakistan after Independence in 1949. We stopped at the Intercontinental Hotel – just for a drink - and then camped in the grounds of the Green Gates Motel. We were allowed to use the swimming pool. It was pure luxury after camping and travelling in dusty, dry desert conditions.

The road to Lahore was extremely dangerous because of the heavy traffic driving at full throttle and flashing lights on and of repeatedly and threateningly, to clear the oncoming opposition from the road. It was the game of chicken that we had experienced in Afghanistan already. They meant it, and were good at it.

We nearly lost the road a few times but developed the knack of dodging the oncoming vehicle at the last minute, as they did sometimes. They were better at it. The flashing light by night was particularly dangerous - blinded by light the next by darkness.

We camped in the huge sports stadium at Lahore. We felt very safe. The girls were having the same problems as they had had in Tabriz. We were besieged by students from Lahore University. I visited the 11th Century Lahore Fort before we moved out.

We crossed the Wagha border post into India in the queues of people trying to get to their own side of the border; almost climbing over each other to get their passports stamped, despite the occasional pot shots and shells I could hear being exchanged. Pathetic bundles of possessions being checked by customs officers. It was a surreal and very depressing sight. The fighting between the two countries did not look to be over yet.

It took hours for us to get through, and when we did we made off for Amritsar on the road to Delhi – about 275 miles away. Amritsar was amazing and the Golden Temple breathtaking. Indeed, I later saw - luckily by full moon- the Taj Mahal, which though breathtaking in itself, and a wonder of the world, was not as wonderful as this Sikh creation. The golden temple was awesome.

I went to the scene of the famous massacre in Amritsar. A British disgrace; murder at the hand of General Edward Dyer in 1919. We were guilty of murdering unarmed men, woman and children in gardens; 400 killed and thousands injured by bullet. I was embarrassed and uncomfortable.

Sightseeing in Delhi was a real break and pure relaxation. We camped in an open air theatre, the Rangshala which accommodated 10,000 people, on a hill overlooking the city.

Both Dave Greening and I drove a Pedi Cab with the driver in the passenger seat. We saw all the touristy sights but went into the darker parts of the city as well. Cool!

From Delhi around a dozen of us headed off to Agra to see the Taj Mahal – simply incredible - and then on to Benares (Varanasi) to see the Temples of the Kama Sutra – naughty! The temples were actually en route to Benares; at Khajuraho. The eroticism etched on the temple walls is best described by an expert. All I will say is 'woooow'.

En route we travelled some thirty miles along a dusty single track road only to find that a bridge had collapsed in the monsoon and a river crossing was impossible. I was astonished to see woman carrying heavy bags of soil on their heads - they were building up the entire bridge and the river banks without any mechanised support. We turned round and travelled 30 miles back along the road and took another route.

In Benares we met a few students from the University and one of them hitched a lift back with us to Delhi and received our hospitality – he was the ungrateful thieving basket that stole my shoes from beneath my sleeping head and disappeared from our base camp in Delhi.

Benares is on the banks of the Ganges River where I watched, with respectful interest, the dead being carried, garland-laden, in procession and through the narrow streets to the bank of the river where they were ceremonially burnt on timber fires before their ashes were cast into the sacred river.

It was an unforgettable sight that I photographed without appreciating the insensitivity of having done so. I tried to be discrete but it was wrong. Fortunately I got away with a few glares from those on the fringe of the ceremony and they exercised restraint and tolerance. It is easy for a tourist, fascinated by such an alien scene, to see it as a photo opportunity. On reflection I should not have taken those photos.

Next Lucknow, the city that was the birthplace of the Great Indian Mutiny, and then Delhi where Charles Kjewelski and I decided to travel, on our own steam, to Nainital where we would meet the rest of our contingent.

Delhi was hot and humid and a journey up into the cool foothills of the Himalayas would be a welcome experience. We travelled by train to Moradabad and then bus to Nainital stopping en route at several villages. The train journey was an education and we travelled third class but could not resist hanging off the side of the train and sitting on the roof – fourth class. The steam from the engine did cause a few minor burns however.

A retired Sikh British Army Officer approached us in one village and asked us back to his farm for tea. To our amazement, in these humble surroundings, he produced a silver Victorian tea service and we drank local tea, with and without milk. He showed us photographs of his tiger hunting days and reminisced with great emotion and pride about his days with the British. He thought life was the worse for their absence. We were not allowed to leave without trying his home made potato whiskey – my word. We took a rickshaw to the bus station giggling and joking on route. It had some kick.

We arrived at the Corbett National Park ranger's offices and after much persuasion, because the Park was closed by the monsoon damage to roads, reached agreement that we could walk in the Park provided we were armed and under escort. More about our search for a tiger later.

The further we journeyed, the higher we got, and the air got thin and dry. The bus, with its peasant passengers, chickens, a goat (strapped on the back) and Charles and I, wound its way around hillsides and reached its destination on the banks of the beautiful Lake Nainital; snow-capped Everest glistening beyond the surrounding mountains.

This was truly the playground of the British Raj, like Simla, peaceful and clean. An unbelievable journey, accompanied by unbelievable friendliness and hospitality, was capped; completed with this unbelievable sight.

For a good twenty years afterward I pledged that this was the place of my retirement, but consideration of a quality health service quelled my enthusiasm in later years.

From Nainital we returned to Delhi to perform a concert, and I reluctantly played a minor part; miming in the choir.

My money had been stolen together with my shoes. Money that had been posted to me by my Mum and Dad never arrived – the accompanying letter did, but the envelope had been expertly opened with a razor blade and cleverly resealed after the expert thieves had removed the concealed cash. The British High Commission were very helpful in trying to secure funds before I left Delhi – NOT. I eventually collected some from their offices in Lahore after a panic phone call home asking for more! It was wired to the High Commission.

On our return journey to the UK we stopped at a village, and I went to the police post to introduce myself. I was greeted as a brother and presented with a wonderful Sikh police hat complete with badge. That pride and joy was stolen by somebody in our party during the journey.

Illness, dysentery, hepatitis and even typhoid hit our ranks during our time in India and our top driver, Kevin Sparkes, spent weeks on his back, with our doctor, Anne Roberts nursing him. He had hepatitis. The typhoid victim was hospitalised.

Bad temper was the main enemy. Moodiness and irritability were all normal human responses to tiredness and fatigue, and we all battled against it, but there were flair ups. Kevin Sparkes, quite reasonably, threatened to hit me over the head with a cooking pot during one such disagreement over dinner. He later apologised.

We all got accustomed to this cycle of minor upset and reconciliation. Our self discipline prevented such outbursts with local people, although the border police, customs and immigration had a real habit of giving their fellow countryman a bad reputation. They were arrogant and egotistical arseholes who seemed intent on creating delays and obstacles when none were necessary.

Our return journey was via Baluchistan taking the road to Quetta via Multan and Sukkar. Baluchistan was experiencing political unrest and foreigners were not particularly welcome. It was Ramzan, and Muslims were fasting from sunrise to sunset, and this didn't help the overall climate. The locals get irritable at this time of year.

Many places imposed the fast on non-Muslins by the simple act of closing down all shops and restaurants despite the fact that under some circumstances there were exemptions. For example, travellers or women with periods were exempt from fasting.

As we headed for the Sind desert, the Pakistani state subject of serious flooding recently, the road became narrower and the deep dust on the verges presented a hazard. It got worse in the Great Sand Desert, when there was no easily recognisable road at all.

We spent a night in Jacobabad, by reputation one of the hottest places in the world, and froze in the night. It was so, so cold and, against the best of advice, travelled through the bandit infested Bolan Pass where robbery and murder were a serious threat.

In Jacobabad a large crowd attacked one of our vehicles and put out some windows – it reminded me of a journey back from Wolverhampton to Coventry in a football supporters coach with not a single window undamaged. On that occasion we all lay on the floor with bricks and stones flying over the top of us. This was, I guess, nearly as bad.

49

In Quetta we rested before the assault on the Great Sand Desert into Iran and on to the capital, Tehran - 1,200 miles of desert. It was here that Tom McCauley and I were invited to fly gliders and Tom dramatically crashed and seriously damaged his. Hair raising but exhilarating, only the wind broke the silence as we sailed our gliders, side by side, through the sky with a backdrop of the Mountains of Afghanistan in the distance. Mind blowing stuff.

On another very memorable occasion we stopped in the Great Sand Desert to await the arrival of two Bedouin riding on that ship of the desert, camels. We couldn't communicate except with smiles and gestures. A smile is, as I have repeatedly said, a great communicator of good will.

We gave smiles and chocolate and water. They stayed mounted on their camels high above us, smiling occasionally but peering down at us as we peered up at them in a feeling of mutual respect admiration and gratitude. I was given something that they demonstrated I could chew, and kept it uncomfortably in my mouth until I had the chance to discretely turn and eject it on to the ground. It was nasty.

Those two guys on their camels presented one of the most romantically rugged and exciting sights that the desert could have offered me. These two lone rangers of the desert reminded me of Lawrence of Arabia. Where had they come from? Where were they going? We watched them cross the sand until they were just dots on the horizon.

There was a police post in a tiny place called Shur Gas but that was the only building until we reached the border post, on the Pakistani side; Nok Kundi. There was a 75 mile no man's land, where a compass was more useful than a definable road, until we reached the border post of Iran, which we passed through into the village of Mirjaveh, before returning to the border post to formalise the entry into Iran - weird hey!

In Mirjaveh a border policeman politely 'ordered' our doctor to tend to a sick relative and we duly resumed our journey without hassle. We spent time in Isfahan to see the magnificent mosque and continued through to Tehran after being absolutely sick, sick, and sick of desert sand.

We spent just a couple of days in Tehran, not too long because it was starting to get cold, and winter would soon be closing in on the Turkish mountains. It was November.

I had never really got to know the Colonel, or he me. I wasn't sure I liked him. Was he pompous? Was he aloof? Too full of his own self importance? He came over to sit with me one evening. We chatted alone for about 30 minutes. He was OK. What about me?

It seemed we had common ground. He wrote of this chat in his book, "I was able to appreciate more the youthful enthusiasm of Dave Wakefield who wanted to make Singapore at all costs or cross the monsoon drenched mountains into Nepal. What a pity the many preoccupations before departure acted against us getting to know each other earlier".

Once across the frontier into Turkey we had some big decisions to make. Weather conditions were getting worse and the Colonel knew that certain roads would and could become impassable very quickly – he had crossed the Asian Highway over 20 times before – he should know.

We travelled from Refahiye to Ankara via Zara to avoid the treacherous Karabayir Pass that had been so troublesome, even in good weather, on our outward journey. There were still no guarantees, but it was the right call.

We had big problems and there were times that we thought we might need to abandon the vehicles but we did it. On one occasion we came across a stretch of gravel road that had deteriorated into a quagmire of mud. Heavy goods vehicles were littered, axle deep in mud, for fifty yards either side of the now indefinable road. Bulldozers were being employed to pull vehicles out of the mud. Do we turn around or do we try to get through? We went for it with Wayne Merridew at the helm, and fingers crossed. We made it but another of our vehicles suffered serious delays waiting their turn to be pulled out.

The rain turned to snow as we climbed through the mountains. Excitement got the better of Tom, the Aussie. He had never seen snow let alone touched it. We simply had to stop and watch him playing in it like a five year old.

It was freezing and camping out was an ordeal; winter clothing had been kept to a minimum and I just had a pullover a waterproof jacket and trousers and a pair of thick socks - my call!

Coughs and colds spread through the camp and misery set in, not helped by the period of Ramadan that was nearing its end. There were no shops or restaurants open to break up the day with a welcome hot meal and drink during the journey.

Arriving in 'Old Blighty' at the end of November was such a joyous relief; I was exhausted and so desperately excited to see family, friends, and the bottom of a pint of beer followed by fish and chips. It was the first thing I did on our shores.

I won't labour the sentimental stuff, and will spare you the drama, but if I was to close this chapter on any note at all it would have to be through the words of Lt Colonel Lionel Gregory, who I came to respect and admire.

It is a pity that my life moved so fast that I didn't have another occasion to catch up with him again after the expedition. I don't know what became of him or most of the people that I shared my smells, bad habits and irritating attitudes and comments with, during that incredible journey. Comex was a journey in more ways than one.

"There is something more at stake than the contemporary preoccupation with economic survival, and it takes a man of courage to use such expressions as 'the brotherhood of man' which, ironically enough, is precisely the message from the majority of the human family – the young. The largest and most elaborate international army in the world – the corps diplomatique - has yet to come to terms with it". Lt Col. Lionel Gregory.

I was home to fish and chips, British beer and family. I was home to my beloved Coventry City Football Club. One letter from my Dad wetted my appetite, City have bought a striker, Colin Stein of Glasgow Rangers for £140,000, also Tommy Hutchison, a winger from Blackpool for £100,000. To raise the money they sold Blockley to Arsenal for £200,000 and Rafferty to Blackpool.' Tommy Hutchison is my all time favourite Coventry player!

Before I was eighteen years of age I had been to Sweden, France, and Spain and travelled the Asian Highway. I mixed with many people from many cultures and backgrounds exchanging views and stories. It was a foundation for great understanding of the diversity that life provides, and a realisation that, despite, in some cases, significant apparent differences, we are all the same.

My immediate conclusions were that I didn't much care for Turks or Pakistani's and loved Iranians, Afghans and Indians. These were the immature views of a teenager. The truth is there are good and bad people in every race, colour and creed. Our illustrious leaders, religious and political, influence who are our enemies and who are our friends.

Chapter Four
A Police Officer

At the age of eighteen years and at a height of 5ft 7 ½" I walked through the gates into the Police Training School at Ryton-on-Dunsmore. I am sure that I was the shortest policeman in the country at that time, although I did put on an inch over the years.

At the Training School I learn the theory and practice of policing and made an ill fated return to the boxing ring; this time as a reluctant volunteer. We were in barracks at Ryton. The school was, for me, best remembered for pillow fights with new friends like Brent Kirton, and the array of practical jokes, the most notable of which was a commendable stunt by the police women who hung the woman Commandant's knickers from the parade ground flag pole.

I wanted to do well at police training school but at no time over the thirteen weeks did I really exert myself. I think my expedition had tired me. Crucially I cruised through the course. At that time I was more interested in having fun with the new friends I had met from Forces across the country. I entered the boxing ring as a volunteer. Again I was keen to demonstrate to other people that I was not lacking in guts. Who the hell wants to volunteer to get hit around the head by someone who is himself trying desperately to avoid getting knocked about.

My fight was spectacularly embarrassing. Nothing I ever seem to do passes without incident. I lost in typically dramatic fashion.

No surprises, I was fighting a taller man. What's new? This time it was the turn of the 'exhibition boxer'. This guy suggested to me before we went into the ring that we should 'put on a bit of an exhibition'. What a prat! 'Avoid hurting each other' was his comment.

I just looked at him, I couldn't say anything. Me, fight. I build up a last minute head of steam and, as before, came out of my corner like a windmill. I came out fighting like a man possessed, expending a great deal of energy and giving this guy one hell of a shock. I should have won in that first round. The second round started much the same way but this time the guy was clearly rattled and intent on fighting back to avoid humiliation. I was tiring. I didn't have a strategy. I wasn't a boxer at all. He was beginning to get the better of me. I had spent a few months sitting on my arse as I travelled the Asian Highway, and I had lost fitness. I was tiring. As I threw out a left hook, he punched me in the left shoulder. The momentum of my left arm going forward resulted in, yes; you've guessed it, a dislocation!

To massage my ego and again demonstrate my courage I agreed to have my dislocated arm 'pulled' in the changing room, to avoid further a time wasting trip to hospital and further discomfort. The PTI clearly relished it!

I passed out, regained consciousness and walked into the bar with a sling on my arm to a chorus of laughter led by my new friends Bob and brother Steve Swain, of Birmingham.

I had heard them laughing earlier at the ringside. Bob had been with me on the Commonwealth expedition and we had a similar black sense of humour. I would have been happy to have laughed at myself if I had been ringside.

I was again disabled. However I was reasonably happy to be incapacitated on this occasion as it was winter time and I had lost some of my appetite for physical exercise of the extremely strenuous kind. I was happy to have had avoided the parade square for a while to give me a little extra time to catch up on my studies. As long as I was fit to complete the thirteen week course that was all that mattered.

Unfortunately the injured arm didn't keep me off the parade ground for long, and I was back on the drill square with the Drill Pig; not as bad as the guy in the film Full Metal Jacket, but close! I tended to be a bit of a clown on the parade square and this got me in a little trouble. We had some great fun moments, but I sailed a little bit close to the wind on occasions. I had developed my sharp wit to the point of getting in trouble with staff who did not appreciate having the piss taken out of them. My Instructor, Sergeant Kennedy, took me to one side and quietly reminded me that I 'should watch it'. There was no offence intended, but I apologized and eased off, choosing to take the piss out of others in the class rather that the main man.

I finished the course, doing just enough, and couldn't wait to get out on the beat.

I enjoyed training school, but was anxious to get on the streets. Eighteen months later I returned to police school for a refresher and it was far less enjoyable. By that time I had tasted something of the real world.

I recall a journey from the training school that was quite shocking. The police van was following a mini. A vicar was driving the mini. His wife was in the passenger seat. The mini was following a lorry with overhanging girders. The lorry braked and the girders went through the window screen. The vicar was decapitated, his head ending up in the shopping bag in the back seat. The wife in the passenger seat was hysterical. Human tragedy had become part of my daily life during the first eighteen months of my beat bobby days.

My first ever patrols were with John Oatridge, a tutor constable at Fletchamstead Highway police station, nicknamed the 'Ponda Rosa', in Coventry. The station was not as busy as the one in the city centre, hence the nickname, implying it was quiet and laid back. By the way, on account of my raincoat and the fact that I was partial to the odd cigar, I got the nickname of 'Colombo' during the first couple of years of my career.

In 2003, when I returned from Indonesia, I met quite by chance and became friends with, John's daughter, Trisha, and subsequently his ex-wife Gloria. John had died a couple of years earlier, but after retirement. He was an ideal tutor constable. Coincidentally, Gerry Whittaker, who had driven me and his son, John, to school almost daily, was Superintendant in charge of the station. Gerry was also a real gentleman, known to my Dad, Mum, and Uncle Eric through his support for Coventry Rugby Club. Gerry had a great big Lord Kitchener style moustache and a kind rounded Father Christmas type face. It was good to think I might have a guardian angel watching over me, but it also made me feel uncomfortable. I needed to be further from home so that I felt less inhibited and more independent. I didn't want help. I wanted to be 100% self made.

I think it was when I was at The Fletch that I got my first inkling of what a serious and dangerous world I was entering. If the cadets made a man of me, real policing was to educate me. Policing was a serious business but larking about and sharing black humour was quite normal. It was a kind of release from the harsh realities of the darker, sadder, side of life that the work engaged. But make no mistake, when the serious business was called for, when the siren sounded, professionalism instinctively kicked in.

The larking about did not replace the job that had to be done. We knew that at any time something serious would happen and that might mean risk and danger. One example, close to the heart of any police officer serving in Coventry at the time, was when Pete Guthrie, married only six weeks, was brutally shot down and killed at Davis's sports shop on Gosford Street, and Sergeant Gordon Meredith was shot in the leg when disarming the intruder. It all happened following a routine; everyday burglar alarm activation.

Gordon was awarded the George Medal for holding onto the shotgun despite being wounded. Pete was posthumously awarded the Queens Police Medal. I met Gordon last year and his leg still troubles him. Pete's wife, Marie Ann, eventually joined the force some years later.

The shock reverberated through the City and the realities of apparently routine policing hammered home to every officer in the country. You never know what will happen or when.

I was transferred to Sutton Coldfield, in the Birmingham conurbation, but still in the Warwickshire & Coventry Constabulary force area; my career really started.

Chapter Five
Sutton Coldfield, Erdington, Aston to Hong Kong

My family, friends, school and the cadets had all helped to define me as a person and shape me into a proud, principled and confident adult. I held myself in high self esteem and I was determined to put my values, including those of fairness and justice, into practice. Sutton Coldfield was the place where I started to learn about the harsh realities of working life. In the course of this development I was to become disillusioned and disappointed with the quality of some colleagues, and learn that I had not yet made that huge step from boy to man. It is a painful step to negotiate.

Sutton was a quiet Royal Borough in the County of Warwickshire at the time of my arrival, but was later to become swallowed up together with Coventry and other parts of Warwickshire to become The West Midlands Police. After that amalgamation I chose to move to Aston, Birmingham, via Erdington.

In Sutton I was lucky to have a gentle baptism into my new career alongside friends old and new. I was pleased to team up again with Ian Brierley who was luckily on my shift. Knowing him made it easier for me to get to know, and get accepted by the other lads. My reputation had preceded me. Sutton was to become a fun posting.

Before my move to Birmingham I had found police officers to be good and fundamentally honest. The Sutton division was not overwhelmed with violent incidents on a daily basis. Domestic fights, road traffic accidents, burglar alarms, lost dogs and sudden deaths comprised the average day. There was time to enjoy a patrol and get to know the community of residents and businessmen and learn about the beat.

I had not arrived at Sutton as a rookie in the true sense, and so the initiation was a little inappropriate for me. At Sutton they had an initiation for new recruits, but I did not quite fit that category, so I simply enjoyed the spectacle from the warmth of the first floor police club window with other laughing onlookers.

The concept was a straightforward one and typical of the services; attempt to make a complete fool of the new recruit and have a great laugh at his expense. The vehicle of this humiliation was the pedal cycle. The recipe; take one pedal cycle and half a dozen traffic cones strategically placed in the yard to represent an obstacle course, place one rookie on the pedal cycle in full uniform, complete with handcuffs, truncheon, whistle and 'tit helmet,' and time trial him during a cycling proficiency test.

Add to this a few 'police specific' manoeuvres, such as removing handcuffs and truncheon from the trousers, whilst on the move, removing and blowing the whistle whilst signalling a left turn and you have the makings of a real crack – if the candidate is stupid enough. Most catch on early, but the 'odd' one doesn't. My particular favourite was the attempt of one guy to remove the truncheon whilst on the move. A truncheon was about fourteen inches long, and kept in a sleeve sown into the trousers. I must emphasise, particularly to the ladies that a truncheon is a fourteen inch piece of hardwood used to hit a naughty man across the shoulders, and not the average man's dream! On another occasion the guy failed, and the expression on the guys face was priceless. He couldn't manoeuvre around the cones, let alone pull out his truncheon!

Sutton Coldfield is a wealthy town on the perimeter of Birmingham that is home to soccer players, celebrities, entertainers, rich businessmen and politicians. It has few council estates and might have been considered by some to be a quiet trouble-free town, and to be fair they wouldn't be far wrong in comparison to 'the city'. The division included a large rural area. Our patch stretched out as far as 'The Belfry' hotel and golf course.

In point of fact, from a policing point of view, Sutton provided a wide variety of interesting work that could be comfortably undertaken in a professional way. Unfortunately the lower than average crime rate meant that greater emphasis was given to 'petty offences' mainly involving the motorists. This is why, in my view, underworked rural police are more likely to stop you for an incorrectly sized number plate, or a cracked tail light than in the city, where the uglier side of policing preoccupies the time of police officers. Sutton was a far cry from the tough, depressed areas of Aston, Nechells and Lozells. It is unfortunate that poor deprived areas receive, in my view, poorer and tougher policing, but I can fully understand why.

Sutton offered a good working environment and I was never too busy. There was pressure to produce traffic 'offence reports', and undertake 'stop checks' as it was the only way to measure how hard you worked. Issuing tickets for trivial and technical offences might have been good for experience, the government coffers and statistics, but does little for good public relations. I have long been in favour of separating these functions from the police service.

I was comfortably engaged in my duties, with a little time to have fun as well. Yes, police officers are human, and they can be mischievous and naughty too – don't tell me you are too naïve to realise that!

When I arrived at Sutton I shared digs with my old mate Ian Brierley who had been stationed there direct from training college. It was great to have an established friend there. I later rented my own place, a flat on the top floor of a three storey Victorian house owned by a scout leader and his cheeky wife. It reminded me a little bit of 'Rising Damp' although the place was a bit more up market. I generally returned to Coventry on my days off, so I spent nights at my parents' home, and, of course, had my washing and ironing done free, gratis!

I was a very confident chappy. I struck up a good working relationship with the other guys in the team. The shift inspector was known as 'the smiling assassin'. I was later to experience why he had the nickname.

Bert Murray, or 'Uncle Bert' as Ian liked to call him, was the station sergeant; the stereotypical friendly round faced experienced cop of the kind that everyone would want to see standing on their street corner. A lovely, lovely man. Alongside big Bert at the helm of the station was 'Bunny' Green who greeted the public at the front office. I can't remember Bunny's real name. He got his nickname after he fell victim to an early morning telephone call from a newspaper during the great myxomatosis outbreak in the 1960's when a healthy rabbit was newsworthy. "No healthy rabbits in Sutton Park! There are, I saw one myself coming in to work this morning!" was his remark. The newspaper article read 'a police spokesman said.....'. He got a knuckle rap and a lot of piss taking afterward and of course the nickname 'Bunny' for life. Bunny had a serious whispery side, and a dry sense of humour. He was also a gossip that you could rely upon to pass on a little bit of 'confidential information'!

Familiarisation was the business of the first few months at Sutton and I 'walked' the High Street for days and nights occasionally walking out of the town to a satellite shopping district of Boldmere, getting to know shopkeepers, publicans, garage owners, tramps and thieves in every nook and cranny, every alleyway, yard and garden. I even got to know the ushers at the local cinema where I stood in the shadows and got the occasional film preview. My real business was keeping an eye out for 'molesters'. Many boys encountered cinema weirdos when going to the 'flicks' to watch 'dirty movies'.

I watched 'X' rated movies as a thirteen to fourteen year old during school holidays at the old Paris cinema in Coventry. Entering an empty cinema, sitting down to watch a movie, and then being approached by a 'perv' was not unusual in those days. They would sit right next to you and start to touch your leg. Even if you moved across the cinema you would sometimes be followed to the new seat. They disgusted me.

I drank gallons of coffee walking my beat, and got a great deal of satisfaction from knowing so many people and knowing so much about the place. It was good to become something of an expert on an area, and to be approached by other officers to be asked questions about people or places on my 'beat'. However, there was one upsetting occasion when the Warrant Officer asked me to help him, based on my beat activity. It was only a few months after my arrival in Sutton, and I did something for him that I deeply regret.

The Warrant Officer, a station based 'old boy' that had responsibility for enforcing Court orders, asked me to execute an arrest warrant on a guy that I soon got to know as a relatively harmless rogue; a small time petty criminal. He was a bit of an arsehole really; a prat! But he was nothing more than of nuisance value to the public and the police. He was simply a waster. Chris R was also a decent enough guy if you took the time to talk to him and understand him.

I walked down to his house to execute the arrest warrant for non-payment of fines. If I had known then that Chris was to go to prison over the Christmas period I'd have told the Warrant Orifice (that really was a typographical error) that he wasn't at home. Instead I did my job and arrested Chris, denying him his Christmas with his wife and children. If I'd had the opportunity I'd have sent the Warrant Officer to prison with him; the nasty bastard.

I felt like a shit. I never executed another warrant for that lazy arsehole, who didn't have the courage to do his own dirty work. He could have left the whole matter until after Christmas. I later apologized to Chris and thankfully he accepted my apology. My reputation was not too badly damaged.

If I wasn't in the police club on completion of my shift then I was in the local pubs and off into the big city to the clubs, usually with one or two of the lads on the shift, more often than not with Ian Brierley or Bill Guest, an ex drug squad officer who arrived as a newly promoted sergeant on our shift.

Bill was from Coventry, and when he arrived we shared petrol costs travelling daily from Coventry, a round trip of about 24 miles, and I scaled down my use of the flat, because by then I had met my future wife, Nikki, and she had moved to Coventry; renting a room from my parents. It's complicated!

Nikki had worked as a hairdresser at Simpsons hairstylists on the High Street, just along from the Cottage Hospital. When she went to live with my Mum and Dad in Coventry, she worked in Coventry at the Midland Educational Book Store under the management of 'Mr. Mac'. The circumstances that brought about our first meeting make interesting reading, and more will be said about that later, suffice at this stage to say that they were a bit bizarre.

I've changed my mind. I'll write about it now. At around 4.00am one morning, a baker arrived for work at the bakery adjacent the hairdressers. The baker arrived on a moped bearing 'L' plates. To arrive he needed simply to turn off the road into a driveway alongside the hairdressers that led to the back of the bakers.

He somehow contrived to miss the driveway, overshooting it and accurately hitting the front door of the hairdressers' shop with the front wheel so as to force it open (with no damage to the door) and drive into the shop, down a step, and park his moped in amongst the hairdryers! Don't ask me how. He had no idea, and neither did I when I turned up at shortly before 8.00am to investigate.

He was a very embarrassed lad. Mr. Simpson, Nikki's boss, was happy to deal with the matter through the insurance and I was happy to see them all shake hands. Most importantly, and significantly, I had found an amazing new 'tea stop' with half a dozen or so sexy hairdressers!

I visited the kitchen at the back of the shop regularly, and sat supping tea with the girls on many occasions. Nikki and I never chatted and she never showed any interest in me – so I chased her mates!

One day, I was sitting alone with my cuppa when she came into the room and we started to talk. I was taken aback with her willingness to engage in conversation with me and was surprised when she agreed to go to 'the pictures' sometime. She was gorgeous. I set a date, we went to the pictures and that is how life with my first 'real girlfriend' started.

There were a few other notable 'tea stops' on the streets of Sutton. My visits to the dentists' surgery came about as a result of an emergency call to the flat above. A guy had taken barbiturates in a suicide attempt. I got there before the ambulance, and kept him lucid, and then followed the ambulance to the hospital where I helped the nurses to hold him down while he was having his stomach pumped out.

The guy was very grateful for the help and wrote thanking me. I visited afterward to provide a little counselling and keep an eye on him. Fallen apart because his girlfriend had left him! A classic. He was seldom about and so I had coffee with the dental staff.

Police work was of course often exciting but it could also be boring and tedious; particularly on a night shift. We therefore had some irresponsible fun, but make no mistake, the business of policing was very serious and we all switched to 'professional mode' when the occasion arose. Oh and 'yes' the blue light occasionally went on when I was late for breakfast; police, fire, ambulance, we all did it.

A police officer enjoys exciting chases, thrills and spills; it was glamorous stuff at times: but it wasn't all 'Life on Mars'. A lot of work was very tedious indeed. 'Feel a collar' and there was mounds of paperwork. We complained about it then, and police officers are still complaining about it nearly thirty five years later – nothing it seems is ever done. 'Book' someone and there is paperwork to be done, and a diary to be maintained – the policeman's pocket book! This was the place where contemporaneous notes were kept. The contents of the pocket book would be reproduced in the form of a statement and report. Contrary to the 'old chestnut' statement, 'lessons have been learnt' – lessons are NOT learnt – lessons are seldom learnt. They are more usually repeated. How had the problem of excessive paperwork, a massive problem in the 1970's, be as big a problem now as it was then; particularly given the 'paper free' society that the computer age promised us. Civil servants, notably those responsible for the Social and Police services; those bureaucrats given the job of freeing up time, have a lot to answer for!

My operational shifts were: 2.00pm – 10.00pm, 10.00pm – 6.00am and 6.00am – 2.00pm with opportunities for overtime at football matches, carnivals, the RAC Rally, etc. I was required to report for duty fifteen minutes before the shift commenced for briefing, but we weren't paid for it. The R.B.O.s (Resident Beat Officers) worked during the daytime and evenings – easy peasy.

The quieter times were the best times for paperwork, often after 2.00am and before 8.00am. But I didn't like leaving my paperwork until the next day, and certainly not the next shift. I liked to do it while it was fresh in my mind and would rather work an extra half hour for nothing than put it off. I didn't like a backlog of work. Of course if I made an arrest late on in the shift, the prisoner had to be processed, and that often meant working paid overtime. There was also the prospect of a Court appearance during the daytime. This might also represent overtime work if working a 2.00pm – 10.00pm or night shift.

I found the disproportionate amount of paperwork frustrating. Some of it was a wasteful use of time. I hated processing minor traffic offences simply because it demonstrated that I was actually doing something. Much good police work is intangible and impossible to quantify. I liked to be out and about on the street, talking to the community and searching for 'real criminals'. I always wanted CID work, but needed to serve my time in uniform. This meant menial tasks – directing traffic - and booking motorists – I didn't like that unless it was for, the more serious offences of 'driving whilst disqualified', no insurance and/or tax.

Spot checks of pedestrians and vehicles produced excellent results; gut instincts worked well with me. I had a good return on arrests for 'crime' during regular 'spot checks'. More's the pity that these 'spot checks' and searches have all but stopped. If they are untaken professionally, politely and considerately then no damage is done. The problem was they often weren't.

There were times when standing around on a street corner, or some inconspicuous and quiet spot, watching the world go by, reaped dividends. At night-time the town and country has an eerie silence that you grow to love. To enjoy the night while the world sleeps is a different kind of experience. Most of us have walked through deserted streets; heading home at 3.00am or 4.00am and those walks offer a taster, but you really feel the solitude by standing in the shadows for an hour or two.

I can remember one dark winter's night standing in a shop doorway smoking a cigarette when 'Charlie' jumps over the fence into the road with his bag marked 'swag'. Charlie and 800 cigarettes from the newsagent's yard landed right into my arms!

But waiting round could be very boring too. Sitting in an open timber yard for three successive nights waiting for an arsonist to turn up was no fun whatsoever, and neither was the night I was assigned to protect a judge at his home, although it was a bit warmer, and he did leave me 'a gottle o geer'

Things happened at the least likely times, and in the most unexpected places. My partner and I went to a Poodle Parlour. There had been a report of an intruder in the flat above. It couldn't be anything I thought. The building was virtually derelict. I went in the insecure door. It was unoccupied even if it wasn't quite a derelict building. I went up the stairs. My partner followed on a distance behind. We joked. I entered the lounge. My

63

partner was trudging up the stairs. Behind the door was a guy holding out a knife toward me. I backed into the corner. "Bill" I shouted. "There's a bloke behind the door with a knife. Be careful". "Oh yer. Pull the other one".

He appeared by the door. I pointed to behind it. He still wasn't convinced. I took out my truncheon and told the guy to put the knife down. Bill could tell by my face that I was serious, but then again he knew me so he still doubted. Then he caught sight of the guy through the door hinge. He took out his truncheon, rammed the door open and trapped him. I dived in to take away the knife. It was hairy, and I'm glad I had company that day. We received a Chief Superintendent's commendation for our efforts. It was very heartening to receive those little distinctions and have them published in the monthly reports. I'd had others for burglary, theft and drug arrests. The Poodle Parlour arrest was just another example of what would be regarded as 'a good', albeit fortuitous, days work.

Flashers were common in and around the park area. Plain clothes observations were sometimes called for when a pattern emerged. One night 'matey' and I were sitting in bushes at the side of the road; strategically positioned, and perched, to survey the relevant length of street where a flasher habitually operated. I sat reasonably comfortably in thick branches on a bank, away from street lighting but opposite a popular pub. The guy tended to flash his tackle to woman walking along the street late at night and usually after the pubs had closed.

For two sub-zero winters' nights, we froze our goolies for three hour stretches, torch and walkie-talkie in hand, so that we could communicate privately between one another. We had one network radio to call for assistance. It's amazing what you see on the streets as the night wears on and the town settles down for the night. I saw two woman kissing in the darkness and saw how indiscrete people can be when undressing in the bedroom! Draw your curtains!

The second night one of our lads turned up in his panda, a Mini 850, and parked it in the alleyway alongside the pub. His presence would interfere with our operation. We had to move him, but I thought of a fun way of doing it – he was going in for a crafty pint with the landlord! Before you gasp in disapproval, it was very common in those days for police officers to drink on duty. It is important to read this account in the context of the 1970's. Indeed it was normal for uniformed officers to drink on duty, albeit against official regulations. However, our gaffer, despite indulging in a drink himself from time to time, didn't like it, and he would administer disciplinary action if he caught you. Quite rightly too.

64

Mischief was in the air and I made a suggestion to my mate. We left our positions and crossed the road to the pub. We lifted the tail end of the car sufficiently to the right to make the car undrivable – it was trapped between walls. We returned to the bushes to wait and watch. What happened next was unscripted, but it couldn't have been better. It was sods law.

He received an emergency call to attend a burglar alarm activation at a golf club that the inspector 'had an interest in' and the inspector usually attended these alarm activations.

We watched him come out of the pub and were close enough to see the look of horror on his face and hear the subsequent radio message. He paced rapidly backward and forward, held his head in his hands, and even made a futile attempt to move it.

He went into the pub doorway, turned and went back to the car, sat in it, got out, looked up and down the street, swore and suddenly, looking inspired, radioed in and said that his car wouldn't start! Another officer was sent in his place. At that point we came out of the bushes and over a barrage of abuse, helped him return the car to its rightful position. The language was rich!

Now please don't be too judgmental about these pranks – nobody's safety was compromised – it was a quiet night and we had a full complement of officers. Black humour was all part and parcel of the job.

You see you really must put these stories in context even if they do seem to dominate my account of life in the force. And drinking on duty was 'the norm' for many officers – even senior officers. If not participating, most turned a blind eye because they knew the importance of good intelligence and that the source of much intelligence was the local pub landlord and his staff. A lot is overheard in a pub. A lot of business is done in the pub. That's why CID officers spent so much time in the pub; getting to know the people and their affairs, either directly or indirectly. Intelligence information was collected from civic minded citizens or 'snouts' or 'grasses', paid or unpaid.

The police response to drinking generally was liberal too. The entire nation was drunk-driving; from judge, jury to housewife and cleric. The breathalyzer test existed, but was seldom used, and in most cases the 'drunk' driver was either given a lift home, or surrendered his keys, confiscated for collection at the police station the following morning. I agree with the strict measures that were subsequently implemented, but I'm not sure that drink- driving is responsible for quite the number of accidents that the statistics attribute to the offence. Statistics are manipulated. Times haven't changed in that regard have they.

There were just a few occasions when I arrested someone for drink/driving; I could count them on my hand. On one such occasion I was driving along and a guy waved me down and insisted I help him bump-start his car. He could hardly stand. I told him he wasn't fit to drive and to give me the keys. He got in the car and tried to bump start it down the hill. I trotted alongside and stopped him. He argued and had his collar felt.

Others I arrested for similar reasons; stroppy or nasty individuals who wouldn't or couldn't see that I was trying to provide some sensible guidance. One guy was actually slumped over the wheel while the vehicle was moving at about ten mile an hour – he was incapable of walking let alone driving – that was unforgivable excess! He wasn't even capable of giving a breath test. A blood sample, taken by a doctor called out to the police station, was the normal procedure that would follow, but he was even too drunk to agree to that. He slept in the cell and was charged the following morning.

I think that greater discretion should be given to police officers, they don't seem to be given enough these days. In the context of drink-driving I accept that it is unacceptable these days, and accept that it should be in the 'criminal' category of offence, but I struggle to recognize that the Courts have ever treated it proportionately. Yes, death by dangerous and drink driving are serious offences, but when thieves, murderers and rapists often suffer less severe treatment in Court, sometimes just a slap on the wrist and the services of a counsellor, it sticks in the throat of the average person who is caught marginally in excess of the legal alcohol limit, but pays for his mistake by losing his job, his mobility, his job prospects and otherwise clean criminal record. There can be a further knock on effect; the financial implications can mean the loss of the family home, and penalize the entire family. Family breakups can follow a relative misdemeanour.

I sometimes despair at sentences dished out by the Courts. I remember reading in 'The Police Review' , back in the 1970's, of a man who received a £30 fine for sticking a glass in a police officer's face resulting in the need for thirty odd stitches, at a time when £30 was the standard 'careless driving' fine. They don't get things right in the 21st Century either – nasty evil people are pampered to by well meaning but misguided do-gooders, who blame society for their dastardly deeds. Nobody tries to stand up for 'Mr. Average'. The motorist is simply seen as an easy source of revenue.

I'll stay on the soap box for another paragraph or two. Slow and poorly trained motorists are the biggest problem on the roads in my view. I don't believe that excess speed is as big a cause of accidents as is suggested. A fast, yet competent and safe driver is usually well trained – as a police officer is properly trained to drive at high speed to attend emergency calls.

Slow drivers slip under the radar and leave devastation in their wake. They cause frustration and congestion on major roads and motorways, forcing lorries into the middle lane of motorways, and therefore all cars into the overtaking lane (it is not a fast lane). It is apparent that some drivers lack confidence, training and skill on unfamiliar roads and motorways and that is reflected in their over cautious and dangerous, yes dangerous, driving.

In my view driving tests should comprise urban, rural, motorway and night driving in all conditions, each module of the test qualifying for insurance discount. Drivers should also be taught to drive a route using their own navigational and road sign reading skills, and be taught to overtake safely. Drivers should also be taught how to drive in snow and ice and be taken on a skid pan. It's not rocket science; properly train motorists for all road conditions and reduce accidents! Everyone over sixty five years of age should be re-tested annually, supported by a medical report.

I have been trained to drive at speed, although I hated my short period as a traffic patrol officer. I have learnt about the capability of the car I drive (an S2000) and driven it on the Silverstone circuit and have been on the skid pan. Like motorcycles, car drivers should be graded, and nobody should be allowed to drive high speed cars until they have undertaken stringent testing and taught to distinguish between driving techniques for front, rear and four wheel drive cars. Pilots (glorified bus drivers) get 'type rated', or tested, before they are qualified to fly that category of aircraft. My mate the pilot, John Cushing, captained 767's and other aircraft – all different and all subject to separate tests as a prerequisite to flying.

I believe that the Chief Constable of Durham Constabulary undertook a study of speeding and the effectiveness of 'cameras' and that he concluded that speeding 'contributed' to accidents but caused around 5% of accidents rather than the national statistic of around 25%. Lies, damn lies and statistics I think! The propaganda concerning 'excess speed' is, I suspect, yet another 'easy earner' designed to raise revenue.

Anyway, I digress slightly. What was worrying about my first couple of years in 'the job', was the pressure to produce results; prosecutions. As I mentioned earlier it was perhaps the only way to measure performance at the time but we should really have

67

moved on and learnt over the years. The truth I suppose is that the target was really to raise revenue because the pressure was directed toward motoring offences – the easy option – and regrettably officers were caused to concentrate on prosecuting the normally law abiding motorist. It was persecution, and nothing has improved since.

I joined the police service to catch criminals and not to persecute Joe Bloggs. I never joined to persecute the general public and my eventual departure was in part because of my unease at the attack on the motorist. It is the source of most ill feeling between the average guy and the police and I never had my heart in issuing tickets for driving up 'one way streets', parking illegally, or failing to indicate when turning left or right. I suggest there remains a strong case for separating 'the police' from traffic enforcement duties. I was not interested in giving the community a hard time, although I saw the value of searching suspect motors for 'contraband'.

No law abiding person with an interest in the safety of the community in which they live should object to being stopped for security reasons. It is in the interests of the public at large and should be a source of comfort. I will never understand the logic of arguing against 'spot checks' and the odd road block. We will be stuck with the society we create unless we concentrate on protecting the majority at the inconvenience (not expense) of the few.

Unfortunately I had to do my time as a young copper and did as I was told, but my focus was on 'intelligence gathering' and the arrest of criminals; thieves, violent offenders and crooks in general. Arrests of this kind gave me immense satisfaction and pride. There were numerous collars that felt my glove. This was real police work that was aside from, but also a part of proper beat work. The Criminal Investigation Department was the link. I was destined for the CID and a step toward the real police work that the public most wanted to see. Police association with the motor car created conflict and the disrespect of the police.

Having said that I did, as admitted earlier, serve a few months on attachment to traffic patrol working out of Chelmsley Wood, and drove, unauthorized, the Triumph P.I. a great car in its day (but a rot box of an investment). I was officially the observer. It was simply license for speed cops to speed – in pursuit of the speeder – and a buzz!

The prerequisite, apart from the serious matter of dealing, very professionally with road traffic accidents, was that you ticketed every driver you could for everything from an illegal defect in the vehicle bodywork to the much more satisfying 'disqualified driver.

68

Of course there was the thrill of the vehicle chase – the movie favourite. That was fun, no doubt.

I drove at high speed courtesy of my partner and absolutely loved it – most people would – what a thrill. But it was not me. The only truly memorable moment was the escort of Father Fell – the infamous Coventry priest – to Wakefield Jail to serve eleven years for conspiracy to blow up Coventry police station – he was an IRA cell lieutenant!

But dealing with road traffic accidents was not the sole responsibility of the Traffic Department, although they always dealt, ultimately, with fatal accidents. I handled accident investigations involving four, five and six vehicles, albeit injury and not fatal accidents. It is a complex and involved investigation and report if handled properly (using the brain).

I recall with pride the occasion when a young mother was injured with a deep cut on her head. She was distressed and I sat with her to reassure her and comfort her. She was supposed to be giving me a statement but I could see that she was more concerned about her wound, and whether it would scar. I said it should heal nicely; I'd seen worse. She sent in a lovely letter to the Superintendent about me, telling him how I had made her feel so much better and helped her through a terrible ordeal. I wish I had kept that letter. It made me feel so, so good.

The Bungalow Fire. Fact and Fiction

Another exciting incident occurred, albeit tragic, while I was attached to the traffic department. It happened in Meriden, near Coventry. I was first at the scene of a fire after receiving a 999 call.

The Birmingham Evening Mail reported, 'Birmingham Policemen who risked their lives in city fire dramas are to get special bravery awards'. The article went on to say, 'Another act of heroism involved a policeman risking his life to rescue a 88 year old woman from a smoke filled bungalow......the bungalow rescue was carried out by PC David Wakefield who made two unsuccessful attempts to rescue a woman. His third attempt succeeded but the woman was found to be dead'

The Coventry Telegraph had reported a vaguely similar story, but eventually got quite close following the award.

Entitled, 'Fire hero' the report read, ….not yet twenty one, PC David Wakefield of Torbay Road, Allesley Park, Coventry, holds the Certificate of the Society for the Protection of Life from Fire as the result of his bravery in a house fire at Meriden.

He was in a patrol car on the M6 on a February night when he heard a radio call about a fire in Meriden. He arrived first on the scene and forced his way into the bungalow ….. where a ninety two year old…..lived.

After several attempts, being beaten back by smoke, PC Wakefield found (the woman) by crawling, with a wet towel round his face, and pulled her out, but she had died. He needed stitches to an arm cut by broken glass and hospital treatment for after effects of smoke. His rescue efforts were praised at the inquest. He received the certificate at a Birmingham civil ceremony'.

The truth was part farce and part keystone cops comedy. I went to the side door and my partner to the front. I cut my arm using a truncheon to smash a glass panel in the door. My truncheon caught on the handle and my arm was pulled on to the broken glass. I banged my head on the door frame when I pulled my arm away and nearly knocked myself out! To add insult to injury I found that the door was already open!! Perhaps I should have tried it first?

Like a fool I entered standing up! I wandered around like a blind mole. I eventually used my brain and crawled under the smoke. There was no wet towel. I was no hero.

The 'traffic department' interlude was interesting, but no substitute for 'real' police work and I was relieved to return to my normal uniform duties in Sutton.

Have I mentioned Stacey D yet? I'd be surprised if I hadn't. He was a harmless friendly man. He was a 'simple' middle aged man still living with his domineering mother. He would hand clover leaves in at the police station as lost property. Bunny would pretend to enter them in the lost property book. Sometimes he would hand in some stones. One day I was dealing with a traffic accident on the Boldmere Road junction with Station Road. I had the 'tit' on my head when he walked up to me as I was writing a driver's name into my note book. He stood next to me. "I'm busy now Stacey. I'll see you later in the Oak (the local pub). OK?"

He looked at me, licked his right forefinger, looked up, and rubbed my tit helmet badge with his wet finger, "Like yer badge" he exclaimed. That was Stacey - harmless.

70

La Gondola

One of my favourite restaurants was the La Gondola in Mere Green, Sutton Coldfield. I would quite often end up there late at night as their alarm would go off; early alarms were very susceptible to wind and were too sensitive. I was invited, to pop in for a cup of coffee when I fancied one. This was not unusual, but a high quality 'tea spot' was a real treat, and the staff were good fun.

Sometimes I would be given a nice slice of cake or a sandwich. I enjoyed visiting the place for obvious reasons, but there was never considered to anything wrong in the public creating good relations with the police any less than the police creating good relations with the public and local small businesses.

It would be surprising if the La Gondola didn't hope for prompt service, and it would be surprising if they were let down. Getting to know the 'patch' is part and parcel of good policing; an essential part. Refusing hospitality, even if duty required it, would in many cultures, including our own, create a barrier, and can be uncomfortable for both parties. As long as it is not excessive and disproportionate there is no harm in accepting a small gift or hospitality.

I ate at La Gondola quite regularly and got to know the staff very well. I took Nikki there for a regular treat and she got to know them also. I can't recall ever having received a free meal but that would make no difference to my thinking.

One of the members of staff was Renato. He was a rounded Italian with a voice to kill for. He would walk from table to table singing with Italian musicians in support; you are probably familiar with the romantic nature of this musical interlude when dining with your wife/husband, or loved one (not necessarily in the alternative).

Renato couldn't make it to my wedding day but he was invited as he was regarded by Nikki and I as a friend. You may remember Renato. He went on to sing, "Save Your Love" with Renee. They took number one slot in 1982 and topped the charts for four weeks over Christmas of that year.

Pranks

Police officers can be lunatics and sometimes their mad behaviour is relief from the serious side of life. A madness that keeps you sane and is encapsulated in the art of the practical joke, usually black humour.

I was a master of black humour but some of the lads engaged in behaviour that I was less impressed with, but nonetheless represented some relief from the stresses and strains of everyday policing. I didn't express disapproval; you see team work involves some degree of flexibility and might explain why disciplined services close ranks when under attack or under critical scrutiny. As long as it is not too offensive I go along with it. We are all human and imperfect.

I refer to the one or two guys who would, on quiet nights, drive around the multi storey car park in the centre of Sutton 'Italian Job' style in the minis; they were nippy panda cars and ideal for urban policing. It was all a bit irresponsible but even the best of guys can be a bit naughty.

We held keys for Sutton Park, the setting for a stage of the annual RAC Rally. At night it was fun to drive around at speed and without any danger of hitting another vehicle. So quite how three police vehicles shunted each other I will never know! Fortunately we were, with the help of the skipper, following a 'serious chat', able to repair one car at a 'friendly garage' early in the morning, and then separate the instances of minor damage to the other vehicles by designating them as different accidents on different dates. This involved the assistance of officers on other shifts, and the hope that the 'chief wouldn't notice. Boys will be boys!

Me? I was more for practical jokes. My idea of fun is best illustrated by the stunt I played one night with Roy Bolton, an ex South African policeman. We were doubled up (two in the car). It was a quiet night and I had a mischievous streak. I had an idea for a practical joke. Roy was an older, more mature and serious guy so I depended upon him to pull it off. I had a reputation for playing the fool and for this one Roy was more plausible. He radioed in. "Delta Two to control".

Receiving Delta Two".

"Yes control. We've just spotted a woman running across the road near Sutton Park Boldmere Gate. She seems in some distress. She was seen heading toward Boldmere Road but we've lost sight of her".

"OK Delta Two I'll send assistance. Description please?"

"Well she's no clothes on – fairly distinctive control. Blonde in her 20's I guess"

We were actually parked in an alleyway at traffic lights on the junction of Jockey Road and Boldmere Road. We listened and waited. There must have been some discussion in the control room.

"Control to Delta One. Boldmere Road, Sutton Park end. Delta Two has seen a distressed woman in the area can you take a look please".

There was a pause while Delta One answered. He asked for a description. There was a further pause. Control (Bunny Green) responded. He dropped the vital punch line.

"Well she's naked but she's a blonde haired girl in her 20's."

Within ten minutes the area was the most thoroughly policed in the town. Police vehicles criss-crossed the junction in scenes reminiscent of the chase in the Pink Panther. You remember, the guy in the gorilla costume, another in a zebra costume and Peter Sellars dressed in medieval armour- all driving back and forth at speed through a town centre

It was hilarious. A CID vehicle even turned up – no doubt abandoning a pint on a bar somewhere.

After a few minutes we wiped the tears from our eyes and went for the jugular – the pièce de résistance. "Delta Two to Control. We've found the woman. We're bringing her in. PC Wakefield has covered her with his tunic but have some blankets ready please."

"Control to Delta One. You can resume as normal. Delta Two has found the girl and is bringing her to the station."

We waited a couple of minutes. Long enough to allow the anticipated charge to the yard at the back of the nick. There were already three cars in the yard when we arrived

73

and another behind us. We went directly to the rear of the cell block where I could see Bunny peering at us through the little window. I could see Bert on his shoulder holding blankets. They couldn't see in the car. We had the headlights on full beam. Roy killed the lights. We were rolling about laughing. The realisation on the faces in the window was apparent by the smiles and foul mouthed language that didn't need you to be an experienced lip reader to understand. We howled. Faces appeared at the side windows and the same foul language was again muttered, this time we heard it.

It was the talk of the shift for days and Roy and I took 'the proverbial piss' whenever the opportunity arose. Even the 'smiling assassin' joined in. the stunt was well received but we had been close to 'dropping in it'. In those days policewomen didn't work nights. They were just on call. Bunny was poised to wake one up!

Sailing close to the wind has been the hallmark of my sense of humour all my life. Ninety nine times out of a hundred I get away with it. It is a hazardous path but reaps great rewards when you get your calculations right. I have had a talent for it.

One day I got the sharp end of Bert Murray's tongue. I'd never seen him in such a rage. My close mate Ian Brierley was with me in the parade room at the start of a shift waiting for briefing. Ian was messing about on the radio. I don't know what he was saying – I was talking to someone else. Whatever it was Bert stormed in red faced finger pointed directly at me as he walked toward the table. I was so surprised, taken aback, that I can hardly recall what he said but he was threatening me. Ian nervously said. "Sarge. It was me".

"Don't you start protecting him" said Bert with a much quieter tone.

"No Bert. Sorry it was me".

Bert didn't quite know what to say. He looked embarrassed, turned and walked away. He later apologised to me.

The reason I tell that short tale is that people are inclined to jump to conclusions if 'you fit the bill; if your reputation precedes you. I also tell the story because Bert had believed that Ian was 'covering for me' that had some significance a few months later when I went sick in the early hours of a morning during a night shift. I signed off and went to Nikki's place (she was living with her Mum at the time). I parked my car, an Austin 1300 as I recall, on the road outside.

The following night I returned to work as normal. Bill Guest asked me into the 'assassins' office. The 'assassin' was at his desk. I was asked where I was when I signed off sick. I told them. They said they had driven past my place, and then checked at Nikki's, and my car wasn't there. Bill later told me he thought I had nipped down to the city 'clubbing it'. I still have difficulty understanding how Bill thought that, but again put it down to reputation.

They were bemused and clearly believed that I was not at Nikki's. I can't explain why they didn't see my car. I told them that apart from Nikki only one person could confirm where I was but I would have to ask if he is prepared to do so. Ian had popped in to see how I was.

The meeting ended. I went into the parade room and was asked about the mysterious 'behind closed door' meeting. I told the lads. I actually wondered if Bill was trying to score points with the 'assassin'. He was a new sergeant and on probation. I waited until Ian said (in front of the lads) that he'd been along to see me. I didn't say that somebody had done so.

Ian volunteered to tell the 'assassin'. Technically he was well off his beat and a vindictive moment could get him in trouble. Ian told him. I felt uncomfortable about the whole affair and knew that they thought Ian was 'covering up' for me.

I recalled, sometime later, popping out to get something from my flat, so they could have missed me as I drove between the two places. Anyhow I never bothered to tell them. I should have done. It was case closed but I was equally unhappy that Bill was uncomfortable with my explanation. I really should have told him, but I just let sleeping dogs lie. I was a shade disappointed that they thought I was lying, so I left them with their discomfort.

Bert Murray was not beyond a little mischief himself, although it was generally designed to help the young constable learn a lesson. I was, as I have mentioned, a little 'green' and my inexperience was highlighted when Bert sent me to 'a domestic'. Neighbours complained about the noise! A husband and wife were having a right blarney. When I arrived they were going at it like cat and dog and neighbours were at their doors waiting for me. I spoke to the neighbours briefly and then went to attend to the 'happy couple'.

I knocked the door and a short muscle man appeared at the door, bare from the waist upward. Abuse was hurled at me from the outset. Then he shouted abuse into the street, for the benefit of the neighbours. Then he turned, went in and started to blame his wife. I asked if I could enter, I didn't get a reply so went in anyway. I was confident I could get the couple, locked in argument before me, as if I wasn't even there, to calm down and be quieter - nothing of the kind. My touch was about to fail me.

I couldn't get a word in edgeways, when it looked although I had the attention of one, the other abused me, if it wasn't one it was the other. She tore up a full packet of his cigarettes and threw them in my face. He tore off her pearl necklace and threw it at me, pearls stinging my face. It was like a scene from a black comedy. A full ash tray, a table lamp and a picture in frame crossed the lounge narrowly missing me. I was too close to the action so I stepped back toward the door. I tried everything I knew but nothing was working. She pushed past me and stormed up the stairs and he followed – was I invisible?

I stood at the foot of the stairs with the front door behind me. A tiny crowd of neighbours had congregated at the gate and they had decided to give the couple a bit of their own mind. I asked them to be quiet and go home-they weren't helping.

The couple had disappeared into the bedroom but the screaming continued and he bellowed. I wasn't going upstairs. I did just a few steps. I took a firmer hand, "Now that's enough, the pair of you. Anymore and I'll have to take action. This is a breach of the peace and has got to stop".

I might as well not have been there. He shot to the top of the stairs and started to come down. Another table lamp crossed his path, hit the wall and ricocheted down toward me.

"Now that's enough" I said firmly.

"That's enough is it?" He said as he brushed me aside on the staircase.

He went into the lounge and turned the radio on and turned it up. "I do what the fuck I want in my own house. Now fuck off".

He took me by the arm and pushed me toward the door.

"That's it" I snapped, "You're under arrest for breach of the peace".

I took his arm. God he was strong! Ooooops! I pulled and he resisted. I was getting nowhere. I stood on the door threshold. He held on to the door frame. He was locked like a limpet. I was never going to move him. I went for my radio to call assistance as I did so he let go of the door frame and, locked together, we fell out of the house, down the step, across the rose bed and on to the lawn where we rolled until I got a firm lock around his neck. We lay motionless, my legs wrapped round his body.

I had dropped my radio. No radio, a struggling Mr Muscles, and nowhere to go for either of us. It was looking very undignified for both of us – stalemate! I asked a neighbour to call the police – then I couldn't believe I'd just done that!

Assistance arrived and he calmed when it was two against one. This 5'2" guy was the strongest man I can ever remember wrestling with. Fully restrained we got him back to the station and into the charge room. Enter Bert.

"Hello Bob" Bert said with a broad smile on his face. "Wife giving you trouble again?" My jaw dropped.

Bert gave him a good talking to and he was released 'no charge'. Bert drove him home at the end of the shift. Bert laughed and pulled my leg about my inability to handle this guy. He could have warned me - I'd been had! I was a little embarrassed but I had registered the lesson, and I could laugh about it.

Operation Julie

In March 1977 the biggest drug bust in the UK and possibly the World took place. It is estimated that something like 90% of the world's production of LSD originated from a farm house in Tregaron in mid Wales where the big raid took place. The raid and ultimate convictions of scores of people received worldwide publicity and resulted in a film and BBC documentary. The investigation lasted some eighteen months. Praise was heaped on those police officers leading the investigation, and justifiably so.

But where did it all start? Did the investigation start at the manufacturing plant in the farm house where the ring leaders, most notably Mr Kemp operated? I doubt it. Most investigations, unless there is a huge piece of luck, start on the street, and, in the case of drugs, are traced back to source. This is where I claim a huge slice of credit, which prompts me to suggest that I might have been the person that initiated, at any rate played a major part in, the early stages of a limb of the operation. How could this be so?

In 1974 I was a 'green' and young uniformed officer on the streets of Sutton Coldfield. One day I picked up this sad bedraggled lad off the main street. He had a little cannabis on him, looked like a vagrant and so I arrested him and took him to the station for a chat. He was a really nice guy with a very serious drug problem. He was charged with 'possession' by Bert Murray toward the end of the shift and I left the station with him and brought him a beer at the Royal Oak next to the station. He was homeless. I took him to my place, fed him and let him have a bath and a few clothes. He started to talk to me frankly and honestly. If I could remember his name I wouldn't mention it, as it happens I can't remember, but we'll call him John.

John told me that drugs were being distributed across the city by a guy named Preece and Richard Green of Sutton Coldfield. They were readily available from the ice cream man in the bottom of cones. He also knew of a marijuana farm on the Walmley Road, Sutton. This sounded sensational and very sound information. He had no other reason to give it to me other than because I had helped him and he liked and trusted me. After all, I had just busted him!

I didn't want to put in a normal 'intelligence report'. It sounded too big for that. I spoke with an ex drug squad inspector who was a uniformed inspector at Sutton. I also spoke with Bill Guest, my skipper, who was also ex drug squad. I agreed to pass the information on to the drug squad. We talked and they were clearly very interested. There were exchanges on the phone, and, against all the unwritten rules of the game, I agreed to let them meet my informant. We met up in a parked car. The DS was impressed with what John had to say. He wanted to test the information by raiding the marijuana farm where 80 or so plants were seized. Trumps! I was promised some involvement in that raid, for experience. It went ahead without me. I was pissed off and felt betrayed but it was too late. John was quite rightly put into rehab and I heard nothing more until around 1980 when I read that Preece and Green had been sent down for about ten years apiece.

I didn't mind being blown out so much as being cheated of valuable experience. I didn't mind that the DS and his drug squad team had been commended for their part in 'Operation Julie', just that they had failed to report, and recognise my role in it. The information that led to that farmhouse in Wales can undoubtedly be traced back to information from 'the street', possibly, and given that the information preceded the farmhouse investigation, probably came from me - I mean John!

I had stopped Richard Green as he sped through Sutton in his green coloured Range Rover. It had personal number plates as I recall. I chased and stopped him. He had a young giggly girl on his arm. He was taking the piss. I was with Bill Guest and told him who Green was. We took the smile off both their faces by suggesting to each other that we take the vehicle in for a 'strip search'. He went quiet and the girl pale. We had overstepped the mark but went no further. We had let him know that we thought he might have drugs in the vehicle but left it at that. We didn't want to jeopardise the 'operation.'

I don't think I'd have stopped him if I hadn't been left out in the cold by the drug squad. The whole thing might have been blown if we'd done any more than just put him in his place. I never stopped him again. I had a sense of duty but always felt that I could have been better rewarded by the drug squad.

They were plain clothes plods because they didn't have enough brain. I would have taken care of a young enthusiastic bobby that had come across such important information – rewarded him with a little experience as I'd requested. They were never to have any more information from me. They had denied me a chance to join 'the big push,' as Colonel Melchet in Black Adder would have put it.

West Midlands Police

There was some sadness on amalgamation of some of the Warwickshire and Coventry Constabulary divisions with Birmingham, and some other force areas, to form The West Midlands Police. Warwickshire and Coventry officers felt the same way when their two forces amalgamated years earlier. It was the end of an era and many felt it was for the worst.

Coventry became a division and Sutton Coldfield a sub-division of a monster force under the 'demon Brummies'. I actually embraced the changes, as do most youngsters, but I was also apprehensive. I wanted to serve in Birmingham to see how 'thick' these Brummie cops were; whether their reputation as thugs was warranted.

In Sutton we were pussy cats. The nearest thing I had experienced to 'police brutality' was in the context of 'effective administration of street justice'; close to what most people would like to see now.

Of course the people of Sutton were a cut above the high rise council estates such as Castle Vale, for behaviour, but there were still 'scum' elements, and certainly cheeky youngsters that needed to be taught a lesson or two.

In Sutton, my mate, who hailed from Durham, got some lip from a gang of youngsters outside a chip shop in Mere Green one night. He grabbed the biggest by the scruff of the neck and banged his head several times on the bonnet of the Allegro police car. "Don't you talk that way again you cheeky young shit" he said as he did it. Everyone in the chip shop stood watching. The youths stood looking on, jaws dropped. My mate sent him on his way, "You lot behave yourselves. If I catch you messing about round here again I'll knock your block off". They all left. There was not a single complaint.

Of course the older reader will be well aware that the bonnet of an Allegro was so thin and bouncy that no harm whatsoever could befall the hapless, terrified teenager. The springy bonnet and the youth parted quite unharmed. It was in my view excellent policing. He knew the lads and his approach had a lasting and positive effect on their behaviour.

But my mate's style wasn't mine. Not least because I didn't have the physical presence that he did. But I did use a glove or two around the ear on the odd occasion. I repeat, not my style, but on reflection it worked, and for my part I believe that a clip around the ear, from a teacher, parent or police officer, never does anyone any harm.

There is a place for brutal policing. There has to be. There are some extremely evil and well organised brains out there that see softness as an exploitable weakness. The inexperienced, the idealists, the naive amongst us may disagree, but there are facts of life that are as brutal as the fiction, and there is little point in pretending otherwise.

I was eventually to get a transfer to Aston, the 'D' divisional headquarters, next to the Villa ground in Queens Road. What was that place going to be like?

There had been an early influx of 'Brummies' to Sutton, all trying to escape I guess, and it was never to be the same again. Nobody wanted to go in the other direction. I had worked in Erdington on occasions, but not in the real city. I requested a move to Aston. Nobody could understand why I would want to be transferred to a reputed hellhole.

Erdington

Erdington was an interesting little nick and a part of the old Birmingham force. It was there that I met my first Brummie nutter by the name of Sgt 'Mad Mitch' Mitchell, the station sergeant. He had a mean looking face, bloodshot and wild (he was a Scotsman). To be fair he clearly had a health problem; probably blood pressure. 'Mad Mitch' had an awesome reputation for blowing a gasket. I remember one day Mitch at the counter with a little old lady. I can't remember what her query was, directions I think, but Mitch lost his patience with her when he found that he was failing to communicate. He exploded,

"Get oot of my police station, get oot oot oot I say". I felt so sorry for the little old lady as she scurried out through the door at high speed. It was like she was on casters. But it was nonetheless very amusing.

Mitch came out with me on a 'sudden death' one day. He was the last person I wanted in the car, but I could do nothing about it. He had wanted a lift to the bank and was in the car when I got the call. We turned up at the house and walked in. Mad Mitch (Mr Insensitive) looked down at the body lying in front of the open fire and turned to the deceased's wife. "Well he's dead alright Mrs and there's noot we can do. If you put the kettle on we'll have a nice cuppa tea, just one sugar for me hen". I met a few crazy old cops like Mad Mitch, but none quite as nutty and insensitive as Mitch.

Erdington police station was the scene of one of my most shocking police experiences, not least because it had a profound effect on my thinking and taught me a major lesson in 'reading' people. Two years on from 'muscle man' and his neurotic wife I learnt how powers of persuasion can have catastrophic outcomes.

Police officers spend an inordinate amount of time dealing with disputes between boyfriend-girlfriend, husband-wife and other everyday disputes, in restaurants over unpaid bills, outside pubs between drunken friends or at taxi ranks between cabby and customer. It is in no police officers interest, or the interest of the parties, to arrest anyone in minor, albeit heated dispute. So often charges were later withdrawn once temperatures had lowered and all too often a little mediation and dispersal, sometimes expressing firm threats, did the trick. Conflict resolution is a major part of a police officer's work and they get little credit for it. There are few statistics you see. It's often an intangible. If you are good at it you are generally a good policeman. I was.

None of the disputes that I dealt with in my career affected me more that the one in the early hours of a Monday morning on the last night of a night shift.

I was doing a little paperwork in the station. The skipper, not Mad Mitch I hasten to add, came into the parade room and asked me if I'd help deal with a guy that had been arrested for putting a brick through the window of a car occupied by his girlfriend and her new lover. He wasn't coping with being jilted.

The three of them, all coloured (I'm afraid I can't be done with too much political correctness), maybe Indian, maybe Pakistani, but second generation British, were brought to the station. The girl didn't want to press charges but she was frightened of the

81

assailant, her ex boyfriend. I spoke to the boyfriend and the skipper spoke with the girl in the other interview room.

My job, as it unfolded was to convince this guy that we didn't want to charge him and that his girlfriend (and lover) didn't want to press charges providing he promised to leave her alone. It wasn't easy. In fact I sat talking to him for well over an hour, exchanging notes with the skipper, and feeding messages between the parties. He loved her. She didn't love him. It was over, I convinced him.

Over the duration of the chat he became increasingly and visibly saddened, at the same time calm, cool and collected. He gave me a guarantee that he would leave peacefully and go home. I had to plead with him to do so. They left, and the boyfriend was released about half hour later. A successful outcome I thought.

I finished my shift and went back to my digs to sleep. I slept, as usual, through to nearly 5.00pm. I then drove over to Coventry to be with Nikki, who was living with my parents at the time, with the intention of returning to work on the Wednesday for a 2.00pm start. I was listening to the local radio as I drove along the motorway. I was stunned by what I heard.

The guy had visited his girlfriends flat. Poured petrol over her, and her boyfriend, and then set them alight before pouring petrol over himself and setting fire to himself. They all died. I was shocked and upset. I pulled onto the hard shoulder, took some deep breathes, and reflected. Was it my fault?

The Road to Aston

One fine afternoon I was walking the beat some distance away from the town centre, indeed on one of the few council estates. I came across a car, very badly, like ridiculously badly parked, with the rear end at some 40 degree angle to the kerb, with the tail end obstructing the flow of traffic along the road. The car had a sign 'Doctor on call' on display. Just as I was about to go the doctor appeared. He said he was sorry about the parking and that it was an emergency call. I thought he was lying and I wasn't going to let him get away with that. I said no problem if you are on an emergency call, what happened? He told me it was none of my business. I said it was my patch and that I was surprised I hadn't heard of an emergency. He changed his tune and said it was just a house call; it wasn't an emergency. I then told him that if that was the case he should have taken the time and trouble to park properly.

82

He didn't like me chastising him. He started to get stroppy and I took out my book. I was going to give him a ticket to produce his documents –there was no way he was going to talk to me like a 'shit'.

I asked him his name, got it, but he became increasingly impatient, sharp and then rude. He pushed my book to one side, got in his car and drove off almost running me down as he went. I was fuming.

I was back at the station a short time later with the intention of submitting my report and issuing the doctor with a parking ticket. I was still angry.

I walked down the corridor to the report room. Baker, an 'admin inspector' and ex Brummie dinosaur, came out of his office as he saw me approaching. He wanted a word with me. He had received a complaint from the doctor, a police doctor as it turned out, who took blood samples from drink-drive suspects.

He was taking a firm tone with me and giving a clear impression that I was in 'hot water'. He was bullying. I took an equally confident though submissive tone explaining how the story went. He started to warn of the implications of putting in a report; frighten me. He reminded me who the doctor was. I said that made no difference but that if the doctor was cautioned then I didn't mind, it was a senior officer's prerogative. I was just going to put in my report. He started to criticise the evidence. I told him once I detailed my report he could read it. His tone then mellowed and he asked me not to put the report in – it was too late, I was on his case. I was even madder.

I said I would put my report in, and if 'my' inspector wanted to caution the doctor, then he could do, and that I was disappointed that I didn't have his support when I had been verbally and physically abused.

I walked along the corridor back toward the front office. I wasn't even going in the right direction. I was upset. Within seconds, not minutes, my own inspector, the 'smiling assassin' came in to the corridor from the front officer. "Now PC Wakefield I understand that Inspector Baker has asked you not to put in that report. Now I'm ordering you not to, and if you don't like it you can go and see the superintendent"

I simply replied, "OK. I will", turned to my left and walked up the stairs and knocked the superintendants door. I told him calmly and respectfully what had happened. He called in Baker and the 'assassin'. Baker said that 'never in 30 years of police service had his authority been challenged in such a disrespectful way". I said, " I have no respect for either of you" and continued to say that if my evidence was flawed, so be it, but I had a right to put the report in, that I could not be ordered not to put in a report, and that I expected a senior officer to support any junior officer that receives abuse from a member of the public whether he is a police doctor, judge or simply a friend.

The superintendent was in a very difficult position. He asked me what had happened again but this time he was looking at the evidential value. I knew I was on safe ground and that I was right, but that the superintendent was looking for a way out.

I gave it him, and agreed that I would not put in a report, but demanded that I have a transfer. I refused to work for either of the two inspectors because I didn't respect them. I made it clear that if I was made to I would resign. I said I could not work for senior officers that I had no respect for whatsoever. Baker was seething and the 'assassin' looked quite humbled. He knew word would get around about him. He cared, Baker didn't. I suspect he was a corrupt cop, if not a brown nose.

The 'super' looked relieved. He could do nothing about these dinosaurs, they were virtually un-sackable, and I'm sure he knew that they were wasters in the final years of their careers and just waiting for retirement.

I got the move to Aston that I was looking for, not yet CID, I didn't squeeze that hard, but that would come. There had been the influx of City cops into Sutton but I was the first into the City. Why? I thrived on new experiences, stimulation, new challenges and excitement. I was usually prepared to go where others weren't, and it always proved to be rewarding. I needed to see these notorious Brummie cops at close quarters; were they really thick thugs?

Aston

The Chief Super at Aston had a good reputation as was reflected in his nickname, 'Gentleman Joe Matthews'. He greeted me with a wry smile, knew about by encounter with 'Baker' of course, but was impressed I think, with my conduct and my reasons for wanting to move. He liked me, but he soon retired and was, fortunately, replaced by an ex Coventry cop, Tom Meffin who later went on to become Assistant Chief Constable (Crime). He was a 'Coventry Kid' and ex CID Coventry; well respected and liked by many. We liked each other and met up on the terraces at Coventry City matches from time to time, chewed the fat and yelled support for the Sky Blues. Tom thought highly of me as a copper.

I joined a shift and made good friends early on with Tom Clark, and 'Scooby', who became a flat mate at my place in Sutton. Although I was never certain as to his sexual persuasion, Scooby was a very likeable and excitable 'loony'. Sadly, he was later to turn on me.

Tom Clark worked in the front office at the station; Queens Road. I did my firearms training with a 38 calibre Smith and Wesson revolver at the range in the yard. Co-incidentally the control room sergeant was by the name of Weston (sounds like Wesson ha ha). He had a very sharp wit and he was a fast thinking smart cop. I liked and respected him a lot.

Tom was a keen First Aider, and I enjoyed First Aid. I had the St John's Ambulance certificate, and so, at Tom's request, I joined the First Aid Team and qualified for the Advanced Certificate. Ian Brierley shared my interest and also joined the divisional team. Tom was a gentleman with over twenty years in the job. He had sensitive eyes and so wore dark glasses and worked indoors.

I got a 'second place' in the 'individual' part of the force First Aid competition, to the amazement of the better First Aiders in the team. The team got a third place. The test, on an individual and team basis involved dealing with an accident/incident with actors playing the part of injured people and onlookers, on an elaborate set. I/we were then sent onto the set, as first on the scene, to deal with the incident, treat the wounded (if not dead) and make all the right decisions, at the right time, and in the right order.

Judges watched and marked the performance. It was necessary to give a running commentary of what you were doing to make clear to the judges what your diagnosis was, what your treatment was, and thus maximise the mark. It had been necessary to do a running commentary when doing the advanced police driving test so we were experienced in doing so. It was theatrical really, and very enjoyable.

There wasn't really much foot patrolling in Aston; too risky. There was good overtime at the Aston Villa matches, I joined the CID for a spell, and became acting sergeant directing operations in the control room for a few months before I resigned and went to Hong Kong, otherwise I got little enjoyment or satisfaction out of working at Queens Road.

Experience in abundance, but no enjoyment. I only saw the worst of policing; over-zealous and lacking warmth and respect. There was inability, and of most concern disinclination, to diffuse difficult situations. All too often heavy handed talk, or action, inflamed situations. The Handsworth race riots were no surprise to me. Confrontational and dictatorial approaches seem to suite those with an appetite for fighting rather than calming. It disappointed me; these guys were not of the quality I had been accustomed to.

Most in Birmingham were not Britain's best, but then I suppose many weren't the brightest bulbs in the room. Good officers were thin on the ground. The patrol skipper, why I can't remember his name I don't know, was a good guy, an honest capable cop, and a laugh; but aging and limited in intellect. I needed his confidence, but hadn't yet got it. I think I was seen as a physically short guy wearing a broad non-stop smile that ill suited the hard world of inner city policing. Aston, Nechells, Lozells were rough, derelict and deprived areas, rife with gang activity and populated with tough people. He wasn't sure about my credentials.

I earned his respect firstly with my report of a suspicious death. I was called to the flat of a guy that hadn't been seen, unusually, that morning. I went to the door and was surprised that it was open. A fat black guy lay, dead, across the bed, fully clothed and in a state of rigor mortis. His position was in itself suspicious, as he appeared to have fallen across the bed and he had been bleeding from the mouth.

I asked for CID and a pathologist but he was sent to check up on my report. He agreed that it was a suspicious death and I sealed off the area and started to keep a log of comings and goings and an account of my own involvement.

A posse of cops tried to enter the room – I knew that was wrong, and took charge and stopped people coming in, to the indignation of many, until the senior investigating officer and the pathologist arrived. There would be no contamination of this 'crime' scene.

He was taken aback, but supported what I said. He began to take the same stand. He started to look through some belongings, but I didn't stop him. That would have been difficult for him to take.

The dead guy turned out to be a slim Caucasian Irishman and not a fat West Indian! It turned out that he had had a massive thrombosis and his body had been blown up like a balloon. I had never seen anything like it in my life, and neither had anyone else. Even the pathologist had early doubts. So it was a sudden death, but I had performed professionally and with confidence, authority and wisdom and I won over many people by word of mouth.

Around the same time I got called to a reported murder. It was a sound report, if it wasn't a hoax, because the report had been made by the murderer, who was waiting for me. A rough tough cop got there before me. I arrested the guy, Dove, but the rough tough cop went down as arresting officer. He was desperate to get into CID and wanted as many arrests for crime as he could get. I didn't get upset.

Dove wasn't going to go down for murder. I was sure of that. He owned a small back street motor repair business and after a dispute with his partner, who hit him with a spanner, knocked him to the ground and dropped a bench vice on his head. His head was crushed like a melon. It was a hell of a mess.

I sat with Dove for some time. He was devastated, very sad and very remorseful. He'd done it on the spur of the moment in rage. He was really quite an ok guy. I felt sorry for him. He got just two years for manslaughter.

I got asked by the 'Super' if I wanted do some plain clothes undercover work for them at nightclubs in the City centre. I agreed and got some good overtime, free beer and food on expenses. I liked it. Sometimes I would be given a policewoman to take. I liked it even more. Problem was word got back that some underworld characters had heard about me and wanted a photo. I was taken off the job. I was later told there was a price on me. I don't know if that was true.

My inspector in Aston was Jack Crow, a quiet guy who seemed to let everyone else run the shift. He looked and drank like Danny Parker; grey haired, wide mouthed and a keen card player. He'd want to play cards all through a night shift, and would do if we didn't get out of the canteen of our own volition. He'd never order us to leave the card table. If it wasn't poker then it was snooker. Was any work done at this nick at night? But I enjoyed it and went along with it.

On a night shift the gaffer would visit Nightingales, a gay nightclub next to the Villa ground, and play his banjo to whoever would listen. We knew where to find him. I went in there from time to time, on and off duty, on one occasion I took Nikki in for the experience. It was very gay, transvestites serving drinks and lesbians strutting their stuff in gents clothing, and giving you a tough eyeballing. It was a bizarre place, but I wasn't homophobic and enjoyed the gay company.

I got into a few scrapes on the terraces at the football, as all coppers did, and got myself on the TV apprehending a pitch invader during a cup semi final game at Villa Park; I enjoyed that. I hated everything else about the place. It was depressing. There was however a little camaraderie, and banter on the odd occasion.

The police held the keys to the mortuary in Steelhouse Lane for those occasions when it was closed, for example, on Bank Holidays. We would arrange for the stiffs to be checked in. I remember occasions when I visited during opening times. The attendant was a gay guy who kept photographs of huge dicks on the office wall and delighted in showing me his 'record holder' a fourteen inch black stiffy complete with ruler strapped to the side. I must admit it was humbling.

One night a new recruit was given the keys to check in a stiff; a new arrival. Of course this was a fictitious new arrival. We arrived at the mortuary early and I got underneath a sheet on a slab alongside the dead. Lights out door locked I waited. The guys waited in the office in darkness. The new recruit needed to pass me to get to the office to check the stiff in. It was a cold eerie place; horrible. He entered. I timed it to perfection, giving it a few seconds from when the main light went on. He would be just in front of me to the left. I sat upright under the sheet and made 'that noise', you know the ghostly deep groan out of the movies.

He shot off at high speed out of the door and past his car to the street beyond. Only a radio call from control got him back. He had been petrified, didn't see the funny side, so didn't fit in and so, eventually he resigned. Black humour is endemic in the services. It is a defence mechanism; it's part of the job.

Racism in the city was particularly apparent. One night I was in the report room of Canterbury Road nick. One of our guys opened the telephone directory, and randomly picked out a 'Singh', rang the number (at 3.00am in the morning) and hurled racist abuse down the phone. I looked disinterested as another guy laughed. I felt very awkward and angry but engaged him in conversation to disguise it.

It was apparently one of his party pieces. I spent days wondering what to do. Not too long afterward the Detective Chief Inspector (DCI) came into the canteen and played the recording of a man that had made a bomb hoax call to the Villa ground and as a result the stadium was evacuated. I thought it was him, and discreetly told the DCI. He asked why I thought it was him and related to him the incident in the report room.

It turned out it wasn't him, but nonetheless he got fined £5 for the racist telephone call. I knew I would have a rough ride thereafter even though I was assured that he had been ordered not to tell anyone about it. The DCI asked me to tell him if I had any shit. I didn't care. Racial abuse from a person duty bound to uphold the law is simply not on!

A couple of months later Scooby came right up to me in the pub and asked me straight out. "And did you?" "Yes I did". "You bastard" he stormed off. He had already moved out of the flat, so there was no moving out, but he didn't speak to me again. I didn't give a monkeys, but knew the word would spread. I am proud to have told him straight. There are certain standards that officers of the law must adhere to, and there is no place in policing for racism. I didn't mind racist, sexist, or any kind of joke, but active racism is insidious. I would not tolerate it. I held my head high and told him. Scooby was not the guy I thought he was.

There was a later incident that disturbed me. Not because of the incident, it was minor, but rather the disproportionate publicity that it received. I am sure that it was 'spun' by the person that gave the information.

The Birmingham Evening Mail front page headline was, 'City Mob Clash', an article by June Walton on 8th April 1976.

'Two injured policemen had to be rescued by colleagues in an incident involving a screaming mob of 100 teenagers' it opened. 'Two officers, PC David Wakefield and PC Colin Partington, went to the scene after complaints from residents in Stoneleigh Road, that youths were running wild, armed with sticks and bottles. The two officers were set on, and needed treatment for cuts and bruises. No one was arrested'.

Poppycock! Nonsense. How did this story get into the papers? There were maybe a dozen or so youths. I didn't see a bottle or a stick. They surrounded and jostled us. My helmet was pinched, and eventually found in a hundred pieces. We took a few punches, held them back by drawing truncheons. I can't recall an injury, but somebody insisted we go to the hospital for a check up.

The article explained, 'the incident happened in Perry Barr last night after a disco attended by hundreds of West Indians.'

The article highlighted that they were West Indians. The Handsworth riots, when they came, were no surprise to me whatsoever. Black guys were subject to racism. On the other hand, many of these guys were searched for understandable reasons; violence and

89

the use of weapons were common in the predominantly black areas of the city. The crime was disproportionately high in the black areas, so it follows that searches would be disproportionately high. I support random street searches.

I had my application for CID approved and 'moved upstairs' working with James, about the only guy I really trusted. He was smart and educated, and he knew about my scrape. He didn't seem to care.

I was involved in one of the most disgusting cases that I can recall. A woman reported that her brother-in-law, aged sixty, his two sons, fourteen and thirteen, had forcibly raped and sexually abused his daughters, their sisters, aged twelve and eight. Regular sex sessions followed the 'breaking in' process. The Social Worker had known about it for three months but had decided that he could deal with it himself.

The old man was disgusting and quite unrepentant. He smiled his way around the nick although he was enjoying some wonderful adventure. He got seven years. I had interviewed the older victim and took a statement from her. She was flirting with me throughout, and her eyes were piercing in to mine; she wanted me. She had been seriously affected by her year long ordeal. The Social Worker was reprimanded by the judge and the kids taken in to care. The 'lessons' that we are still repeatedly told are being 'learned' by social services, politicians, police, council workers, etc, are, it would seem, never learned.

I was uncomfortable working at Aston, not just because of the brave stand that I had taken in relation to the scum in our ranks, but because the style of policing was depressing, uncreative and draconian. I could do nothing here other than sink to their level and exist. I thought of a move, an exciting and unusual move.

I was better than most of these guys, and things weren't moving fast enough for me. I had passed my promotion examinations and needed promotion quick. But it would take another year. I couldn't wait. I needed a new challenge and travel was now in my blood. Pay was awful, I was disillusioned with my lot, I couldn't afford to get married or have a house, and the country was falling apart under Government mismanagement and excessive union power.

I looked into the idea of becoming an officer in the Hong Kong Police. I enquired, went with Nikki to a seminar at the High Commission in London, got the job and resigned. Hong Kong offered me command experience, higher salary and a 25% gratuity on earnings over the term of a three year contract. And oh, we had free flights for Nikki, and any children, if I was married, plus free accommodation. This was virtually irresistible given my credentials and background; I was adventurous.

Long before I thought about Hong Kong, in 1974, in fact, I flirted with becoming an RAF pilot. I passed the initial interview stage and was asked if I was interested in anything other than flying. I would not entertain it. I wanted to be a pilot, not a navigator, air controller or anything else. I wanted the glamour of flying.

Nikki wasn't prepared to move from the Midlands, to Swinton, I recall. I kept on postponing by trip to Biggin Hill for the aptitude test. I had lost interest because I was in love with Nikki. I had the railway warrant, but it appears, from an old letter that I found, they were already fed up with me. The letter of February 1975, opens, "since you did not attend this centre <u>once again</u>, on the date arranged, will you please advise us whether, or not, you wish to continue with your application for a commission in the Royal Air Force".

The tone of the letter says it all doesn't it. I will never know whether I would have made the grade as a pilot. I suspect not, certainly not a fighter pilot, but that I did not test myself on the issue, leaves me with a little regret. C'est La Vie.

"You're Nicked"!

One afternoon Pete Wilford travelled over from Coventry and we went out for a beer that night. I was on a 6.00am – 2.00pm shift the following morning so needed to be up for 5a.m. Pete had to be back home that night. We intended to have just a couple of pints!

We went to the Horse and Jockey on the Jockey Road, Sutton Coldfield in Pete's car. At closing time we were invited for George Rafters (afters). I said I would go to get a takeaway meal for the staff. Pete gave me his car keys. Out into the car park I went. The car had gone! Pete double checked – as you do. It had been nicked!

I telephoned my old nick – Sutton – and reported the theft to my old shift colleagues. We decided that Pete would stop at my place, drop me off at Queens Road nick and borrow my car to travel back to Coventry. We had a few more beers and walked, no staggered, back to my pad.

I felt rough, and when I got in to work I was happy to hear that my car was off the road; a chance to do paperwork and have a walk. The downside was that I was given a point duty on the Aldridge Road at its junction with College Road during the rush 'hour

91

and a half'. Nevertheless with a couple of aspirin my monumental hangover would have cleared for a late breakfast break.

Aldridge Road was an arterial dual carriageway road into the city centre that was often bumper to bumper in the weekday morning rush hour. College Road fed into Aldridge Road from the right and so traffic queuing to get out of College Road had to cross the outbound carriageway of Aldridge Road and merge with city bound traffic.

Without assistance it was difficult to get out of College Road; you depended on courteous and patient motorists to let you cross the carriageway and to let you into the traffic flow.

Having said that, I think that the idea of a police officer directing traffic at this junction was to make sure that the Chief Inspector got to work on time! At any rate it was not a daily routine, the presence of a cop depended on availability. I was available.

Now Birmingham is a city of several million and at times they all seemed to be amassed on the Aldridge Road – at least that morning they did.

Believe it or not in those days there was no real guidance given as to how to regulate the flow of traffic. The success of the operation depended on the commitment and judgment of the officer conducting the duty. I wasn't taught how to tackle traffic flow, the only tuition related to the disciplined manner in which you should quite clearly and deliberately, confidently and authoritatively direct it.

Surprisingly I had only conducted traffic, except at accident scenes, a couple of times in my career and this was to be the first prolonged spell. Despite my hangover I started to enjoy it. I always try to make the best of a bad situation. I was intent on stamping my character, by way of style, into the task. I smiled a lot and tried to joke where possible.

Any naughty behaviour – I waggled my finger and smiled. I put on a sorry expression when I had to stop traffic. I smiled at motorists as they passed, especially the women. Most smiled back but then there were the inevitable miseries. I was more like an Italian traffic cop in Rome than a British Bobby. I wasn't exactly dancing but I, no we, were enjoying ourselves; and why not? A smiling face is a good start to the morning.

One motorist was about to make my day! I had stopped the College Road traffic to allow the two lanes to flow normally again. My right hand was moving at the speed of a geisha girl fanning her face, to keep them moving. My smile was broadening as my hangover was clearing.

Vehicle examination was habit. I looked at oncoming cars, the make, the model, the registration numbers, the tax discs, carefully but surreptitiously, the occupants with a smile. Then I saw it. My eyes were transfixed on the vehicle – it passed me. Pete's car!

I looked over my shoulder in disbelief. My eyes widened and I momentarily froze. It was, it was Pete's car.

I abandoned my post and legged it along the road in hot pursuit, helmet in hand. They had a tendency to fall off during a chase. The traffic stopped, started, stopped started but I was slowly catching up. I prayed for a prolonged jam. I passed one, two, three cars; just three to go. The traffic slowed. I was going to make it. I eased up, the traffic stopped. I'd got him.

I walked the last few steps; he might not have seen me running up the side of the cars. I tried to regain my breath and composure. My fear was he'd try to make a run for it, maybe he was violent. Surely he wouldn't think that I already knew it was stolen, or would he? I needed to buy time so that I was ready for a struggle. The best option was poise and any element of surprise that I could muster. I tapped the window and gestured for him to lower the window. He did. He looked calm. He was a normal looking sort of guy and quite well dressed. He wasn't going to be trouble I concluded.

"Morning Sir", I said. "Could you pull in to the side and turn off your engine please". He did. It was a tricky call to ask him to move because he might have panicked and taken an opportunity to shoot off but I thought the traffic too heavy for him to do that. I stayed close to the open window in case.

I had now got excited about this and I wanted to enjoy and savour the moment, but I still double checked the registration number. I just couldn't believe my luck. I looked down on him. "Could you open your door please sir". He did. That was it. I was in. He was going nowhere. Elation was the feeling.

I leaned forward, left hand on the roof, right on the door. My helmet had been returned to the 'tit head' position. "Where are you heading sir?" "To work" he replied.

"Is this your vehicle sir?" I asked. Oh how I enjoyed asking that question.

"Yes" he replied.

"Are you sure" I teased.

"Yes".

And now the pièce de la résistance. I slipped into Sweeney talk – corny and never before or since uttered by me. "No it isn't. It's my mates and you're nicked!" Yes, yes yes - it was better than an orgasm. His response disappointed me. I wanted face in hands shock. He said nothing.

I had no animosity toward this guy at all. No ill feeling, no anger; only gratitude and it must have been the friendliest arrest on record. I felt like he was a mate.

"You are so unlucky mate. I was with the owner last night when you nicked it". Then I noticed minor damage to the car. "When did you do that?" I asked.

"I didn't. It was like that when I took it".

Now I didn't feel quite so good about him. "Look mate. I was in this car last night and there wasn't a mark on it when we left it. This has been caused since you pinched it from the car park of The Horse and Jockey. Now there is no need to lie, you're not going to get in any more trouble than you're already in."

"I'm not lying" he said, "but I didn't take it from The Horse and Jockey anyway. I took it from (forgotten) Road this morning." I was sceptical but didn't push the matter too hard. I'd got my mates car back.

I radioed for a car. He was taken to Queens Rd and I followed in Pete's car. There were incredulous looks on faces but I was floating on air. Pete's car went in the property book, and the prisoner went into a cell. My skipper let me charge him – icing on the cake. A sergeant would normally do that.

Pete was gob smacked, almost speechless. He collected his car later that day. I thought he would have been delighted but he seemed disappointed that I hadn't got the guy to admit to doing the damage. I can understand that, I should perhaps have tried harder. It is likely that a mate of his stole it initially, and he made the mistake of using it the following morning.

94

Now if he was telling the truth, an already remarkable situation was even more bizarre. But this was already amazing. This was a quite astonishing chain of events that culminated in me recovering my close friends' car. Not only that, arresting the man that had stolen it. The odds on that happening could hardly be calculated.

Now the reader could be forgiven for thinking, "Bullshit". I would understand. But frankly and honestly, some simply ridiculous things were happening to me at this time of my life. Vehicle incidents in particular.

Some of these incidents were embarrassing, some as a result of intoxication some fluky and some I am confident in saying were just down to plain common sense and good police work.

One night I went to a party above a shop. I came out of the party worse for wear. My car had gone! I reported it stolen. It was found the following morning where I'd left it!

Early one morning I received a tap on the door. I'd been asleep for about an hour. It was a sergeant from my old nick. At once I noticed my car missing from the road in front of the house. He was there to tell me it had been used to race around a field at the back of some nearby houses. I'm sure he was thinking it was me. Fortunately I was able to give him my keys so he could return it for me.

I came out of a club one night. I was sober and relatively drink free. I reversed the car some twenty yards back to the main road with the intention of slowing and reversing around the corner. My crook lock was round the brake pedal! I crossed the main road – without being hit by oncoming vehicles- and buried the rear of my car in the corner of a brick wall. The car was a write-off.

My car was parked at the foot of the hill outside my Dad's house. A council gritting lorry skidded down the hill writing off my Dad's car, my car and damaging a neighbour's. I could be a disaster at times.

In the quietness of a winter's night I was walking the streets of Sutton and stopped in a dark corner by a builder's yard for a cigarette. Chummy jumps over the wall into my arms with his bag marked swag. Another time, on a busy shopping afternoon I saw a badly parked car in the road. I checked it out. It had been reported stolen. I thought, "What if he's in that shop?"

I went in and angrily demanded, "Could the driver of this Ford Capri please move it now. It's causing an obstruction". A man stepped forward. "You're lucky you're not been booked". He said sorry and I followed him to the car. He got in. I nicked him for Take and Drive Away!

Arresting the guy that stole my friends' car takes the biscuit!

The Birmingham Pub Bombings

There is one last story to be told before I jet the reader off to Hong Kong. In the early to mid seventies the IRA were extremely active in mainland Britain. In 1972 rioters and protestors were brutally gunned down by Britain's finest troops; paratroopers. No thinking person felt comfortable about the explanation for it, and most questioned how the hell it could have happened. I felt ashamed.

Many fell victim to the propaganda machine and the slender unconvincing excuse that they had been shot at first. Whatever the truth, this 'Bloody Sunday' was hailed a massacre and Republican opinion swung heavily in favour of the IRA and their ranks were swelled. British action played into IRA hands.

The act of brutality on Bloody Sunday, in my view, caused the problems that followed. It was disgraceful and unforgiveable, and yet I have some sympathy for those responsible. Trained killers should not have been put on the streets to confront a crowd of civilian demonstrators; they were not properly trained for such a situation. It was a political mistake.

After Bloody Sunday there was a hardening of Republican attitudes. There were now victims, and martyrs, and the IRA had been handed a recruitment drive freebee. However, the IRA could find decent excuses, however feeble, for their own brutal acts of retribution. The sympathy for the IRA was understandable, but when they opted for acts of violence, some indiscriminate, the pendulum of British public opinion swung against them and further entrenched the positions of both sides.

Any attack on civilians is evil and wrong, and frankly a war crime. The IRA claimed they were at war; those responsible for such acts, particularly of the kind I am going to write about, should be held to account; I don't care how long ago it was.

Coventry had a very large immigrant Irish population and it was no surprise that a Coventry based IRA cell commander, was arrested with the plans to Coventry police station. The only surprise-no shock- was that it was A Man of God; Father Fell of Hearsall church was that man. He got eleven years and I was honoured to escort him part of the way to Wakefield Jail. After his release he resumed preaching in the name of God in Donegal! Is that right?

I had been in Coventry on the night that James McDaid had blown himself up carrying a bomb to Coventry Post Office. The citizens rejoiced, but were shocked. Bits of him were found all over, and a guy I knew found an eye outside the Penny Black pub some distance from the scene. There was outrage at the proposal that he would be carried through the streets of Coventry by his family, friends and sympathisers after his funeral, a week later, and before his bits were flown back to Northern Ireland.

As it happened, the funeral cortège walked, walked and walked. In the early 1980's a friend, Jack Murphy, a Scot, and my economics lecturer at Lanchester Polytechnic, told me he was in the cortège. He was an IRA sympathiser. As long as he wasn't a man of violence himself, I could accept him for that.

The body was late getting to Birmingham airport for the flight to Ireland. The police presence on route was unprecedented. All leave was cancelled. I was one of many uniformed officers at Birmingham airport on that fateful day of 21st November 1974.

Nothing had happened on route and many had been stood down, but we waited and waited. Baggage handlers in Belfast had apparently refused to handle the body off the plane. The plane was awaiting take off and clearance from Dublin. Press men suddenly started dashing to the bank of telephones in the departure lounge. "What's up" I asked. "A bomb has gone off in the city centre" I was told by a notebook wielding 'press pig'.

It was another half hour before we were officially told that we were heading for Birmingham Centre and that bombs had gone off in packed pubs; The Mulberry Bush and Tavern in the Town (now the Yard of Ale). Twenty one were killed, including a young engaged couple, and over 180 injured. The country was outraged, the atmosphere that night sober and sombre.

We arrived at Digbeth police station from where I was later to operate as an undercover officer for the Licensing Branch. There were scenes that night that have haunted me ever since, most of all a policewoman wearing a white shirt that was blood soaked from

97

shoulder to shoulder top to bottom. I will never forget the empty look on her face. Dead meat was easy to deal with; the true horrors are seen through the faces on the victims.

Watch a post mortem and you get a preparatory feel for police work and body bits amongst rubble, but the sight of the shocked policewoman that night was the most haunting of all. As is so often the case, it is the living, the survivors, the witnesses that suffer the most.

Another bomb had been planted on the Hagley Road but it didn't go off. The city was like a ghost town, silent and eerie except for the sound of sirens. I don't know what time we finished our work that night. It's a bit of a haze.

I next remember an early morning shift at Queens Road, arriving to be met by my good honest friend Tom Clarke. He looked and sounded shocked. He was always quietly spoken but on this occasion he was almost whispering. "The bombers are here. There are armed men on the roof and dogs in the cell block". I walked into the front office. I can't remember who was there; the station sergeant I think, but I'm not sure.

A sad looking washed out individual dressed in a raincoat appeared at the counter, "That will have been Callaghan" I was later told by Devon and Cornwall officers investigating allegations that they had been beaten. I think Callaghan was the alleged leader, the lieutenant. "He did not have a mark on him", I told the two officers at my home in Coventry, some thirteen years later. He didn't.

Tom was featured some years after the bombings, in the mid 1980s I guess, on ITV's World in Action. He had, in my view, been framed for stealing £5 from a prisoner after twenty odd years' service, lost his pension and spent some months in prison. He denied the theft and I believe him. I knew him.

He alleged that there had been card board boxes across the entrance to the cell block. I couldn't remember that. He alleged that the prisoners had been set on by dogs. I can remember him saying that. His allegations helped reopen the case against the Birmingham Six.

He was later to be a discredited witness (because of the theft conviction) for the Birmingham Six during their appeal. That's rough on a really decent guy.

I remember seeing the 'Six' pictured in the local newspaper upon their first appearance in Court, bruised and battered. There were rumours that they had been beaten by

98

prisoners and prison officers alike at Winston Green Prison. Based on my experience and knowledge as stated, this must have been the case.

There was not a bruise on the guy that I had met after his arrest and interrogation. Yes he looked tired and frightened, but he showed not a sign of having been beaten. There is nothing, and I mean nothing, apart from intense torture, that could ever get me to sign any statement admitting to the deaths of so many people in such a cruel manner; you?

The Birmingham Six were released, their convictions overturned, in the face of damning evidence of a serious case of injustice.

I was interviewed for nearly three hours, thirteen years after the events that I have just summarised. I was entirely honest about my recollections but told the officers that if Tom Clark said he saw card board boxes across the cell block, then there were indeed card board boxes over the front of the cell block. Of that I am sure.

The six men did not commit the atrocity; that is official. They were just IRA sympathisers simply travelling to Ireland to attend a service for James McDaid when they were arrested bound for the ferry at Liverpool; case closed.

The 'real' bombers have never come forward; have never been identified. Surprised? Dismayed?

At Sutton I learnt hard lessons, before facing some huge and difficult decisions at Queens Road Police Station in Aston; a Birmingham crime heartland. The choices made would eventually result, in part, in my decision to resign and join the Royal Hong Kong Police (RHKP). It was time to move on to fresh pastures; mature and continue to learn. I left with the blessings of the Assistant Chief Constable (Crime), Tom Meffen, who told me to watch my back and expressed the hope to see me back someday. I had been an exceptionally good police officer in every sense of the word, and I knew it.

I think I left Britain for Hong Kong a politically and socially well balanced individual. I was developing views that transcended party politics. I was a 'lawman' so my leaning, and learning was heavily influenced by my chosen career, but I was healthily open minded.

I was becoming tolerant to certain law-breaking, and recognizing that everyone and I mean everyone, broke the law. Before the reader becomes indignant about my comment, take time to think about it.

I retained a hardened attitude toward crime committed by persons in positions of authority, trust and power. I loathed corrupt officials who hid behind the very uniform, authority, that people turned to for help in times of trouble. I hated cronyism. I had no real problem, animosity, toward clever non violent criminals that stole from the rich (but not from their homes), and those that stole from banks. I was also becoming a bit more socialist, despite having been a conservative voter, and an admirer of those that fought battles against injustice. Politically I was becoming right, left and centre!

Was my future with the police? Was I ever going to properly fit in (without opening my mouth)?

Chapter Six
The Royal Hong Kong Police

After over 3 years together, Nikki and I married in May 1977 and left for Hong Kong to begin married life in probably the most exciting city in the world. There was a lovely photograph and write up about us in the Coventry Evening Telegraph, 'Newly-Wed Man for Hong Kong'. My old friend Richard Lynes wrote a very touching reference that helped me get the job. The final paragraph read,' I consider myself lucky to have such a friend and I am only too pleased to have the opportunity to give David a personal reference'. I left good friends and family behind.

Hong Kong was, at that time, a British Crown colony, consisting of 236 islands and a portion of the Chinese mainland, known as The New Territories. The colony lies on the south coast of China, just south of the Tropic of Cancer; latitude 23.5. The most important island was called Hong Kong Island the island was ceded to the British, in perpetuity, in 1842 by the Treaty of Nanking. The population was about 5 million. The police had about 20,000 officers.

We met John and Liz Walsh on the plane over. They were to become good friends to us, Nikki becoming God Mother to their daughter Liette. Coincidentally John was also joining the Royal Hong Kong Police (RHKP). We shared a taxi to the Peninsula Hotel in Causeway Bay on Hong Kong Island, our home for several weeks, and where we were to meet other new recruits and their wives. They also became good friends.

We were in that hotel for about six weeks, and believe me, six weeks, even in a top hotel, can soon wear very thin indeed. We moved to temporary accommodation in Homantin Hill Road, in Kowloon, and this accommodation at least allowed us to unpack some of our belongings and stop living in a suitcase. Boxes that had been shipped out could be delivered and opened. We had still not opened some of our wedding presents.

Within a further couple of months we had chosen our accommodation from 'an availability list'. Allocation of government accommodation was on a 'points' basis and we were mid table. We moved to 153 Green Lane Hall overlooking the famous Happy Valley horse racing track and Hong Kong harbour beyond. The view was breath taking; the parties on the balcony fun.

The Wong Nei Chung Gap Road ran through the mountains behind us providing me with convenient access to the Police Training School (PTS) in Aberdeen on the islands south coast. Nikki found a job in Stanley, for a fashion designer, Jenny Lewis, and it was also convenient for her. Nikki had found a job she enjoyed, as a beautician. Stanley, which was beyond Repulse Bay on the far south eastern corner of the island; was quite a distance. She did some modelling work for them; mainly shoes, although with confidence she could have strutted the catwalk wearing anything (or nothing). Nikki was beautiful; Spanish features. She performed a ballet solo at the Birmingham Hippodrome at twelve years of age! She was fit! Her lack of confidence came from her experiences during her cruel upbringing.

It was also convenient to travel down to Causeway Bay, Wanchai and Central districts of Hong Kong Island from where the Star Ferry shuttled people back and forth to the Ocean Terminal and shopping centre on 'Kowloon Side'; the Chinese mainland.

The location was idyllic and the apartment, on the top 15th floor, spacious with fabulous views across the harbour to Kowloon and the mountain range beyond. Kowloon translates to nine mountains.

We settled in very quickly and our social life throughout our stay in Hong Kong was phenomenal. The only terrible sadness during our stay was the death of Nikki's Mum just months after our departure. A brain tumour; it was tragic.

We travelled the length and breadth of the colony, enjoyed beach days, walked the markets and sailed the seas. We took trips to Portuguese Macau, to gamble the casinos, and partied, and dined. There was a packed sporting calendar. We did what all kids in their 20's do, or should do; enjoy life to the full.

For the first two months at PTS I was in a classroom learning the Cantonese language, 9.00am to 5.00pm and five days a week, with the expectation that I would practice when out socialising and going about your everyday activities. Practical use of the language was the key to improvement. I really became quite proficient, and could hold simple conversations in some subjects, and get by on most.

PTS was tough and there were regular examinations. Failure and you were out! The contract was for three years service; but conditional on 'passing out' of training school successfully.

The training school was at the foot of 'Brick Hill' the scene of a famous Second World War battle between the Brits and Japanese when a guy got the VC for fighting off the 'nips' singlehandedly. Just behind the hill was the 'Ocean Park' a fantastic dolphinarium and aquarium accessed by cable car over the hill. 'The Hill' was a PTS punishment run' up and down' in the humid heat of a Hong Kong Summer!

The RHKP was a para-military force and there was a heavy military style slant to the training. I was trained in the use of the Federal Gas Gun, the AR15 assault rifle, the old Sten gun, the Remington Pump Action Shotgun and of course the pistol that I was already familiar with from my UK police training.

I was trained to a Company Commander level, and operated to platoon commander level. Riot drill was the main discipline that we practiced time and time again. However, it was always envisaged that I would enter directly into the Criminal Investigation Department (CID) and the training was therefore somewhat surplus to my requirements and those of the RHKP, nevertheless it was interesting, and enjoyable.

All the guys that had lived with us at The Peninsula and Homantin Service Apartments had become firm friends and they were on the same intake as me. At training school we met up with 'the single' guys that had joined the force, and of course the staff supervising our intake.

The training was to last six months. Most of the single guys were ex-servicemen or raw recruits from 'Civvy Street' with an impressive academic background. Most of the married guys were ex-UK cops although none of them were as well qualified as moi!

I had my UK police promotion exams behind me and so got more money, more accommodation points and, if I performed, the pick of the jobs after PTS.

Of course the married guys became the closest of friends. We bonded from day one. As couples we were all anxious to make new friends for our wives as much as ourselves, otherwise, from day one they would have felt very lonely thousands of miles from the familiarity of our homeland. Nikki was not an extrovert and so needed this introduction.

It was good to know that Nikki was amongst friends when I was at training school. Because we were married we were allowed to travel back to our homes every night rather than to barracks. That was a major plus, although the instructors made sure that we were 'gated' regularly; possibly more regularly than the single guys.

'Gating' was a punishment duty. Manning the gates at the entrance of the training centre during the evenings kept you behind and messed up your travel plans and social plans for the night. It could come without much notice.

Steve Ward was an ex Strathclyde cop. A cool, larger than life guy; quietly spoken but harsh and hard. He became a great friend who I would have trusted with my life. His wife was a sweet 'girl next door' who was always subservient to the Steve growl on the surface but I am sure in charge when necessary. Steve finished his contract and went back to Glasgow. Putting his language skills to good use he set up a Triad Society Bureau and became a bit of an expert. He would be retired now but the last I heard he was a DI (Detective Inspector) and living in Hamilton in a nice little house overlooking the soccer ground. I miss Steve.

Jack Ballantyne was a qualified chemist and another Scot. He was a very bright guy with no previous service experience but was such a whizz kid that he would cruise along and deal with anything that was thrown at him; except as it subsequently turned out 'discipline'. Just days before finishing at PTS he cracked up in the face of parade ground discipline and complained.

He was in line for the coveted 'baton of honour' for being the top of intake, but resigned and went on to become a Forensic Scientist with the LAPD in California. Jack's wife was also a very bright individual but although they were fine people we didn't have enough in common with either of them to socialise too much.

Andy Neilson was yet another Scot! He was an ex marine commando although a smaller guy than me and, sorry Andy, not as fit! Andy was also a commercial artist and magnificent cartoonist; a very interesting chap indeed.

Laura, his wife was equally interesting and, I have to say, attractive. She had a great business brain, drive and a character to match. Not to say Andy didn't, but Laura was certainly a 'driver'. When Andy decided to leave the police after completing the course at PTS it was me he came to, to discuss how to set up business in Hong Kong, and suggested to me that I might join him in setting up the pub business we had talked about. Amazingly, there was only one English 'pub' in Hong Kong and Andy and I had seen a gap in the market.

Andy was a doer and he didn't have the commitment to the RHKP that I had at the time; although I was teetering on the brink of leaving to do something else. Hong Kong really was a land of opportunity. Andy left the police after completing the training, and I think it was always his intention to do so. He went on to work as an artist developing a business called 'King and Country' making top quality model soldiers and battle scenes designed by Andy, and hand-made and painted in Canton. He went global. His work can be seen on King and Country.com. You can thank me for the plug Andy!

Andy and Laura had our problematic cat when we left Hong Kong. Laura adored cats and had dozens. They separated and divorced in the mid 1980's but remained friends, which was only befitting the maturity and genuineness of this fine couple.

Laura and Andy set up the pub business just after we left. They called it 'Mad Dogs' after the song Mad Dogs and Englishmen'. In 1990 they were interviewed by Alan Whicker during his series 'Whickers World' on Hong Kong. They had made over $HK30 million; £3m in the years since I had left. Mad Dogs became a pub chain. Both businesses still thrive and Andy also owns 'Joe Bananas' that can be found in Wanchai district. Andy still lives in Hong Kong (HK) and Laura lives in Texas - Crawford - Bush's home town I believe – I am told she married an aging billionaire!

Andy Gordon (oh not another scot) was married to Marion. Another fine couple that will no doubt share some fine memories with me. It would be good to catch up with these guys one day, but we haven't been in touch since the 1980's. Andy was another quietly spoken man with a lovely wife.

All these guys were on our party list, and we theirs. We had a lot of laughs in those days and some outrageous parties. We only had a small balcony, but it was enough to cook a barbie if necessary and certainly enough to line up a crowd to enjoy the City lights during the evening. John and Liz were in the same block but lower down. The other guys were living 'Hong Kong side' but little better off for partying. The mega rich had terrific facilities with gardens and even pools, but land was so expensive in HK that 'houses' were never a realistic proposition; far too many government points for those on first contracts.

Johnny Walsh was an ex Lancashire bobby from Preston who had met his French American wife on holiday. They married and left for HK just as we had. John was a big tough guy and a good footballer. He was a 'rum' bloke as he would put it. We had a similar sense of humour and many common views; we also had wives that got on well with each other and we dovetailed nicely as foursome friends. Much of our socialising included them, and although I didn't seek many friends outside the force when in HK John and Liz introduced us to another two couples that we became very pallie with.

106

Dave and Kate Palmer had moved out of a motorway construction site caravan in the north east of England to Hong Kong with Gammon Construction. Within 20 years he was in charge of their Far Eastern operation with homes in Singapore, UK and Hong Kong. He was very career focused.

Dave hit the jackpot, and probably rivals Andy for wealthy outcome. Problem was that Dave always seemed 'up his own' with an arrogant air of self importance. He could be a fun guy and interesting to talk to, but sometimes too serious for me and too upwardly mobile in his social networking. His ambition was apparent.

Kate hit the bottle big time and was always very 'wealth conscious' but good fun and more down to earth than Dave and less serious. When I was last in Hong Kong for the international rugby 7's in 2002 I felt that Dave was not too interested in my company, although Kate was still Kate, and still very friendly. She was a genuine good fun girl. I caught up with Andy Neilson during that visit but was too drunk to have any in depth conversation, and flew out before I had another chance to arrange a meeting.

Nikki introduced me to an interesting couple, Martin and Barbara. Martin was in charge of Marks and Spencer in Hong Kong – his Dad owned Marks and Spencer at the time! They were lovely genuine people, but alas we haven't seen them since we visited them in London in the 1980's. I think they are separated now.

Dave Palmer had use of the company junk. There were some fantastic trips out to the outlying islands, and swimming off the side of a boat was a new and exciting experience. He also had good access to tickets at the Hong Kong Football Club and watching top European Football Clubs and National Rugby teams posed no problem.

The only single guy that I really got to know well, and truly warmed to, was a laid back ex metropolitan cop who just wanted the easy life. He made no secret of his wish to have a relaxing time in Hong Kong. He joined the Marine Division and was in charge of a police gunboat patrolling HK waters. He was mainly looking for illegal immigrants arriving from mainland China and refugees from the Vietnam War. He took me out on the launch on a few occasions for a drink, swim and social chin wag. He sometimes came in useful as a water taxi!

Many 'illegals' swimming across from China were attacked by sharks; mainly Tigers. They were that desperate to earn the fortunes of HK. The Vietnamese refugees were fleeing the Communist Government in the aftermath of the American defeat. They had been fighting for, or supporting, the wrong side.

The journey across the South China Sea was treacherous and they made the trip, having paid top dollar, on overcrowded unseaworthy craft that often didn't make it. They went straight into detention camps. I didn't fancy joining the Marine Division because it was a somewhat dead end job, although the chance to become trained in mastering a vessel did appeal to me.

My neighbour, Ken Lau, was a uniformed Chief Inspector and son of a defeated Nationalist General that had fought with Chan Kei Chek in the Chinese civil war. Having fled the communists in the aftermath of the war in China his father settled in Taiwan.

By association, Ken was worried about what would happen to him and his family after the British handed HK back to the Chinese in 1997. He asked me to look after his son if he went to study in UK. I agreed but he never took me up on it. Ken and his wife, Rosy, were lovely people and great neighbours.

Jack Ballantyne rejected the 'baton of honour' in disgust at the degrading manner in which he was treated on the parade ground. He decided to resign, and I tried to talk him out of it, but I had some sympathy with his view; then again that is what the disciplined services are all about. My instructor subsequently called me to his office, sat down with me and asked, 'Would you be proud to accept the baton of honour?' and I replied, 'of course but I don't think I deserve it'. I didn't get it!

I was certainly in the running, but I was one of the lads – I didn't want my head above the parapet! In any case, I had been up to my old 'piss taking' tricks again at PTS, joking, but sailing a bit close to the wind again.

My instructor whispered in my ear when I was at 'attention' on the parade ground, "Wakefield. Live By The Sword – Die By The Sword". I thought long and hard about what he had said, and trod very carefully thereafter. Thankfully he came to realise that I wasn't being disrespectful, just a cheeky comic, but I have always marked his words. They were wise words. Push things too far and you pay the price!

I came top of the course in musketry; I was a very good shot since my Dad brought me a competition rifle when I was about twelve, and I had been firearms trained when I was in the UK police at Queens Road police station. My classroom examination marks were consistently high – in the top two or three, and I was hard working during physical fitness exercises. I had demonstrated that I was a good leader in all kinds of practical leadership

108

exercises and the feed-back from all my tutors was good. I had definitely been in the frame. But I had not put everything into it – I enjoyed my social life too much.

On one of the training exercises, we were sent to the Siekung peninsula for jungle training. This was where the Ghurkhas were given their training. It was thick jungle, swamp and tall elephant grassland. We set up camp. One night, about half an hour after we had all gone to sleep, we were awakened and ordered out of our tents into the darkness. We were immediately blindfolded and manhandled into trucks. About ten minutes later, after a couple of stops, I was pulled out of the lorry and the blindfold was removed. I found myself with three other guys. "Make your way back to camp" was the order. The direction was pointed out to us but by the time the truck had left over the hill none of us could be sure which direction had been indicated. It was pitch-black and I wasn't sure who I was with. I lit my cigarette lighter and we briefly saw each others' faces. We stumbled through very thick jungle in total darkness, the guys following my lead by sound, and then swamp, in moonlight. I think it took us about an hour. WE could see the camp ahead of us. It turned out we had been only about half mile away. We were cut to ribbons but we faired very well indeed. Other groups were out most of the night. I was alarmed to see leaches on my ankles!

On mess nights traditions were followed and the mascot, a duck, was passed down the centre of the table and everyone was expected to touch the terrified little bird on the head for good luck. He was a privileged and well kept duck. He had his own private quarters, his own mess boy, and attendant, and was under constant surveillance and protection.

It didn't help him when it was our time to pass out. The poor little bird was released from its home and consumed by a 'hungry python'. 'I know nothing' was the message repeated by the massed ranks on the parade ground.

I genuinely knew nothing, or at least very little. It was rumoured that one of the mess boys had it in for that little duck, but to this day the reasons for the critters fate remains a mystery. It was no accident. The pen had been deliberately left open; at least that was the outcome of the thorough investigation. Whether a hungry coolie or large snake had eaten the duck, we will never know.

We all waited for our assignments. I was offered a position in Special Branch, dipped my toe in but found it too boring. It sounded all very glamorous but it wasn't 'real' police work. It was political. As things turned out I should have stayed in that job, it might have kept me out of trouble, but instead I asked for something more policeman like. I accepted a job in the Headquarters based Commercial Crime Bureau (CCB). This was also a mistake but it did however at least give me the opportunity, indeed the honour, to assist a visiting Fijian officer in his investigations. Inspector Singh was a gentleman, and we parted friends.

I went to Detective Training School and was also trained as a negotiator (which stood me in good stead for my future career in Loss Adjusting). I was part of an exercise to test security at Kai Tak airport before kicking off at CCB. I was a bit too frisky and young for sophisticated crime and the complex desktop work involved at CCB.

It is just as well that I had been headquarters office based. At PTS I had again dislocated my arm during a soccer game after a tackle by big John Walsh. It dislocated again during my sleep. Nikki had rested her neck on it, woken, and readied herself for work. I woke with my arm out 90 degrees to my body and dislocated – I couldn't move! Since breaking it in the cadets it had dislocated more easily and more often year by year, until it was simply slipping out when I lifted something- like a suitcase. I simply pushed it back in but this time it had frozen solid and I was in great pain.

When the paramedics arrived they wouldn't move me because I was groaning. They called a doctor who gave me a jab in the arse, which numbed it, my arse that is, and pulled my shoulder. I passed out.

The communist newspapers milked it for all it was worth. The government became involved and the story hit the South China Morning Post, in an item headed, Policeman's Case was 'Storm in a teacup'.

The article read, to my embarrassment, ' Government officials yesterday dismissed as a 'storm in a teacup' reports in the Chinese press that a European police inspector had received special treatment from medical personnel.

Banner headlines in several Chinese newspapers reported that three ambulances were sent to pick up inspector D.I. Wakefield from his Happy Valley home.

In addition, a doctor from the casualty department of the Tang Shiu Kin Hospital had to make a special house call to treat the policeman.
Chinese newspapers said it was "the strangest tale in the history of Hong Kong"………
bla bla bla'.

There were paragraphs of the nonsense. Bottom line was they couldn't or wouldn't move me, through either incompetence or fear. Anyhow, no ambulance at all was needed.

The doctor pulled it and I decided it was time to get a Bryan Robson style 'putti plat'; an operation to tighten the ball around the shoulder joint. I had it done at the British Military Hospital - on a very entertaining Ghurkha Ward. The doctor, a captain I think, had never done the operation before!

The Commercial Crime Bureau was, as feared, still too boring for me, and after a few months dealing with frauds, involving dodgy watches and scams, I asked for a move to a conventional CID role and transferred to Wanchai Division, just down the road from Arsenal Street, where the Police Headquarters was located.

Wanchai was an exciting station and where things happened. In 1977 Wanchai police station was on the waterfront. When I returned in 2002 it was 100 yards inland! Such is the constantly changing skyline and general landscape of Hong Kong. Build, demolish, build, demolish, reclaim land, build demolish, etc.

The station was colonial style with a balcony to the Officers Mess overlooking the harbour road with the water a stone's throw away. Many a glass of beer was drunk in this mess. Indeed too much beer was drunk; beer in the Officers Mess became mess in the officers!

There was usually no service required in the mess except for food, and the mess boy, a man in his 50's, would order and deliver. We generally asked him to leave us to our own devices. We would sign 'chits' for drinks we consumed, and left them behind the bar. We served ourselves and the 'chits' went into an honesty box. We settled our bills with the mess boy at the end of each month. They were a fortune!

We all drank too much. Frank Murphy, my boss, would start morning prayers (daily briefing) at 8.00am every morning with whiskey topped tea and we followed the leader. Very little got in the way of drinks at lunchtime, and if we hadn't left the mess in the afternoon, we would return in the evening. God knows how we did any work, but we did.

We worked very hard indeed. We would work twenty four hours on, and twenty four hours off. It was a tough shift. If something serious happened toward the end of the twenty four hours duty, the need to work overtime could mean that the two shifts merged in to one mammoth seventy two hour continuous duty. This happened to me on just one occasion, but was not uncommon.

If there was a level eight typhoon warning, all personnel were required to report for duty. All leave was cancelled. This meant that we had to remain on duty, at the station,

111

throughout the entire duration of the typhoon. We had two such 'confinements'. One as I recall was Typhoon Rose. They were boozy affairs. There was lots of time for making merry! CID got very drunk indeed during a typhoon.

A typhoon confined any sensible self respecting criminal to his home, so little if anything ever happened to involve CID. If anything was going to happen it would probably have been looting in the aftermath of the typhoon, not during it, and it would be more a matter for the riot police than CID. When riding out a typhoon we did little more than catch up with paperwork.

I can remember one boozy afternoon when Alan King, 'Kingy' as he was known, stood on the bar and leapt across the room toward the air conditioner above the balcony doors.

He swung from the top of the air conditioner through the balcony doors onto the balcony. In the process, the air conditioner was pulled from its housing in the wall, and he fell onto the balcony floor with the air conditioner falling behind him. He slid, legs open, between the railings. Ouch!

We always had an explanation organised. The hole in the wall left by the air conditioner was as resulting from the force of the typhoon winds blowing it clean out of its housing – it was plausible and had been known to happen before. The sore bollocks were put down to normal rowdy mess behaviour. A bit of a scrum down; we had those in the mess as well!

'Eddy the Bucket' as he became known, was the prim and proper uniformed divisional deputy commander. Eddy enjoyed a quiet drink in the mess and generally tried to avoid us. In any case, during a typhoon he needed to be available sober and prepared. We set up an elaborate trap over the door for when he arrived for his lunch, involving a bucket full of beer, paid for by the boys I might add. It's a childish trick that quite simply meant that when he came through the door the bucket discharged its contents over his head.

It worked too well. He was drenched. His black afro style haircut straightened by the beer rolling off his head. We were hysterical. He was livid. He stood there, shocked, and looking like a drowned rat. It was like a scene from a slapstick comedy. It had worked like a dream. Eddy could do nothing about it. We would all deny it, and reporting it would have caused too much embarrassment. He changed clothes and never spoke to us again.

112

The mess boy had a very good looking daughter. One of the single guys, living at the station got caught with her. The mess boy chased him through the station, meat cleaver in hand, and out into the street. Chinese are sensitive to these things, and in particular loss of face. To us, well it was very amusing watching the chase from the balcony overlooking the rear yard, and then moving to the mess balcony to watch the action at the front of the building as he sprinted along the harbour road with the old mess boy in hot pursuit.

The food in Hong Kong was amazing. I don't eat Chinese food in the UK because it is simply not the same. There were some very unusual foods indeed, and the markets sold everything from giant toads to snakes. Snake eating is a winter activity. Snake restaurants, and there were quite a few in Hong Kong, depend on a cold winter, for snake is a warming dish with many believing that the food aids sexual prowess. It worked for me, aphrodisiac or not. I ate it almost daily in the winter!

Hong Kong winters are more like British summers but usually dry. A cardigan or coat felt comfortable but was not essential; not to me anyway. The snakes are slow and fat in the winter so they are easier to catch. Even the proud King Cobra finds itself on a plate.

My 'local' restaurant was in Causeway Bay, 'The King of Snakes'. Snake meat, snake soup and snake wine were consumed in great quantities; snake being caught locally but mainly imported daily from mainland China. It was a fast food joint and you could 'pick your own' snake. You just pointed to it. Queues were often long. Python was officially 'off' because it was 'protected' but a few of my lads had tried it before at a high price.

The snake soup was my usual at about 50p a bowl. It was a rich soup, almost as thick as a congee, with shreds of snake, chicken and sweet corn. I seldom had the full snake on the plate (it was too long to sit comfortably at the crowded tables). When I did it was usually decorated in chrysanthemum petals and served with tree fungi, lemon leaves and flour paste crackers with of course boiled rice.

I am told that the classic snake dish comprises snake, chicken and cat (tiger) which is illegal of course; although so is dog eating, but you could find dog easily enough if you wanted to. I did, just once, but felt very woof afterwards.

Any self respecting snake eater will take a dram with it. Snake wine is a wake-up call to those considering themselves to be seasoned drinkers. I drank my last bottle in 2006; shared it with the Monday Club boys in 'The Barrels', Berwick upon Tweed. A superbly presented bottle with copper decoration and whole snakes, including cobra, elaborately and painstakingly arranged in the bottle so as to look like an attractive buy. I bought it in Vietnam for about £2. It went down well, but didn't if you understand me. It is awful!

Snake wine is essentially rice wine with the bile of about five different snakes, including cobra, flavouring it. Although not at the 'King of Snakes', I have had it served to me with the bladder from the snake; cut out from a live snake, next to the table and before my very eyes. And no, I didn't drink it; one too far.

Seemingly bizarre, but a meal at a snake restaurant is well worth it if you get the chance to overcome the mental challenge.

Police Five

Some of you will remember the TV programme, Police 5. It was just five minutes long and was introduced by Shaun Taylor. The programme comprised appeals for witnesses following brief summaries of crimes. The programme was the forerunner of programmes such as 'Crime Watch'. There was an identical programme in Hong Kong, introduced by a man called Matthew Oram, who styled himself, and sounded like, Shaun Taylor. It was screened weekly. He was a sports journalist, and it has to be said, a shade effeminate.

At morning prayers, about 8.00am, we were gathered round for the briefing, having tea and scotch forced down our necks, when out of the blue, Frank turned to me and said, "The Commissioner wants us to talk on Police 5 about the theft from vehicles in the Happy Valley area and your name came out of the hat. You're on tonight". Laughter, particularly from Johnny Walsh.

"Hang on" I said, "You're the boss. You should do it?"

"No" said Frank, "I'm busy, and you would be just great Dave".

"But I know nothing about car crime in Happy Valley; I didn't know we'd got any".

"You can read up on it, and anyway the Commissioner suggested you". More laughter.

"Bollocks. Now I know you're jokin'. Bollocks".

"No honestly" said Frank, with a serious look on his face.
"I haven't got a tie!"

114

"You're doing it. No argument" said Frank. "Get over to the studios in Kowloon this afternoon. You've gotta be there for 3 o'clock. Ha Ha Ha"

Laughter and discussion followed.

"I'm watchin' that," said Kingy.

"What times it on" said John.

"8 isn't it" said Frank..

"What channel" said Kingy.

"HKTV"? Why was I joining in?

"Yer I think it is. We'll check. We can watch it in the mess".

"It's on at 8 you can be back for then Dave. Watch it in the mess," said Frank.

Now a little clue as to the reputation of Roy Henry, the Commissioner. "Ooooh! You are awful.....but I like you". Kenny Everitt if you haven't guessed.

"Hey Dave. Commissioner's suggestion hey. Feather in your cap mate" said Kingy. John agreed.
"Bollocks. Bollocks. Oh God"

"You'll be asked to a dinner party I bet. Perform well tonight and you're on the guest list. Could be the start of a career in TV Dave. Go for it" laughed Frank.

"Hey if you can catch Roy's eye he might put you up. Nudge nudge wink wink."

"Dave if you can get in a "Wwweelll Matthew" in the conversation at some time, and cross your legs quickly like this" said Frank, "You'll get him hot".

"You're going Dave" Frank barked. "Now.....next item".

I 'agreed' to do it and took a bet that I could slip into the conversation with Matthew Oram a very familiar "Wwweelllll Matthew.....," accompanied by a tricky' left over right'

115

with the 'old pins', Kenny Everett style. Ten dollars apiece. A couple of my DC's accompanied me to the TV studios and I went in to this glass bubble, the studio, while the lads stood the other side of the glass with beams on their faces.

"You're going to have to lose the shirt. Have you got a jacket?" asked a technical type guy.

Because of the studio lights etc I had to borrow a jacket from one of the boys – a size too small but with the buttons open I looked OK.

I sat to the left of Matthew Oram. He asked me a series of questions about the thefts from vehicles and I answered. He asked the questions again and I answered. "OK let's try it again. This is a take" he said.

"Take" raised a voice from the darkness.

We went through the questions again but broke off." Cut".

"Relax. Better take a drink of water. Turn your chair in slightly" said Matthew, "That's it. Good." He laboured the effeminate tone in his voice.

"What was wrong?" I asked.

"It's OK. That was good, but the problem was technical. Don't worry. We'll get it this time"

I talked clearly precisely and confidently throughout. My body language demonstrated how relaxed and confident I was. I didn't know an awful lot about the details of the thefts so I just decided to answer with a crime prevention and awareness theme. It was actually great.

The rehearsal had really done the trick, and I felt sharp enough during the interview to think about how I could win the bet. I knew I couldn't afford to look a fool or make it too obvious, so I needed to subtly comply with the conditions of the bet. It was an 'in' joke so it would be enough to say "Wwweelllll Matthew" and cross the legs, slowly, in a less effeminate way. It would qualify.

I had recognised a slot about four questions in. When the opportunity came I executed it to perfection. The only difficulty was not laughing, so I just broke a confident smile".

116

With slow cross of the legs, "Wwwweeelllll Matthew. It is simply not possible to have a policeman on every corner and therefore there is a responsibility in the community......
...."

The crowd in the mess erupted in laughter when we watched it later that night. You couldn't hear what I was saying for a few moments after that. The money was passed to me at the back of the room, in dribs and drabs, some of it thrown at me. The drinks flowed. Frank left the room to take a call and then came back in.

"The Commissioner passes on his congratulations. Dave".

The room erupts in laughter and "ooooooooowwwwws"!

"You bastard," I laughed, "Don't give me that crap" I said.
"No really. He was very impressed". The banter and mickey taking went on through the night and got bluer and bluer.

Frank always maintained, in company and in private, that he wasn't telling porkies; the Commissioner really had phoned to congratulate me. I don't know what to believe. I knew I had sounded very professional, but I know I didn't get a dinner party invite!

I quite enjoyed working at Wanchai and should have stayed there. I had had the distinction of becoming the first officer to process the conviction of a man for raping a prostitute for the first time in Hong Kong. I had some good convictions, and some interesting encounters. My men could get a little cowboy like, but then Wanchai was like the Wild West.

I remember reading of one of my guys in the newspaper over breakfast – to my alarm! The report read, 'A detective constable fired a shot inside a Wanchai nightclub as five men attacked an employee in the Club Capital 187, Lockhart Road at about 2.00am. Reports said 'five men had gone to the nightclub for drinks when a row started. One of the five allegedly grabbed a bottle and hit the club captain on the head. As the five started to attack the captain, a detective constable, sitting nearby, revealed his identity and ordered them to stop. They ignored his warning before he pulled out his revolver and fired a shot in the air'

When the 7th Fleet hit town Wanchai rocked and it really was like the Wild West. The aircraft carrier Constellation and escort ships, including the missile cruiser Sterrit, were

117

amongst them. The fleet were regular visitors during and after the Vietnam War. It hit off virtually every night, but there were two notable occasions.

One night a dozen or so sailors were arrested and were followed back to the station by the usual posse of Chinese men and women seeking to cash in on their arrest. A window and a door had been damaged, and the wailing crowd demanded their pound of flesh. That generally meant money – they would screw as much as they could out of these poor hapless guys.

There is no doubt that the culprit was one or more of these men, but in true services fashion they weren't going to grass. Enter Chief Dunkerton of the missile cruiser Sterrit. He was on shore patrol. He was doing his best to keep these guys out of the brig, and avoid them getting a good 'kick in' when they returned to their ships. If they ended up in Court in Hong Kong they would be severely dealt with by the US Navy. The Chinese knew this well. They were there to extort money from these 'trapped' guys.

I had to help. I suggested to the Chief that my guys negotiate 'damages' on behalf of his men. We left the office for a coffee, returned when the negotiation had been completed and the men had been ripped off. Everyone was happy. The Chief was elated. Although stung, so were the sailors. There are few perfect outcomes when negotiating your way out of trouble.

Chief Dunkerton had dinner one night at my place, and left us with an invitation to stop at his place in San Diego sometime. We did subsequently get there, but I had lost the Chief's address and didn't get to share a beer with him.

Another evening all hell let loose. I was in a topless bar when a gang of pissed up Yanks appeared at the bar beside me. I joined in the banter. One of the gang took a bet. We all chipped in $10 a piece and left the money behind the bar with the European barmaid. The Yank nipped off to have the bell end of his penis tattooed with a rose! He returned about an hour later, very pissed, and red around the eyes. He slapped his tadger on the bar for inspection. God what a messy sight. I cringed and so did everyone else. It was red and blue. He duly collected about 100 bucks from the barmaid.

Minutes later it was fight night. The resident Royal Green Jackets, the HMS Tamar crew, Australian submariners and a French ship were also in town. US marines and sailors joined them in a pitch street battle, although it was clear to me that nobody was particular about taking sides – it was a free for all. Oh yes, and the police, shore patrol and Military Police arrived to join in. I stood pinned against the outside wall of the club and slid along to the safety of the side alley where an eighty odd year old lady, keen to continue business, asked me, "You like sucky sucky, better with teeth out"? I went home as I wasn't quite that drunk.

When my Mum and her mate Jan visited us a trip to Wanchai red light district was a must, and they loved it. So did my old mate Pete Wilford when he visited.

Chapter Seven
Principles or Career

The Hong Kong Police had an awesome reputation for corruption. In the UK things were done differently thank God, and although corruption in the Met hit headlines in the 1960's and early 1970's, the minority scum were just playing at it in comparison with their colleagues in Hong Kong. Corruption was rife, and to help eradicate it, an Independent Commission Against Corruption was set up. The ICAC as they were known were rubber heels; corruption fighters.

My old mate Mick Agar, a sergeant I knew from Birmingham, was seconded to the ICAC during the period I was in Hong Kong, and although some of my colleagues didn't like it, we would meet along with our wives, on a Thursday night usually, to play ten pin bowling with his mate Charlie Slater, a retired Superintendant, also of the ICAC. We got on well, and never spoke about work. It was better that way. But my association with them, and my outspoken views on corruption would cost me dearly; Hall, my next boss was to refer to me as a 'Skunk'.

Although the ICAC were also getting a reputation for corruption, they had had early successes, and even sent a superintendent Godber to prison. I think his arrest was connected with the gambling racket.

I'll give you an example of the corruption. In the UK, selection for identity parades was made on the streets. Volunteers, of similar description to the suspect, were asked to stand in one. They were paid expenses afterwards. In Hong Kong they employed professional actors through an agency. The police, and the crooks, made good use of these actors. The link is this. In Hong Kong, surprisingly, gambling was illegal unless through the Hong Kong Jockey Club. The Chinese of course love gambling and will bet on two flies in a teacup. Illegal gambling dens were everywhere and of course the police were obliged to be seen to do their job. They would raid gambling dens. Here's the scam. The police would warn the gamblers in advance of the raid; for a princely sum of course. The gamblers would pay actors $30 to sit at tables in the gambling den waiting for the raid, and the real gamblers would relocate, or take a night off until the heat was off. The actors would be arrested and charged to appear before the Court. They would all plead guilty because the fine was $20, giving them a net profit of $10. Most actors would actually arrange for somebody else to plead guilty on their behalf, for a dollar. It was always acceptable to the (bent) magistrate. One guy could plead guilty for up to 30 or so others,

120

so he made a few bob as well! The magistrate was of course in for a cut and so repeated offenders were never jailed, and the fine was standard.

Enter the complication; a new, and straight, magistrate. He noticed one particular repeat offender and demanded he appear before the Court, and promptly sent him to prison. Of course the poor actor was horrified. He was having none of this, and spilled the beans. Enterprising lot aren't they.

I encountered 'bent' solicitors. Labels on evidence exhibits were exchanged during a break in a trial. I had left an officer to keep an eye on them, but he abandoned his post it would seem. Upon resumption of the trial, as brazen and direct as you could get, the solicitor immediately asked for the exhibit to be produced and identified it as falsely labelled. I knew he knew that I knew. He didn't care. The prosecution service had deliberately withdrawn from the trial the night before, and left me to prosecute five guys singlehandedly, with five solicitors representing them. I was lucky to get just one convicted when it should have been a very straightforward case. I had been well and truly stitched up. Somebody was trying to tell me something.

I knew John McClelland briefly. It had to be briefly because he was shortly to be dead. John hailed from Glasgow. He was waiting for his fiancé to join him at the time he met his fate at the hand of bent coppers. John had been assigned to a team especially assembled to investigate 'homosexuality in the government'. Homosexuality was still illegal in Hong Kong. It is said that some big names were uncovered and that John refused to cover them up. He was found with all six rounds of his revolver discharged into his chest. The verdict was suicide. They brought an expert from the States to say that it was possible to discharge six rounds into your own chest. John was alleged to be a homosexual himself. Even a public enquiry endorsed the original verdict! Criminal.

You see, working in the Royal Hong Kong Police was perilous, but somehow, I didn't watch my back properly, as I had been warned by Tom Meffin. That's inexperience for you.

At the time things started to get scary I had been offered a new contract, but events resulted in my career in the Hong Kong Police ending abruptly, and for me, somewhat tragically. I wanted to leave, but not in quite the way things turned out. The circumstances had a profound effect on me and changed my thinking forever.

Mention of crime in Hong Kong would be incomplete without a mention of the Triads – the Chinese Mafia. Chinese communities all over the world are terrorised into paying protection money to the Triads who also operate two other highly profitable businesses - gambling and vice. Triads maintain discipline among their members by elaborate oaths and blood rituals. Once initiated, a Triad member may never leave. There are many Triad 'Societies' the largest probably being the 14K. The Wo Shing Wo is fairly big in Britain and Europe. Attempts to infiltrate them have had little success; officers doing so are killed or corrupted. Such attempts are said to have been responsible for much of the widespread corruption in the Royal Hong Kong Police. It is almost certainly the case that officers who worked with me were members of a society, and equally likely that officers for another squad were members of another. I believe I underestimated the strength and depth of their network.

To break the Triads, the police must overcome the fear built up by one of their oaths, 'I must never reveal triad secrets or signs when speaking to outsiders. If I do I will be killed by myriads of swords – death by 1,000 cuts'. It is no surprise that little is seen or mentioned of them in Britain, but they operate here big style, believe me.

Whilst at Wanchai I had been twice approached to join the Crime Squad by Superintendent Hall. I was flattered. I knew I was good at my job, and he knew it too. But I didn't like him, his style or his reputation, and he didn't like me either; referring to me as a 'wide boy' didn't help. He also had a dodgy right hand man, a DCI, appropriately nicknamed 'Harry the Rat'. I declined. Hall was an ex metropolitan policeman, fluent in Cantonese and was reputed to be the only 'boollay' (Cantonese for white devil – a name for whites) member of a triad society, which said a lot. He had attracted the close attention of the ICAC and had made a name for himself on the popular BBC documentary series 'Hong Kong Beat', although most colleagues thought that he made a complete prat of himself. I certainly did. He appeared in the programme in an almost ankle length leather coat as he was searching suspects on the street. He had them stretched out 'Yankee' style against a wall. We simply didn't do that 'Starsky and Hutch' nonsense. It was laughable, embarrassing also, but Hall was dangerous. The Hong Kong newspapers described the 'Hong Kong Beat' as 'a public relations exercise that backfired'. One Scotland Yard Commander was quoted as saying 'I watched with dismay. I couldn't believe that a police force had so laid itself open to potential disaster. The show illustrated blatant disregard for many basic law enforcement principles'.

Me being me, and seeking excitement and action, I ignored all the danger signs. Not too many months later I had a rethink and I phoned him to say I was interested. Within a couple of weeks I was operating a squad from Victoria Barracks on Hong Kong Island. It was to be the biggest mistake I had yet made.

122

The barracks were exactly that. Disused Army Barracks dating back to the Second World War and beyond. Our H.Q. occupied just one of the many deserted building. 'Harry the Rat' showed me round on the first day. Ominously he showed me basement shower rooms that he referred to as being easy to clear blood from. From day one I was uncomfortable and realised I just needed to keep my nose out, and keep it clean. Was I capable of doing that?

I headed one of several squads. I didn't know any of the guys so I tried, unsuccessfully, to get my sergeant to follow me from Wanchai. Another Crime Squad DI, an ex British Rail police officer, warned me about Hall. He shared my concern and discomfort.

He told me the story of his hush – hush kidnapping case that Hall intervened in. Hall arranged, as many Chinese businessmen preferred, to pay the ransom money. The pick-up was to be at the island star ferry terminal at peak hour travel time, when traffic is at a standstill. He arranged a stake out with patrol cars at strategic places. "How the hell", I asked, "did he fail to have motor cycle cops on standby"? It was either incompetence or deliberate. The ransom money was collected by a guy on a motorcycle who left the scene at high speed through heavy traffic never to be seen again! What a surprise.

I had done OK at Wanchai but I didn't suffer fools easily in those days, and my propensity to treat fools as such, irrespective of their rank, had attracted the interest of a head quarters 'uniform'. I knew this pen pusher had it in for me and that if he had the chance he would 'stick the knife in'. This is why,months earlier, the pen pusher, a Headquarters Chief Inspector, had wanted me to act like a coolie. He phoned me, when I was upstairs in the CID office, and asked me to run downstairs to the station reception to pass on a message, because nobody was answering the phone in the police station. I told him 'No. I can't do it, I was too busy'. He 'ordered' me, and I repeated that I couldn't. I was too busy. He irritated me and I suggested he phone back later. I hung up.

He complained, perhaps justifiably, to Frank about my insubordination. Frank warned me to take care, and not to be too cocky. My mission while working in the crime squad was to do just that; keep my head down and my mouth shut. I wasn't able to do it.

I had hoped that I could wile away most of my time looking into the existing caseload of murders and robberies but of course this was unrealistic, and new work would come my way. I just hoped to steer away from controversy, and turn a bit of a blind eye to 'matters that should not concern me'. Wrong I know, but believe me, this was the smart option when your contract is up in just a few months. Not long to wait.

One day I dealt with an armed robbery at a fur shop. There were no immediate leads by the close of my shift. That evening I attended a celebratory dinner party with CID Wanchai colleagues.

During the evening I had just a couple of drinks and kept sober as it was not intended to be a night out drinking. I was technically on call 24/7 and 365 days of the year; that was the nature of the job, but being called out, particularly when everyone knew I was at a prearranged dinner, was very rare.

Late in the evening I received a call at the restaurant from Harry the Rat. There had been an arrest in connection with the robbery earlier that day. 'Get back to the office immediately' he said in a provocative aggressive tone. He found my Achilles heel. I was annoyed. I questioned the urgency. When was the arrest? Where are my guys now? When will they have the suspect back at the office? All these questions, that were quite reasonable and pertinent given that I was off duty made him annoyed as well. He 'ordered' me to get back to the office immediately.

I agreed to return to the office straight away but ignored him and stayed an extra fifteen minutes to wind up my conversation and finish eating. When I got back to the office, just five minutes away, nobody had returned. The place was virtually deserted. Nobody who worked for me was there, and nobody knew anything about the case, or an arrest having been made. I was expected to wait around.

I expressed my anger to a fellow DI who was in the main office and asked where my squad were, and if he knew when they would arrive. He knew nothing. I sounded off about Harry the Rat demanding I return immediately, then went through to my office and checked for any clues as to what had been happening.

I then went through to Dave Edwards' office. Dave was a seasoned DI who had been in Hong Kong some years. He was just coming off the phone. I sounded off again. He said that I had upset the other DI. As I was explaining, and saying 'I didn't think I had,' he got up from behind his desk and knocked me to the ground 'for upsetting his mate'. I was kicked and punched and every time I tried to get up he hit and kneed me in the face. 'Stay down' he insisted.

If only I had stayed down it might have ended at that; I would have been put in my place. But Dave Wakefield can't do that can he; determination, stubbornness and stupidity prevented me from doing that.

'You're a tough little bastard' I remember him saying (and I quite liked that). I was going to get a beating but I was going to get a good decent beating if I was to be defeated. There was no doubt I was. Honour in defeat. It would have been 'honour in defeat', and it would have been over, but for the arrival of Harry the Rat. He joined in and I raged.

He kicked me about the head. I knew then, in a moment, that my future in the Crime Squad was over. I was soon to realise that my future in the Hong Kong Police Force was also over. I was about to be humiliated and I could never maintain any authority in their ranks again.

I would not stop trying to fight back at him so Harry arranged for me to be handcuffed by his lads. I was moved to a chair with my arms behind the chair. Junior officers were left with me while I 'cooled off'. I didn't.

I struggled and demanded removal of the cuffs. 'Harry said not until he says so'. I was mocked. 'You are very strong sir' I was complimented. I feared that I would be set up or something worse.

I demanded I speak on the phone to my wife. After some time and after repeated demands I was told that Harry had agreed. I told Nikki to contact Charlie Slater at the ICAC. She did. That act also signalled the end of my career with the RHKP.

It caused all sorts of high level shit! Hall was called out and he drove me home demanding I hand him my gun and warrant card. He informed me that I was to take some holiday and wait until I'd heard from him. I went to the hospital the following day to get a medical examination and I photographed my injuries.

The exercise in attempting to 'bring me to heel' went wrong. They had misjudged the situation and more importantly me. I was not going to take it and had consciously made the decision not to give in; my Achilles heel.

My mate Johnny Walsh had joined the crime squad from Wanchai after me. He fed me news of what was happening. Dave Edwards wanted to speak with me. He regretted the misunderstanding and allowing things to get out of control. He was not happy with the way Harry had behaved or the situation as it was unfolding. They were trying to frame me with the allegation that I was drunk.

They had tried to persuade John, who had been with me at the dinner party, to give a statement to that effect. They wanted Dave Edwards to say the same. John told me that

125

he had refused. Dave Edwards, I was told, wanted to admit that he had started it and to get me off the hook. I asked John to thank him, but declined a chat. My fate was sealed. I had declined a possible way out of the mess simply because of my dignity and pride.

I was ordered to attend Headquarters where I was given my cards by the very Chief Inspector that had complained about my insubordination. Take that! It was the Christmas holiday and this guy had been given the 'honour', presumably at his own request, of terminating my contract.

I was told it was for 'being drunk in charge of a firearm' but this wasn't true. It was later changed to 'insubordination' then amended to general unsuitability. He was gloating. I was paid off to the end of my contract and given my substantial gratuity. I had a right of appeal but it never took place. I was never interviewed or asked to give a statement about the incident.

I left the colony a few weeks later and a small band of supporters; including a couple of my team from Wanchai, saw me off. It was a bitter and humiliating end to an enjoyable three years in Hong Kong, but I left with my head held high knowing that I was true to myself, even if I did regret getting myself into the pickle in the first place. I had been foolish and had paid the price. I'm not sure whether it is quite appropriate to say it, but maybe I had 'lived and died by the sword'. I rather suspect however that I lost my job not because of the huge miscalculation on the part of a genuinely, although mistakenly aggrieved colleague, but because of the cowardly Harry 'the rat'.

A subsequent look at Peter Hall's report on the incident confirmed my worst fears; the report contained a complete pack of lies and a complete reversal of the truth. There were no statements from 'the rat', or Dave Edwards. They were virtually written out of the script. They were praised for their conduct under difficult circumstances.

You see, the story according to them is that I had turned up late, remonstrated, left the office with four D.C.'s, arrested four men and seized exhibits at a property in Wanchai, popped in to the celebratory party, returned to the property in Wanchai, returned to the office with the men and the exhibits, remonstrated again, attacked Edwards and was then restrained by him and 'the rat'.

I had been well and truly stitched up. Facts that he could not dispute, were interwoven into a fabricated web of lies, and he neatly incorporated the old chestnut; drinking too much. If there are two people on earth that I have hated its 'the rat' and Hall; they are evil

126

men. Men that held authority, men that were there to serve the public, but only served themselves. I believe that Hall was actually awarded the Queens Police Medal!

There was one little bright spot in this pathetic little saga. I do believe I managed to get a good right hand twist on 'the rats 'balls as he kicked me!

I'm a great believer in fate. Nikki had announced her pregnancy and she wanted me out of the police. I was ready to move on in any case, and, painful as it was, I was now being catapulted toward an exciting new future, in a successful new career. The dismissal did not ultimately affect my ability to re-join the West Midlands police but it did, in my view, ruin any chance of holding a high rank. My police career was behind me, but could I put all the stain on my reputation behind me?

I festered for years afterward. Resurrecting events for the purposes of writing these memoirs rekindled old bitterness, and new anger, so the account has been précised. If I pause to think positively, I did not end up like poor John McClelland.

PART TWO

Chapter Eight
Bouncebackability
1980 – 1984

Our return journey to UK included holidays in Sri Lanka, Seychelles and Kenya. Then it was back down to earth. After my setback life was all about getting back on course.

We had money, a good gratuity from my contract with RHKP, and I was paid up for three months, but this money was earmarked for a deposit on a house. We had left a UK in 1977 that was in decline through industrial mismanagement and union stranglehold. We had been unable to buy a house on a meagre police salary and the police had been poised to strike. We returned to a Thatcher government and higher house prices. Thatcherism was taking its early faltering steps.

We lived with my parents for some months before we found a house later that year. I couldn't make up my mind exactly what I wanted to do but was pretty firmly settled on soliciting, so I would need to wait until October to start a degree (three years) and then follow on with a year at law school. Nikki was pregnant. She had set her stall out and wanted me to become a responsible father and leave the police. Policemen were unsuccessful in marriage, statistically, and there was a high divorce rate. CID work was not at all conducive to marriage and family life; long unsociable hours even if it wasn't particularly 'shift based'. CID was all I wanted out of the police service.

It didn't take much to persuade me to seek a change. After leading complex and major criminal investigations a return to uniform, junior status, and training school for a refresher did not appeal, even if for just a year. Promotion would follow, but again into uniform, and again a wait. There were few fast track schemes in those days so there was little alternative. If I did a degree I could always return to the police later. As my reputation had been tainted I discounted the police. It was decided - a law degree.

I was however intrigued as to what kind of report I would get from the RHKP. I had been booted out – they could do it for no reason if they wanted - and I decided to check out prospects in the police. I also applied for jobs with Thomas Cook Investigations (they were looking for a Far East investigator), Abel Alarms in Leicester, and as an Operations Manager overseeing the cleaning operations at the National Exhibition Centre in Birmingham.

'The Rat' had been at work trying to stick the boot even after my departure from Hong Kong. He'd told me shortly after my arrival in the squad about his 'cousin' who worked with Customs and Excise in Felixstowe. I knew then that he was putting one across my bow, and now, on arrival in UK I was to experience the meaning behind his need to mention it.

Our boxes of personal possessions, furniture clothing and bedding arrived at Felixstowe. P & O, the shippers, tried it on first. The boxes were retained by Customs and Excise(C & E) for inspection. P & O tried to bill me for the period of storage in detention. I knew they couldn't (I'd read the contract carefully). They appointed solicitors when I refused to pay the bill. I got the solicitors letter and I replied 'I'll see you in Court'. I heard nothing further.

I then received a telephone message via my Mum to phone this guy, I forgot his name, from C &E in Felixstowe. I phoned that afternoon. I was asked which box the cigars were in. I knew it was a strange call. When the boxes arrived the cigars were missing. The phone call was an introduction – a message. The real business was to come.

I got a visit from C & E in Birmingham. Two C & E officers sat in my parents' front room asking for an invoice for a purchased Hi Fi. I had no idea where it was, but I knew I had one, and that the Hi Fi had been purchased in my first year in Hong Kong and that no duty should have been payable. They weren't prepared to wait for me to find the invoice. Pay £150 duty and they would not 'look at the wife's jewellery' then the matter would be closed.
These officers were of course being 'used' and I think that they could have been real bastards if I hadn't deliberately manoeuvred into the conversation the fact that I'd had that strange call from Felixstowe and told them about my 'fall out' with crooked cops. They seemed genuinely uncomfortable, interested and surprised about the call I had had. They knew something wasn't quite right.

I later found the invoice (it was in one of the boxes) and sent it to C & E but they weren't interested in dropping the duty charge. I dropped the matter. I knew that I had no invoices for many of the other items, and if they wanted to they could make my life very difficult. The last thing I wanted was for Nikki to be subjected to an inquisition. But I was very angry with 'the Rat'. At that time I felt that one day, when I had raised a family, and had no responsibilities, I would re-visit Hall and 'the Rat'. I suppose in a way that's what I'm doing now; in a non-violent way.

Thomas Cook asked me to join them as a travel cheque fraud investigator. They thought my links with RHKP, my commercial crime squad experience and my language skills ideal for far eastern operations. They discussed starting dates salary, etc etc, and then I told them that my ties might be weakened as a result of the bust up. They thanked me for telling them. I didn't get the job.

I provisionally accepted a job with Abel Alarms, as a sales representative. I could have made heaps of money with them, and there were real long term prospects, but I only wanted a stop gap. I took the Operations Managers job at the National Exhibition Centre (NEC). I'm not sure I made the right decision. I needed a job that would last up until my start at college and this one fell short by a month due to my employers, Servicesystems, losing their contract, and some of my work colleagues were envious of the fact that a newcomer had walked straight into a job that several of them had been vying for. Resentment became a spoiling factor in an otherwise easy and straightforward stopgap earner. Nevertheless those few months represented an interesting and new experience.

It's difficult to take contract cleaning seriously as a profession, but I learnt from the senior technicians who were responsible for chemical technology and manufacture of cleaning products and started to appreciate how important the choice of materials and techniques can be. It was an eye-opener.

Operations Management was quite different; the cleaning crews were rough and ready guys, mainly off the local housing estate. Some were decent enough and likeable guys, others backstabbing types that would do anything to gain favour and others lazy. I made no secret of the fact that I was an ex cop and I'm sure that won't have helped me, but that's life. It was really my first taste of the nasty competitive world that is 'industry and commerce'. I needed to harden up. But could I, should I?

One of the office based supervisors wanted my job. Her mates would fall in line with her views once she'd spent time on making a case for them. She could be a bit of a flirt really but had decided, consciously or unconsciously, that she wasn't going to get on with me. She loved her previous boss, and she wasn't going to accept change easily. She created the illusion of making an effort, but never had her heart in it.

I liaised with a NEC employee responsible for cleaning operations. She was the NEC's answer to Mrs Slokeholm (Are You Being Served). Mrs Molden was a chav but snooty woman, attractive in her day, and still attractive in her, I would say 50's. Tall and well dressed with black stockings, high heels and face (caked with makeup). I don't mind tarty. Mrs Molden was an OK woman actually, and my boss, Dave Richards was also a decent guy to work with, but the politics, backstabbing and squabbling was like nothing I had experienced before. Quite sad really, quite an insecure environment in which to work, and that impacted on my ability to enjoy the work.

I was pleased to meet Ken. He had been a crime squad officer in the Warwickshire force and was now head of security at the NEC. Ken had had a chequered history and one worthy of mention later. Suffice to say Ken was a decent honest guy and someone I felt comfortable being around.

I was still troubled by my rough justice in Hong Kong. I was intrigued about how it was sitting with the boys at home. I sent in an application form for the police and then phoned Tom Meffin, who was by now Assistant Chief Constable (Crime) to tell him about Hong Kong and discuss how my career might unfold if I returned. I told him that the RHKP report would be unfavourable and why. He reminded me that he had warned me before I had left for Hong Kong to 'watch my back'.

The RHKP had been damning and I could not accept the allegation that I had been dismissed for 'drunk in charge of a firearm' I wanted to sort the situation out. I did not want to swan back into the police, as I am sure I could have done had I played my cards right, with the situation unresolved. I went to see my M.P. John Butcher, an industry minister under Thatcher's Conservative Government. We were eventually to become friends. I was sad to hear of his death in 2006, leaving his wife Ann, and three kids. I can tell you now that he did a lot to help me, and also taught me a few things. He was a clever hard working man. He also had a wicked sense of humour and a taste in music that ranged from rock to classical; apart from being a Birmingham City fan, we had a lot in common and enjoyed each other's company, especially over a drink.

John forced the issue with the RHKP so they withdrew the allegation and wrote confirming that my contract had been terminated for 'insubordination'. I could live with that. It was later changed to 'unsuitability'. A result? Yes, but not justice. John appealed to the HK Governor, Cater. That came up with a big '0'. Eventually solicitors were appointed and they confirmed that although there was a strong case, and there was, as I suggested to them, a breach of natural justice; the case could go nowhere under English Law! Oh well, get on with it.

Unfortunately John had misread my wishes in relation to the handling of the matter and had mishandled an enquiry that he had made with Tom Meffin, I suspect by repeating a confidential discussion between Tom and I. Oh dear. I hadn't asked John to do that.

When I next met John he was visibly embarrassed to see me. Tom had clearly given him a piece of his mind. He had apparently asked for copies of the correspondence from the RHKP. I let John off and said I no longer wished to pursue the matter. I think he relaxed.

When I next met Tom, in our usual meeting place (on the terraces at Highfield Road Football Ground) he 'deafed' me. "I have nothing to say to you Mr Wakefield", and that was it. I never got a chance to explain the mistake, although I didn't understand it, and I guess he would still have ill feelings toward me. I can't change things, but I regret that mistake, and missing the chance to explain it. It hurt me. If we had spoken he would have realised that wires were crossed and 'confidentiality' hadn't been best handled.

I was interviewed for admission to Lanchester Polytechnic by Bert Raisbeck, a man I admired and respected from my first meeting. He also became a good friend. Bert was a politically well balanced guy who had been a policeman and magistrate. Bert, unlike most academics, had seen something of life. He wasn't just a brilliant academic and well qualified lawyer; he was a social drinker like me, and very down to earth.

There were formalities, but I was accepted into the faculty that day, over several beers in the Sir Colin Campbell pub. I turned down an earlier offer of a place at the much more prestigious Warwick University. There were two reasons; (a) the university was two bus rides away and 'The Lanch' was one, and (b) the degree at The Lanch was a Business law degree, one of only two available in the country, and this was a much more practically based degree than the one at Warwick. Warwick taught the traditional jurisprudence, and I thought that to be surplus to my requirements. The Lanch approach was practical and modern, and they were the leaders in this area.

I got my degree but only after a massive argument with the faculty head over how he should behave toward guests. I was so angry. He was a prick; up his own arse with self importance and very rude.

The trouble started when I was asked by the faculty 'student's graduation dance committee' if I knew anyone decent to invite as a top table guest. I did, "Yes, a Government Minister".

I asked John and his wife if they would attend as honoured guests. A formal invitation followed from the committee. An embarrassing verbal attack on John was made mid speech by one or two students. The faculty head, on the top table, joined in. I was incensed.

133

It is one thing for young students to let off a little steam, perhaps expected, but not the faculty head, a man of responsibility and in his 50's. It was the height of bad manners to invite someone, as a guest, accompanied by his wife, to a social occasion and abuse him. The evening was politicised and spoilt. I could see that John was taken aback, and that his wife was uncomfortable. It was wrong.

I told Bert that I was going to complain to the faculty head on the Monday morning. He counselled against, but warned me to keep my cool. I sort of kept my cool, although I wanted to hit him over the desk, but I told him how I felt and suggested he apologise. He thought that impertinent and showed anger. I then told him that his behaviour was unbecoming a man in his position and that I had no respect for him. It cost me.

I also had a scrape with the DHSS at the end of my first year. They refused to pay money owed to me, and I went to appeal at tribunal, representing myself. They had in my absence, earlier ruled against me, and had further decided on another issue that was not a matter that had been put before them. This was outside the power of the Court (ultra vires), and I told them so. Unbeknown to me a faculty lecturer, Ben Broby, was on the tribunal bench. He directed the others that I was correct, and the tribunal advised that I would need to apply to the County Court to reverse the decision. That cost money and time and it was not worth it – a victory was sweet enough and the money was not a large amount. It was a point of principal! I was being cheated.

Ben Broby later taught me land law, and told me of his admiration for my stand.. He was very impressed. But then I knew that I was better at understanding than regurgitating the law – onto paper. Ironically my worst subject at Uni was criminal law, and that weakness cost me a grade. I froze in the examination room.

I read an awful lot during my Uni years, and knew my law well. I understood it , but my memory was crap. Revision was always difficult for me. I got bored with it. I just wanted to learn, understand, and get on with enjoying my life. Education is not an exercise in memory retention parrot style, it is more about retention for an appropriate occasion when circumstances arise – my problem was that when the occasion arose in examinations I wasn't quick enough or thorough enough. My memory has always been bad. I was more suited to the autonomy of a post graduate course, and later I did in fact start one at Warwick University but pulled out after a few weeks – I had no time for it.

When I had a pint after studying in the library it was generally with a couple of the cooler guys on the course – both Welshman from Cowbridge, Bert Raisbeck, or Jack

Murphy, my economics lecturer during my first year. Jack was a bearded Scot and IRA sympathiser, but we were able to talk and debate with respect for each other's view.

I didn't see eye to eye with everyone on the course. Elizabeth Sewell, daughter of the TV actor of Z-Cars fame was a feminist of sorts and an idealist; young and radical. That's all fine, and typical of youngsters with healthy attitude, but she had no tolerance for the views of others. I held a door open for her once and she scolded me!

I'm sure that those three years that I spent at Uni were difficult for Nikki but I can't remember her complaining once. She went without a lot in the interests of our future prospects, but I could see she'd had enough by the time I had finished and I had to remain true to my promise (to myself) that I was going to lead a balanced life and be a decent family man.

I decided against taking a place at Chester Law School and lost the deposit for my place of £25. It would have meant me moving to Chester for one year and away from family. It was too much of a sacrifice. Anyway, I had been questioning why I had wanted to be a solicitor anyway. I thought that bargaining and academic argument, more often brought about outcomes, rather than justice.

Justice was for those that could afford to pay for it. If I had wanted to sue the RHKP I had been advised that it would have cost around £20,000 – the cost of the average house at the time. I was never going to make a top lawyer, and most lawyers were overworked and pressured to capitulate. I wouldn't find that very satisfying after a while.

I owed it to Nikki to go out and earn some money. Money had been hard to come by for three years. How we survived is clear; with the help of my parents and Nikki's step–grandfather, Joe. We had a mortgage, two children and a dog by the time the three years was up. Income comprised a local authority grant, social security by the way of child support, and donations from the aforesaid family members. It couldn't have been done without them.

Zoe had been born in my first college year, Katy the third, and in between, we had the dog – Johan Sebastian Bach; Sebastian for short. He was a Labrador pup. I wanted to call him Bach, but it's a strange name to call out to a dog. He had been superbly trained during college breaks and was a wonderfully disciplined loving and faithful dog. He lived just eight months. During a visit to the in-laws he followed the children out on to the street and was hit by a car. I was distraught.

Despite being broke, the college years were fun years. I took on an allotment for fresh fruit and vegetables. We partied a lot with friends and neighbours. We visited the local Working Men's Club with the kids when we didn't have a baby sitter or the local pub. In the summer we walked to The Rainbow pub, a good walking distance across the 'wedge,' a beautiful greenbelt unchanged in hundreds of years, through the churchyard of All Saints, where we were married, and into Allesley Village.

I did a lot of walking from our new home. It was about a mile walk to my parent's home. I walked over the fields with the kids, the dog, or on my own. I walked to my parents and to the allotment. I used the bus to Uni but sometimes walked. Nikki did even more walking, and was a wonderfully devoted and loving mother. We were reasonably contented. The 'Wedge' was a beautiful green belt, unspoilt and typical English countryside leading into Allesley Village. A stream ran through it where a kingfisher could occasionally be seen – just yards from the edge of Coventry City. Jaguar won their campaign to run a service road through the 'Wedge' – essential for expansion of a factory (they told the council) and giving jobs to the people of the area. The plant closed a few years ago!

I made a little extra money in the summer growing coleus from seed, potting them and selling them on to greengrocer shops. I could get 100 times the cost of the project. I also worked a short spell at the Jaguar factory as a plumbers mate during the 'breakdown' when the factory was closed for a fortnight.

Joe often visited at weekends. His wife, Nikki's grandmother, Edna, had recently died of cancer, and he was alone in retirement. I insisted to Nikki that we have him for the weekend at least once a month. In fact he visited more often. Joe was a great guy; a real gentleman with a naughty side to him. We were extremely close and the children adored him. He, like John, Nikki's Dad, was a good friend. However he was not exactly a stabilising influence: he enjoyed pub life as much as I did!

We lived there, until my new job took us closer to my office in Northampton during the late 1980's. I have very fond memories of our days there. Nikki was at her near best, and certainly contented. In fact, her best was probably reserved for the first few years that we were living in a small village in Northamptonshire, our next home. She loved being a mother and her time was devoted to the children. As the children got older, in an ideal environment, my wife blossomed.

Our early family holidays were fun. We took our kids on holidays to Dyffryn, in Wales, and Snettisham, in Norfolk, for holidays that linked with my childhood, our courtship and the children. We took them to Devon and Cornwall, where we had great memories of our first holiday together as boyfriend/girlfriend. We had taken a three week coastal drive that took us from Bristol to Plymouth. The children will particularly remember successive B & B holidays with Mrs Moore in Cawsand. Gracie Fields had lived next door, and Admiral Lord Nelson and Lady Hamilton had done some courting in this quaint little seaside village.

We later managed holidays in Spain and Disneyland, Florida. These were OK times.

Chapter Nine
Insurance Loss Adjusting
1984 - 1997

I had decided that a solicitor's life was not for me. I wrote upward of one hundred and fifty letters to insurance companies, brokers and Loss Adjusters and advertised my talents to get a job. I had about thirty replies, including three interviews. I had done a week's sales course with a doorstep sales company and had been taught that 10% (3 out of 30) was an expected conversion rate. Interviews were in Plymouth, nearby Kenilworth and one in Birmingham with Howells & Co.

John Lewis interviewed me in Kenilworth. He had been a Director with Howells and left to set up his own company. He said he hadn't got a job for me but gave me a lot of advice and invited me to call him if I needed more. We got along fine.

I attended the other interviews, in Plymouth with Davis and Co. and in the Coventry office of Howells with a cigar wielding 'flashman' who appeared to be a complete prat; but a likeable one. I had job offers from both. The bigger company offered more money but the smaller company in Plymouth better prospects. I phoned John Lewis to ask his opinion. He agreed that Plymouth offered the best career move. He said he had been thinking things over and that he might have something to offer me. I went to see him again, accepted his job offer and joined John Lewis & Co for the 'middle money'.

I cut my teeth on domestic work in Kenilworth. It was quick turnover work. John was something of a pioneer offering insurance companies cheap 'fixed fee' single page hand written reports for domestic insurance claims, providing settlement could be agreed after a single home visit. If matters couldn't be sorted out in this way the claim would be taken out of the 'scheme'.

He had recognised the direction the insurance market was heading and was ahead of the pack. The effectiveness of the scheme depended on a flexible negotiated settlement on a cash basis. It saved the insurance company money and, in my view always left the insured with a little more than necessary. It produced a very amicable and quick resolution to small claims handling.

The work was ideal work upon which to cut my teeth and my background lent itself well to the job. I had good investigative and negotiation skills and a nose for when things weren't quite right. I knew I was good at this work, and progressed to bigger losses. John asked me to move to a new office he was opening in Northampton; his business was fast growing.

I was working at both Kenilworth and Northampton offices. I hadn't been attending Northampton for long but had already attracted the attentions of the offices of competitors Howells, located just across the Market Square. Dave Fisher, who was eventually to become a close friend, asked me if I wanted to join them and I politely declined…for the time being.

Not long afterwards John made a mistake that affected my relationship with him, and saw me move to Howells. He was having problems meeting reporting timetables agreed with his customers, particularly his biggest, the General Accident. At a critical point yet another complaint was received and he decided that he would cover up for the delays in the system caused by a typing-pool backlog. He was in danger of losing the company's business.

When I had occasion to return to a 'closed' file I discovered that such a complaint had been made about one of my reports. John had telephoned the insurance company, and then written to them, indicating that the delay was the fault of the Loss Adjuster – me – and that he had bollocked me (there was no reason to do so). He had used me as a scapegoat! I took the file through to his office and opened it on his desk in front of him. "Can you explain this please John?"

After an uncomfortable period of silence he said, "What else could I do?"

"Tell me John. I would have fallen on my sword for you?" And I would have done. Had he told me that business was on the line I would have willingly, if begrudgingly, taken the rap for the good of the company. He had stabbed me in the back. He had never spoken to me. He had never bollocked me. He had hoped that I would never have known what he had done. This betrayal hit me hard. It was alien to me. Welcome to the commercial world!

I told John that I couldn't work for him anymore and that I would be looking for alternative employment. He made a further mistake. He offered me more money.

I had been with John for about eighteen months before I moved to Howells in Market Square, Northampton. For a few months I commuted daily the twenty two miles back and forth to Coventry before I moved the family out of Coventry and to a small village in Northamptonshire close to the M1 motorway and not too far from Rugby in Warwickshire. It was a super move in every respect. A period of calm, contentment and normality entered my life for the next five years. It was time to raise a family in a stable environment.

The village life was great, and I enjoyed working with my new found colleagues who became friends. I was only firm friends with Mark Holland when I was at John Lewis's. The office atmosphere at Howells was like that of a family. Moving to a village can be dodgy, but the locals were very friendly and not at all cliquey.

House prices were rising fast and gazumping was common, but an earlier attempt to buy a bungalow in Yelvertoft, a village just a short distance away, ended in an unexpected disaster when the Lay Preacher who was selling to us backed out the evening before the day of exchange. His wife didn't want to move any more. I could have crucified him on his own for sale board, but just picked up the bill and got over the disappointment. We consoled ourselves with the thought that 'it was clearly never to be'.

Nikki was apprehensive about moving to a village but we both quite fancied the idea of a better environment in which to raise our children than in a city. We were delighted and so were the children. We fitted in brilliantly. Katy started at infant school and Zoe juniors – all in the same small school just around the corner from our house; a three bed roomed semi.

Our Coventry home had served us well and we were sad to leave the house and our good friendly neighbours but it was a superb quantum leap into country life that could only be good for the children and none of us ever regretted it.

Village Fetes, barbeques, country walks, street parties and house parties – we loved it. The Grand Union Canal and a marina were just on the edge of the village and I would take the girls fishing. The village, of just about 1,500, had three very different pubs and an ex-serviceman's club, a very beautiful old church, a post office and a village co-op. There was a 'top', and 'bottom' end of the village in the minds of many – we lived at the top, in the posh end! Everyone, millionaires to grave diggers mixed without real exception; such is good village life. Everyone knew everyone. It was perfikt!

Nikki made friends at the school gate and I was making them in the pub. By being tolerant and patient we developed good relations with neighbours. We helped to create a friendly little community in our little cul-de-sac; it hadn't always had one. When we had a party everyone in 'the close' was invited, and I mean every one. Most turned up.

Neighbours on our left were 'the George family' Willie, a little Glaswegian, his wife, Ivy, a cockney. Their lads, John and Ian, both born and bred in the village were in their thirties and still living at home. Ivy was a rounded woman with a sweet heart of gold and a round cherub face to match. Willie was a bagpipe wielding little Scotsman with a heart of gold and a smile that showed his dignity, warmth and decency.

The Georges lived in a, let's say, interesting house. It was an Aladdin's Cave. You couldn't move for moose heads and muskets. It was so cluttered you couldn't get through the door, and how anything could be found was beyond me. It was like a ram jam full antique shop – just like 'Bits and Bobs' the village antique shop. Bob, Willie and Ivy have all passed on. John and Ian still live in the house and the garden still looks like a garage mechanics yard.

Both Ivy and Willie might have passed on a lot earlier in life if we hadn't encouraged them to insulate the walls and repair floorboards, put in central heating and put in double glazed windows before the old ones fell out. Willie wasn't short of a few bob but he wasn't keen on spending it; he was a Scotsman! Ivy and Willie became our very dear and close friends although they were both a good thirty years older than us. After Ivy died we nursed Willie through his grief and he was a regular for Sunday Dinner – after the pub! They had been married since they were teenagers.

Graham lived to our right. Graham was a quiet former school teacher. Regarded as 'odd' by some he was in fact simply a bit shy, but one hell of a guy when you took the trouble to get to know and understand him. He lived with a former Sixth Form pupil – his reason for packing up teaching. Graham was a good gardener; a home brewer; a VW enthusiast; a very intelligent and knowledgeable guy.

Pete and Hazel lived over the road. They had two great kids. The family became good friends. Kit and Les lived opposite. He was a carpenter at Gartree Prison and she taught 'handicapped' kids. We now call them underprivileged of course. Kit played Nancy in Swallows and Amazons, the film, her claim to fame. I was really impressed. They were both the salt of the earth. They rented their house out just before we left the village, to do voluntary work in a small remote village in Zambia. Quality of life meant everything to

141

them and not money. They taught me a few things in life; concentrated my mind. I respected them both. And they were also great fun.

Malc kept the garage and petrol station on the outskirts of the village. Malc was a likeable guy and a good friend. I recall one guy in the Oak (the local's local), referring to Malc and I, saying, "This must be the only village in the country with two village idiots". Malc was nick-named 'Proudman' by Des Gray, another good guy. I joined them at times as an honorary 'partners in crime', or rather drink! Looking back none of us have really grown up! Many fond memories emanate from the Royal Oak, and the kaleidoscope of characters within. They call it 'Weasel Central' and a plaque on the door is testimony to that.

Malc was the only guy in the village that would pat all the school kids on the head at the school fete – just in case they were his!

I had met Malc long before it even crossed my mind to move to the village. One night, a few weeks after Malc and I had met and hit it off, we were sitting in the pub with our respective wives and I asked him if he remembered me. He looked surprised at the question and I left him to think about it before explaining. I gave him a few clues. The penny dropped. "You! You crafty bastard. You cost me money you did. Damn you had me".

You see, Malc had had a break in at his garage a few months earlier and I had been the Loss Adjuster that had visited and settled his claim. In relaxed conversation he dropped his guard, and admitted to something that cost him a few hundred quid off the claims settlement. He knew he had been manoeuvred into the slip up. That night he forgave me. I think he eventually got his money back by servicing my car!

The list of 'characters' in the village was endless. 'Tunner', God Rest His Soul, was the village grave-digger, hedge layer and poacher. He actually lived in the almshouse in a neighbouring village, but had earlier left our village when the undertaker ran off with his wife. Tunner always, like always, wore the same Werzle Gummage cap, complete with field mouse. One Sunday he came to our house for Sunday Dinner. Shirt, tie, freshly pressed trousers and cleaned shoes. He still wore his tatty old cap! He took his cap off as he passed the threshold with flowers for Nikki. Tunner was an unexpected gentleman. If you took the trouble to get to know him you realised how thoroughly decent he really was.

I once asked Tunner if he'd ever buried a live one. He gave a lengthy and chilling story of a burial culminating in his final chore – filling the hole. 'Tap tap, tap' he heard from the coffin. So engrossed and attentive were I that I demanded anxiously, 'What did you do? What happened?' He leaned in across the bar and whispered in my ear, 'No reprieve'. I howled, he had taken me in as few can. It was a brilliant story and told superbly. My account cannot do it justice, so you need to use your imagination a little.

Our life was 'perfikt'. The village was well balanced and so was my family. I even went to church on a few occasions! The pubs were of course the heart and soul, but everything about the village was good, friendly, and almost idyllic. It was a true and complete community. There were of course busybodies and gossips, but that was all part of the package. But one thing is for sure – the gossip was generally correct. Nobody could afford to rumourmonger with duff information. Being caught spreading a malicious rumour was a serious offence and in a village it wasn't difficult to identify the originator of any such rumour. In a town it is, and in a modern city there is no community left to be interested. Everyone keeps themselves to themselves.

Hamsters and Chickens

Bringing the kids up in the family home would not be complete without pets, and living in a village would not be complete, and in harmony with the countryside, without chickens and an allotment, oh yes, and a little indoor activity in a hamster.

I had never kept chickens. I built a fine hen house in the garden and promised Nikki the chickens would be controlled and that I would keep them clean, fed and watered. They would be fun for the kids I assured her. She reluctantly agreed. Our girls named the four or five chickens.

Things were fine and the chickens lived with us in peace. They were no bother and it was a delight to collect one or two eggs in the morning, even though productivity was well below expectation. Only Henrietta, the Warren, a beautiful brown coloured commercial breed, lay reliably. The breeds; including a Rhode Island Red and Suffolk let us down. The Rhode Island Red was a complete dud!

We went through a winter and one spring day Graham, my next door neighbour was chatting with me in the Red Lion when he raised the subject of the cockerel in the area. "What cockerel?" I asked. "Yours" he replied, "haven't you heard it?"

No I hadn't. "Most mornings at around four or five" he said.

"Oh God. No. I haven't heard it. It's not causing you a problem is it? Nobody's been complaining have they?"

No problem Graham assured me. I concluded that Nikki didn't know either.

"Has Nikki mentioned it?"

"No" came the reply.

"She can't have heard it. She would have mentioned it. Hey Graham, keep it under your hat hey. If she doesn't mention it the chickens are OK. If she finds out the chicken gets it!"

I made the mistake of telling the kids. "Don't say a word. Mum'll go mad."

Nothing was mentioned for a week. She may have heard it herself or Katy, who couldn't keep quiet about anything, may have let slip. Even Zoe, who saw the funny side of it, might have sold me out. Anyhow Nikki quite casually calmly and unexpectedly asked me what I was going to do about the cockerel. I swallowed. "What cockerel?" I asked, in the faint hope that she hadn't got an ID on the source. "You know which cockerel David; don't think I'm a fool"

"Ohhh, that cockerel. Well it's not causing a problem is it?" A potentially inflammatory question, but one worth posing.

"No David" she snapped, "But it might be to neighbours".

She had hit me with an 'old chestnut' and she was right. "Well we've had no complaints so far have we so how's about we see how things go and keep it. He'll encourage laying" I said with a positive bounce. She agreed; miraculous (but I feared the worst for the future. Her patience would lapse!).

As it happened we decided to move before it became an issue and the 'herd' were packed off to a reliable friend Des Gray, who agreed to keep them in his own henhouse. "Look after them Des for Christ's sake. If anything happens to those chickens the kids will be devastated. They all have names you know!"

Disaster struck a week into their move. Des left the henhouse door open overnight; presumably following an alcohol overdose. All the chickens were killed. The locals in

144

the Oak (weasel central) howled. A fox's tail was placed through the henhouse door and a photo taken. Des was mortified and suitably embarrassed. The fox had had the lot and Des was gunning for it. He was very apologetic. When I learnt, I was head in hands. I cringed. How could I tell the kids? The story ran for days over copious amounts of alcohol. It was disastrous but funny.

I had kept tropical fish in Hong Kong and continued to do so throughout the 1980's keeping a large four foot long tank, packed with colourful fish. It was very therapeutic to watch fish, but whilst they were cheap in Hong Kong they were prohibitively expensive in the UK, particularly given the mortality rate. I haven't kept them since.

The hamster is an essential member of any family. Katy was just an infant when she arrived in the village and despite my reservations, she had one. Zoe had had one, so she would too.

We went away on holiday for a fortnight and Kit and Les offered to look after the hamster. On our return Kit took us to one side and explained that she had had the hamster out and it had vanished. A crisis; not so much for the hamster as Kit. She felt awful and I felt awful for her. I don't like to see well intended helpful people beating themselves up over a mistake. "Don't worry" I said. "We'll just say it died and that it was buried in the garden".

We decided on one last search. Nikki and I checked all the usual hamster haunts. Curtains, floorboards, cushions, cupboards, etc. No sign.

We were just about to give up when I spotted the garden lounger bed. The stitching had come apart. I suggested we check by 'feel' to see if the hamster could be inside.

We laid the bed on the floor and Nikki knelt at the open, damaged, end in case the hamster came out. I slowly advanced over the surface of the foam bed from the other end, feeling thoroughly with outstretched hands, in gentle sweeping motions so as not to hurt the hamster if I found it. We were quiet as mice listening out for a 'squeak' or a movement that might betray its presence. Nikki couldn't help but do the same at the other end and she swept across the surface with her widespread hands. "Be careful" I said, "you don't want to press down too hard".

As I advanced toward the centre on all fours sweeping my hands across the surface, gently but firmly, Nikki farted loudly. My head lifted in shock. My eyes met hers. "Oh

No" I exclaimed, as I briefly thought she had squashed it. We both broke into uncontrollable laughter. The hamster was never found.

April Fools

I enjoyed playing and having fun with my kids and their mates. I wanted them all to feel at home in our house, as my parents had done for me. One 1st April I pulled off a very effective 'April Fool' by sending this letter to my daughters. Chris, the Post Master was in on it.

Doat Hall,
Dryswell,
Nr Plymouth
Devon
PD1 2FG
30th March 1995

Dear Zoe and Katy,

I hope you do not mind me writing, I obtained your name and address, and the address of some of your friends in the village, from Guildford School, Northamptonshire.

As you may know the Northamptonshire Botany Society has recently found an extremely rare plant, Hicofical Crocusus (formerly known as Frog Lettuce) in three Northamptonshire locations including your village.

The spring affords the best opportunity to find the little plant in amongst the common grass and I intend visiting the three locations in Northamptonshire this weekend to undertake a search.

I shall be visiting the village pond on the Green at about 11.30am on Saturday until about 2.30pm when I must travel to another site in Long Buckby.

I would very much appreciate your help in finding these plants and hope you can meet me on Saturday. All you will need is a magnifying glass and some old trousers. Please bring a friend.

My local club are not at all wealthy but I am authorised to offer you and your friends £5 each for your help as the plants are highly prized.

Until Saturday,

Kind Regards

Mrs Betty Gorf
(Amateur Botanist)

Chris also had a poster in the post office window. There were a couple of clues in the letter, Toad (Doat) Hall and Mrs Frog (gorf), but these were missed and the girls and a couple of their mates fell for it.

When Zoe started secondary school in Guildford village, and I had toured the pubs in neighbouring villages, we grew to know more people. I would often stop at The Crown or the Hotel in Heldon on my way home. Stewart kept the Crown and Jimmy the hotel. They were great meeting places. We made good friends through the pubs and on 'the school gates'.

I had known Roger, headmaster of Heldon School from my days in Coventry. Steve Parker introduced me to him. Roger was a very likeable and intelligent guy. He was also a bundle of mischief. He was, like me, flirty, lots of fun and, he would admit, totally irresponsible with money; he loved to gamble.

The Crown was buzzing in those days, and Stewart, the landlord, made a mint. He was a terrific host. He took his best customers and mates to London on an annual excursion, and a couple of times I joined 'the gamblers' to visit the Rubicon casino in Northampton, spending only my standard £20. Stewart now lives somewhere in Wales. I met Graham Dixon after I'd settled his insurance claim; Graham is a very well spoken chap with a real down to earth mentality. He was one of the 'gang'.

Jimmy had a couple of race horses; neither had been anywhere close to getting 'a place' let alone a win. One night Jimmy confided that his trainer believed his 'top' horse would win the coming weekend. It was priced at 33:1 and held its price as the rumour passed through village to village, and money was piled on. I put a 'tenner' on, and I suggested to my friends at work that they have a dabble.

147

It won! Payouts were suspended until Tuesday because of the 'strange pattern of betting'. Bookies aren't very gracious in defeat.

Roger moved from his post in Heldon under a cloud. He had injected new life in to the school and the village, but he was unconventional to say the least, and his parent evenings turned in to 'parties' and 'fund-raising' schemes. He was a decent businessman as well as teacher you see. Pompous 'governors' criticised his activities and he moved to a school in The Scilly Isles with his wife Kate and three kids. I am Godfather to his son Scott. Roger and I had great fun.

On one occasion friends, Clive and Sally had a barbeque. They kept around a dozen scrambling bikes and had a motor-cross circuit on their land. We all had a go, but neither Roger nor I had ridden a motor cycle before. Appropriately and not unexpectedly Roger and I made complete idiots of ourselves. To everyone's amusement I was dragged some distance- clinging by my fingertips to the handle bars – and lived to tell the tale. I was very sore indeed for several days. Roger thought he might have broken bones!

Chapter Ten
The Truth about Loss Adjusting

It seems the general public have a very limited understanding of the profession that I entered in the 1980's after I'd completed my degree. Bad news travels fast and is very newsworthy, so claims that are turned down – repudiated – are better remembered. Unless there is fraud a Loss Adjuster will not want to disappoint an insurance policy holder. The bad stories shape public perception – not the thousands of claims that are approved; most rubber stamped.

Having become an experienced and highly qualified Loss Adjuster over a career that spanned fully twenty two years I can with conviction and certainty, state that the aim of a Loss Adjuster is to get an amicable settlement as soon as possible. The Chartered Institute of Loss Adjusters, have a motto that sums up principles that are close to my heart; 'Truth in Equity'. I adhered to this motto almost to the letter. Fairness took a strong hand when I could 'arrange' it, even at the cost of a little generosity with insurance company money.

You see, the Loss Adjuster's role is the investigation of an incident to determine if any damage, or loss arising from the damage, is insured under the terms and conditions of an insurance policy. It is then the Loss Adjuster's job to identify the financial extent of the insured loss as precisely as possible, and within reason. It is not the function of a Loss Adjuster to seek out ways of denying anybody their entitlement. I couldn't do that. It is to identify a valid claim, and if necessary negotiate the claim.

By now the reader should have recognised my integrity and honesty, but if you cannot grasp and agree with my explanation of what my job was for over twenty years, you are perhaps a 'nut' that I am never going to crack. No offence or pun intended.

In a nutshell (still no pun intended) it boils down to this. The insurance company employ 'Loss Adjusters' - a title that I have never liked and always thought misleading - to determine by investigation how much they need to cough up! The Loss Adjuster receives a fee for completing the job to the point of agreeing the payment with both parties. It is a misnomer that a Loss Adjuster's fee increases the more they save the insurance company. That's nonsense. There is however, in this country, a person, that anyone can employ, called a Loss Assessor; a character that will present a claim for you, just as an accountant calculates your tax return, but will want a percentage of whatever you are paid by the insurance company and sometimes a contracted fee.

These guys chase fire engines and turn up at fires, usually at factories or offices, tooting for business, but why an honest and well organised business would want to hand over part of their 'entitlement' I would never know. Unless of course, they feel that they don't have the time, or business sense, to present the claim themselves. Or, as is sometimes the case, they are crooks.

If the Loss Adjuster is honest then they can rely on him, and a Loss Assessor is surplus to requirements. Loss Assessors can be tempted to exaggerate a claim so as to include their percentage, or fee, within the settlement, and this is something that the Loss Adjuster looks out for when examining a claim. It can create difficulties for the innocent insured. It can be heavily disguised. That is my view of Loss Assessors.

An Insurance Broker is an agent of the insured person/company and should look after the insured's interest (so why the need for an assessor). They are liable to their customer for negligence. They should monitor the progress of a claim and help their client if they need it. An insurance 'agent', on the other hand, is in the pocket of the insurance company and his loyalty will lie with them.

The Loss Adjuster should be independent and any advice given to the insurance company and/or the insured should be based on entitlement; that is the framework within which a Loss Adjuster works. When all is said and done an insurance policy is a contract, and although I might have sympathy for the view that some, if not most of these contracts, contain too much small print, that is what it amounts to. I would generally try to skew a policy interpretation in favour of 'Joe Public' when vulnerable householders were involved.

The fundamental approach that I took to every single claim I dealt with was fairness and did my utmost to get a fair settlement for unfortunate victims of accident, fire, theft, subsidence, storm etc. It was an overriding consideration that I always hoped my talent for 'creative' report writing would deliver. If I was forced by circumstances, to abandon hope of applying this principle, I was disappointed if not mortified. I got no satisfaction from selling anyone short of what was fair, particularly if they were good and honest people. Integrating 'fairness' into a settlement relating to a commercial insurance contract was difficult; consumer law does not generally apply to companies.

During my career I rose to the near pinnacle of my profession, both academically and practically. I dealt with multi million pound claims across the globe, and did so, if I may say so, with great skill and satisfaction. I took great pride in accepting the Presidency of

150

the Chartered Insurance Institute of Northampton in 1995 after serving as Dinner Secretary for two years and being an active member for ten. Try arranging dinner and guests for six hundred people!

I was, by examination and experience, an associate of the Chartered Insurance Institute and the Chartered Institute of Loss Adjusters. I worked extremely hard in my spare time to pass these examinations and I am proud of the achievement.

I have an amusing account of the Loss Adjuster's work written by an unknown author; however I have a much shorter version – juggling six balls and avoiding getting two of them kicked!

I was leading a much more regular life during the 1980's and early 1990's. I was reasonably responsible and, I believe, a decent father. I was comfortable leading a standard family life; life was still full of fun and the workplace provided some of that fun.

Initially, our office 'Christmas Parties' were wild; very wild, and skiving on the odd afternoon perfectly acceptable as long as it did not impact on work. This all changed in the 1990's and the fun started to leave the workplace, in the name of so called efficiency. I've never seen insurance premiums come down because of efficiencies!! Only job losses.

I remember one disastrously funny 'birthday' celebration at the office. Denise Andrews (another friend I've lost to cancer) asked me to arrange her husband's 'entertainment'. I arranged with a mate to 'deliver' a beautiful blonde stripper that I'd seen before. He phoned last minute to say she couldn't make it – she'd injured a boob - and would the 'belly dancer' do? I was disappointed, but agreed as it was already laid on my end. Unfortunately the belly dancer doubled as the 'Rolly Polly Gram'! I was concerned for the office furniture, once she started to move there was no stopping her!

A Perilous Profession

Site visits could be perilous for a variety of reasons. Aggressive people and dangerous structures were an occupational hazard. So were women.

On more than one occasion, I was compromised by housewives. Most advances were subtle but some were much more up front. On a couple of occasions I was greeted at the door by scantily clad ladies that ignored my suggestion that I might give them time to change, invited me in and then proceeded to assume a variety of seductive poses.

151

Innuendo and naughty jokes were commonplace, but combinations of these together with requests to check pipes in bedrooms and bathrooms (that weren't subject of any claim) were more blatant.

I once delivered some bad news and was asked, "Is there anything I can do for you that might change your mind?" On another occasion I was invited into the lounge and sat on a three piece settee with my note board on my lap and invited the lady to sit and answer a few questions. She didn't sit in any of the arm chairs. She sat right next to me on the large settee and placed her hand over my thigh and gave it a little squeeze. She got nothing!

I must admit to having been tempted on occasions (but like the cop in 'The Wicker Man' – what a great film) I kept my discipline.

On another occasion I visited a house to inspect damaged roof guttering. I laugh about that day as I write. To get a clear view I needed some height. I didn't have ladders so I asked the woman if it was OK to stand on the concrete slab coal bunker in the yard so I could see, and take photographs.

I placed my notepad on the top of the bunker and the camera strap around my neck. I placed both hands flat on the top of the bunker and, as I lifted my left knee onto the bunker my body weight transferred onto the top of the bunker which suddenly collapsed under my weight - it had a hairline crack in it.

I disappeared, head first, into the empty bunker, my legs dangling out of the top. To get out I had to get fully in, turn myself around and stand up. As my 'coal dust covered' face appeared out of the bunker (like one of the flower pot men) my eyes met those of the woman who was standing watching from the kitchen door. Clearly holding back laughter she asked if I was OK. I climbed out, sore but intact, and brushed myself down.

She invited me in to the kitchen. She thrust a clothes brush against my trousers brushing vigorously. "It's OK" I said. "Please don't worry". She spotted a tear in my trousers. "Take them off" she said "and I'll stitch them up". "It's OK" I said, but she was going for my belt and what followed was a tip toe type dance around the kitchen as I tried to kerb her enthusiasm to undo my belt.

I didn't think she was propositioning me, although she must have known that the gutter was just old and leaky, and certainly not damaged by storm, but the last position I was

152

going to allow myself to get into was with my trousers off in a strange woman's house, however innocent and genuinely helpful the woman's offer!

We would share a lot of our stories in the office and I was not alone in my experiences. They were not always good. There were dangers, hidden and otherwise.

Inspecting severely damaged premises, particularly after a fire, could be hazardous; unsafe roofs, smouldering debris, nails, glass and unexploded pressurised containers of various descriptions. Yet injuries were scarce. Lads might put a foot through a roof, and occasionally fall through it during inspections, or they might tread on 'nasties', but generally we were a careful crowd.

I am reminded of the girl, Julie I think her name was, who I met when dealing with claims in Essex after the great storm of 1987. She was walking backward on a lawn with her camera raised to her eye to take a photo of a damaged building. To the delight of the householder she fell backward, handbag, note pad and all into the garden pond. For a lady, particularly undignified, and dare I say it, funny.

A bigger danger could be the insured (claimant). I remember Richard Blackshaw returning to the office looking dishevelled and shaken. He had entered an office and the insured locked the door behind him and then set about trying to give him a good thrashing. Rich was not a walkover and managed to fight him off, but fighting off, without retaliating, is difficult for the untrained. The incident was reported to the police, but in a somewhat bizarre twist the matter was settled the following week when the assailant dropped dead with an apparent heart attack. Case closed!

I didn't have too many close calls, and I was experienced at seeing problems before they arose, but on one occasion I was pinned against some garage doors by a builder that attempted to intimidate me by wielding a hammer above my head whilst leaning in to me. I didn't show fear, kept my cool and continued to talk to him as if I hadn't noticed. I didn't move an inch. Nothing happened. He backed off.

My good friend Jon Cushing, now a commercial pilot (Captain Cushing) was a young Loss Adjuster. I was his mentor and responsible for his training. We went out one day and I asked Jon to deal with his first 'flat felt roof' claim; a type notoriously difficult to deal with if a good clear explanation is not given in the case of claim repudiation. Jon did the job well, but I did warn him not to inspect the roof and communicate bad news when the claimant was standing at the foot of the ladder. There had been cases when the ladders were removed and the Adjuster left stranded – very embarrassing. He did, but on this occasion I was on hand to intervene. The funniest moment was when he was trying to explain, and at the same time try to collect pages of notes that had blown from his pad - I couldn't contain my laughter. Jon saw me, and started to crack up himself. I moved out of view because it was getting out of control.

There were plenty of opportunities to work away from home, for weeks, if not months, and earn a lot of money, doing catastrophe work. I worked long periods, living in hotel accommodation, in Brighton, Plymouth, Exeter, Edinburgh and Chelmsford. The fun we had at Chelmsford was amazing, and the work exhausting. Many great stories emanate from the Great Storm of 1987. I worked on the International Catastrophe Team the following year and spent a long spell in Jamaica, based in Kingston dealing with Hurricane Gilbert claims. The claims were interesting and often settled on the spot. Dealing with loss of coffee crops took time and careful consideration.

Much of the work in Kingston was during a period when there were curfews and helicopters patrolled the night skies shining lights onto the street below. Getting out to the clubs was hazardous, but we dodged the searchlights and had a ball; albeit in dangerous clubs. One night an arsehole left Gareth and I in the club, at a time when Gareth was getting a little fresh (on stage) with an exotic dancer; we were advised to leave 'quickly' but the guy had cleared off in the taxi and left us alone. We were close to the blade of a knife that evening.

Relationships with contractors were always fraught, unless they were really honest. Unfortunately insurance companies have formed close ties with some of them, and as a result the pricing and quality is uncompetitive. The only contractor that I ever formed a trusting relationship with was a small industrial cleaner; Alan Eaton, a guy that had pride in his work, competitiveness and honesty. I am still good friends with Alan.

Chapter Eleven
A Perilous Path: Milton Keynes

My Mum taught me a few things in life. She taught me that if you 'do good' to others the chances are you will reap the rewards, and they will 'do good' by you.

It's not an easy philosophy to adopt. It requires courage and perseverance for there are disappointments on the road to those rewards. But it does work. At fifty seven I continue to cautiously give everyone the benefit of the doubt. None of this first impressions nonsense, although I am not saying it is a factor that should be ignored. No, log it, and be patient. There are many reasons why people can give bad first impressions, not least nervousness or shyness.

I have had my fingers burnt, but continue to wear a smile on my face, and a small corner of my life is reserved for the bad guys, at a comfortable distance. Another good piece of advice- keep your enemies close enough for effective 'neutralisation'. It makes it more uncomfortable for them to bad mouth you. In the workplace I have actually 'courted' the friendship of people I know to have a dislike for me; some of them I dislike myself. The tactic tends to disarm them, and in some cases can reap rewards. You might gain respect, even become 'kinda friends'. I believe this is particularly important in the workplace where you may need support, and you can't always choose your workmates.

If you cannot make any headway with a bad guy at work then build up a case. Make sure that your case is so solid that there is no way back. If you must fight then be prepared to fight till the death, because your enemy will not forget, and will always be looking for the opportunity to put the knife in. You'll be looking over your shoulder for ever more. When you do battle make it decisive. Make it the last battle. Make sure that you are the winner.

Now I don't always follow my own advice, and I have made mistakes; but not on the occasion I moved offices from Northampton to Milton Keynes. Shortly after moving I was asked to work with a younger, yet more experienced Insurance Liability Specialist. This was because I had decided to specialise in Product, Public and Employment Liability work.

It was ideal work for me as I was very good at 'general' liability claims work and enjoyed it. I had my commercial law degree (LLB) and very significant investigative skills; a unique combination.

In Hong Kong I had attended an extensive detective training course learning the theory and practice of criminal investigation; as a chief investigating officer. Exercises involved simulations of murders and the associated crime scene. I would be responsible for preserving the scene, directing collection of evidence (exhibits) and directing simultaneous and subsequent investigations by an assigned team of detective officers. It was not dissimilar to the kind of simulation that I encountered when being 'tested' in First Aid Competitions. I recall arriving at the scene of a mock airplane crash with my team colleagues and on another occasion a mock passenger train crash.

The Loss Adjusting profession was poor at investigating fraud at the time that I joined the profession; there was insufficient formal training and what training was given was given by inadequately qualified people. I had massive advantages, and was a great asset, if I'd been properly used as a resource. In any case, team work was not a well recognised concept. It changed, although insurance companies are more concerned with the bottom line, 'profit' than honesty, and too often let fraudulent claims through the net. They change their minds when they want to make a case for increasing their premiums!

Anyway, Ian W was very good at liability report writing and, outside the workplace, very pleasant on most occasions. In fact there was much that I liked about him. His problem, and it was his, was that he was an arrogant power crazy bully. He adored himself. He had the title, 'Manager', but there was just me and two secretaries in this newly established department. He was the most obnoxious man I have ever had to deal with in the work place.

He was desperate to use every opportunity to show that he was boss and enjoyed demonstrating his seniority. In point of fact I think he was actually a very insecure guy. Despite numerous efforts to sort our differences privately, it became intolerable and he seemed intent on winding me up good and proper. I can be wound up; my Achilles heel.

I sent a knock-out blow of a letter to the Director of Liability in London. I had had enough! I did, as I tend to; go for the jugular. If there had not been a positive response I would have resigned. This is a summary:

You asked me on the phone to make a few notes regarding my concerns about Ian. I have.

As you know I have tried desperately to work with Ian for fully four months, and the position has now become intolerable. Ian must agree to the points listed below, to ensure the office environment is improved.

1. *Stop the racist, homophobic comments and jokes.*

2. *No more 'orders' - they are incompatible with a small office environment. Ian should make his own tea like the rest of us – we are all busy!*

3. *Ian should not use me to issue his own directives to secretarial staff – he can do it himself.*

4. *Similarly, if Ian wishes his files to be returned to the proper place he should do so himself, or instruct his secretary to do so. If he wishes to have each and every piece of correspondence of his read to him over the phone when he is out of the office, then he should ask his secretary to do so. I am not his PA.*

5. *While I am in my office I wish to remain undisturbed by him unless the matter is one of urgency. It is impossible to concentrate when I am constantly harassed by his comings and goings. He is to stop shouting for me like a master calls his dog!*

6. *I am becoming increasingly unhappy with my use of English and writing style being constantly attacked. In relation to' personal injury claims' I bow to his superior experience and knowledge, but in relation to legal matters generally, and my command of English, I am afraid he better keep his nose out.*

7. *I ask that he refrain from criticising the manner in which I set out my office. I consider that it is easier to find a file in my office than his.*

8. *I wish him to refrain from making unnecessary derogatory remarks concerning colleagues within the company such as 'Margaret Clubfoot' and, 'Noddy and Big Ears'. Some of these references (although funny) are to personal friends, and, irrespective of the technical merits of the criticism towards these colleagues, there is no need for these issues to be dealt with so disrespectfully. I must admit he does make me laugh though!*

9. *He must desist from making mocking and derogatory remarks about me in the presence of other persons. He is getting on my nerves.*

10. *Ian well knows that my work hours are above and beyond those expected under my contract and considerably longer than those worked by the majority of people within the company. He must therefore cease making any remarks concerning how hard I work. I know that he also puts a lot of hours in, but he makes sarcastic comment that is designed*

to irritate. I have not retaliated by pointing out to him the number of days he takes off to be entertained by solicitors!

11. *I will not be told that I cannot fill in expense forms in work time.*

12. *If Ian wishes to criticise any of my work he must desist from using the phrases, 'crap', bollocks' etc. He is really getting to me!*

13. *Ian W must stop telling lies to me. He must stop calling me a liar.*

14. *I am sick and tired of Ian criticising the way things are done in the company. Please ask him to button it. Not everything he did, and does, is for the better.*

15. *Ian W is not always right. If I have a view, that view should be discussed and debated. Like mine, his technical knowledge is less than perfect on occassions.*

16. *Whilst I appreciate that Ian is very proficient within a narrow specialist field of employers' liability / personal injury, it must be appreciated that the somewhat regimented approach that he takes is not necessarily appropriate in relation to all matters. He must stop wielding the stick. It will not work with me. No more threats.*

17. *Ian W must stop telling me that I cannot see a colleague in the neighbouring office at my chosen time.*

18. *Ian W should concentrate on keeping his own house in order rather than mine; I do have some degree of ability, and I for one wish to adhere to our clients' instruction and not his. They are the customers.*

19. *Being obstinate with regard to 'outside branch instruction's only creates difficulty and I would much prefer a clear agreement to change established procedure rather than employ a flagrant disregard for them.*

At present I have no respect or trust for Ian, or his 'managerial' abilities. He is a rude, pedantic, patronising and condescending individual who does nothing for the image of the company that he now serves. He really must desist from his arrogant air of self importance, his bullying and harassment. If he does not I fear that I shall be provoked into striking him!

If I am to share a cordial working relationship with Ian then I would prefer that he be available to me on a consultancy only basis.

I confirm that, as discussed, I wish this matter to remain unofficial at this stage. I am deeply saddened that I have to bring this matter to your attention but it is serving no ones interest to allow things to continue the way they are.

158

I apologise for the difficulties that this must be causing you, particularly in the light of the fact that Ian is, as I have indicated, technically very good at his work. His reports are excellent, and the benefit that his experience in 'handling solicitor's is bringing to the company, and indeed myself, is valuable'.

As the saying goes, "You live by the sword-you die by the sword"! Ian was visibly shaken after hearing from the 'boss'. He was a quieter person. I hope that by now he has learnt his lesson. Ian had taken advantage of my tolerance and good nature; my easy going and friendly style. He saw it as a weakness I think. He got both barrels!

The letter was the final solution. I had had stand up arguments with him. I had tried to reason with him. I tried to beg him; all to no avail. In the end I felt like dropping one on him – something that really would sound the last post on our ability to work under the same roof. On more than one occasion I had to tell him to "Fuck off out of my office and stop pestering me".

Ian failed to take notice and he failed to recognise my experience and long service. He was tactically inept, insensitive and thick skinned and was always there for the taking. I could have made life very tough for him, but I didn't. I am not like that. He was initially welcomed with open arms.

That I had to resort to the above letter, gave me no satisfaction or pleasure and in my view such a letter suggests a degree of failure to communicate and 'get on' with colleagues. It is not a step that I would recommend to others unless they are really desperate.

I was later promoted overseas. The office was closed, and Ian moved down the road to the larger 'claims management' offices where he sat alone with nobody to manage or administer orders. I understand that he eventually left the company under a cloud having been caught fiddling the record books! The arsehole!

I have never been afraid to stick my neck out and at the turn of 1994, I had occasion to complain about the company's propensity for 'beating willing and hardworking horses'. Terry Flood, the office manager, asked me to write down my feelings. I wrote, 'Personally I am incapable of working any harder without further detriment to my family and private life generally. The volume of work is such that every day my target is simply to keep my head above water and hope that major complaints are avoided..........morale in the company, and most importantly my office, has become intolerably low, and systems appear to have been introduced at customers whims, and promises made, with either a

159

total disregard for the effect on the workforce or a complete miscalculation of the resources available to deliver on promises'.

My much respected boss (and friend) Terry Flood, was sympathetic to my complaint, which was on behalf of all employees. I appeared to be the only one prepared to stand up and say what needed to be said. He let Bev 'Champagne Charlie' Fitzgerald, the incoming Operations Director knew of my feeling and Bev came up to the Northampton office to see me. He cracked a bottle of wine and we sat in the board room with his secretary. He listened to my complaint. He later wrote:

13th January 1995

David,

I very much appreciated your open conversation yesterday. Over the next few weeks, I shall be visiting offices and listening to other genuine, committed Howells Adjusters like you. Positive, constructive exchanges like this will then help define what we need to do to make working here enjoyable again!

With very best wishes to you, and especially for a happy and successful CII (Chartered Insurance Institute) Presidency in April,

Bev Fitzgerald

Bev was` perhaps one of the last of the old school of bosses that valued employees forthright attitude, view and dedication. In the early 1990's we were taken over by a re-insurance company (they knew nothing of our profession) and later an American company. American style management and systems arrived in UK changing the face of my profession forever, and for the worse. Indeed the fully qualified professional Chartered Loss Adjuster was to become virtually extinct. The days of 'rationalisation' had arrived.

In February 1996 I wrote to Pete Ward, the Regional Director based in Birmingham. I knew Pete, not that well, but well enough to know he was a well respected and reasonable guy. He was a good man, a fellow Coventrian and another ex Northampton office guy. Northampton was the breeding ground of most of the best of Howells, and the breeding ground of the most promoted and respected within the company. Honest and brave voices

160

working in the most profitable of UK offices. I complained, tactfully about my level of remuneration.

'I am not unappreciative of the 4.6% increase received. I understand that this is above inflation and incorporates a merit award that some adjusters have not received............... you will have been told that I have been disappointed with my salary reviews for the last few years'.

I made reference to the Retail Price Index and pointed out that for the ten years ending December 1995 my pay increased 13.7% in real terms, averaging out at 1.3% per year, and that most of the increase was weighted into the 1980's. I pointed out that during this time my qualifications had been achieved and that I was an Associate of the Chartered Insurance Institute and an Associate of the Chartered Institute of Loss Adjusters.

I pointed out that other companies were offering significantly more money and that I could command a good 50% extra if I defected. Pete phoned and said he could do nothing about it. It was the time when the owners, SwissRe, were preparing to sell off the company - to the Yanks!

Nineteen ninety seven was a good time to get out of Loss Adjusting in the UK. I did, with the help of my supporters in high places. I was never to return to the World of UK Loss Adjusting again. The profession was in decline.

I had been geographically handicapped throughout my career because of my respect for Nikki's wishes; that we have a period of stability in the interests of our children. Indeed I agreed with her at the time. This however had not been good for career prospects. I always knew this. Northampton had been a settled, well run office, with 'top guys' in top positions. There was nowhere to go in Northampton. Milton Keynes had not worked out.

I could see that the take-over by the Americans (the CCS Corp) would mean a future based on systems driven claims handling that, unless I avoided it, would result in me wasting the years of study and hard work. I had spent evenings studying to pass examinations. I wanted to do the traditional skilled work of Loss Adjusting. If I was to apply these skills it would need to be overseas. There were more limited opportunities in the UK where the need for traditional Loss Adjusting skills was being diminished and the rewards devalued.

My good friend Gareth, a 'Jamaica team' veteran and colleague from Northampton had already made the move. He went to work in Bahrain. I went out to see how he lived, but

161

primarily to be his 'best man' when he married Wendy. I found he was operating with some autonomy and enjoying it. Shame one of his mates stuck laxatives in my drink the night before the wedding! That's another story.

I met with the Managing Director for Asia and Pacific region, Richard Solomon, in London in October 1997. He was a guy I felt I could trust. I instantly liked him and respected him. He offered me a post in Indonesia. Indonesia was in crisis. I knew that 'fools walk where others fear to tread' and also that 'he who dares wins'. Indonesia loomed large.

This opportunity knocked, at an opportune time. The opportunity needed to be taken. I didn't see another coming along, and I needed a fresh working environment. A new challenge was needed and on ground where I could express myself and fulfil my potential. I knew I was underachieving and that I had been doing so for too many years.

My years of 'consolidation' and 'training' were over. I had ACII and ACILA professional qualifications to my name, had sat course after course; negotiation and 'time management' being the most notable, and made a name for myself. Somewhat surprisingly I'd won an 'ideas' competition (a customer questionnaire) and an article and photograph of me appeared in the 'Intercity' train magazine. I'd shown my 'sales' ability by securing the exclusive rights to 'domestic claims work from a small insurer in Milton Keynes; only about £30,000 worth, but nonetheless additional business. I had waited a long time in the interests of the family. I was truly ready for promotion to the next level-even if this meant working overseas!

Chapter Twelve
Indonesia
1998 – 2003

By the summer of 1997 Zoe had successfully completed her school years and had achieved spectacular results in her GCSE's on the back of tremendous resilience and determination. She was exhausted by her efforts.

I didn't think that she should do it, and counselled against, but she wanted to go to college and she did. I didn't think she had thought long enough about what she really wanted to do. She started college in the autumn only to drop out after couple of months with a real desire to leave home and see a little bit of the world. She wanted to go to Chicago to see Liam, her cousin. I supported this view but Nikki didn't. She was worried.

Meanwhile Katy was performing well below her potential at school because, in our view, she was entangled in the family problems affecting two of her closest friends. Katy being Katy she shouldered their problems, on her shoulders, as if they were her own. Katy has always been a loyal and committed friend.

The situation here was quite a simple one. The parents of two of her friends in the village had, in effect, 'wife swapped' on a permanent basis. I will leave this one to you to imagine how difficult that was for their kids. At any rate Katy was not performing at school, and her projected GCSE results were at best D's. Under normal circumstances a move at this stage might have been to the detriment of Katy's education, however things could not have got worse in that regard.

Insofar as the domestic scene was concerned our marriage had been a little rocky for a few years. My career had not been blossoming. I was not happy at work, and I had put any career ambition on hold while we brought up the children in a stable environment. My marriage and family were priority.

Finances were not very good, in real terms my income had not increased, and had been pegged back. Our marriage was, in my view, an unhappy one and we needed to freshen it up. In fact I think it was in freefall and recall a few years earlier asking her to show commitment and arrange a meeting with 'Relate'. Nikki said she had had an appointment but that 'I wasn't needed'. I felt a major change was necessary. A move might inject a

163

new life into our marriage. Our life together needed a boost. A new environment and job might save our marriage and I discussed it with Nikki.

As it happened, and with the help and good support from trusted and supportive work colleagues, the prospect arose to work overseas with the substantial benefits that it provided.

I discussed this with Nikki and after speaking with Richard Solomon was offered the Technical Directorship in Jakarta, Indonesia. I again discussed this with Nikki and persuaded her that a move of this kind would be good for our finances and our relationship. She was understandably apprehensive but agreed to go. We rented the house out on a three year tenancy; the minimum period of time that I agreed to work in Jakarta.

On reflection, it was around this time that the serious psychological problems that were affecting Nikki first manifested themselves. On the particular day that the question arose concerning Zoe's wish to leave home, Nikki spent some considerable time trying to dissuade Zoe from leaving and when she failed to do that, came to me.

There was a scene in the kitchen where she demanded that I stop Zoe leaving home because she was too young. I said I couldn't, and more importantly I wouldn't, because at one stage or another children need to fly the nest.

Nikki found this almost impossible to deal with and she fell to the floor with both arms clutched around one of my legs begging me to stop Zoe leaving home. I liken the response to the reaction of a mother to the news that her daughter had just been fatally injured in a car accident. It was more proportionate to news of death. That's how dramatic and hysterical her response was. It spooked me. It was almost terrifying. I thought back to her family history, I knew there was something not right about her behaviour, but disregarded it. I shouldn't have done that.

The plan was that I would leave for Indonesia, in January, as required. That Katy and Nikki would follow on at the end of the academic year; around June 1998. Zoe was persuaded to modify her travel plans, and work in the Yorkshire Dales in one of Ray Chandler's hotels. Ray, an old school friend, would keep an eye on her for me. She would then visit Ollie, my sister's first husband, and her cousin Kim in Ireland.

I travelled to Indonesia as planned and stopped for some weeks in a hotel in Jakarta.

164

You may recall that in July 1997 the Far East experienced the Asian Economic Crisis and Indonesia was probably the worst hit. The economic position was dire and there had been demonstrations on the streets before my arrival. The Indonesian Rupiah had plunged from 2,400 to 5,600 to the dollar that year. Prices had soared. Businesses were bust and unemployment rife.

Indonesia had been ruled by President Soeharto since the mid 1960's. The attempted coup of 1965 had been blamed on the former Indonesian Communist Party, the PKI, but the latest version of the events that led to the murder of some 500,000 suspected communists, suggest CIA involvement. Sukarno was unseated, Soeharto, who at the time was a General in charge of the Army's Strategic Reserve (Komstrad) became President. PKI members, and Sukarno loyalists including seven Generals, were slain while millions more were persecuted for years afterward.

Soeharto was a dictator and ruled with an iron fist. Nevertheless Indonesia was in 1998 developing into a prosperous country, and had been growing at a rate of some 7-9 % a year, for some ten years, and the population of some 230 million were obviously prospering and were content. However, when a currency collapses so much that it is worth less than half of its value six months earlier then there is clearly a recipe for unrest. Imagine that happening here – or can you? Read on.

It transpired that Pres Soeharto, his family and his cronies were creaming off billions of dollars from the economy and had been putting it into their own pockets for years, but the system had worked, everyone was better off, so why worry?. Only when the economic crisis hit did the people start to ask questions. The UK in 2008 sounds familiar?

Indonesia is, to those who are unaware, that group of some 17,000 islands strung across from west of the Malaysian Peninsula (Singapore) to Australia, in the east. Indonesia is the fourth most populous country in the world, and the size of the US east to west. Of its 230 million citizens, 95% are Muslim. It is the biggest Islamic country in the world.

The major islands are Sumatra, Java, Sulawesi and Kalimantan (Borneo). For those who think Bali is a country, it is not. It is an Indonesian island to the east of Java. To correct another misnomer, the famous volcano of Krakatau is in fact 'west' of Java and not to the east, as the Hollywood movie, 'Krakatau East of Java' suggested. That's Hollywood!

I felt very lonely during that first six months of 1998 and missed Nikki and our family. I was also worried about Nikki. I had spent about six weeks living out of a suitcase in a hotel room, but then moved to a temporary apartment adjacent the arterial motorway from the City to the airport. It was just a couple of hundred yards from the Government Assembly buildings where Soeharto and his government sat. The apartment was conveniently located for travelling to the office in the centre of Jakarta. The apartment had all I needed; three bedrooms, a communal shop, tennis courts, gym and a swimming pool in the grounds.

That first six months was devoted to my work; morning, noon, and night. It was probably better that the family were following on. I could concentrate on my new job, find a suitable home, and generally prepare for their arrival.

Our company was 50% locally owned and therefore I represented the 50% interest of the parent American company, CCS. Handoko was the local Managing Director. A member of his family had been a student activist in 1965 – 'The Year of Living Dangerously'. Remember the film of that name? Indeed Handoko had told me on my arrival that one of his relatives had recently been arrested for speaking out against the President and on suspicion of conspiring against the government, and had been linked with bomb conspiracies.

My remuneration package was probably worth about £100,000, and represented the pinnacle of my career based on remuneration. I was paid in dollars, and so conversion was subject to the exchange rate mechanism. I was receiving something like £45,000 tax free plus bonuses, free accommodation, electricity, gas, education for my daughter, flights backward and forward to UK for my family, two cars with chauffeurs and household staff. A far cry from the poultry provincial sum I was earning in Milton Keynes. My big break, financially and professionally had arrived.

Before deciding to move to Indonesia I had done my homework. I had read the Economist magazine Intelligence Report on Indonesia and other publications. I had discussed life in Indonesia with those with past experience and read books. I had prepared well.

There was a technical advisor who was working in our Jakarta office at the time and I spoke with him. He provided me with good advice and supported me before and during my time in Indonesia. We hit it off well, and understood each other well, but then that might not be so surprising given that he was also a 'Coventry Kid', hailing from Keresley; just a couple of miles from my parents' home. What a coincidence. Paul H was, and is, a very good friend and confidante. Amazing, is it not, that I should take a job half way across the world only to work alongside another Coventry Kid.

Paul provided me with a lot of level headed and sensible support throughout the years I was there. Nothing could have been achieved without him. My eventual accomplishments are also his. Richard Solomon, my boss had also worked in Indonesia; he had established the company there. He was also a great help, offering empathy and wise guidance.

I was replacing the outgoing Technical Director, John Seddon, who had been in Indonesia for several years and had considerable experience working overseas during his extensive career. He was retiring. He provided me with precious little help; few words of encouragement, and was clearly very unhappy with the operation in Indonesia and in particular Handoko. He had been unable to get on with Handoko or his staff, and had effectively given up, choosing to work on his own portfolio of work rather that engage with those around him and tackle the greater responsibility to the business. He had ceased to function effectively and should have left earlier.

John provided me with negative feedback during the hand-over period, save to provide me with a number of tips that I simply logged for future reference. I did not allow the tips to cloud my judgement or allow the negativity of them to deter me from my game plan. I kept my focus. However, it did subsequently turn out that a lot of what he had to say was correct, and I began to understand why he had behaved the way he did.

John's remarks reflected bitterness and anger towards Handoko and I could not afford to ally myself with his position, particularly as he was the outgoing Director. Handoko would have been very well aware that John would be giving me a very bad account of him. I did not particularly like John but I never forgot what he said. He was not a stupid man.

During the first few months it was very clear to me that I was taking over a business that was hamstrung by a lack of desire to change in any way, and this flowed almost exclusively from the stubborn resistance of Handoko, a man that I was later to understand, and whose position I since have sympathy for.

Handoko had, over the years, tried to keep very tight control over the company and the individuals within it. This was not entirely for selfish reasons, or because he was power crazy. It was simply very Indonesian.

Indonesian People

In the main, Indonesia comprises a population of 230 million villagers! They are of native origin with a flavour of those immigrants of Arab, Chinese, Indian and Eurasian origin. The tribal nature of the population means that some 600 local languages are spoken with Bahasa Indonesian as the national language. Although nearly 90% of the population are villagers, only about 15% of the population own the land!

There are some 400 ethnic groups ranging from cannibal 'Bataks' of Sumatra to Dayak head-hunters of Borneo. They are a highly superstitious people.

The Bahasa Indonesian language is easy to learn although if I told you that there were twelve ways to say 'No' that might be difficult to believe. I learnt Cantonese, so believe me when I say that Bahasa Indonesian is easy. Bahasa is used by 80% of the population. It is not tonal, like Cantonese, and the grammar is straightforward and is basically phonetic. Some words sound very similar so it is possible, given that 'Kunci' means 'key' and 'Kelinci' means 'rabbit', to ask the chaffeur to 'get the rabbit to start the car'.

My 'starter' words were 'salamat' (a greeting) and 'Apa Kabar' (how are you) and 'Terima Kasih' (thank you). 'Salamat' preceding the word for morning, afternoon and evening completed 'day one' learning.

Indonesia is not famed for its food, and that is understandable; in some ways it is to Asian food what British food is to European food. Like the British, the Indonesians are fond of their 'home food' and have difficulty with foreign foods. I found only a limited range of dishes that I enjoyed, and found my favourite foods in local 'Kampungs' (villages). Catfish with lime leaves and chilli was a personal favourite. An interesting dish is 'Usus Gajah', which literally means 'elephant intestines', and apparently it started off as such. These days the same dish is made with 'beef'.

The squat toilet terrifies most Brits, but they are common in Indonesia as they are over most of the world. Never offer an Indonesian your left hand; that is the one that is used to wipe the bum!

I lived and worked with mainly Javanese people (Jakarta is on the island of Java) and these people were known to mask their feelings. It is hard to get to know them, but once you do, they are good friends. Status is a big thing in Indonesia, and no-one is equal.

168

'Respect' is however almost tangible. 'Asal bapak senang' (keep the boss happy) is a prominent concept that is woven into the fabric of business and the community.

The Indonesians are generally extremely polite and good mannered; qualities the British seem to have lost. Punctuality is also important, and the need to 'forgive' is very strong. Greeting cards, exchanged between friends at Lebaran (the end of the Muslim fasting month), not only reads 'Happy Lebaran', but also 'Pardon my mistakes'. Apologies must be accepted. Handoko once shamed himself with an outburst. He felt that 'malu' and asked me for forgiveness. I respected him for that and I did so; although I wanted to throttle him!

Indonesians believe in ghosts as the medieval Brits believed in witches. They have 'dukun', medicine men, to deal with serious problems with 'ghosts or spirits'. It is a mistake to mock. The head and the hair are thought to possess life force, so it is a bad thing to touch somebody's head; especially a child's. They love to gossip, but not to discuss scandal.

My staff called me 'Bapak' or 'Pak' for short. It literally means 'father' but is used in the context of seniority in a work environment. On the basis of respect, I would call an old man selling goods from a cart, 'Pak'. You'd address a waiter as 'mas', a simple address to a man.

Indonesians practice the state philosophy of 'Pancasila' a term for the five principles; including freedom of religion and generally a kerb against extreme ideologies. That might surprise those Christians that condemn Muslim peoples 'en bloc'. Let's not forget that Britain has a state religion. In Britain you couldn't be Prime Minister if you are Catholic, that's why Blair converted to Catholicism after he resigned.

Handoko felt genuinely threatened by the US owned partner, CCS, whose powers in Indonesia were vested in me. He also enjoyed being revered, Godfather style, by the staff. It would be difficult to convince Handoko to swim in unfamiliar waters; the business was very profitable and it had always provided for all. Why should there be 'changes'?

The staff was technically very well qualified, lawyers, engineers, accountants, but were otherwise devoid of imagination, the ability to think laterally or to act on initiative. Initiative was virtually frowned upon let alone encouraged. Reports were 'cloned'; paragraphs pasted from one to another. In many cases it suited, but it was a dangerous practice and inaccuracies occurred.

169

As a result of a practice that allowed laziness, they did not have a great deal of self belief, and even in the case of the most experienced personnel, they were lacking the art and craft of negotiation. They were not in the practice of negotiating for fear of upsetting ''powerful forces'.

They were not confident people. They were suppressed. I grew to understand why. I had done a lot of research before I took on the assignment but nothing prepared me for the fact that 'to question', to challenge, was dangerous.

The development of business, and its resulting profits, would flow from the cronyism and nepotism endemic in the system. From that would flow good salaries for the employees. It had always been that way, and to Handoko, would always be that way. If it wasn't routine he was a fish out of water. The market was not dog eat dog, and it did not need to expand. There was food for all, and in any case I suspect that Handoko did not want the business to grow because if it did he might lose control. The office was 'contented'. Why upset the applecart?

As I reflected on this situation years later I concluded that there was much to commend in this system. There was no need for competition! However, 1998 was to be a year of massive change for the entire country, and my arrival was necessary and well timed.

In addition to the plentiful supply of business, courtesy of friends and relatives, there were political difficulties in doing anything that the government, in particular the army and police might frown upon. They had a major stake in big business. Upset them, and you might end up wearing concrete shoes, let alone losing business.

Contradicting a police report was dangerous, and conducting any form of investigation out with official approval a 'no no'. I needed to demonstrate that we could do more without provoking catastrophic response.

I had a big job ahead of me, and I had a lot to do to get the operation to function as it should; I repeat, the business was hamstrung by a refusal to change in any way. The terms of reference given to me by Richard, the regional MD (Asia Pacific) were to improve systems and efficiency and grow the business. There would be opposition from within.

The first few months working with Handoko were extremely difficult. He clearly thought that John Seddon would influence me. He tried hard to intimidate and provoke me. He did not want me to leave the office for several months. I chose not to. It actually suited me to get a good handle on what was going on in the office, and I restricted my communication with customers to business functions, be they through the Embassy, British Chamber of Commerce, corporate or private. I made no formal approach to any of our customers; existing or prospective.

The Curry Club provided a good opportunity to meet insurance industry ex-pats, and 'local' introductions, meetings, were generally left for Handoko to decide upon and arrange. I was patient. I waited for him to make the moves. I wanted to diffuse any thoughts he might have of John Seddon influencing my own behaviour. I was intent on being my own person, applying my own ideas, thoughts and actions, based on my own experiences. I shelved all the advice and views of others; stored them for further consideration, save for the instructions that were given to me by my boss Richard. I never lost my focus.

Handoko tried to make my life as uncomfortable as possible. It was his way of asserting his authority; of exercising his muscle. I allowed him considerable slack. He was not a Brit and could not be handled like one. He insisted that I 're-use' paper. Use the reverse side of typed paper. It was expensive he said, we could not afford to waste it. Austerity measures; nobody else appeared to be doing it, but I did. Why not? It was not an unreasonable request or suggestion, but if I'd have argued? Well, conflict might have been what he wanted. I did not give him the opportunity.

I boxed a very clever early round. He rejected any suggestion that the office was less than perfect, even before any such suggestion had been made that it wasn't. He was not only provocative, but he was extremely aggressive in his defence of 'the way things were done'. There was 'no need to change anything' he said. 'Just relax and enjoy yourself. Help the guys, educate them and leave everything else to me, this office has been very successful for a long time you know?'

I was disciplined in my responses. Listening, saying nothing in reply, or offering a compliment, praise, or a measured comment that suggested I wanted to help .build on that success. I never, never, used the word 'change' the word would have been a red rag to a bull.

When the time was right, when I had a good understanding of how things worked in the office and I had got to know everybody I asserted myself, in a controlled firm but non aggressive way. Gentle persuasion was what was required with a large measure of patience. 'Softly softly catch a monkey'.

171

There was a point when I actually showed Handoko the instructions given to me by the MD. I did so at a strategically opportune time when it was suggested that my nose was where it shouldn't be. It stopped him in his tracks - for a while.

Showing Handoko my terms of reference in writing; my authority, had maximum effect. He was left in no doubt that I was going to take my role seriously and that I was determined to carry out my mission. I knew that my effectiveness had a limited sell by date and that after four or five years the business would need an injection of new blood. Handoko was resilient and determined. Ex-pats were often here today and gone tomorrow.

After my departure someone else would need to pick up the standard and underpin gains made. Unfortunately Handoko saw the CCS partners that I represented as a necessary evil. I am sure that he would have preferred to head a 100% Indonesian operation.

Before I start to sound too negative about Handoko, it has to be said that he was a wonderful guy, a religious and honourable man. Socially we got on fine and on most working days we got on fine, however, we had some serious differences and Handoko was extremely stubborn in his resistance to any 'change'. The word' change' was never used by me for that reason. Handoko could always rely on me as a friend. Paul was also loyal to him.

It took months, and in some cases years, to get any change on key subjects. It was a difficult job and required a great deal of diplomacy, a great deal of patience and a great deal of personal skill and craft. Nevertheless, with Paul's support, for which I am eternally grateful, progress was made and Handoko was persuaded that we could improve our service to our customers, and in many cases make life easier for us all. We started to do things that should have been done, that hitherto, hadn't been done. I emphasise; nothing could have been achieved without Paul.

Referring back to the six months before Nikki arrived; these were worrying, and at times extremely traumatic. I had found friends, I loved my work, but I missed my wife and daughters, and Indonesia became a dangerous place to be.

It has always been very clear to me, since the early years in Indonesia, that the United Kingdom would eventually face bankruptcy, and will probably have done so by the time these words go to print. I have had first-hand experience of the effects of an economic

172

collapse on a gigantic scale. To give you some idea, and a taste of what I shall be writing about a little later; in July 1997 the Indonesian Rupiah exchanged at the rate of 2,000 to the US dollar. In the January 1998 the Rupiah had been devalued to something around 17,000 to the dollar. So how did this affect the local populous?

If I give you a feel for what the place was like for the poorer locals, compared to the wealthier Indonesians and ex-pats, then you will understand their anger, and the reason for the later uprising. It could happen in UK!

If only £6 is the minimum wage in this country; it's still a lot of money if you haven't got it. The Indonesian masses earn little more than £6 per week! Imagine then in this country if the £ is devalued and a loaf of bread suddenly costs £6 a loaf! How would you feel paying a week's wage for a loaf?

Imagine conversely, the pound suddenly being worth more to dollar owners? Imagine that you didn't spend $60 on your recent trip to Disney, and brought it back. Your $60 is worth £360. You go to Curry's and you buy a new laptop computer!

The big dollar earners were not adversely affected in Indonesia and there was resentment. I was better off than envisaged in the first eighteen months. The natives were suffering price hikes that were 'crippling' for the average man.

Given that only about 3-4% of the population earned dollars, or held dollar bank accounts, the vast major were paying massive amounts of money for any goods or food that were imported, or depended upon imported parts. Imports were at a dollar rate. Payment had to be made in dollars. Nobody wanted the vulnerable Rupiah.

There was massive inflation. Goods and components for locally produced goods increased in cost eight fold. In a nutshell the majority experienced massive price increases whilst the dollar earners were unaffected. Indeed, as the crisis had such a sudden impact, there was a period when dollar earners, ex-pats generally included, were raiding the shops to buy goods that retailers had maintained at the old price; whist stocks lasted. Suddenly, TV's were eight times less expensive for the wealthy!!!

When I arrived in the January of 1998 foreigners and local dollar earners were having a field day. On 8th January the Rupiah plunged further to 10,000 to the dollar – halved in value again and as I have pointed out, it got worse! They were plundering the shelves in Shopping Malls where goods had not been re-labelled on the new import pricing basis. The scenes were almost obscene and in many cases people, mainly Indonesians with

173

dollar bank accounts, were insensitive and brazenly loading vehicles with TV's, radios, Hi Fi's computers and just about anything that would be increasing in price over the coming months. This was not panic buying for survival; this was frenzied buying for greed. This would understandably cause resentment.

It was estimated that some 80% of businesses were bankrupt, although still trading. By 11th January all but 22 of the 286 companies listed on the Jakarta stock exchange were technically bankrupt. On the 21st January, in a single days trading, the Rupiah fell 23% to 17,000 to the dollar!

The country's economy was disintegrating, and all this had been overseen by a corrupt greedy family, crony friends and business associates that had laundered billions of dollars to Swiss and other overseas bank accounts, and businesses. The prognosis in January 1998 was not therefore good for Indonesia, its people and its economy.

There was in fact significant risk of civil unrest, and this settled uncomfortably on my mind and stomach. I was at times very depressed about the prospects for my family's happiness. I was worried. I had to make a decision as to whether it was wise for my family to live in Indonesia. It was a mess that made me feel doubt and guilt. Had I made the right decision by convincing my family of the benefits of a family move? I was worried that I had let my family down. When not working I was lonely and a tiny bit depressed, and so I worked hard and got out and about as much as possible in my spare time.

Was my decision a bad one? Time would tell, and there was no need to make early changes to plans. Let's see how things were in May and early June.

You could feel the tension 'on the streets' in the months before Nikki arrived. The tension had spilled into violence in May. I could sense trouble was afoot.

I knew that serious civil unrest was likely, possibly in the form of a coup that might even develop into Civil War. It started on 12th May 1998 as a result of a clash with students and 'a week of living dangerously' followed. A Civil War was averted, but only after violent revolution on the streets, and a stand-off between opposing military factions outside the gates of the Presidential Palace.

The events of May were extremely worrying, at times frightening and very traumatic. Thousands were killed, injured or raped, assaulted and traumatised. I had arrived in Indonesia during one of the most violent, yet interesting, periods in its history.

174

The Uprising

When I arrived in the January most people thought the president was toast, and that his thirty years as ruler were over. The burning question was, 'Would he go peacefully'?

The People's Consultative Committee had met in March concerning his re-election and few thought he would be unanimously re-elected. He was in ill health, the economy was in dire straits and the country was facing 'El Nino' climate conditions that severely affected the rice crop; the country couldn't feed itself. If he couldn't be convinced to resign there would be a political crisis.

Contenders were the Vice President Habibie, General Hartono (not the military's choice) and Generals Wiranto and Sutrisno, but nobody challenged him. Thousands of troops were deployed to protect the VIP's from a hostile public as they arrived at the Assembly building (just down the road).

There were large student demos. Suharto was not trusted and the people had no faith in him. Worryingly students started to 'disappear'; chilling echoes of Chile and Indonesia in the 1960's.

Even though the situation was tense in May 1998 I had no reason to feel that my Dad's scheduled visit to Indonesia should be cancelled, although I explained the position to him. He arrived in early May with his good friend Colin Wardle.

I decided to take my guests to Yogyakarta by plane and arrange for my driver to meet us there and drive us back through the mountains to Bandung, and then back to Jakarta. As we were driving back to Jakarta news came in that on 12th May, the day before, troops had shot dead a number of students at Trisakti University.

My apartment was on the main airport road and between the University and the Parliament (Assembly) building; within a couple of miles of each other. The burial ceremonies were taking place that day, and rioting erupted all over the capital, and I later heard, the country. We were driving in to the city as it was happening!

We drove through frightening scenes and managed to get through makeshift roadblocks, through back streets to my apartment where we were secure behind steel gates manned by security guards. That night we watched the city burning from the rooftop. My Dad likened it to the Coventry Blitz!

There was an apparent loss of control. I decided to assemble the residents and agree an evacuation plan in the event it was needed. It was literally women and children first, through a whole cut into the tennis court fence. We discussed how we would defend ourselves if attacked.

We agreed to 'keep watch' in shifts at night-time. The security guards were nowhere to be seen. A Malaysian guy had a pistol, otherwise we had no weapons; we improvised. We planned to 'torch' petrol at the front gate if attacked.

That night I met, and got to know properly, Brad Berg. He worked for one of our customers, and lived in the neighbouring tower block on our complex. He was married to an Indonesian and he assured me that if needed, he could have a contingent of crack troops at the gates 'in no time'. That was reassuring.

There was serious rioting and looting at the nearby shopping mall where many were killed. The buildings burnt through the night and gun shots rang out regularly. The following morning troops moved toward the shopping mall followed by water-cannon and tanks.

I had all the provisions you would expect a man, living alone, to have in the home; about a dozen cans of beer, a few tins of baked beans and water! We had had no time to shop before they all closed.

Some of our number left that day, and others were planning to leave during the night. The Malaysians had sent a c30 aircraft that was waiting on the other side of the city at the military air base. They were going to try to get to the base. Our own Embassy had no such facility, only a simple instruction to get to the airport if safe to do so, and if a ticket had been secured, or stay indoors and listen to the radio and TV. The airport road was known to be unsafe but with the help of a wonderful woman in our London office, Sue, the company secured tickets for a flight on 15th.

Colin had been getting an increasingly severe case of the 'screaming ab dabs'. I had tickets to get my Dad and Colin out but wondered whether Paul thought we should go too. I consulted with Paul and we decided to go. We hoped that the airport road would be passable.

176

Paul drove to my place, which was en route to the airport. Perhaps reflecting the traumatic nature of the occasion I recalled that Brad drove us to the airport. Paul has recently reminded me that he drove. My dad and Ken must have travelled with Brad. We had seen convoys of cars being driven toward the airport with military escort. It was a perilous journey to the airport. Paul reminds me that we had to divert from the main route to enter a kampung (district) to collect his exit visa from a contact close to the immigration department. We sat in the car waiting for the contact to come out of her house with the visa. The streets were crowded and we felt unsafe. Paul described it as the most uncomfortable wait he has ever had. After negotiating our way past corrupt airport officials demanding money for departure we flew to Kuala Lumpar.

That day Suharto was arriving home from his meeting in Egypt with their, President Mubarak, so we were pleased to have got out. Thousands had left with us that day but from Halim military airport and by sea. Civil War was feared.

Many had thought the rioting to have been instigated by the military and there were fears of a military confrontation. In the days after the 12th to 14th May riots it was clear that a move to a new political order had begun and that it was already a bloody one. Thousands had lost their lives.

We spent time in KL (Kuala Lumpar) and a few days on the beach in Rangoon where my Dad tried paragliding for the first time, before they flew to the UK from KL. I flew to Singapore to meet Paul. The old boys had not moaned once, or shown any fear, during traumatic times, but I could see that they were both very relieved to have made it to KL. To be honest, so was I.

Paul and I took stock of the position and decided to return. Soeharto had resigned on 21st May after 32 years in charge. The future was still far from certain, but we couldn't just wait, we had work to do, and it was going to be very busy indeed.

The events of May were critical when it came to considering the exclusions in an insurance policy. Was the damage caused during the 'struggle', the transition of power, caused by, riot, civil disorder, revolution, coup or Civil War? If so, some policies did not provide cover.

Ultimately this would be a matter falling for the consideration of lawyers and insurance companies but I was asked to provide a 'company opinion'; after significant discussion and debate we sat on the fence; ironically, for political reasons of another kind.

177

'It was not possible to draw firm conclusions' was my message. I wrote to Joe Van Savage of AIG stressing that it wasn't surprising that economic conditions had brought about rioting. I pointed out that the IMF, by insisting on the removal of fuel subsidies, that had been removed a week before the riots, had not helped. I mentioned the 'racist element, enclosed a few local press reports and added some personal experience. My Slipi apartment was right at the centre of the stage.

Riot cover was normally provided in commercial/industrial insurance policies, sometimes civil commotion, but not normally civil war. Did events amount to 'civil commotion, popular uprising or an act directed toward the overthrow of the government, or the influence of it by violence?

To my mind these questions were best left to those with a clearer vantage point and therefore we sat on the fence. I think that this was a correct decision; we didn't try to be too smart. My report went to London, The States, and Singapore. In order to understand the probable motives for the riots it was necessary to understand Indonesia, its culture, its economy, its people and most importantly its politics; this was for expert commentators.

The week in May was dubbed 'The Week of Living Dangerously'. After May 1998 the country started to take on a distinctly Islamic character that I hadn't seen before. I saw Jilbabs being worn on the streets, I hadn't seen that before. I felt that extremists were seizing the initiative and taking advantage of the political instability and uncertainty.

Troops remained on the streets for months afterward and periodic riots broke out; some serious. I was trapped in the Mercantile Athletic Club, when troops battled a large crowd in the street outside. There was a new feeling of hostility towards foreigners; because of the resentment I think.

That Soeharto had survived so long was because corruption and cronyism didn't matter that much until the crash of 1997; then it mattered. Crony capitalism is based on personality ties between political and economic powers. The crony's and the corruption would still be there when we got back. Incidentally, all these ingredients are woven into our own country; Britain is not so different, just more sophisticated. All this could happen in our country following a financial crisis. Our political system is rotten to the core.

They asked in 1997 why all this could not have been predicted. Ring any bells? Indonesia had enough resources to pull out of their crisis, with IMF and World Bank help. Does the UK?

Strong contenders in this new environment, was Amien Rais , the head of the 28 million members of a strong Muslim organisation, Megawati Sukarnoputri, grand-daughter of the previous president, and Abdurrahman Wahid; but Habibie, the vice president took control.

One of the first things Habibie did was to publically strip a General Prabowo of his command of Kostrad, the largest single troop command. Prabowo had apparently led his tanks to the gates of the presidential palace but was turned away by General Wiranto.

As a member of the Soeharto family Prabowo was spared, but banished to Jordan. The president was in Egypt at the time that a military confrontation between Wiranto and Prabowo would have spelt Civil War.

Wiranto is said to have slapped Prabowo on the face at the palace, whether he did or not, he is accredited as having averted civil war. Prabowo backed down and withdrew his troops. Habibie was close friends with Prabowo, and some suspect he was involved in Soeharto overthrow.

Indonesians of Chinese origin had been targets during the unrest and hundreds had been raped and tortured or killed. Many of my Chinese colleagues told me stories of horror, the worst being a case of a red poker being inserted in a woman's vagina before she was killed. Tension remained under Habibie's rule. The military rounded up 'trouble makers' and some troops 'disappeared' from barracks.

President Habibie's government was on shaky ground and couldn't survive long without serious trouble. East Timor erupted in revolution, Christians were clashing with Muslims in Sulawesi and the Malacca's, and tensions between the Chinese entrepreneurial minority, and the 'native' majority were almost tangible. Most of my office were Chinese, and would turn up for work wearing old worn clothing so that they didn't look wealthy.

Doing Business

Despite the unstable and uncertain state of affairs I was loving work, and had an enjoyable social life. Working in Indonesia was interesting to say the least. Misunderstandings were a feature of everyday life, not just in the office. The reasons are to some extent cultural and too often a result of language difficulty, all of which boil down to the fundamental old chestnut, communication. Overcoming misunderstandings and communicating well is the only basis upon which business can be successfully done. Learning the local language helped, and so did having a massive chunk of patience.

I have offered some background on cultural difficulties that westerners experience in Indonesia. Now an insight into the business approach. On a business level there are a few important rules to learn and observe and one should never talk business on social occasions. An expatriate is regarded as a guest in the country. Foreigners are well received, but noses are not welcomed where they shouldn't be.

Ex-pats are perceived as experts; that is supposed to be why you are there. They expect you to know everything. They also expect you to understand that relationships are hierarchal and not democratic. It is important to recognise in this context that a government official, or civil servant on almost any level, has a higher status.

Maintenance of face to face harmony of feelings takes precedence over the business task to be performed. Westerners have difficulty with this one! You will not fit in if you 'command' rather than develop supporting relationships or if you display a need to be superior in knowledge and technical skill.

The boss or 'Bapak' is entitled to expect deference and obedience. They often treat an employee like a father does a child. If the boss calls, he is obeyed; all other plans or appointments are postponed unless he gives the nod.

Although punctuality is expected of foreigners, the Indonesians tended to be late, and adopt a practice they amusingly call 'Jam Karet' which literally means 'rubber time'. The most common excuse I would suggest is the old chestnut – the traffic jam! In Jakarta it was not only plausible but probable.

Getting things done 'on time' could be extremely difficult unless you did it yourself – and, in extreme circumstances, it sometimes came to that. To work in Indonesia you have no choice but to accept a much slower pace of life in the office. Indonesians do not work at the same pace as Westerners. No amount of pressure will change that. Things will simply not move at the pace you are accustomed to. Western-style pressure on schedules and deadlines are not welcomed.

Attitudes to deadlines are extremely laid back. There is a long tradition in Indonesia of being tolerant to delay. It is a testimony to my success that our report issue times were cut in half.

For all the above reasons, and more that will become apparent, my relationship with Handoko was going to be a tricky one, and it was vital that I was on my 'cultural toes' constantly. There were great dangers in forgetting my relationship with him, and his with the local staff. It was a minefield that demanded alertness and careful thought. Operating in a foreign environment can be impossible unless you learn 'local rules'.

A major difference between working in Indonesia, and what I had been used to, was the travelling. The time it might take to travel to and return from a 'loss' could be literally days. Many mines, dam projects, construction projects and production facilities were located in remote jungle areas and on other islands. If you look at the map, and compare Indonesia with Australia, the United States or Europe you will see that Indonesia is large, very large indeed. Sometimes it could take two or three flights to reach the scene of a 'loss'.

You might need to drive for fourteen hours or more following the flight. You might need to take a similar journey by speedboat along the rivers of Kalimantan, rather than car. I have done it, and I can tell you it is very tiring and uncomfortable indeed. And try dealing with an insurance claim when you arrive! Many of the remote jungle locations could only be accessed by company owned/chartered light aircraft or helicopters.

When an adjuster returned to the office he was generally exhausted, but then there was the business of producing a report. Generally the Indonesian adjusters would submit their reports to Paul or I for approval. When we recruited a third ex-pat they were split three ways. The reports were written in English, their second language, so patience was required. Writing technical reports in a second language is tough and the guys had my utmost respect for doing so.

Our office in Jakarta had seventeen local Indonesian adjusters, and when my Dutch and English colleagues or I were not preparing our own reports, we were checking reports of our Indonesian colleagues.

When it came to the size of losses in Indonesia they were large. Some so large that I thought little of the figure work, otherwise I would have been overawed. Most of the office claims were over £50,000 in value and many over £1 million. My predecessor handed over to me two outstanding claims of over £20 million. It was necessary to remind myself that the principals of loss adjusting, and insurance generally, are the same irrespective of size.

There were very few household claims. It was all industrial and commercial work. There was not a lot of legal or product liability work, but it was likely to be a category of business that would grow and I wanted to develop our capability to deal with it. I had dealt with industrial accidents, interestingly some involving deliberate injury; the guy that deliberately put his finger in a garlic slice, and the asthmatic that deliberately sniffed molasses to irritate his ailment. Liability work would be lucrative and I was to learn that I was the only guy in the country that knew how to deal with it properly.

The range of work that I personally dealt with was beyond the dreams of most ambitious adjusters. For example, I dealt with a machinery breakdown and profit loss at a pulp and paper mill, bomb damage to the Jakarta Stock Exchange Building on 13th September 2000, when thirteen people lost their lives, damage and profit losses at a gold mine as a result of rioting by 6,000 people in December 1998, a furnace explosion at a nickel ore processing and smelting plant, a fire at a gold mine, damage at shoe factories, cigarette manufacturers, and cold steel rolling mills.

On several occasions there was widespread earthquake damage, pollution damage and injury resulting from a noxious gas escape from a 22MW (megawatt) thermal power station, death and injury on off shore oil rigs, losses at the Hard Rock Hotel resulting from the 'Bali Bombing' and many more. It was extremely interesting and challenging.

We had a contract to provide services at a 1200MW coal fired power station that was under construction at Probolinggo in East Java; the Paigton Energy project. It was through this connection that I was to get to know two guys from Marsh McLellan that were to perish in the World Trade Centre on 9/11.

I dealt with flood damage at a thirty one storey twin tower office building in central Jakarta that Handoko and some of my senior colleagues thought to be impossible to settle on amicable terms. All the building's support systems were in the flooded basement and the building ceased to function. They wanted 'the world'. The big honcho, a Chinese Mafioso type character, flew in from Hong Kong to take personal charge of the claim during one of our meetings.

People were suggesting I might care for a gift, or concrete boots. There was amazement when it was settled, on the correct basis, substantially less than envisaged, after intensive and close attention over a number of months. One of my proudest moments was when a senior 'local' colleague in the office came up to me and shook my hand and said that he did not believe it could be done.

182

There were claims adjustment considerations that I had never experienced before. For example, the currency issue. The Rupiah, the local currency, had fluctuated, at times almost daily throughout my stay. Imagine what that does to a business, importing goods for payment in foreign currency. Imagine what that does for someone attempting to quote a price for his product. Imagine, finally, what implications it all has for the adjuster attempting to identify the replacement cost of goods, and the loss of gross profit over the duration of a business interruption! The variables were wild!

I'll be writing about one or two specific cases later, but suffice to say at this point that working in Indonesia was extremely interesting and very exciting. I loved it, even when it was a little hair-raising!

Chapter Thirteen
Ex-pat Life

I had spent a lot of time during the early months learning as much as possible about everything. Every conversation and every turn of a page, in a book or newspaper was an education. I needed to know as much as possible as quickly as possible. I would advise any person considering a move overseas to consider carefully possible consequences.

When being overseas, and for a limited duration, there is a need to get off the blocks as quickly as possible. Learn as much about the place, and how it works quickly, and as a matter of priority. If you don't, you will be leaving before you have made optimum impact. Don't settle in slowly or gently. Throw yourself at the job and at the lifestyle. Be bold and get involved in all you can as much as you can. The more people you get to know the better the chance of meeting good business contacts and good friends.

I threw myself into everything. I learnt to Scuba Dive (a must in tropical waters like those around Indonesia) and I joined the Jakarta Hash House Harriers (cross country running, drinking and networking).

It was imperative that I built up some kind of social network for when Nikki arrived with Katy. Katy would get to know people through the British International School but a broad choice of options needed to be open to her upon her arrival. I needed to be able to take them places and meet people. I just hoped they would settle in.

Work was an excellent vehicle for this. It was essential that I establish a network of contacts as quickly as possible in the interests of the business, after all I had agreed to give Indonesia three years, and three years passes in a blink of an eye. Handoko was against this, for a few months anyway. He didn't want me to get out and meet business contacts before he felt I was ready. I tolerated this for a while and then asserted myself a little with some persuasive argument and he relented.

I wanted to schedule visits to meet all our customers. Handoko accompanied me to meet the Indonesian customers and Paul the others. A visit to meet customers in Singapore was arranged for later in the year. Other regular visits followed. I set about putting my name on the map.

I joined the Curry Club; a monthly lunchtime get-together for the Insurance Industry ex-pats organised by Bernard Sherriff MD of The Royal Sun Alliance. I met important people informally, and they became friends as well as existing or potential customers. I eventually became the club organiser, and this kept me in regular contact with them all, as I held the database of members and used it to good effect.

I inherited membership of the British Chamber of Commerce from John Seddon, and although Handoko wanted me to give it up because it cost too much, I kept it and persuaded him that Paul should be a member too.

Similar opposition was given to the membership of the Mercantile Athletic Club located on the top floor and roof of the World Trade Centre complete with swimming pool and tennis courts, but Paul, Nikki and I had membership, that was crucial, not only for sport and fitness, but also socialising with some VIP's. It was exclusive. I was actually in this top floor club at the time the planes were hitting the other World Trade Centre in New York

I visited customers and potential customers at their offices and then over occasional lunches. As a means of maintaining contact with claims departments and demonstrating managerial control and commitment to maintaining standards, I initiated a programme of monthly visits with a full report on the status of the portfolio of work that we retained on the customers' behalf.

I was only partially successful in getting others in the office to share the burden. It went down very well with local claims staff. It gave them the opportunity to ask questions and comment on progress. It gave me the opportunity to meet eye to eye and 'get into their minds'. There is no substitute for face to face meetings. I could also apply pressure for payment of outstanding fees! It worked. We were the only company doing it. Our competitors were, for a time, being left in our wake.

We halved the time it took us to issue reports by fast-tracking some and introducing time saving procedures. The market loved it. Paul was showing confidence in my ability to deliver and he became enthusiastic again about his role and new opportunities that my predecessor had denied him. We were working well as a team and we were good friends. Not to say Paul was easy to deal with. If he had something to say he'd say it, and if he didn't like something you'd know it. I liked that spunk and enthusism.

Paul and I started to network with vigour. We went to the pub in the adjacent building after work most nights and mixed with the Willis Caroon guys and through them others in the Industry, and their clients. We sometimes went on to the bars in the red light district and drank till late. We were buzzing. Could we keep up the momentum?

Handoko never stopped giving me the occasional hard time, but eased off, and confrontations were infrequent. Paul and I were making real progress on productivity and quality, by making changes that we were careful not to call 'changes,' and we started to see new business coming in. Handoko started to show confidence in me and that really was the key nut to crack. The three of us started to work well together and enjoyed socialising.

I joined the St Georges Society and the St Andrews Society and got invited to join the ANZAC's for their bashes. I got into our Embassy regularly where they had a great little pub where you might occasionally meet the commercial attaché and Robin Christopher, the Ambassador.

There were spin offs from the society and Embassy connections. I was an occasional visitor to the Australian Embassy, had invites to the French wine tasting parties, the American Embassy and their Chamber of Commerce meetings.

On one such American Chamber of Commerce meeting, the President of Indonesia attended at the top table amidst great security and gave a speech. There were just a couple of hundred tickets so I was really very honoured. Just a stone's throw away, the President of the fourth biggest country in the World; addressing me over lunch! Who'd have believed it a few years earlier?

I joined the Hash House Harriers and tried to run every couple of weeks or so on a Monday night but it meant leaving the office at around 3.30pm generally and I couldn't run as often as I would have liked. In any case after a strenuous run through jungle and paddy fields, sometimes in complete darkness, we consumed copious amounts of alcohol. Tuesday mornings were rough! I met an entirely different kind of guy through the HASH, a lot of them oil men and a couple of eccentric Japanese guys. Everyone had a HASH name. Mine was 'Blackbum'; one of the least outrageous.

By the time Nikki had arrived in the summer I could introduce her to scores of people that I knew personally and regarded as good company. Most importantly some had wives that I could introduce her to.

We enjoyed some terrific nights at the New Zealanders wine society dinners as a guest of my mate Ross Keenan of Marsh McLellan brokers and his wife, and other good

186

evenings through the Wine Tasting Society, a branch of an exclusive British club. A top wine expert from the Burgundy region of France was flown out to present Burgundy wines at one amazing tasting dinner hosted by the French. She went to some lengths to explain what to do and how to do it and we sampled some wines worth hundreds. I fell in love with white burgundy.

I loved the new life. I had been catapulted into the social and business elite, and I was not only keeping my head above water but I was becoming a popular and respected socialite and businessman. I was in heaven. I was as confident as I have ever been in my life.

The Dinner Dances were extravagant affairs with little expense spared. Tickets were popular and could be scarce, but if I wanted one I could probably get one. There were St Andrews Day Dinners, Burns Night Dinners, Trafalgar Night Dinners, Melbourne Cup Breakfast and Lunches, Aussie Rules Football Final breakfasts and lunches, and an annual end of term dinner organised by the British International School.

The annual Highland Gathering brought people in from all over the Far East. The social calendar was always full.

One or two of these events require some explanation. They were 'firsts' for me and I must confess I knew precious little about them. Burns Night was never really understood by me.

Robert Burns, I think we all know, was a Scottish Poet whose turn of phrase is little understood by the average Scot let alone the English, and the rest of the world. At any rate he lived in the 18th Century and one day in the 18th Century he was invited to dinner and rather than toast the guests or host he gave a poem dedicated to his dinner; a haggis. A few years after he died a few of his fans decided to have a dinner every year and toast the haggis as Burns had.

Now a haggis is little more than spiced offal stuffed in a lambs stomach although I have quite successfully convinced children and adults alike that it is a cute little animal that was almost driven to extinction in the 15th Century as a result of over hunting and the animals propensity to stampede toward winter pastures on the Scottish coast where, because of their heavy weight and short legs. They invariably ended up being slow to stop; and fell over the cliff edges rather like lemmings. They once wandered the highlands in large herds.

187

Burns week culminates in Burns Night on 25th January when, in one way or another Scotsman get pissed drinking whiskey and eat some haggis so they can have something to bring up later that night. But seriously I love haggis; it's like the Rolls Royce of faggots. But here's a tip. Eat it with gravy (not whiskey covered) otherwise it's too dry. You buy it cooked and just need to heat it for about forty five minutes.

The posh Burns Night in Jakarta is a wonderful ceremony and exercise in restraint, for the poshest. The formal gathering of several hundred was as authentic as any. The haggis was flown in from the UK. 'The Supper' included the 'Address to a Haggis', a speech to 'The Immortal Memory of Robert Burns', a 'Toast to the Lassies' and a reply from the 'Lassies'. I went during the year that Gus Roberts presented the haggis to the top table. Gus had just been 'pipped to the post' for the honouree position of 'chieftain' and I think the consolation prize on the eve of his departure to Shanghai, was this particular honour.

Anyway, the formal procedure was for the piper to lead a procession of three to the top table, the cook carrying the haggis on a plate. Gus followed the haggis. After the 'address', all three would be offered a glass of whiskey and everyone would stand to toast 'The Haggis'.

There isn't much Burns that I understand but the first verse, and please try to understand it, goes like this:

> Fair fa' your honest, sonsie face,
> Great Chieftain o' the pudding-race!
> Aboon them a' ye tak your place,
> Painch, tripe or thairm;
> Weel areye wordy of a grace
> As lang's my arm.

Now you don't have to understand this verse to like it and be amused by it. But there are eight verses that lose all but the connoisseur completely. During the third verse, at line two, Gus was expected to cut the haggis. I quite like this third verse as well.

> His knife see Rustic-labour dight,
> An' cut you up wi' ready slight.
> Trenching your gushing entrails bright,
> Like onie ditch;
> And then, O what a glorious sight,
> Warm-reeking rich!

Bizarre, mad and so British isn't it. The assembled kilted masses then proceed to get drunk on whiskey. That night was the only occasion that I have been seen in a kilt.

To experience the eccentricity of a formal Burns Night; Haggis 'neeps' (turnip) and 'tatties'(potatoes) and half a bottle of whiskey for about £75 a head ils a bargain. A well organised Burns Supper is something to behold.

The Trafalgar Night was, in contrast, a night worthy of celebration with more than a hint of formality preceding the more traditional piss up. The Admiral of the British Fleet or a very senior stand-in would fly in to give the speech. Massive paintings of 'the action' would adorn the walls of the hotel banqueting hall and flags would be draped around the wall spelling out the message, 'England expects that every man will do his duty....' (No mention of the Scots Welsh and Irish then). All the finery was courtesy of 'Asian Tigers' the 'local' International Removal Company; the sponsors.

Hundreds would sit along tables, seaman style, drinking rum from souvenir pewter engraved totty cups. 'Yo ho ho and a bottle of rum', it was a singing extravaganza by penguin suited 'men behaving badly' amongst women throwing in the towel and going with the flow.

Just to remind you of what Trafalgar Night is all about, you may recall that Admiral Lord Nelson beat the French and Spanish fleet singlehandedly off the south west coast of Spain on 21st October 1805 and lost his life in the process despite Hardy's attempt to revive him with a snog and Nelson's belated declaration of his love for him. What would Lady Hamilton have made of that?

Not one British ship was lost and the enemy lost 22 of the 33 that started the fight, and most of the others were captured. He was Britain's greatest ever war hero. A really sound reason to celebrate and get pissed!

Using the Curry Club, as my social marketing medium I became a well known figure and I organised a terrific golf weekend in the mountains outside Jakarta involving many people, including some that didn't like golf or had never played it. Copious amounts of alcohol was consumed 'on course', normal in Indonesia, and at the presentation meal afterward. I had deliberately arranged prizes for the worst golfers, rather than the best, which put the entire weekend into perspective. For once the serious golfers came second. Bernard Sherriff came first and to my knowledge never played again.

189

We had an annual Curry Club Christmas Dinner that I helped to arrange, and twice acted as Master of Ceremonies. There were ridiculous annual awards announced, after deliberation by a committee, of which Bernard was a key figure. With limited consultation I received an increasing number of awards year on year, until it became a farce with me taking a near clean sweep in the last two years. The awards were very popular because they created a great deal of laughter and story-telling. The awards were usually derogatory.

My awards, that must be the envy of Oscar winners, included 'Best Dressed Man in His Wife's Knickers Award' that followed my admission that I had 'accidentally' put on a pair for work one day, 'The Bintang Star' Award (Bintang being the local brew), and 'The Curry Club Man of The Year Award' on no less than two occasions. We had some great laughs, and some very elongated lunches with yes, you've guessed it, copious amounts of alcohol. All my awards can be attributed to outrageous behaviour!

I was happy to have the piss taken out of me - I didn't mind playing the fool. One or two felt that I had helped to rejuvenated the camaraderie amongst the insurance industry ex-pats. The Curry Club was the centre of our industry banter and piss taking; the place to let your hair down and try not to talk shop.

Christmas Club Dinners, in my last two years in Indonesia, were held in the red light district. Dinner was served by beautiful babes in little Santa mini skirt outfits with stockings and cute Santa hats – very tasteful and a recipe for drunken debauchery.

On the first of these two dinners the New Zealanders got a little bit over zealous during my welcoming address. I welcomed the German lads to the do for their first Christmas Dinner. The New Zealanders response was "Ziegh Heil Ziegh Heil". The dangerous humour did not go down well, but the boat race did. The Germans excelled.

I used my email a lot to keep in touch with the ex-pats, and when the tragedy of the Bengkulu earthquake in South Sumatra hit, I immediately set up an appeal for money, having arranged a suitable bank account through the HSBC. The donations were transferred directly into the account and within just a week ready for immediate distribution to the victims. The problem was how.

Ten thousand Rupiah had been raised and I wanted it to get to the victims directly; by hand if possible. A long drive to the east coast of Java, a ferry ride past Krakatau, and an even longer drive to the affected area, was considered, but it was impractical. I didn't have the time, it would take a week out of the office, and neither did anyone else.

I contacted the British Embassy to see if they could help and explained what I wanted. I didn't trust the Red Cross or any of the other organisations; I had heard of the corruption money required by police, army and local officials before the needy could get anything. I wanted direct distribution – cash.

The Embassy produced an answer for me. There was a reclusive type Brit that tended the British War graves in Bengkulu. He knew the area, the people, and was trustworthy. He lived amongst the victims.

It was arranged. I felt great knowing that individuals would receive a personal handout without local government and other official interference from a knowledgeable local contact that I could trust.

Toward the end of my time in Indonesia I was invited by Arumugam, MD of an Indian Insurance Company to join the Rotary Club; Rotary Gambir in Jakarta. I was immensely honoured, particularly as there were only another couple of white faces in the Club. I met some really good, honest and decent people including a charming and attractive looking TV presenter of some fame.

The 'Rotary Call' was very flattering and maybe a little over the top, but I am proud of it. Here's an extract:

'You have been chosen to membership.......because your fellow members believe you to be a leader in your special line of activity, and because you manifest those qualities which fit you to interpret and impart the message of Rotary to your fellow men..........we believe in your ability and sincerity as well as integrity.....we admire your enthusiasm and look to you to help carry on with the activities of the club'.

Rotary gave me a platform and opportunity to engage in some meaningful and well informed charity work which of course involved me parting with some cash and getting involved with some hands on support. I visited villages and schools in the East Java area to consider and review projects. It was extremely rewarding, humbling and emotional. I shall never forget those visits.

Unfortunately I had to leave Indonesia before I was able to become heavily involved as I would have liked. That disappointed me.

Most of my socialising was high octane. I joined my Aussie mates to perform a 'Blues Brothers' song and dance at the annual 'Melbourne Cup' day. Five hundred people sitting round tables for breakfast, booze and the race. We wore identical outfits. Nick Van De Venne was the ringleader, and the embassy 'federal policeman' his deputy. The Aussie Rules grand final was, as you would expect, another great day. Both these events were lavish fun days involving an outrageous amount of alcohol.

There were one or two outrageous outbursts by me, such as the time that I did a strip to music at Kirk's party; poolside. It went down very well actually and the applause was genuinely warm.

Indonesian Cricket

Believe it or not there is, or was when I was there, a small but thriving and enthusiastic Indonesian cricket scene amongst the locals. This was all possible because of the enthusiasm, and passion of my mate James Arthur; a gentlemen and a scholar. He set up the Indonesian Cricket Foundation and, with the usual need for sponsorship, held an annual dinner. As a friend, and not a cricket enthusiast, I attended with Kirk Austin. Keith Stackpole MBE was the guest speaker, and Mike Chick, James's right hand man with PT Synergy, James Company, sat on the top table and presented the awards.

The Austin/Wakefield table was a bit rowdy that night. The usual ten around the table got slowly, no rapidly, inebriated. There was an auction of some marvellous cricket items and one, a cricket bat, signed by the entire Bangladeshi second X1, became the target of Kirk. Kirk threw everything at it, and secured it with a bid of $2,000. He woke up the following morning with a hangover and an arm round an extremely expensive cricket bat. Kirk is not a cricket fan but entered the bidding war with only one thought in mind – that prat on the next table is not having it; the wanker! The 19th May 2001 was an expensive evening for Kirk, but then most evenings out with Kirk were lavish affairs.

I gate crashed the team photograph; my beaming face appearing on the back row between two genuine and deserving Aussie cricketers. Kirk and I never failed to enjoy a night out!

192

Golf

My eventual departure from Indonesia in February 2003 was appropriately 'celebrated' with a game of golf. All my friends and customers were invited and about fifty turned up. Indonesian golf courses have a 'bar' every four or five holes, and on this occasion Kirk had arranged a 'drinks' buggy driven by mini skirted waitresses. The caddies were, as usual, brilliantly skilled, female and mini skirt clad.

A friend videoed the hilarious proceedings in the club house at the end, one of the girls presented me with her underwear, paid for by Kirk, and I wore them, on the outside of my clothes, for the remainder of the day.

In some ways there was nothing special about this golf day; they were always fun, and usually finished off with food and copious amounts of alcohol! This one though was a little emotional.

The golf courses and facilities were magnificent and it was a privilege to play them. Most games were informal and fun.

One of my early 'locally' arranged golf days, and an eye-opener, was hosted by a well known Indonesian insurance company. At the end, everybody, and there were maybe 100 players, got a prize. There was no fee, it was by invitation, and I played badly, but I still got a rice steamer. This year's 'hole in one' winner (I think they had one every year) won a brand new four wheel drive. The 'hole in one' was of course well witnessed!

Holidays and Visitors

The most important issue for me was Nikki and her happiness. If she was happy and involved then Katy would be fine. Nikki was not the sort to seek a large circle of friends and I knew that, but I hoped and expected that she would find one or two close friends through the network available. She did eventually do just that, but she became more insular as a result, and this was not the outcome that I had wanted. Nikki was becoming increasingly withdrawn.

When we were living in Hong Kong our holidays were to Thailand and the Philippines, with weekends in Macao or the new Territories. It was a little claustrophobic. In

Indonesia we were not only financially better off, but we could drive off for miles, or take flights to exotic locations.

We drove to the west coast of Java and had hotel beach weekends overlooking the smoking Krakatau volcano. We could venture into the Ujung Kulon national park; the last refuge of the Java rhinoceros.

We could take a boat trip to 1,000 islands off the coast of Jakarta, or take a car or train journey to Bandung in the mountains. In the cool paddy field terraced hills outside Jakarta there were 'playgrounds of the rich' and the fantastic Taman Safari Park where I have never come closer to animals in my entire life.

Beyond Bandung in the mountains, on the south coast, a long drive away, was Yogya, a seaside city in the shadow of Mount Merapi, another active volcano. Nearby was the wondrous Borobador Hindi temple; discovered not 200 years ago when tons of volcanic dust was removed to reveal an ancient undamaged place of worship.

A hazardous journey through the mountains to Prabarahanratu, also on the south coast gave the opportunity to bathe in the volcanic springs and geysers, and visit 'the bat caves', where millions of bats 'clock out' of the cave, punctually at 5.15pm like a massive swarm of bees.

A flight, via Yogya, took us to Lombok, the next island along from Bali, and its unspoilt beauty. It has been described as the new Bali. We stopped at the Sheraton, on the beach, and at the foot of another amazing volcano. They're everywhere in Indonesia.

A direct flight, just about an hour and a half, took us to Bali, where we stayed in other wonderful hotels in Ubud and Denpasar. Commercially exploited these days; Ubud still holds a special charm. Denpasar caters for Aussie and Jap hoards.

A flight to Surabaya, the second city, a long drive or short flight east, took us to a marvellous golf resort, one of many in Indonesia, on the slopes of yet another volcano. A short drive away was one of the most spectacular, amazing wonders of the world; used in several films.

Mount Bromo is a large volcano ten miles across with smaller smoking volcanoes within. As a backdrop, is viewed a constantly smoking volcano several miles away. When you stand on the edge of Mount Bromo you feel that you are on top of the world. The moonscape panorama is breathtaking.

194

For the wealthy, these excursions were accessible and affordable. For the masses? Well they had perhaps never even heard of these places.

We travelled further afield and holidayed in Thailand nearby Singapore and Australia. Our first Christmas in Indonesia was spent in Freemantle and Scarborough, just outside Perth. We also holidayed in Sydney, and later, for our 25th wedding anniversary, New Zealand.

We went with Katy to Phuket where she revised, sat (and passed) her International Baccalaureate examinations. The opportunity to see the world, from the other side, was too big an opportunity to miss. Nikki was less enthusiastic.

Our first Christmas, in Freemantle, Australia was disappointing. Nikki was miserable all of Christmas Day, and wasn't even keen on leaving the hotel room. I had great trouble even raising a smile from her. I know that Nikki missed Zoe, but so did I, and the only difference was how we handled it. All I ever wanted was for my family to be happy, and when things turn miserable I feel hurt and sad. I try hard to provide the best for my family.

It wasn't apparent at this stage that Nikki was slipping into mental ill health, but she deteriorated throughout our stay in Indonesia, and in the end it was clear there were serious problems psychologically.

We were leading 'the good life', and were proud to receive guests so that they could share the benefits of our presence 'miles from home'. My sister and Pete visited us, my Mum and Aunt Brenda, Ann (Nikki's step Mum) and Nikki's half sister, Sarah, Joe and my neighbour Willy George (twice), Chris from the village Post Office, Rick Bennett - a fellow City away game travelling companion, and Zoe on two separate occasions with her 'fiancée of the day'.

Nikki had to share her time with her visiting daughter with accompanying boyfriends, and I sensed that she realised her daughter to be independent. I don't think that I ever saw the 'old Nikki' again after these visits. Zoe obviously wanted the company of her 'betrothed' during her holiday and I'm not sure that Nikki was comfortable sharing her. For me, well I was working for the most part, and so shared the evenings. I was content with that. Katy was at school and seemed contented.

I arranged for Zoe, and her partner, to spend some time in Bali. I travelled with her and her second partner to a small jungle village in the Leuser national park in North Sumatra

195

to see the Orang-utans. They loved that. They also loved the day out at Taman Safari, where they were able to hold white tiger cubs, leopard cubs, and play with naughty baby Orang-utans. Opportunities that are rare in the UK.

Katy and I had a mate at Taman Safari. She would take him walks and I would share a cigarette on a bench in the sunshine. This friendly, but nicotine addicted adult Orang-utan was a real character. He didn't seem to forget me, and he had to be prised away from Katy. Incidentally, I didn't give him the cigarettes, the keeper did, and the Orang-utan offered to share!

On the occasion of our first ever visit to the park, Nikki and I had a series of photos taken of us mounted on a camel. To my horror, embarrassment and great amusement, years later Paul came in to my office with a Taman Safari brochure with one of the photos on the front! It was also emblazoned on bill boards in the city of Surabaya! The embarrassing bit is that the photo was the most uncomplimentary photo that could have been taken of either of us- it was horrific! It was also hilarious. We didn't even get free tickets!

As Nikki drifted into depression she became more withdrawn. I tried hard not to let Nikki's condition stop me 'living a life' and in the last eighteen months of our stay Nikki was either absent, in the UK, or absent in another sense. I couldn't motivate her, by encouragement or demand. I was fed up with her attitude and took trips on my own or with friends.

I travelled to Japan, to see England beat Argentina 1-0 in a World Cup game in Hokkaido, and to take in some sightseeing in Kyoto. I went to Hong Kong to catch up with some old mates, new mates, and watch the Hong Kong Sevens - England won! For my last Christmas in Indonesia, with family in the UK, I went to Christmas Island and watched one of the natural wonders of the world, the crab migration.

When I eventually left Indonesia I made sure that I visited a French mate in Cambodia, a mate in Saigon, a mate in Hanoi, and from Vietnam took a few days in Laos. A goodbye to mates in Singapore and my far east fore was over.

And Nikki's Welfare

Keeping Nikki occupied in the daytime was important. We had servants; something that it was difficult to get your head around, so housework, gardening and cooking was taken care of. To work in Indonesia it was necessary to have an expensive work permit, and to live in Indonesia you needed sponsorship from a company. The company paid for my permit and a 'bond' against good behaviour of the 'guest' to their country. Family of permit holders were welcome. Perhaps that would be a good idea in the UK?

Nikki had left school with reasonable qualifications and had despite this, been a hairdresser, shop assistant, beautician, part time model and barmaid in the period before and during her time as a housewife. Nikki couldn't work unless she had skills that the country needed, and she hadn't. However, at least three years in Indonesia offered her a great opportunity for further education, but she didn't take this opportunity.

There were so many opportunities for Nikki in Jakarta, and it is a real pity that she didn't take to ex-pat living more readily; only her 'home' and her daughters counted. Her social life would need to be active, but even this aspect was neglected by her. There were occasions though when she really enjoyed herself, but these appeared infrequent.

One of the last social functions that she attended before she left Indonesia semi-permanently, was the 'Absolutely Fabulous' Fashion Show in May 2001; the year Katy completed her education at the British International School.. Oh she did enjoy that. She was with friends, got a little piddled and was in her element. Like all major functions it was at a hotel; the Kempinski, and was on a grand scale.

It was actually a British Women's Association production. Nikki was a member but not that active. She found some of them a little bit too stuffy. Some referred to the British Women's Association (BWA) as the Bitches and Witches Association, so she couldn't have been far wrong. Ex-pat women had the chance to model the clothes themselves, but although she fitted the bill, Nikki wouldn't.

All ex-pat nationalities would have a chance to attend these kinds of functions. Cocktail receptions, musical entertainment, raffle prizes, and decent dinners were usual, with dancing till late. All the big name clothing stores were represented, including M&S, Next, Emporio Armani, Escada to name just a few.

The raffle prizes at these events could be superb. At the above event you could win two business class tickets to Paris, a two night holiday in Lombok, mobile phones, nights at top hotels, club membership, and 'a string of pearls'. All were sponsored prizes and like most events, the proceeds went to charity.

Just two days before the Fashion Show we attended the International Baccalaureate Graduation Dinner; Katy had passed with flying colours. I was so immensely proud of her.

There was a group of ex pats, led by true professionals, that formed the 'Jakarta Broadway Singers' group and presented the 'A Little Night Music' cabaret at the grand Borobudur Hotel. It was, according to Nikki, a little pretentious.

I had encouraged Nikki to take a degree of some kind but she chose to get 'a little' involved with charity work instead, and on behalf of the British Women's Association and the Red Cross visited village communities to oversee distribution of aid. That was very satisfying for her but it simply wasn't enough to fill her week, and she only did it for a short spell.

Nikki particularly enjoyed the Beatles Dinner; the entire theme was 'the Beatles'. We enjoyed a Choral Jazz Concert at the Dharmawangsa Hotel; a grand hotel to roman design, where Nikki enjoyed a full range of exotic and expensive beauty treatments. Songs from the forties to the Eighties were performed.

To Nikki's credit she tried golf, and actually started to enjoy it, as long as she was in the right company. Her best mates were both lovely people, but both were 'low' if not depressed. I felt that they fed off each other in a negative way. Lydia was married to William, M.D of Chubb in Indonesia and Australia. William was Burmese born and 'connected', through family, to the military there. They were both lovely people, but they were 'drifting apart'. I was quite close to Lydia.

Marie was married to a HASH mate, Alex, MD of a wire rope company. She was also a lovely woman. We met them often at our favourite curry house/bar in Kemang. I am reminded of the occasion when Alex had a visitor from the UK. He was introduced to me as a town planner and we chatted. He had designed the Plymouth city centre he told me. "What's your name again?" I asked. "John Reid" he said. I gulped and with a broad smile on my face said, "Not the John Reid, town planner that is reviled for planning Coventry City centre in the 1960's?" "Yes" he laughed.

Nikki was reasonably contented enjoying her tea mornings, shopping plaza trips and afternoons and occasional nights 'with the girls' - when she was not sharing time with Katy. Unfortunately she didn't get to grips with any activities on a regular basis and she couldn't even get involved in sporting activities. It seemed that nothing interested Nikki and by 2001 it was clear that she was becoming apathetic, and slipping into depression.

In 2001 Katy returned to the UK with her school mate, via Vietnam, Cambodia, and Africa. Nikki lost interest in everything and just about everyone. She could have done so much – but didn't. She just wanted to go home. She did later that same year. She just couldn't be away from our kids.

It would be easy to say that Nikki's feelings toward our kids was normal (I understand that, we discussed it) but it wasn't. Nikki had arrived in Indonesia depressed, raised her game after I 'lectured her' about the effect she was having on Katy, and returned to the same state prior to Katy's departure. I was starting to conclude that Nikki was clinically depressed and that the reasons were more than just the craving for her kids.

Chapter Fourteen
Work In Indonesia

There were political tensions throughout my stay, and by 2000, although Abdurrahman Wahid had succeeded Habibie as President, his popularity waned and new political insecurity emerged. A struggle to loosen the militaries strong hold on political power followed. Censorship was abolished, but religious and ethnic conflict followed. There were mass protests and violent and racial confrontations. But we felt quite safe, and life went on.

Between 1998 and 2001 efforts were made to crackdown on corruption, and 'disassemble' old 'contracts' and start afresh. The economic climate was a breeding ground for potentially fraudulent claims by desperate companies seeking to survive. We had to be mindful of that, but handling 'suspect' claims was extremely difficult, and even dangerous.

The water companies suffered cancelled contracts just days after Soeharto resigned. Each of them had a foreign partner, Lyonaise des Eaux and Thames Water. I dealt with an extremely difficult and complex claim submitted by the French company for 'loss of revenue'.

The water companies had been accused of neglecting their contractual obligations. The state electricity company, PLN, and other massive state companies such as Pertamina Oil, and Garuda Airline were also targeted by the government. I dealt with claims made by PLN and Pertamina.

PLN had outright ownership of power stations and shared ownership in some private power plants. They were liable to pay a high fixed price for the private electricity. The private plants were financed by foreign capital and had been commissioned at a time when demand for power was greater than supply. When demand dropped the private electricity was not needed, but PLN remained liable for a fixed amount of electricity whether they needed it or not. The cost of this 'private' electricity was higher than the price paid by the public!! It has been said that the price charged by the companies included a payment for 'Mr 10%'; a member of the Soeharto family.

I listed a few of the claims that I had dealt with on an earlier page. Here are a few in a little detail.

200

One of the most interesting claims that I ever dealt with, and there were many, arose as a result of an incident in Sumatra in April 2000.

The Japanese had built a huge foundry on the coast at Kuala Tanjung to produce aluminium for export to the massive Japanese market. The factory produced a large percentage of the Japanese demand for aluminium. The factory needed massive amounts of electricity to power the plant. It took its electricity from two hydro electric power plants that they also built especially for the foundry. The power plants were about 130 miles away in Sigura-Gura and Tangga, on the Asahan River downstream from Lake Toba.

Lake Toba is the largest volcano caldera lake in the world and the Japanese built two dams across the river flowing from it to facilitate the power stations. The power stations were capable of producing enough energy to power the factory, the township that was built around it, and provide electricity for the local Batak people around the lake.

Interestingly the Bataks were cannibals, and a German missionary provided an account of the last known act of cannibalism in the hills around the lake. He witnessed the feast, and is one of few Europeans to have done so. Franz Junghuhn lived among these people for eighteen months in 1840. He wrote: "When an enemy is captured the day is set upon which he should be eaten. Then messengers are sent to all allied chiefs and their subjects inviting them to be present at the feast......the captive is bound to a stake in an upright position...then the chief draws his knife and steps forward to address the people. It is explained that the victim is an utter scoundrel, and in fact not a human being at all....at this address the people water at the mouth and feel an irresistible impulse to have a piece of the criminal in their stomachs.....all draw their knives. The radja (chief,) cuts off the first piece. He holds up the flesh and drinks with gusto the blood streaming from it..... now all the remaining men fall upon the bloody sacrifice, tear the flesh off the bones and roast and eat it.....the cries of the victim do not spoil their appetitive. It is usually eight to ten minutes before the wounded man becomes unconscious, and a quarter of an hour before he dies".

That must be a long ten minutes! Anyway, I again digress. The Japanese had therefore invested vast amounts of money in damming the lake, building a hydro electric power station and supplying electricity to a gigantic factory at Asahan on the coast 130 miles away.

The incident occurred at the power station. A fire knocked out two of the four banks of turbines that produced the electricity at Tangga. Although the physical damage was very significant in itself, the real loss occurred at the factory where production was hit as a result of the reduction in the amount of electricity being generated.

Apart from the investigations to determine the cause of the fire, some considerable investigation was required to identify to what extent the reported loss of production, and therefore profit, resulted from the fire. Believe me it wasn't as straightforward as you might think, and the claim took over two years for me to settle.

When we received our instructions to handle the claim the Japanese invited us to a meeting at the factory. I didn't decline but I told them that we needed to visit the power station and inspect the damage first, and I asked Paul who is of course an engineer, to attend the scene with me and take charge of the technical investigation. We spent a couple of days at the power station and then left for the factory where we held preliminary discussions and were shown around the factory. It is always imperative that you make yourself as familiar as possible with the processes and the business. Unless you understand the business you cannot settle a loss of profit claim. By the time I was in a position to consider calculation of the claim I knew just about everything there was to know about producing 'a pot' of aluminium ingots.

We left after listing requirements to progress the claim – everything from technical data, reports, statements, production data and financial accounts for the preceding five years and all actual production and financial data for the period going forward, known as 'the interruption period'. Paul produced a long list in relation to the power station and the fire, and I produced a list in relation to the production plant with a view to considering the loss of production and its implications to the profitability of the business. Paul and I made two further separate visits several months later; to the power station, with consultants from Australia and Japan, to consider the cause of the fire, and to the plant to discuss the implications, and 'demand' further and better information that had so far not been forthcoming. Subsequent meetings were held in Jakarta.

On examining the production figures there was little doubt that production levels were down following the fire, but then there was evidence that production had been falling beforehand. Why? And if production had been falling anyway, to what extent had the fall in production after the fire been attributable to the fire, and for how long after it?

To be fair, the Japanese had acknowledged the decline in production before the fire and attributed it to a fall in demand, rather than any extraneous cause. Enquiries confirmed that global demand had indeed fallen, and of course the Japanese consumed most of it! They claimed however that demand had increased after the fire and they couldn't meet that demand.

My investigations involved a lot of research and looking at the entire process to identify factors that influenced the levels of production possible at the plant over the period that the production was 'interrupted' by the fire damage.

As I improved my understanding of electricity generation, supply on overhead cables over 130 miles, and consumption in the factory relative to output, I began to see flaws in the argument. I also identified efficiency fluctuations at the plant prior to the fire, and seasonal influences on the ability of the power station to supply electricity to it.

Paul had, during his own investigations at the power station, identified a correlation between electricity generation and water flow rates through the turbines and I then remembered reading, or seeing a documentary, about a potential environmental disaster at the lake because the lake was drying up following years of unseasonably low rainfall – drought.

I researched the subject and found that water levels in the lake had been suffering badly, and some alleged that the power station was, at least in part, responsible. Flow rate, we found, would influence production. We examined daily flow rates recorded over the previous two years and the two years following the fire and Paul, who was brilliant at extrapolating data on computer, produced graphs and we concluded that production would be impaired by the flow rates during the interruption period. Again, to their credit, the Japanese conceded this point. But it was like pulling teeth!

Within months of the fire, and following repairs, a breakdown occurred that they attributed to the fire damage! We didn't quite see it that way. Paul was also finding evidence that the fire might not have caused all of the physical damage alleged; most, but not all. It began to emerge that the power station manager might have been responsible for concealing some of the facts because of job threatening ' mistakes' that had been made.

It was a fascinating claim to handle, and we trawled through reams of statistical records and data in our appraisal. The negotiation story is taken up later in this book.

If the claim was a drawn out affair, as many were, one of the quickest resolutions to a large claim that I have ever handled came less than 48 hours after our appointment and following intensive investigation involving transcontinental phone calls and faxes.

I was summoned to the offices of a Korean Insurance Company with Handoko. They were in deep do-do's, having insured a couple of valuable paintings for $1.5 million dollars in return for a peanut premium payment. They had done so a day or two earlier, and now they were being told that the paintings had been lost/stolen in transit from Jakarta to New York where they were to be auctioned by a well known international auctioneer. Could we help them? Handoko asked me if I could do anything and I did. In fact I did everything.

The Koreans were clowns. They didn't know what the paintings were named, who painted them and how much they were worth. They had no documentation whatsoever. I think they were pocketing the premium themselves, and the business was not going through the books, but I don't know. I do know that we never got paid by them!

I got in touch with the owner who identified the painting – one by Chagarl, and the other by Renoir I think. He produced transit documentation and the auction catalogue showing photographs and providing descriptions. This was the only evidence that they existed, let alone that they had indeed been dispatched. The boxes might have been empty. I was suspicious, after all I was an ex cop!

I contacted the New York auctioneers and they confirmed that the consignment had not arrived. I circulated the paintings as 'nicked / awol' with the Art Loss Registry in London. I contacted all those parties involved in the transit and was able to confirm that the crates got as far as Frankfurt in Germany.

I sent threatening letters to the airline indicating that legal action would follow within days if the paintings were not found, to motivate them into action. Bizarrely, the paintings were eventually found in a nuts and bolts factory in Belgium! Spectacular, efficient, and professional success achieved within hours. I had stayed up late at night waiting to hear from the German airline. And the Korean company didn't even pay us!

A lot of heavy machinery was damaged on remote jungle sites and these machines could cost hundreds of thousands of dollars. A lot of them are used for illegal logging. The local adjusters generally dealt with these relatively straightforward claims that were usually as a result of malicious damage by tribes resisting illegal mining or deforestation – why the hell don't insurance companies refuse to insure such activity. Superstition played a major part in Indonesian culture and it was not uncommon for causes of damage to be attributed to 'ghosts'. To villagers in places such as Kalimantan (Borneo) this was an entirely plausible and reasonable explanation and they hoped that convincing people that supernatural forces had been at work would take the heat off them.

The Diyak tribes of Kalimantan were feared by other Indonesians because of their famous supernatural powers. They were able to produce magic and witchcraft. Indonesians took this very seriously.

I remember sitting in my office one day and listening to an Indonesian director of one of our competitor companies, telling me a story about one of his adjusting staff who had flown to Pontianak in Kalimantan to deal with a loss in a small village. The adjuster concerned, so the story goes, was a bit of a lad, and when he arrived at the village where the loss occurred, he took a bit of a shine for the village elders' daughter. Sensing that the adjuster might overstep the mark the village elder 'magiced' away his meat and two veg. According to the adjuster they simply vanished from between his legs, and only reappeared after he boarded the flight back to Jakarta.

I laughed. The director, very seriously indicated to me that the adjusters colleague had witnessed this (not sure I would want that) and that they were both seriously shaken, indeed traumatised by the entire affair. "Screws lose?" I hear you ask. Well not as many as the director – he believed the entire tale!

Superstition plays a big part in Indonesian life and many believe in ghosts' spirits and magic. There is no point in challenging or mocking such stories.

I am reminded of a woman in Northampton. I went to her house to inspect damage to the ceilings, walls and furnishings in the lounge. She explained to me that the damage had been caused by poltergeists that she had witnessed throwing furniture around the room. I told her that I would report the circumstances to the insurance company but that I didn't think they would pay for damage by poltergeists.

This happened when there was enough fun in the workplace to relieve stress and have a laugh. I sent a detailed report to the insurance company in Wellingborough indicating that the policy was an 'all risks' policy and that all causes that were not specifically excluded were covered by the policy, and that, as poltergeist damage was not specifically excluded, they might wish to consider paying the claim. I didn't charge for the report, and some interesting and amusing verbal and written exchanges followed. The woman was of course off her trolley!

Or was she? In fact I have to concede that I also believe in ghosts – I saw a family of three in December 2008, at my cottage in Berwick. If anyone was to ask me if I believe in ghosts, then I would have to say that I <u>know</u> they exist.

I was in the large claim 'big league' and the incident that summed that up for me was when a friendly insurer from Australia virtually tossed a coin over a $30m claim and increased my settlement offer of $14m to representatives of a mining company that had flown in to Indonesia for a meeting at the Sheraton Hotel near the airport, to $18m within a few minutes of discussion. I had bet him on the outcome. He won a bottle of whiskey from me and also demanded that I write my report around the new settlement figure. I'd been had of course.

Chapter Fifteen
Loose Cannon

In 1999 we were making headway with the development of the Indonesian operation and Paul and I were of the view that it was time for us to get some more expert assistance. We agreed that we needed an accountant; someone with Business Interruption experience to deal with the complex analysis required in relation to calculating profit losses.

We convinced Handoko and we waited for overseas applicants. Roger was introduced to us by Handoko. He was a Dutchman who had emigrated to Australia. He was three to four years older than me with a long history of loss adjusting in Holland. On paper Roger was the bean pusher that the office needed; a figures man who was very experienced in extrapolating financial accounts, he was just the job; he could be of great help to us.

I interviewed Roger and Paul was invited into the room to add his views and comments. We were later introduced to Roger's wife a lovely woman. Roger was asked to consider very carefully every aspect of the move and given the benefit of our experience on matters of money, accommodation and security. Roger was up for it. He agreed the package, and had demonstrated to both Paul and I that he was going to be a real asset.

Roger was told exactly what was expected of him and warned that any failure to 'tow the line', regarding the position taken by us, the advisory team, headed by me, would be disastrous. A 'united stand' was an important requirement and it had been the key to the progress that we had made to that point. We explained our goals, our plans, our strategy and tactics, and it was emphasised that any sign of doubt, of difference in the view expressed by any of us, would be exploited by 'Handoko'.

Roger is one of the nicest, yet the most exasperating characters I have ever met. There was much benefit to his input on matters of finance-he was a wizard with figures. Unfortunately he turned out to be a loose cannon and an uncontrollable force for himself and himself only. He was simply not a team player.

He was unhealthily ambitious and yet failed to recognise his own frailties; his own weaknesses and inadequacies. He tried, but he simply couldn't stop himself. He would often change from the pre agreed course of action, and derail proposals put to Handoko.

He would say he wanted to be fair and balanced, but he didn't understand the importance of solidarity between the three of us, and if he did, I can only conclude it was in the cause of his own craving for power and influence. He clearly courted Handoko and failed to respond to the wishes of Paul and I, openly breaking ranks to my frustration and sometimes downright astonishment.

He worked closely with me on the Aluminium foundry claim. We travelled to Sumatra together on a couple of occasions. So did Paul as he had the engineering expertise, although on occasions you might be forgiven for thinking it was Roger. When I was preparing a presentation to Japanese Insurers and Brokers I liaised closely with Roger regarding the business interruption- loss of profit -aspect of the claim.

We worked hard on it and his expertise was crucial. Extrapolating the data and calculating the loss of throughput could not have been done more expertly, and certainly could not have been done without him.

As is so often the case with profit and loss there was some considerable scope for interpretation, after all it is an exercise in applying expected future performance of a business, taking account of all the circumstances and influences on that business during the interruption period, based on historical, forecast and real performance.

There was scope for negotiation as long as the settlement could be substantiated as being realistic and reasonable. Roger checked my own calculations and was broadly in agreement although his theoretical calculations were much more precise. Roger presented, and I agreed, a range of figures before attending the meeting. I asked Roger to make a presentation of the complicated aspects of our financial enquiries because I knew he would be best placed to deal with questions.

Before the meeting, knowing Roger's propensity to go 'off on a frolic of his own'; I insisted that he present the case that reflected the lower in the range of possible settlement figures, because I knew the Japanese team well, and I had had experience in negotiating with Japanese, and knew that they would always argue for more.

There was no doubt whatsoever that they would want more, whatever the figure. It was imperative that there was some play in the figures; some spare capacity. It was after all only a first phase in negotiation and there was in any case some significant difference between what they wanted and what they had actually lost - in fact many millions.

I went out of my way to explain to Roger 'the bigger picture'. The company was 50% Indonesian owned and 50% Japanese owned. They were disputing their contract. The validity of the claim had been doubtful and we had employed Australian engineering experts to provide a report on the breakdown. They had concluded that it had not been as a result of the fire. The insured had J-Power engineers flown out from Japan to obtain their own report. The two sets of engineers inspected the damage jointly according to my wishes, but were worlds apart. The Japanese conclusion was opposite to the Australians. It took some clever report writing to get the claim approved.

The insurance company was in the same group of companies as the insured. They had every reason to want as much money as possible paid to them. The European Reinsurance Company was bearing the lion's share of the risk, and ultimate payout, and they would not be so keen to have it paid. The report that I submitted concerning the question of insurance liability helped to steer the parties toward an agreement to meet the claim. It was not easy and in the end I made it clear in the report that there would be Court action if the claim was rejected. It was a persuasive argument that Reinsurers would recognise and take account of.

Now this was my case; my responsibility. I repeated instructions in the taxi on the way to the meeting. I begged him to 'stick to the agreed script, do not depart from it. Do not get carried away. Do not turn it into the 'Roger van Gool Show' as he was prone to do. Keep it simple and slow. They have difficulty understanding matters of this kind and are listening in English – or at least trying to'. "I will do the negotiating. Leave that to me. Do not concede anything at this early stage."

I submitted my presentation using handouts and an overhead projector and handed over to Roger so that they could understand in more detail the reasons for the proposed settlement figure. Roger started well but I could see he was enjoying the attention, as he often did. He started to showboat and over-run. I could have taken a nap at one stage.

He was losing me as an audience so the Japanese had to be sleeping! I think that one of them actually was! But the main man, my mate Kasuda, from the insurance companies Singapore office, was not. He was educated in the US and had as good a command of English as any Japanese I had met. He liked to think that he understood Business Interruption losses, and indeed did have a good understanding of the basics.

He was alert and I was keeping an eye on his line of questioning. He was a smart cookie and I knew from experience that his questioning was carefully in series and that there was a grand design.

209

Kasuda, I could tell, was about to ask the penultimate question. He had sussed out Roger. I knew what he was going to ask, "So you are saying there is some other way of interpreting these conclusions?" I tried to interject. There was no stopping Roger, he was showing off.

"Of course there always are different views….bla bla bla" I tried repeatedly to get a word in but Roger was stopping me! He laughed as only Roger could, "For you are trying to say something David?"

Most statements or questions posed by Roger were prefixed by the words, "For you are…" I was furious but couldn't afford to show that to the distinguished audience seated along a massive Indonesian style boardroom table – long enough to play cricket on! They were all awake now.

"Yes Roger" I stared him in the face. My eyes pierced his. "But this represents the fairest and most reasonable doesn't it. You should emphasise that".

"Maybe" he said. "I don't know for sure. I need to look more closely at the figures for there have been some good points made David, and we should acknowledge them".

There had been no good points raised at all. Most of them were bored or asleep. Most of them didn't have a clue what was going on. Roger just wanted to feel important and in control.

I did eventually get the case back on track and a settlement was eventually negotiated to the mutual satisfaction of all concerned. Indeed Kasuda was delighted because he had been told throughout, that there were serious question marks as to whether the loss could be attributed to the generator fire in the first place. A causal link was very fragile and open to serious doubt.

It had been suggested that the production loss had affected the world market price of aluminium, but this was a shade fanciful, and there were other important factors that had affected the price at the time. They had just hoped that we would pay for the drop in the world aluminium price because it was attributed to the fire. I produced convincing research material that indicated the drop in price was as a result in drop in demand rather than the fire.

I had a love-hate relationship with Roger. Roger would often be seen moving from office to office asking advice, going back to his own office and ignoring it. He would often demand an hour or two to discuss something, get a clear precise answer, and then go off and ask Paul the exact same question and consume Paul's time in a like way. Roger loved to discuss, discuss and discuss, debate and debate until you were blue in the face with repeated advice, most of which we knew he would ignore. He pontificated and pontificated about pontificating!

He got himself in scrapes that were very much of his own doing. He could get very stressed and I have seen him sweating profusely in his office and during meetings with clients. He placed himself in some ridiculous situations and under immense pressure. He was the author of his own downfall, as case after straightforward case, became complicated and messy as a result of his meddling.

He tried to be all things to all people and simply tried too hard to please everyone. He wanted win-win at all costs and had great difficulty in accepting defeat, or accepting the consequences of telling somebody that they couldn't have what they wanted. As a result he produced a large case load and could not close files quickly enough. He had a backlog of work that he complained prevented him doing anything we asked him to do. But Roger was his own man. He wouldn't listen to advise, follow instructions or fall into line. Eventually even Handoko, who was milking the good fortune, got fed up with it all.

Within a few months of joining us Roger already felt he should have a better car and more money. He pestered and moaned his way through a couple of years with monotonous regularity, saying how he was thinking of leaving, and no doubt hoping somebody would beg him to stay and throw themselves at his feet. We all told him, if you're not happy leave, but for Christ's sake stop moaning. Of course he didn't do either.

Roger stalled most of our development plans and derailed others by playing politics with Handoko in the hope of finding favour and reward and yet I am very fond of Roger and I know Paul would feel the same way.

He could take a joke reasonably well -in a Dutch kind of way- and once he had understood British humour, was as good as the next man at taking the piss. He enjoyed the banter after getting accustomed to the piss taking and learnt how to participate himself. This I respected, and very much enjoyed. Roger had a great sense of humour. If Roger could be persuaded to stop talking 'work' he was really good company.

211

In fact Roger was quite a sophisticated and successful womaniser. He had an old fashioned approach that endeared him to the ladies. He was a gentleman. It could be a bit nauseating to some of us, but entirely effective and worthy of respect. He had some style with the ladies did Roger. Nikki adored him.

Roger would throw himself into anything and to his credit agreed to take up some golf and do a little entertaining. We had some good fun on the golf course. Roger was not good but it didn't stop him trying, and was comfortable with the piss take.

In Jakarta there was an ex-pat community, and in the insurance industry everyone knew each other well. Roger could even be a liability socially. If he spoke about our office his comments could develop into a blunder. He would be telling people our plans and creating his own vision for the office, that may, only by pure coincidence, correspond with those of Paul and I; the official version.

I am incapable of disliking Roger infuriating as he could be. He was a contradiction and I think he was desperate for recognition and respect. He was a very talented accountant but a poor and weak negotiator. He promised this and he promised that, but the promises were rarely kept and if they were, they often came too late.

He was always busier than anyone else. He was often first in the office and last out, but his level of productivity between times was disproportionately low. He loved to debate and chat over his cases and started off being happy to give valuable advice to others. His problem was the backlog of work he built up whilst seeking, what he perceived as being perfection. It was in fact indecision and a clear inability to close a deal; to bring matters to a close. But when Roger bounced around the office like a cheerful kangaroo it was impossible not to smile as he passed – you just hoped he passed.

The staff in the office grew to avoid Roger. A case on his desk was a case never to be closed, doomed, like the Marie Celeste, to drift through the passage of time in search of an explanation, an answer a plausible conclusion.

I would find it impossible to hear the name Roger Van Gool mentioned without beaming an affectionate smile. Don't ever ask me to work with the man, but please, please invite him to the party. I would love to see him again occasionally, but in small and selected doses!

Roger was thick skinned stubborn, arrogant and at times thoughtless and insensitive in business, but above all, and most importantly, also a deeply caring and sensitive man in friendship. In an entirely heterosexual context, "I love Roger"!

"God bless Roger".

Oh dear, it does seem I am going on about Roger, but I've just thought of another funny encounter. Before I move on, I really do need to relate to you a meeting that I had scheduled, again with Japanese. This meeting was intended to be a two to three hour meeting but it was turning into twice that. Roger was in full flow and causing damage. I had to stop him.

I thought of using a way of stopping him dead (he'd ignored my every attempt to stop him by interjecting) without it being obvious to the Japanese that there was a problem.

I caught Roger in mid –sentence – it was obvious his audience were falling asleep so it shouldn't have been detected. I said loudly, whilst clapping slowly two or three times, "That's Hippo Plop Roger Thank You. Excellent". Roger looked shocked, stalled and then started to laugh quietly saying, "You can't say that David". I asked the Japanese, with a smile on my face, to join me in thanking Roger for his superb presentation.

I had banked on the word being missed, and if the serious look on Koshida's face was because he had recognised what I had said, he was not betraying me to the others. I could see the big Japanese boss consulting the young whizz kid by his side as to what I had said.

The whizz kid was good at English, and had been explaining proceedings to him. He was now looking puzzled and was consulting his Japanese English Dictionary. But I kept going and explained that we did not want to take up too much of their time and there was quite a lot to get through before we could adjourn. Roger was still sporting a smile and the young whizz kid was in the corner of my eye trying to ask me the question that I knew was on his lips, "What is Hippo Plop?" I kept him at bay for fully twenty minutes as I kept up the pace of the presentation, but this little Nip was not going to go away.

"Yes? I think you have a question" I faced him square on eyes firmly fixed on his. "Ah please be explaining 'Hippo plop' what is this word?"

I looked him intensely in the eye and sneaked a glare so that he felt slightly uncomfortable – this guy was a potential Rottweiler - "I am just using a word of

213

congratulation" I said and moved back into my presentation. "Aaah" he said, but whenever I looked in his direction he still looked bemused. However I was confident that he would be quiet now. He would be in trouble for disrupting the meeting for a further English lesson; a matter that had no relevance to the business in hand. I got away with it!

Meetings with Japanese open with ceremonial bows, handshakes and carefully planned seating arrangements. Everyone, moves around the table like they were playing musical chairs exchanging business cards and examining them in great detail whilst holding them firmly in both hands. It is very polite to show this excessive interest in a business card, and very rude just to receive them, glance, and then place them in a pocket or case. The cards should be arranged on the desk in front of you, and it is always good to be seen looking around the seated table and smiling or going "Aaargh so" as you place the cards in the positions corresponding with the table seating positions. They love it. It's a ten minute ceremony at least. Everybody is asking each other what they are and who they are.

I eventually realised that when I chaired these meetings it was good form to ask each 'head' to introduce their team to the meeting. It was often too late to stop the chaos of the musical chairs but it helped bring order to chaos afterwards – and it demonstrated organisation and order – they like that. They also like a little flattery and are delighted when you show some knowledge of their history. I made a point of learning some and I loved to drop them my understanding of their historic victory of the Japanese navy over the Russian navy in the 19th Century – it was actually like another Pearl Harbour attack but I don't think they saw it that way – they were very proud and surprised. A lot of time was spent talking about anything but business at the start of any meeting in Indonesia.

Chapter Sixteen
The Hunter Becomes the Hunted

In 1999 I returned to the UK to meet barristers in readiness to defend the company against grave allegations of defamation of character made by a dodgy double glazing salesman/fitter who had been arrested as a result of information supplied by me on behalf of Sun Alliance Insurance Company.

All the indications had suggested that this man was guilty of forging a signature in order to obtain money directly from the insurance company without doing the work. The insurance company had been invoiced for the work, Mr X had been paid, but the work had not been done.

Circumstances conspired to create a situation where this fraud could not be proven. In fact worse than that, they enabled the accused to turn the situation to his advantage, and make his own allegations and build a case up against his accusers. The hunter became the hunted.

Such was the situation I found myself in at The Royal Courts of Justice in London when I was at the centre of a defamation suit lodged by, the very clever, resourceful and delusional Mr X.

I first met Mr X when he made a dodgy insurance claim in 1989. Having made an offer that should, if justice had been done, never been offered at all, Mr X went ballistic and complained. As was usually the case, support for a correct decision was overturned for commercial reasons and Mr X got a bit more – shout loud enough and you are likely to squeeze a little bit more out of them! A nasty piece of work was Mr X, and it did leave a bad taste in the mouth on that particular occasion, but the life of a professional has to go on.

Five years later, in 1994, I am asked by Sun Alliance, because I had a reputation as a good investigator, to weigh up a case involving a postman who had had his insurance claim for damage to patio doors, settled in principle, but not settled in fact. They asked me to look into why 'Postman Pat' had complained that his patio doors had not been repaired when in fact Sun Alliance had received a mandate, signed by him, instructing the release of money to the contractor, Mr X (trading as BritWindows). Sun Alliance had agreed that the work could be done at the price quoted.

I visited 'Postman Pat' at his home and with an open mind. The doors had not been repaired. The contractor had been paid. 'Postman Pat' wanted to know what was going to happen.

'Postman Pat' was shown the mandate that the contractor had sent to the insurance company and had purportedly been signed by 'Pat'.

 "That is not my signature", he told me.

"Are you sure?"

"Yes"

"Can I have a sample of your signature?"

He wrote out his signature six times on paper as requested.

"That does look very much like your signature", I said. "Are you sure it isn't yours?"

"Yes, it does look the same. But it's not" he insisted.

"Are you prepared to make a statement to that effect; to say this with certainty?"

"Yes I am". He did.

I reported to Sun Alliance and tried to throw some light on the situation. It looked like someone was possibly cheating 'Pat'.

I tried to phone the offices of BritWindows. I resorted to a passing visit. The warehouse unit was unoccupied. He wasn't there.

"Any idea when someone's in", I asked a guy outside the neighbouring unit. "I haven't seen him in weeks. He's had loads of callers. People who've paid the 10% down payment and never had the job done".

"I've no idea where he is", said another guy.

Mr X and BritWindows appeared to be a bit dodgy!

216

I visited the police station and spoke with a couple of detectives who 'suggested' that I might find Mr. X in the village of Little Hobgoblin. I made some enquiries at the post office in Little Hobgoblin. "Yes. I know where he lives" said the lady in the post office.

I visited the house but there was no reply at the door. I left a calling card through the letter box.

"I'm trying to get in touch with Mr X", I told a nosey neighbour. "You should try up there", pointing to a house up the road.

I did. Mrs X was staying there. I was told by the woman at the door that she had left him and I was given a cold reception. I didn't ask any more questions but I did a credit check on Mr X and found out that he had had over £1/2 million in Court judgements made against him under different company names.

The police had also suggested that Mr Y of Frod Finance might be able to tell me about him. I spoke with Mr Y and he told me that Mr X was suspected of getting rid of his financed car by selling it to a local car breakers - dodgy dodging – he owed money to the finance company and had presumably made an insurance claim for the missing vehicle.

Sun Alliance agreed with my suggestion that this matter might be best put in the hands of the police. 'Postman Pat' also agreed. I did so.

Mr X was arrested, but then visited 'Pat's' house demanding that he be allowed to fit the window. He was ready and willing he insisted. 'Pat' phoned me about this. He was a nice normal guy and was obviously very easily manipulated. He was obviously a weak man who could probably be persuaded to do or say anything (that would turn out to be Mr X's argument).

'Postman Pat' told me that he had hidden in the house when Mr X called but that he felt very uncomfortable about the position he was in. "I think I'll let him fit the window. What do you think?"

I was quietly horrified that he could contemplate letting the man that he had accused of forging his signature fit his window and that Mr. X could get off the hook by intimidating him. But I could not take a position on this matter and so very carefully and deliberately suggested to 'Pat' that if he was happy to have the man back in his house, despite all that had happened, then it was entirely up to him. 'Pat' decided against.

217

'Pat' had his windows fitted by another contractor and I was left to try to get money back from Mr X. I sent a letter and nothing more. There was little point in my view.

Nearly a year later I received a telephone call from a chief inspector of police who had on a number of occasions appointed me to investigate claims made against the police force. I had done work for several police authorities. He told me that the police were being sued by Mr X.

It transpired that Mr X had appeared in Court only to be told by the Crown Prosecution Service that the case was being dropped, because the handwriting experts report could not indicate that the signature on the mandate was written by Mr X, who had denied it.

Mr X was suing the police -throwing the book at them- and subsequently I heard that he was suing Sun Alliance and my company for defamation. The audacity, I thought.

Apparently Mr X had repeatedly appeared before the Criminal Court, and had received significant press interest, despite the fact that the handwriting experts report, that indicated that the case could not be proven, lay forgotten/concealed or lost in a CID office drawer. This was not good; policemen were under attack. The Force was being sued. Mr X counter attacked.

I helped with enquiries but it was not until several years later, when I was behind my desk in Jakarta that I received the call to attend Court in London. This guy was a vengeance machine – relentless, determined and he had lots of staying power!

I had no fears worries or concerns about my actions, but I realised how little I could remember. How was I going to be a witness?

The trial date was set. I landed at Heathrow at about 7.00am on the Friday morning. I travelled directly to the barristers Inns in London and sat with the barrister throughout the day answering questions and recapping on events. I left their offices at about 5.00pm and took a train back to Coventry with three bundles of documents under my arm to study before the commencement of the trial on the Monday morning, but I had to meet again with the barrister on the Sunday afternoon to read over the prepared statement, alter or add to detail given and sign it. I had remembered a little more during the short break, I could think of little else despite trying to relax with my family, including Nikki, who was in the UK at the time. I booked in to The Strand Palace Hotel before the Sunday afternoon meeting.

218

After the meeting I went back to my hotel room to try and relax. I didn't sleep much and on the Monday morning arrived at the Royal Courts of Justice at 9.00am after a good breakfast. I had been told that I was likely to give evidence on the fourth day of a five day hearing, but that I should sit in Court every day to hear the progress of the trial, and read the bundle of papers every evening.

After the twelve person jury were sworn in there was a very powerful opening address by Mr X that impressed the judge and must have impressed the jury. I actually started to worry!

To our barrister the judge said words to the effect, "I do hope you have a convincing explanation for this dreadful state of affairs."

I had heard a very convincing and sad story that had not only the jury, but everyone, feeling very sorry for Mr X. The jury and gallery were in his pocket. He had painted a very bleak and convincing picture indeed. How could this happen?

Quite simple really; produce a plausible conspiracy theory, add some belief built on paranoia, exploit the weaknesses of 'Postman Pat', and present the case yourself, with the help of a lawyer. Oh, and add some pretty damning truth to the story too.

It was not too difficult, when I heard his slant on the facts, to understand how the case had got this far. His case was dressed beautifully and accommodatingly. I could see how someone who had not heard the contrary view might see it. It looked dreadful

1. I had persuaded 'Postman Pat' that X was a crook.

2. I had encouraged him to believe that X had forged his signature and persuaded him to make a statement indicating his willingness to take the matter to police.

3. I had told him not to allow X to do the repair work. It would damage the case against him.

4. I had conspired with police, the Sun Alliance Claims Manager and others to discredit him and bring him before the Courts. The police 'had it in for him' based on previous dealings.

5. My actions were motivated by my wish to get at him for causing me difficulties with my boss five years earlier.

It was chillingly plausible had it not been for the other side of the story. It was a frightening position to be in and an example of how someone can easily be framed, or put in a position that looks worse than it is. It was a lesson I'd already learnt at the hands of 'bent cops'.

How could a perfectly conducted, albeit incomplete investigation on my behalf, undertaken with integrity and care, result in me becoming a target for him? Could I become a victim of injustice?

I was knackered after nearly twenty hours of travel and spending all that Friday going over my testimony with the barrister. During discussion things started to come back to me. After a short breather I returned to the barristers chambers on the Sunday afternoon, completed a written statement and lived and breathed the entire case for three days. I was to give evidence on the Thursday morning. I was mentally exhausted.

Witness after witness had appeared. It was day four and I spent most of it in the witness box under oath. I was cross-examined at length. It had been explained to me, and could hardly have escaped my notice, that it was my evidence that was crucial, and the focus. The barrister told me the case would hinge on my evidence...thanks for the added pressure!

furthermore, it had not escaped my attention that X had been building a case around me as the central conspirator in a plot to discredit him and his business. In fact to fabricate a fraud and forgery case against him! Nobody had suggested it, but if he got away with this I might end up in the dock myself!!!!

It really is amazing what you forget to say, and how to say it, when you are under intense pressure. You have to get it right. There is no second chance. If you don't say it, and the prompting from the barrister fails to hit the spot...low and behold...you're sunk.

As it happened, I did forget to say a lot and parted from the script. The barrister didn't need to prompt me, I was fired up by this arsehole and amazingly I found myself remembering stuff that I had not previously remembered. My evidence destroyed him. I could see the jury rapidly seeing sense. It was swinging dramatically in our/my favour. Manipulated facts were now making sense when presented from my own point of view.

"Mr X, are you suggesting to me that because I had felt bitter about having been overruled by my boss when dealing with your insurance claim, that I waited five years,

220

and when I saw the opportunity to exact revenge on you I created a situation whereby you would end up in Crown Court facing possible imprisonment?"

"Yes I am" Mr X declared to the Court.

"Then I put it to you Mr X that it was in fact you who had seen the opportunity after five years to have a swipe at me"! In the corner of my eye I saw a member of the jury nod approvingly. His case was crumbling and his own dodgy dealings were being revealed.

Of course it was more complicated than that but it caused X to break down in tears. The game was up; a technical knockout in 'Round 15'.

The following morning – day five – the judge gave his judgment summary. Vindication was important to me; particularly given the intense personal attack on me, my honesty and integrity. He said exactly what I wanted.

"This is a very distressing case ....there has been gross incompetence and negligence on the part of the police. A report from the forensic handwriting expert lay in a police file undisclosed and forgotten, for eight months. A report which established the claimant's innocence.........The claimant has got into his head a firm belief that Mr B of Sun Alliance and Mr Wakefield of CCS, the Loss Adjuster, had no honest belief that there was a strong suspicion that the complainant had forged the signature of an insured on an authority to pay and had defrauded Sun Alliance......it was put to Mr Wakefield that they were motivated by predominant improper motives; Mr B was motivated by a wish to recoup Sun Alliances outlay and Mr Wakefield was motivated by revenge because some four and a half years earlier his disallowance of Mr X's claim in respect of computer software following theft of hardware was overruled by his manager............I hope, following the long evidence in chief and in cross examination of Mr B and Mr Wakefield, Mr X will upon reflection come to accept that his accusations are far-fetched and bordering on the unreal...............I have reached the conclusion having again pondered on the matter overnight (I expressed during argument yesterday my strong provisional view) and having heard further submissions this morning, that in my judgement it is my duty to withdraw the case from the jury.............."

Game, set and match!

I cancelled my afternoon flight. I had a celebratory drink in the pub with the legal team, and then went home to Coventry with Nikki. I had asked her to come down and support me. I needed her. She wasn't keen to travel down to London, but for the day of

221

my testimony she did. She later stated that she had not realised the gravity of the matter until she arrived to sit in the gallery to hear my evidence. She really was visibly shaken by the experience, and needless to say so was I. I was traumatised.

I flew back to Jakarta on the Sunday…mentally exhausted. I went back in the office Tuesday morning bright and early. What a horrific experience; your entire reputation in the balance. It was another of those occasions when circumstances can appear so contrary to the reality when packaged well. Maybe that's what had driven him so doggedly?

What is really frightening about this tale is that it might, if I had not been a good calm witness under examination, or had not remembered the reasons for certain of my actions, turned out quite differently. I might have faced trial for perjury, perverting the course of justice and conspiracy. I might now have been seated in a cell telling a quite different story!

Mr X had a legal bill of £120,000 and I…………………..left with nothing! Goodbye.

Respect

You have read something about business relationships that may have given you the impression that there was a 'them and us' stand-off in the office. Let me put right any misunderstanding. We were a good team and had good relations; we were friends really.

In February 2003 I left Indonesia with a proud track record, and an elevated reputation. I had become a respected businessman; doing it my way. I was an Associate of the Singapore Institute of Arbitrators and had joined the Association for Conflict Resolution; a Washington DC based organisation dedicated to enhancing the practice and understanding of conflict resolution, with my mediation skills in mind. I had matured as a man and a businessman.

The business relationship between Handoko and I had soured some 18 months earlier when he was forced to announce the opening of a second office in Surabaya. He didn't want to, and blamed me. He shouted me down during a managers meeting. His rage caused him great loss of face and respect, and caused me embarrassment, but I didn't bite. Handoko later apologised and I 'forgave him' Indonesian style. I knew then that Handoko had fallen prey to the Peters Principal; he was frightened of losing control, and he believed that a distant second office meant that. It didn't as it turned out.

222

I had made a positive impression on the business in Indonesia and Handoko recognised my contribution and demonstrated his appreciation with a surprise party at his home when he presented me with a very expensive TAG Hauer wristwatch; a parting gift from the staff. That had never happened before. Paul gifted me a Mont Blanc pen, but most importantly he had given me the honour of being his 'best man'. I would miss my colleagues but I was ready to move on. I have great respect for my old friends in Indonesia.

PART THREE

Chapter Seventeen
Adventure; Food and Travel

I know it's a cliché, but life has its ups and downs, and before I write about my basement downs, I write about some of the memorable experiences during my travels, as a series of light diversions.

Big Cats and Elephant

If you have never read an account of a face to face confrontation with a man-eating tiger I can highly recommend that you read, 'Man Eaters of Kumaon' by Jim Corbett. I read it on the northbound train from Delhi to a National Park that bears his name. I was about to visit the territory that Jim Corbett writes about in his book. The places where, as a famous tiger hunter in the 1920's, he tracked down and killed man-eating tigers and leopards.

It was in October, during my Comex travels, at the end of the rainy monsoon season. The vegetation was thick and the elephant grass long. The roads in and around the park had collapsed and subsided as a result of the flooding. The park was closed, but, as a white, and a British face, we managed to get special permission to enter the park; albeit at our own risk. I say we, I was travelling with Charles Skewalski, a friend from Sheffield.

There was no transport and we were given a guide to walk us the sixteen miles to the nearest forest rest house known as Dikala. It was one of the most thrilling experiences that I have ever had in the wild. We had a single carbine rifle, an Enfield I believe, a bag and strong walking boots. Walking through sixteen miles of Indian forest after a monsoon was no easy thing, believe me, and I was a fit and experienced walker. No lack of stamina.

We were both mad keen on seeing wildlife and in particular the tiger. In case you are in anticipation, despite these efforts, and similar efforts in Sumatra, I never did get to see a tiger in the wild, but the very quest to see one, and the evidence of one being close to us was thrilling in itself.

To have read the book by Jim Corbett, and to have had an insight into the mind and cunning of the tiger in advance of this adventure, gave me a wonderful sense of excitement mingled with fear. I was apprehensive yet raring to go. The book was as much about the forest and its dangers as the tigers itself. Reading the book helped me feel the dangers of the forest as well as appreciate its beauty.

The buzz that I got from our guide showing us a fresh 'pug mark' in our path and indicating that it was that of a tiger, not half an hour earlier, sent a shiver down my spine. I knew that the tiger might be watching us at that very moment, and that it would never show itself – until it was too late. I knew that the rifle we had could be no real defence against a hunting tiger. It was an incredible sensation; one that people seldom experience.

We did view animals on that walk; garial, deer, monkey, monitor lizard and snake but not the tiger.

We stopped the night in Dhakala and had expected to return to the lodge by elephant the following day, but as we approached the rest house we saw the hind quarter of two elephant walking away in the distance. I can therefore quite genuinely say, 'we missed the last elephant'!

We returned the sixteen miles on foot, but not until we had had a great night's sleep at the rest house and been gifted with plaster cast 'pug marks' by the ranger. We had spent a long evening drinking potato whiskey and viewing photographs of tiger trophies.

I was almost equally keen to see leopard when at Wilpattu National Park in Sri Lanka. There is something about dense undergrowth in the forests of India and Sri Lanka that produces an atmosphere that I could not find in Africa. Viewing of animals I found to be much easier in Africa but the forest enveloped me. Whatever lurked beyond was possibly close and I constantly felt that I was being watched.

You never know when or what will appear, just that it will be there one minute and gone the next. I remember being driven along a single path in Wilpattu that was just wide enough to take the Land Rover. I recall the branches of trees bending against the front of the vehicle and sometimes flicking into the vehicle itself. The driver explained to us that, the day before some German tourists had been driving along that very same track when an elephant appeared on the track in front of them. One of the German tourists was killed and the other people injured when the vehicle was turned over by the elephant. Again, I have to say this gave me another buzz, and I think terrified Nikki. When I read an article in the Daily Newspaper I was able to verify what I thought might be a fictitious story.

Although Africa did not have some of the same surprise element of these Asian forests, we had an interesting experience with elephants in Tsavo East in Kenya; this time first hand and really quite life threatening. We had left the Voi Forest Rest House before daybreak on route to see what our guide described as 'the crocodilly' and ' the hippoow' I was driving a vehicle that was neither suitable for mud tracks or indeed any form of off road travel. It was just a saloon. It was a very rough very uneven and very narrow track. There was no going back. It was a windy track with thick bush either side.

I had a camera on my lap as I drove, just in case a photo presented itself. We were nearing the river when we came out of some thicket into a grassy open area to my right. There, standing before us were these huge elephants. A cow elephant moved a step backward and opened its massive ears, whilst a calf scuttled off behind the cow. A gigantic, and I'm not exaggerating, gigantic, bull elephant came past the cow and toward us, as the cow turned to follow the calf. These great wings opened each side of this demon; its tusks, were I am sure, throwing out balls of fire. It stopped coming forward (thank God). It was no more than 25 yards away. It was roaring. Posturing, and stepping backward and forward, its trunk being thrown about as if elastic.

It seemed to be content to hold its ground while the family fled, until that is, to Nikki's dismay, I decided, somewhat foolishly, to stop and pick up my camera. There was more than a hint of concern as the guide said, 'keep going keep going' and Nikki reiterated, 'Yes David keep going he doesn't look too happy'. What a moment! We had caught each other by surprise and oh what an exciting response we got. A wee bit heart stopping, but exciting.

I had one or two more great experiences with elephant; a stand-off between an elephant and a pride of lions. It was in Pilansberg National Park in South Africa. I was working in Johannesburg at the time and had taken a weekend off. The Park was perfect for viewing wild animals because it was relatively small, about ten miles across, and was within the caldera of a volcano, that provided a natural bowl in which the animals were numerous and concentrated. It was near Sun City and therefore popular with tourists, and didn't quite have the same feel to it as the other places I had visited.

Elephants were in abundance here and a couple of rogue bull elephants were the cause of a number of attacks. They were searching for their own herds apparently. It is one of these elephants that we encountered as a guide and I were trying to leave the area that evening. The elephant was in the road ahead. Two vehicles were reversing as the elephant advanced. He didn't look happy. The car I had hired was being driven by the guide. He stalled it. He couldn't start it up. I started to panic a little (quietly of course). He managed to get it going as the last of the retreating vehicles reversed past us at high speed! He thankfully followed. However the elephant kept coming, albeit at a light trot.

228

He was in charge of the road. We must have been pushed back several hundred yards before the elephant decided to leave the road and go into the bush.

A couple of weeks later, after I had visited other offices in Africa, I returned to Jo'burg where a colleague from the office offered to take me back out to view animals again – I hadn't seen a leopard or cheetah! Again as we were about to leave the area there was a hold up ahead. Two to three vehicles had stopped on the side of the road. Something interesting was happening. We pulled along-side, sure enough, in the bush, the other side of a stream, stood a very irate elephant. Facing it, and on the incline beyond, sat, unmoved, but roaring, several female lion. Unfortunately, as darkness fell, we could not wait around to see the outcome, but for a good 20 minutes we viewed the increasingly vocal stand-off and intriguing inability of either side to back down. It became more ferocious, the lion to the front of the elephant, standing from its prone position several times, to roar, before lying down again. It would not let the elephant pass. The other lions had seemed to be spectators, but frustratingly I will never know the outcome. There is no end to the story. It was too dangerous to stay where we were, and in any case the view faded with the sun, and we were in no position to watch in the open.

I have since learnt that the 'stand-off' could have lasted for hours, and even resulted in the death of the elephant had they been hungry and sufficient in number to bring it down. My South African friends had never seen anything like it themselves.

I have always been interested in wildlife, and to have had such great experiences makes me feel very lucky and privileged. I have not given up hope of seeing a wild tiger, and one day hope to return to India with the intention of doing just that.

I particularly enjoyed, as a pure safari experience, my time in Kenya. At the police club in Nairobi I met Buddy Van Rensburg, Assistant Commissioner. He was a South African. He introduced me to Ziggy Joshat, who owned African Tours and Hotels, a travel company. Ziggy loaned me a car, and Nikki and I, following his itinerary, travelled the several miles down to Mombasa, and then south down the coast to Tradewinds.

He arranged for us to stop at Voi Safari Lodge on route. It seemed surreal to see triangular roadside warning signs containing the shape of an elephant! We spent a couple of days at Voi, viewing animals, in the bush and at the waterhole nearby in the evenings, before heading for a beach holiday at Tradewinds.

On the lodge terrace, as we were eating a meal, little hyrax, cute chinchilla type animals sat beside us. The nearest relative to the little hyrax is apparently the elephant!

229

The meal on the terrace under setting sun at Voi Safari Lodge, in Kenya and the joy that the friendly little hyrax gave me reminds me also of breakfast on the terrace in Kingston, Jamaica, when a tiny hummingbird about half the size of a wren, took nectar from a flower alongside the breakfast table. I am reminded also of the sight of the comical little clown fish playing in the anemone on the coral reefs of Indonesia.

After a relaxing time on the white sands of the east coast of Africa we travelled back from Mombasa by train. What a fabulous old colonial train it was, and at that time, one of the great train journeys of the World.

Nature

The most peaceful of nature's experiences can be found in New Zealand where there are no poisonous snakes or spiders – no nasties at all really. We saw beautiful animals in New Zealand in the year of our 25th Wedding Anniversary – sperm whale, penguins, albatross. The cutest was a little bird that mimicked the songs and sounds of all other birds. The sound was quite amazing; a remarkable medley of bird songs.

One of the greatest thrills is to have is a wild bird taking food from your hand. On Christmas Island, the one in the Indian Ocean - not the radioactive Pacific variety, I came as close to nature as possible. The diving was sensational, and the birdlife incredible. There are creatures on this island that exist nowhere else in the World. It is famed as 'The Kingdom of the Crabs', and the migration of over 100 million red crabs takes place around November / December each year. I was lucky enough to see it and I was actually on the island for Christmas!

Feeding wild birds on Christmas Island was a cinch. The birds had no reason to be frightened because there were few humans and they were not attacked by them.

The Nasties

Snakes and spiders have always given me the willies. I remember that as a young policeman I was called to a house in Sutton Coldfield where the occupier had reported finding a strange looking snake in the garden.

I was a confident young man, and mindful of the need to instil in others, a confidence in me. With a straight back, with shoulders drawn back, I strode through the front door toward the rear kitchen door and into the garden beyond. As I walked I received the report from the woman occupier as she followed me into the garden, with her children following like ducklings.

I walked along the narrow rose bush lined pathway toward the lawn area at the top of the garden, the family still following. As I approached the lawn a two foot long snake slithered toward me. I turned, on the march, and faced the oncoming family still unaware of my need to retreat at high speed. I bundled them back toward the house with a close eye over my shoulder. My dignity, poise and confidence instilling presence was in tatters. My humiliation was only partly disguised by my attempt to laugh. I never did find out what kind of snake that was.

I remember walking out from our apartment block in Happy Valley, Hong Kong shortly after a typhoon had hit the island and there was debris all over the approach road. I was walking to the end of the road to catch a taxi in to work. Taxi was a cheap and very convenient way to travel.

A branch collapsed in front of me and there was a great thud on the tarmac surface of the road in front of me. I immediately thought it was a falling branch but this large snake, maybe two metres in length, slithered out from the debris and across my path no more than a pace in front of me. I had a minor palpitation and it had gone. I am told it was probably a rat snake – harmless!

Snake shops are commonplace in Hong Kong. I visited one with Nikki and we ate snake soup around a table. There were cages to three sides and an open frontage. A bald headed man, straight out of a Kung Fu movie, was unloading cobra from the rear of a lorry on the street. Some were loose and he popped them into bags. He had wounds all over his hands and arms from bites and I was told that he was immune to the venom.

The cages were full of snakes of various kinds and the owner produced a Banded Krait that he placed on the table in front of us. He explained that most of the snakes were de-fanged if poisonous but that they didn't bother with the Krait because they were so docile. Had this one been defanged, I asked. No. Nikki flinched. I was reassured. It was motionless. Was it alive I thought? I was encouraged to prod it to prove it was. I did. It moved a little. The Banded Krait was responsible for more bites and deaths in Hong Kong than any other snake. Why? It is nocturnal and sleeps in the heat of the sun on pathways during the day. That was my closest encounter with a poisonous snake. I had bullied it into moving!

231

Incidentally, snake is extremely tasty, like the best chicken you ever tasted, and I ate it as a soup with sweet corn almost every working winter's day.

I have had experiences with baby cobra on the early morning golf course greens in Indonesia. Their teeth can't penetrate the skin so they are quite harmless, but a good check in the hole is always worthwhile if the caddy is not there to do the job for you.

I had a close call with a snake on Corfu. I went for a walk in the hills overlooking Kassiopi. It was a very active time of year for snakes and I had been warned to take care. I walked through the olive groves toward the top of the hill. Nets were set out beneath the trees.

I had already seen one, obviously poisonous snake, small and neatly curled in a gap in a dry stone wall that I was about to lean against. There was much evidence of their presence; shed skins and rustling in the grass as I approached. I saw a tortoise struggling across the path. It was a hive of reptilian activity.

I bent down to pick a couple of fallen olives from the netting that was covering the low vegetation below the trees. As I did so a snake struck at me. The netting lifted against my hand. The netting had prevented me from being bitten. I saw the snake very briefly as it slid away.

In Kemang, in Jakarta, at my favourite Indian Restaurant cum bar, a 16' long python was found in the drain at the rear of the restaurant adjacent the stream. It was available for viewing, in a cardboard box, when I called in for a drink before returning home from work.

Snakes were quite commonly found in gardens and homes in Jakarta but I never saw one – thankfully!

A friend and colleague of mine, Aris, told me of his experience when he was last at a smelting factory that we were visiting in Sulawesi. He was billeted in an old workers hut. Falling asleep, and in semi consciousness, he was suddenly awakened by debris falling from the ceiling onto his bed. He switched the bedside light on to see a massive python slithering off the bed and disappearing under the wardrobe. The ceiling had collapsed under the weight of the snake.
Snakes in Indonesia are amongst the biggest in the World and pythons in excess of 20' long have been seen and caught. The biggest are in the jungles of Sulewesi and Sumatra. At this particular smelting works, on the bank of the Soroako Lake, a long picture graced

the canteen wall. Ten men, standing side by side, were photographed holding a giant python.

Newspapers in Indonesia pull no punches and satisfied the curiosity of an interested public. They were not inhibited by censorship of gory photographs. I remember seeing in a newspaper a graphically gruesome photo of a snake being carried back to a Sumatran village by several men. The snake was still alive and digesting a missing thirteen year old boy that had strayed out of the village.

Another photo was of a crocodile that had been hoisted, dead, onto a boat. It had been cut open whilst hanging, and inside you could see the remains of a middle aged man that had taken his final fishing trip. The crocodile was responsible for several deaths. That incident had occurred just a few weeks before I took a trip on that same river.

I had been flown in to the small island of Taripan by a mining company owned plane from Balakpan, Kalimantan (Borneo). The island had been the scene of fierce fighting between Japanese and Aussies in the War. I was to travel for some five hours up river by boat where I would complete my journey for a bumpy couple of hours by four wheel drive to an open cast coal mine. The river was the only way in. The river was low. It was used by illegal loggers and logs protruded from the river bed below, some above and some just below the water line like great poles.

Apart from the boatman I was the only person on board. Just as well; there was little room for a third person. He fully opened the throttle and never attempted to slow down, weaving in and out of those logs that could be seen. My imagination took hold of me and I started to think about the implications of hitting one of the logs, sinking and being eaten by one of these giant crocodiles. I did mention my concerns to him but he just laughed, and I never mentioned it again – I didn't want to sound like a wus!

The journey was uncomfortable in more ways than one. It was extremely hot and humid. The boat bounced off the water and my buttocks were crying out for a cushion – I was in pain. We didn't see another soul for the entire five hours on that little speedboat! Not even a village. Just thick jungle.

On a trip to Mt Bromo in the east, Nikki went to the loo in our hotel room. The peace was broken by a cry, and Nikki shot out of the loo with her knickers round her knees. She had been contemplating on the loo, as one does, and casually glanced to her side, to face, sitting on the shelf, a bright green coloured frog. Their eyes met in horror, nerves cracked and both hopped off in different directions! Oh we did laugh.

233

Spiders and centipedes have always freaked me out. I have a photograph of a ten inch long centipede that I found in my office in Wanchai police station in Hong Kong. They can give a very nasty bite.

The biggest spider I ever saw, and on numerous occasions as they were quite common in Asia, was the black and yellow coloured wood/bamboo spider. They are commonly seen on webs crossing from telegraphs poles to the wires, but also have a habit of webbing across pathways. I have seen them the size of the average car steering wheel, tip of leg to tip of leg, although most are much smaller. They are harmless but scary looking.

When I overcame my fear of going under water, and learnt to scuba dive, I opened my life up to a whole new underwater experience.

Diving

I never really took to water although I learnt to swim at an early age and passed my bronze life saving award when in the Police Cadets and went on to become a proficient canoeist completing the Boys Club 100 mile canoe test on the River Severn in a day and a half. Being underwater was not my thing, and I was definitely not a water baby.

My determination to scuba dive was a natural extension of my need to experience the World; two thirds of it is underwater. If I didn't dive in Indonesia I was squandering a wonderful opportunity to see the underworld in one of its richest corners.

I was, as usual, a slow learner. I sat on the bottom of a pool in the back garden of a house in Kemang, where a Chinese Indonesian girl had the patience to teach me, 'the Padi way'.

My nephew, Liam, was an accomplished, experienced diver and instructed to a superior, British Sub Aqua Club standard, in cold flooded quarries of Britain. No way José! Not for me. Only the basics, and only in warm water thank you! Fair weather golfer and warm water diver – that's me.

I dived mainly on the Seribu islands, 1000 islands about 100 miles off Jakarta. Not great diving but still tropical and still capable of springing some surprises. Mike, a friend of Brads, owned two ex Japanese coastal patrol boats that had been complete with fast pursuit boat ramps from the rear. He had stiffened up the ramp deck, and the upper deck became a bar and restaurant. The boat had about half a dozen double bunk cabins and a large crew to cater for guests.

The Oceanic Explorer was a classy well fitted dive boat with a hint of 'Daddy's yacht' about it. Mike would take friends out for long weekends during 'the troubles', at cost only. We would sleep, eat drink and dance on the boat, diving when and wherever we wanted. It was wonderful fun. I also dived in Bali, the Sunda Straits, Lombok, Christmas Island and Sulawesi.

I will never ever regret plucking up the courage to dive, although I subsequently learnt that much of what you see when you scuba dive can be seen by simply snorkelling. Reefs are shallow and colourful. Most sea life lives or visits the reef. The deeper you dive the fewer colours you can see. A 120 ft dive is great, but so is a 30' dive, or a 10' snorkel dive.

I had some amazing experiences none more memorable than my week on Christmas Island. How sad that I have nobody to reminisce with. Nikki wanted to return to the UK, and everyone else had something else planned for Christmas. I had invitations, but if I was to spend Christmas away from family, I preferred to do something really unusual and different. I spent Christmas on Christmas Island, about 100 miles off the South Coast of Java, in the Indian Ocean.

Christmas Island was Australian owned. They had plans to build a rocket launch facility on the island, that Indonesia understandably objected to, but otherwise it was a territorial outback more of zoological fame than anything else. It was rich in phosphate, and mining was the reason the Aussies occupied it.

The Indonesian cronies, under Soeharto, found a novel use for the place; it was just a short distance outside Indonesian territorial waters. They built a large casino and hotel complex on the island for wealthy Indonesians to visit, but this wasn't all it seemed. It was more a money laundering facility. The Australian government must have known what was happening, but they got tax from it all. It has been said that more money passed through this single island casino, an island with a population of just 1,500 including a 700 floating population, than passed through all the casinos of Las Vegas!

I had two dive trips during my week on the island, one with a dive boat owned by a German guy, the other one owned by Japanese. Christmas Day morning I was with the Jap and the research botanists and zoologists that were based on the island. We drank champagne and ate strawberries onboard afterward. I saw some very special and secret places on that trip.

I have never dived in any seriously dangerous waters insofar as currents are concerned. I tended to stick to drift and wall dives, or in calmer waters, where you could sometimes just as well snorkel. The wall dives on Christmas Island are astonishing. There are shear drops into the Java Trench, the deepest waters in the ocean. The trench is said to be three miles deep; deeper than the Grand Canyon.

The waters are visited by Whale Sharks, Mantas and a kaleidoscope of fish of all sizes; some gigantic. Because of the walls, all the deep water is close to shore. One particular fish that a fishing boat had landed was unidentified – possibly a new species! It looked weird and was certainly a deep water fish.

I had my close encounter with bronze whaler sharks on my second dive – it happened so quickly that I only felt frightened by these huge killers after they had passed me- too late to be a problem.

I fished for tuna and one day, off a local boat, but every fish I hooked was taken by a shark. The waters were alive with fish; all assembled for one of the greatest feeding times in nature – the migration of the red land crabs of Christmas Island. It occurs annually and is one of the natural wonders of the world.

Some 100 -120 million crabs spawn in the ocean around the island, which is just about ten miles long and three to four wide. The females head off to the beach followed by the males. They mate, the males return inland, and the females stay close to the beach waiting for a full moon and the right conditions to drop their eggs in the sea. After Christmas, I spent an entire night watching the spectacle from a small beach close to the settlement. I filmed it. The water was alive with tiny fish, there to eat the eggs, little fish were there to eat the tiny fish and bigger fish were there to eat the smaller fish; all close inshore so that just twenty five metres off shore there was intense shark activity. Crabs marched shoulder to shoulder down to the beach. There were wall to wall crabs.

This incredible sight is one of my most treasured memories but is tinged with disappointment that I had nobody to share them with.

David Attenborough made a tremendous documentary about it; The Kingdom of the Crabs. You should watch it. The crabs are everywhere. You cannot avoid killing them. They crab their way through gardens, through homes, across roads, golf courses, through offices and the school. They can be found in just about every room or orifices in any building. Cycling is a nightmare –they could have you off your bike! Driving results in inevitable deaths, and when the babies come back from the sea the place is carpeted in red.

The island is alive with animal activity from the (fast becoming boring) red crabs, to the rare blue crabs, Golden Bosunbird and Frigate Birds. I went on a Hash House Harriers run on Christmas Eve. I hop scotched through the crabs over about four miles before settling down to the barbie and beer. There was a poor attendance on that run. Most were food poisoned from the last run – some were in hospital. One of the local gastronomic experts had incorrectly cooked a blue tuna – poisonous if not cooked properly! He had returned to the mainland for Christmas unscathed but there was plenty of banter style condemnation in his absence.

Christmas Day was difficult despite the morning dive experience. Several people had asked me for dinner (Aussie style barbie) but I declined. I did pop into a couple of homes for a drink in the afternoon but otherwise kept myself to myself. An emotional moment was when I opened a bite size Christmas cake sent to me by Zoe. It was a lonely day. TV reception was not good on my hotel room TV so I didn't watch TV. I had a couple of glasses of wine and went for a walk.

The Crabs

I know I might be labouring the point but the crab experience was mind-blowing. Until I arrived on Christmas Island I'd never suffered with crabs!

The crabs were everywhere and apart from directing you to any of the numerous documentaries filmed on the island I can only help you to image the nuisance they cause during their migration by likening it to a flying ant infestation. They were in the roads, on the pavements, in the gardens, shops, pubs and hotels. They were in the bedrooms, the kitchens, the sitting rooms, and the loos, on the curtains the settees and the beds, they were everywhere.

I hired a car for the first part of my week and drove around the island. At first I would weave the car around the crabs like a drunken driver but then realised that there was no avoiding them. Crunch, crunch, crunch. I soon grew to ignore and then forget the carnage beneath the wheels.

237

During the second part of the week I hired a pedal cycle. I wish it had been a mountain bike! I started to weave again. The bigger crabs could have you off the bike. In fact I'm sure my front wheel was lifted off the ground when I paused and parked up to admire a view. It was worse walking about.

You know how a crab has that attitude problem. Approach it and its hands go up like a sumo wrestler poised to engage. Then it moves from side to side as you challenge it; never too sure when to make a run for it and in which direction it should run. Well image several of these encounters before you can get from your hotel room to the bar. You start to get really pissed off.

I did my best to enjoy my short stay on Christmas Island in harmony with the crabs. I didn't want to hurt them.

My patience was tested on the golf course. I was invited to play by a couple of club members but decided to play a round on my Jack Jones beforehand. There were special local rules for the crabs. The red crabs were a nuisance but the massive robber crabs, though much rarer (and very edible), were the real danger. They could crack open a coconut to eat the flesh in a few minutes. If they grabbed your ball you were in trouble!

But the robber crabs were slow and disinterested. The red crabs were mischievous little shits and I grew to hate them. I tried desperately to put up with them on the greens. I would politely marshal them off my 'line' only to take up my position addressing the ball and find they had walked back onto the 'line'. It seemed that they were doing it deliberately. They didn't seem to be heading into any particular direction; the shops, the beach, the woods. They were just being naughty.

By the time I was on the 14th green I was kicking them off into the rough and delighting at their motionless flight. By the 18th I was pitching them into the sand with a five iron. The little baskets were just spoil sports. I will never forgive one small one that popped out of the hole just as the ball was about to drop. It was early on in the round, when I still had the patience to give him a piece of my mind rather than resort to violence.

Food

My earliest experience of bad food came to me courtesy of Pete Wilford. A gang of us had decided to drive over to Sweden for a holiday. It was 1971. John Hamer drove in his car and I drove in my 1964 Hillman Minx, Uncle Maurice's old car. We camped next to the beach in Gothenburg and Pete had decided to cook this particularly strange and horrible dish. He called it Beef Stroganoff and gave us an understanding as to why it was so called. I have photographic evidence of an attempt by the dish to 'struggle off' the plate.

We all turned our plates upside down and the food stuck firmly to the plate. I am sure that it formed the basis for all the major selling adhesives on the market today! It was horrific!

When I was living in Hong Kong Nikki and I decided to take a holiday in The Philippines. We spent some time in Manila then decided to take a train north east to San Fernando on the Island of Luzon. It was an amazing train journey. During the journey, which was long and uncomfortable, we experienced Rail Food Philippine style. A young girl carrying an old cinema style snack tray around her neck and was serving, not confectionary and ice creams, but other strange foods, the most notable and popular of all, particularly amongst the children, being 'balot'.

Balot is essentially a salted duck egg. Nothing unheard of there, I hear you say. But the twist here is that the embryo of the egg is developed, so as to leave a tasty blood ring on the outside of the cute little kid's mouth! The sight, complete with crunchy sound effect left me speechless, and Nikki staring out through the window in an apparent effort to erase the memory from her mind and pretend she had never seen it. Even the Chinese find it disgusting.

When we arrived in San Fernando we travelled by motor bike and sidecar to our beachside hotel where, in complete contrast, we tasted a delicious fresh seafood platter. The meal had been landed, before our very eyes, just minutes earlier. Nothing fresher and nothing cheaper or more delicious. Amazing!

Anyhow, turning back to 'bad' food, experience and the two we had in Sri Lanka. A beautiful island and a people that are amongst the friendliest, hospitable and humble that I have ever met. For that reason the following events that represent the first of these 'bad food' experiences, are particularly distressing for me to explain. I am cringing at the thought of telling you this story.

In Colombo a local inspector of police had provided, for our benefit, the use of an unmarked police vehicle complete with driver and sergeant 'tourist' guide. They took us to Kandi, and upon our return the chief asked us to join him, his family and friends, for a meal at his beachside home.

My recollection is that a railway track ran between the beach and the house and that this track spoiled what was an otherwise idyllic beach setting on a beautiful evening. The home was quite large and charming; sparsely furnished without being unwelcoming. We arrived for the meal and seated ourselves with perhaps a half dozen other guests. Set out on the table before us was this fabulous looking array of food on a splendidly presented table. Around me were immaculately dressed couples; the women looking beautifully resplendent in their colourful saris. We were underdressed.

Everyone waited for Nikki and I to be seated before they sat down; we were the guests of honour. The food looked delicious and I had a real appetite. Most of it was fish. I set about loading the plate after Nikki had been helped to her normal modest and more cautious portion. Oh how I wish I had not declared my appetite, oh how I wish I had taken a smaller portion.

The others helped themselves to the food after Nikki and I had been served. I asked about the dishes as I was loading my plate. I was fascinated; and in my element, real, authentic Sri Lankan family food in a real family home on the West Coast of the Island under a setting sun. It was a real honour and a privilege. I eat, like the others, in the traditional way, with my fingers. Nikki was offered, and accepted, a knife and fork.

The food, mainly curried dishes, was stone cold. The fish full of tiny bones with no chance of extracting them; I simply can't cope with fish with bones in. I prided myself on being able to try, and struggle through, any food dish and situation in favour of good manners and 'not wishing to offend'. Here I was, this evening, meeting my demon, my wall. I needed Nikki to rescue the situation and yet I knew she was a fussy eater.

I tried a little bit of each dish to demonstrate interest and willing but, for the first time in my life, I actually found myself wrenching on the bones. I pretended that a little food had gone down the wrong way. I was offered water. I drank. It tried again. My mind was wondering to the thought of sickness. I was making myself worse, I felt extremely uncomfortable and only hoped that the red face caused by the onset of embarrassment, would be explained by the wrenching.

I wrenched again! Oh no. I managed to eat half the plate but made what I felt was a transparently untruthful excuse – I am full! No, I felt unwell! Oh God what had I said. I had lost it!

I was unusually quiet and 'felt' transparently very embarrassed. I imagined that my face was ruby red – it probably was. I decided that I would try to talk interestingly to deviate from the subject. While blundering through meaningless and trivial dribble my thoughts were on an escape route. 'Nikki please help' I thought.

Normally she would have made her excuses by now. She hadn't, and I had beaten her to it. In fact I had deliberately tried to beat her to it. I felt worse for doing so. 'Please Nikki, please Nikki, keep eating keep eating' I thought. Within moments of my declaration the predictable and overdue happened. Nikki said she was not hungry and couldn't eat any more. She had hardly eaten anything. 'Any desert?' 'No thanks'.

If that was not embarrassment enough things got worse. The entire table stopped eating because we had stopped eating. Please continue I insisted. They were having none of it. A table full of food lay cold that evening – not that it was ever hot! A walk perhaps?

I felt like crawling down into the floorboards and sliding my way out through the foundations of the house to an imaginary get - away car that would speed me back to my hotel bed, from where I would wake in a hot sweat, having suffered some terrible nightmare. I would then sigh with relief, smile and fall into a wonderfully deep and peaceful sleep. When at the table I think I did actually close my eyes, briefly and tightly, in disbelief at the embarrassing mess we were in.

I never recovered from the table embarrassment. I never regained any of my normal composure and, characteristically beat myself up about it. My memory of the after dinner events are hazy. I can't remember what Nikki did. She was probably inside with the women. I remember a short stroll along the beach, and taking a photograph with the host. I don't remember the visit being for long. I decided to use Nikki as an excuse and suggested that she had felt ill for much of the day, and we had even considered cancelling. "We should go. She will feel better in the morning!"

I knew that they knew the truth behind every excuse that was given. I truly believe that this may have been the most embarrassing evening I have ever had. Correction, it was definitely the most embarrassing evening of my life. I have, to this day, shuddered whenever I have thought about it. I did, and do, feel awful. They were such wonderful polite people who felt honoured, as I did, to be sitting around the same table. They did not deserve our ill mannered company. I feel worse because I lost their address and never even managed to write. Oh Dear. My worst dinner party of all time!

241

The second of these bad food Sri Lankan experiences is a somewhat easier account to tell because it was funny and it demonstrates the total commitment of the people to provide unbeatable service. Our hotel in Colombo was marvellous, very old and Victorian. It had a wonderful charm. The lift in the hotel was, like the rest of it, wooden panelled. A little man sat in the corner on a stool to operate the lift and drop you off at the right floor. That was his job, sitting in a lift and going up and down all day. It reminded me of the days when Owen Owen in Coventry had a lift attendant.

On our first day we used the lift and were dropped off in the dining room for breakfast. We ordered nothing exciting, just tea and toast, egg and bacon. The restaurant was beautifully presented and tables were beautifully laid out – but empty. We waited fully an hour, without complaint, for the breakfast to arrive. Again, stone cold bacon, stone cold egg and stone cold toast. The tea – surely not. Luke warm, very milky tea. There was no way in the world that I could complain to these people. No way in the World. The service, the attendants, the politeness was second to none in the world; pity about the food.

The final account of a food horror is set in Indonesia, where coincidentally the service is also superb (I once dropped a knife that was caught by a waiter before it hit the floor!).

You would seldom see any salad on a plate in Indonesia except in some hotels. They grew and ate very little of it. You would very rarely see it outside of Jakarta.

On this particular occasion we were outside Jakarta. Nikki and I were sat at a table with friends and a salad was on the menu. We decided to try it.

It looked absolutely delicious on the plate, and it was a real change, a treat. Not quite the British salad, not the full range, but there was lettuce, cucumber and onion. No sign of radish or beetroot or anything exciting.

Nikki was sitting opposite me eating into her salad with relish when during the course of the conversation I glanced down at Nikki's plate and I saw, walking across a lettuce leaf, a lime green coloured bug, bearing antenna that curled out from its head by at least an inch! The camouflage colouring was incredible but I did feel it necessary to point it out to Nikki – even if the other half dozen (God forbid) had been tasty! There was a shocked gasp of horror as knife and fork were dropped simultaneously before we all burst into laughter. At this point I looked down at my plate and saw a whole herd of them, but my plate was almost empty!

242

In the corner of my mouth I felt some movement. One of these bugs had refused to surrender. I again wrenched.

Trains, Boats and Planes

The train from Jakarta to Bandung in the mountains is a steep climb, and fun, but I've had some great train journeys. The train to the Chinese border from Kowloon, the wonderful steam train from Delhi to Moradabad on the way to the beautiful lakeside town of Nainital in the foothills of the Himalayas, with Everest as the backdrop, and the old Victorian colonial train from Mombasa to Nairobi in 1980, but the favourite, the most memorable of them all was the train from Manila to San Fernando in the Philippines. What a journey! What a wait! Two hours on the platform.....eat yer heart out British Rail travellers. It was a ten hour journey, stopping at every village - epic. About ten hours I recall – on bench seats amongst chickens and delightfully friendly natives. The journey that included an optional 'balot' snack! We had two train crashes on that journey to boot - both horse and carts at crossings, although how a train that slow could hit anything is beyond me. It was also memorable for the trip from the station to the beach hotel at San Fernando, by motorcycle and sidecar. I was so proud of Nikki in the side car that night - a true rough it traveller. She sat in that side car with a suitcase on her lap - what a sight! She didn't have to as she was offered the driver's waist!

It's great to have circumvented the World by aircraft, especially business class, but the truly momentous flights must have a thrill. Landing at Kai Tak airport in Hong Kong has provided more than enough thrills. If the pilot comes in too low, he hits the top and sides of buildings, too high, he overshoots the runway into the harbour. It was a challenge for any pilot to keep out of the drink.

Flying back from my second trip to the Philippines our pilot did both, and we had to fly back to the Philippines because of lack of fuel; mainland China wouldn't allow aircraft to land on their soil in those days.

Coming in to attempt landing, the first time around, in thick fog and darkness, was eerie. One of the tremendous thrills of landing at Kai Tak was the close quarter views you could get into two or three storey buildings. You could undoubtedly recognise a familiar face cooking in a kitchen.

The aircraft comes in a little steeply to clear the mountains that surround Kowloon. Lights out, deathly quiet. You could hear a pin drop. The pilot had warned us of the conditions, and that he might not be able to land – a real confidence builder. After the aircraft had all the makings of touching down it roared off like Thunderbird 3. I could see the tarmac but we were going too fast.

We were told of a second attempt after a 20 minute circuit. The lights never went on, there was the odd whisper, Nikki looked amazingly calm. Did I look the same? The aircraft descended over the harbour. The Chinese guy next to me lit up a cigarette, took several puffs and put it out. Nobody complained. We were over the City, but were we low enough – I couldn't see. Then out of the window, I saw dim lights where there might have been the familiar sight of people and washing on balconies. This time they seemed to whiz by. Too fast. I didn't see the runway this time, but felt Nikki's hand squeeze over my own as we regained height. I heard the Chinese guy exhale above the engine noise. I like to be kept informed but I'm not sure that the pilots English translation of his earlier statement, that, we 'should' have enough fuel to return to Manila' was particularly helpful. Thankfully we got back to Manila.

At Colombo, Sri Lanka tyres burst and fire engines sped along side as we reached the end of the runway – exciting but no other hint of trouble really. I took a seaplane on one occasion, bumpy but otherwise simply an experience. Helicopters, well my first ever helicopter flight was memorable for the fun of it.

I was to handle a claim at a copper mine on Sumbawa, the island neighbouring Lombok in Indonesia. The broker was Ross Keenan of Marsh. We got into this Huey helicopter, Vietnam War style, the pilot was a Vietnam War Vet, complete with haircut. Ross and I sat, looking out the side on these bench style seats. We had ear protectors incorporating mouthpiece and headphones. I spent the 15-20 minutes of the journey talking to the pilot, overland Ross spent his time simulating a machine gunner firing on Viet Kong in the paddy fields below. He looked like a mischievous child. He was subdued as we flew over the sea, as it was explained to me by the pilot that indeed, there was a chance of survival if we went down, he had survived several crash-landings. And 'Yes' there was a back –up mechanism for engine / rotor failure. It was tested regularly – in flight by simply turning off the engine!! The best place to do that was over the sea. He wouldn't be doing it today I was reassured.

When we landed I continued to speak with the pilot on the pad. It turned out he had made several forced landings, some in combat zones. He looked the part. He was fascinating and most of all he was still alive. Ross had done it all before. 'Did yer shit yerself mate' he joked as we strode off to a waiting vehicle.

Ross was a great laugh and a good friend. His sister ran a travel agency in Nelson, New Zealand and she arranged our 25th Wedding Anniversary on the South Island. They did us proud.

Flying over Foxes Glacier and around Mount Cook was another great helicopter flight. We landed on the glacier and briefly felt the isolation. On the same trip to New Zealand we took the helicopter to view sperm whales and flew in a fixed wing light aircraft over the South Island Mountains from Milford Sound into Queenstown and experienced aerial views to die for. We didn't, and landed on a beautiful grass runway. I had stood in the cabin of a 747 as the pilot pointed out the top of Everest peeping out of the clouds. That had been amazing, but there is nothing to beat a low level flight in a light aircraft over a snow capped mountain range. You feel, as well as see, in fact all your senses tingle.

Possibly the only adrenalin rush to outrush the above would be the glider ride out of Quetta in Pakistan, not just for the silent movie view over the mountains of Afghanistan, and the desert below, but for the view of my Aussie mate, Tom McCauley, at the wheel of his glider (not the pilot) as he crash landed onto the dusty desert airstrip. It was embarrassing more than worrying. There wasn't much damage, but we had been flown gratis by wonderfully hospitable people we had happened upon by chance. We thanked them and left them with a wave, somewhat breathless and, for my part, ashamed. Tom laughed as only Tom could, 'Gee mate that was fuckin fantastic. Wow, did yer see that landin?'

I thought Garuda (the acronym is 'Good and Reliable Until Delay Announcement') were bad, but my Aeroflot flight from Moscow to Leningrad (St Petersburg) in 1990 was probably the worst domestic air service I have ever experienced. I couldn't be angry because I was so well travelled, and in any case it was hilariously ridiculous. The flight was about an hour I think. I had heard that the commercial pilots were ex–military cargo pilots. The take off and landings were executed in more the style of the Stuka pilots of the Luftwaffe during the war.

I sat alongside Nikki, or rather just behind, and below her. My seat was broken and would only settle into the 'broken 'reclined position, which was very reclined. I looked ridiculously funny.

There was no other seat to take. The hostesses, retired Gulag guards I guess, handed me a glass of water (the in-flight meal) without displaying the slightest hint that there was anything untoward. Nothing at all wrong. I said nothing. Nikki giggled. I really must have looked ridiculous.

On my flight to Jamaica, where I was to live and work for a few months, the aircraft flew in to Montego Bay where it was to offload passengers and resume the journey to Kingston. We flew in to the sound of that song, 'Oh we're going to Barbados, etc' a great Caribbean holiday song, but we weren't going to Barbados. My colleagues and I had been drinking throughout the flight, as was usual. We might have stopped drinking because we had a long wait on the tarmac before completing the short one hour leg to Kingston. The aircraft virtually emptied.

However we were at the back of the aircraft near the galley. We got very friendly with the aircrew and together with them consumed, according to one of the hostesses, 'Vodka, gin, beer the lot. We swayed through the aisles of that aircraft into the airport building at Kingston. We had been virtually the only passengers on the flight and had drunk with the girls at the rear of the plane for the entire trip. We were all pissed as the proverbial parrot. Immigration had seen it all before – no problem! We rested that night over a couple of pina coladas. In the true traditions of Catastrophe Teams we never failed to work our balls off 'the morning after the night before'. What a journey.

But then there was the one that went sour. I was on a flight to Hong Kong from Jakarta to watch the rugby International 7's, visit my Hong Kong colleagues, and hopefully catch up with an old friend Andy Neilson and his ex-wife Laura. I travelled alone.

The night before I had watched the girl band 'Bond'. They were classical musicians pioneering a sexy classical / pop sound.

They were on the plane. The back-up band and crew were sat behind me. Some faces, I recognised from the bars of Jakarta were seated in the next aisle. They were heavily into a bottle of vodka. I chatted over a few beers with the guys behind, mainly the drummer, a very affable black guy. "What did I think of the performance?" I was asked. I talked in some detail about my thoughts, "I thought they were great" I summarised......"but". I now wish I had never said this.

The cello player was a little overweight to be showing a mid-riff. She had put a little weight on since the album cover photo and I thought that aesthetically this was a weakness in the stage presentation. The girl seated two from him had been listening intensely but hadn't said a word. With an angry growl she rose from her seat and pushed passed passengers and went to the back of the plane. What was wrong? "It's OK, she's is the costume designer" I was told. "Don't worry she just took it a bit personally, but I can understand what you mean".

246

At this point the unruly Jakarta lot decided to join in the conversation; I eased out of it and resumed the journey feeling slightly awkward. I said my goodbyes to the drummer as I walked off the plane. I later learned, having met another guy that had been on the plane, that there had been a kafuffle in the queue of people waiting to pass through immigration. The black drummer claimed he had been racially abused by the vodka drinkers........I did feel sorry for the guy......and guilty by association. Brits overseas I thought!

I had another unhappy ending to a flight on Singapore Airlines to Heathrow in 2001; back to see family for Christmas. I was travelling alone. Nikki had returned earlier to buy a new home. I had had my usual quota of beer and shorts before and during my evening meal. I sometimes found it difficult to sleep, particularly when flying cattle class, although Singapore airlines cattle class is better that most airlines business class. I would watch TV beginning to end; every film showing. The lights went down for the overnight spell. I decided to watch a comedy film. I can't remember what the film was, I never saw the end, but it was hilarious. I sat watching it with a gin and tonic.

Those around me were mainly settled, eyes closed. I was laughing a lot and obviously too loudly for one individual. When I ordered another drink I was refused, 'because I had had enough'. I was fuming. It turned out a passenger had complained. I complained to the chief steward. I was as sober as a judge! No clue yet about the complaint. I asked to see the captain. I stood with him in the galley.

He looked annoyed at being hailed. He threw me a broadside,' You know I can have you arrested on landing?' I kept my cool and firmly said, 'What for? For laughing loudly! I am not drunk. Do I appear drunk to you? 'No' he said. So why was I refused a drink? He mellowed and told me a passenger had complained. He appeared to sympathise. We parted peacefully after my complaint. I walked up and down the aisles for several minutes. I had been excited about returning home for Christmas, I was enjoying a great film and having a few 'looseners'. I felt sad and unfairly treated. A few minutes later the chief steward invited me in to the galley.

The hostess was clearly young inexperienced, he apologised and offered to serve me. I declined, stated that my own journey had been ruined because of the overreaction of a hostess to a sneaky complaint, and spent the rest of the flight in misery. The hostess came up to my seat later in the flight and apologised also. Chinese style she asked my forgiveness. Unusually, and to my shame, I was not very gracious in accepting the apology. It was perhaps because of my underlying feeling of unhappiness with my private life.

247

I was not magnanimous in what might be described as a victory, a vindication. To a Chinese the apology was a major loss of face. I knew that. I have deep regrets about not making the girl feel a lot better.

It was Christmas Eve on landing. The crew bowed as I left the aircraft. Perhaps belatedly, I sent a message to their hotel in London to emphasise my forgiveness. I hope the message got through.

When I arrived at our newly purchased home I had as cold a reception from Nikki as I had ever had. Her deeply depressing demeanour appeared to have rubbed off on our two daughters; I wished I had never returned.

I am not even going to bother about listing great 'four wheel' journeys, there can only be one; travelling the Asian Highway, England to India!

There can only be a couple of memorable boat trips, apart from the one already mentioned (the one in Borneo) although I had been comically and embarrassingly sick 'on a millpond', leaving the harbour in Cromer on Syd's (little)yacht!

I have crossed the Channel a few times, but the only real sea trip was on the ferry from Immingham to Gothenburg in Sweden…around twenty four hours I recall.

I spent the entire trip at the bar and at the roulette table with a very elderly women, and for the most part Rob Wilkinson, before he succumbed to the 'bunk bed' with the rest of the lads. They were all sick! The ship was rolling all over the place.

I sat talking to this old lady. After spending our own money the lady asked Rob and I to place money on the roulette for her. We were lucky. We made her a small fortune. She tried to offer us a share but we declined. A bitter-sweet feeling; but we were both decent guys!

The other one was with a 'white Jamaican' who kept a boat at Ochos Rios on the north coast of Jamaica. He took Gareth and I out marlin fishing one morning. We had such a good trip that he asked us if we wanted to join him in the afternoon. The rum bottle was opened, I drove the Hawaii Five 0 style 'beast of a boat' and we had a ball!

PART FOUR

Chapter Eighteen
Living Under Murphy's Law
2003 – 2009

Well if you've enjoyed the read up until now I must warn you that this chapter gets a little dark. If you find the reading difficult then spare a thought for the writer. It hasn't been easy re-visiting a lot of the shit that went on between these years and as a consequence, what style of writing you might have detected has probably changed. It is this period that inspired me to write these memoirs. To download a troubled mind. To feel better. It worked.

What could go wrong during this time did go wrong. Yes there were bright and light moments but generally my life went into freefall. Even the strong, and I am strong, have a breaking point and I briefly found mine. Fortunately I was strong enough to pull out of the dive with the application of some self-styled self help, and the support of a select few. Without my sister, who took the strain for my entire family at one point, I have no idea whether I'd be alive today let alone what I'd be doing. I shall be forever indebted to her, and her husband for the support he also gave.

Writing this chapter has helped exorcise the demon that has sat on my shoulder and given me sleepless nights and moments, hours, or even days of misery. By the way, for the most part I kept my signature smile, although sometimes it was a 'painted smile'. I was hurting, and hurting badly, but hey, it doesn't end on a sad note, so don't be put off finishing the remaining pages of this book. I survived!

I enjoy music very much. I listened to my parents' vinyl record collection and the radio regularly. My sister is five years older than me and I was on her coat-tails during the early 1960's so was drawn into teenage music ahead of my time.

My neighbour, Alan Bainbridge, appreciated all music and was a keen jazz fan, so he helped me to broaden my range of interest and taught me to give all music a fair hearing. As a result I like the full range of musical sound to varying degrees. My collection therefore comprises everything from Gregorian chants to Eminem, Tchaikovsky to Led Zeppelin.

A line from one particular song by Ralph Stanley, a Bluegrass legend, entitled 'Man of Constant Sorrow' sum up the years after my return from Indonesia.

"I am a man of constant sorrow, I've seen troubles all my days..........for six long years I've been in trouble........."

During those dark years life was tough and I was very unhappy. I felt I was being punished, but could never understand why. There were times that I was angry with my wife, my daughters, and was always angry with those that wronged them. I seemed to be living on a lethal cocktail of sadness, misery, anger, frustration, self-pity and joy, satisfaction and pride, never knowing which ingredients would affect me most the next day!

I was also becoming angry with those that wronged me; those that crossed me in the workplace and those that crossed me in my private life. I had a shortened fuse. I quite understandably became a little paranoid. I was impatient with my Mum and Dad, something I am not proud of, but some of the stories I am about to tell are almost surreal. I have kept most of them short because they are too bloody miserable.

From 2003 through to early 2009 I went through the classic stages of grief; denial, anger, bargaining and into depression; with a great deal of overlap, so that at times I was feeling all stages at once! By 2005 my twenty eight year marriage collapsed. I moved to Berwick upon Tweed (far from the maddening crowd) and by 2007 I had lost my career of twenty three years. During these years my paradise was lost; the walls of my garden collapsed!

Summary

Within a month of my return to the UK it was clear that Nikki was in serious psychological trouble, and that I was going to become a punch bag. Katy was off the rails, and Zoe emotionally and geographically distant in Leeds. There were a series of domestic problems, some financial.

Also within a couple of months of my return I suffered a traumatic personal and very public humiliation; an allegation of incompetence by the Managing Director of our Dutch company; a malicious and unsubstantiated attack made by a reptile of a man. He blamed me for losing $20 million of Dutch business. I proved otherwise but my M.D. abandoned me. I was put out to pasture and given nothing meaningful or substantial to do. I was alienated.

In typical Dave style I fought back after having first offered the Dutchman an olive branch, and only after chances had been given to right the wrong. I engaged the Dutchman twelve months later, insisting that I receive an apology. An unintentional by-product of this 'stand' was conflict with my MD. I paid the price.

The relationship with my wife was rock bottom. I broke off with Nikki. Not long after my separation, Nikki had her long awaited but predictable breakdown and was hospitalised; 'sectioned' and escorted to hospital by police. The doctors, through gross negligence discharged her; she caused chaos, and was readmitted under police escort within three days. I also caused chaos during a mini twenty four hour breakdown of my own. Nikki returned to hospital a couple more times in that year. Inevitably, but not justifiably, I felt guilt.

Within twelve months of Nikki's breakdown Katy had a traumatic breakdown of her own, that I had warned her might happen unless she sought help. She was hospitalised. I couldn't take any more and took three months sick leave while she was in hospital. The company cut my income.

I returned to work with a promise of a meaningful and busy schedule to keep me active and aid my recovery. The promise was never kept and within six months the company engineered my redundancy. In early 2007 I was jobless and alone. I went into freefall.

Career Collapse

In March 2003 I arrived back in the UK from Indonesia where I was Technical Director, to take up a new role as Quality Assurance Manager for Continental Europe, Middle East & Africa. A third of our global operation. My report line was to Mark Halliday, the Regional Managing Director.

The position was offered to me on the recommendation of Richard Martinez, Managing Director, Asia and Pacific Region, who described me as a 'quality individual'. Mark Halliday said that I was the person he was looking for. He asked me to write and roll out a quality assurance programme for the region. Richard Martinez had made Mark aware of the budding problems in my private life. The role suited me given that my wife was ill, and I felt unable to take up that tempting position offered to me in China. I was told I could live anywhere in the region, and would have chosen France or Germany, but my wife wanted to live in UK, so that was that.

The move to Europe represented a substantial reduction in my remuneration, but my family had to come first. My marriage, I hoped, was salvageable.

My work in Indonesia had been done. I had improved the efficiency of the Indonesian company, improved its reputation and helped open an additional office. My own reputation had also been enhanced.

I had handled cases diplomatically and skilfully; successfully negotiating the most political and complex of claims at the highest level. In doing so I created a regional reputation that had extended into the US, an important part of the world. All this was achieved during an extremely difficult period in Indonesian history, from the Asian Economic Crisis of 1997 through a period of civil unrest, the unseating of President Suharto, to the crisis initiated by 9/11 and the uneasy peace, punctuated by outbreaks of violence that followed. I was regarded as a potential 'high flyer' by several important customers. At least that's what they told me.

My appointment was given high profile with a small fanfare of press releases describing my experience and role. Typically they read, "CCS has named David Wakefield as Quality Assurance Manager for the central Europe, Middle East and Africa region.....The position will be key to guaranteeing full compliance with individual client service standards at local, national and regional levels.

David, a seasoned loss adjusting expert, has been with CCS for many years, most recently as Technical Director in Indonesia..............he will travel around the region to develop and roll out a formalized quality control and assurance programme.

"I am delighted that David has taken on this new role" says Mark Halliday, managing director.

"Once upon a time our clients asked us the question' can I trust your organization to deliver?' David has played a major role in our clients being able to confidently say yes to that question. Quality, David knows, is not just about technical competence, but about risk management, customer satisfaction and managing our business in a disciplined way...
...........I am confident that this initiative, under David's leadership, will yield further significant improvements to our business practices and gains in terms of competitive advantage".

These were the last decent and honest words that I was ever to see or hear from Halliday; even though they were standard marketing praise.

253

This is how the trouble started. I had my feet behind the desk for just days. Unbeknown to Mark Halliday, or me, the Country Manager for the Netherlands, Mark Van Persie, harboured a deep seated resentment and hatred for me. This precipitated an email demand to Mark Halliday that I be removed from my position. The email complaint was subsequently forwarded to me. It was a bombshell! A complete and utter surprise and something of a mystery. It read, word for word, as follows:-

'Mark,
I was called by David. I regret that you send this guy to me. He caused millions of dollars (of loss). Every day I am reminded of his stupidity......his stupid laughing during the telephone call supports my initial opinion. I cannot deny access to the building as he is an employee. My personal opinion about this situation is that I will hate him till I retire. Sorry I am very vindictive about people who crossed my pass.

In fact I rather that he does not come to the Netherlands at all. His employment is a waste of the prorations...I have to work day and night to make one million dollars per year extra to cover his expense, whilst this guy is costing me millions in the market already.

I almost explode about this situation. It absorbs management focus, because I am angry about the situation every day. Why do we keep these kind of people on the payroll? Why do we keep these assholes in the group? Really I cannot agree to the soft focus. A talk will not help with me in these situations.'

I asked Mark Halliday to let me handle it. That approach was consistent with my confident manner and style. I did so and, according to Mark Halliday, in an 'exemplary' fashion, despite the fact that I was shaken, and angry. I was feeling vulnerable in my private and working life.

It transpired that Van Persie had lost millions of dollars of business and he had blamed me. The odd thing is that this had supposedly happened five years earlier and he had never mentioned it to me! It seemed he had used me as a scapegoat, and I guess my appearance on the European stage was going to cause him embarrassment.

I checked with my then Managing Director, Richard Solomon, and he knew nothing of any complaint against me. I asked my Indonesian colleagues to review the file subject of the allegation. They wrote confirming that I had done nothing wrong or untoward, but it seemed Van Persie's own staff had!

I wrote to the Dutchman, I flew out and met with him in Rotterdam. I tactfully asked him to demonstrate to me my error by producing some evidence. I was puzzled and perplexed. I needed recognition that I was not responsible. He would not give it; evidence or recognition.

There was an uneasy peace declared, it was agreed that the matter would be put behind us, but it was clear that he was never going to be my friend! I felt aggrieved and it affected my confidence, nevertheless I moved on.

Assuming the matter had been resolved, for business purposes, I decided to move forward, and, a few weeks later, in May 2003, I was scheduled to present a plan of action to the regional meeting in Madrid.

All the Country Managers, with whom I had to build up trust and confidence, were present; the most senior staff from every country in the region; from South Africa to Bahrain.

Van Persie chose, in the middle of my presentation, to stand up and repeat the defamatory accusations about me, and he was allowed to do so, unchecked by Mark Halliday for longer than was healthy. I did not retaliate.

I found the entire experience highly embarrassing and sickening. I can't remember ever having felt so physically sick. I had been humiliated in front of the very team of people from whom I was seeking support, confidence and respect; all the people that I needed 'on my side' if I was to succeed.

On the final day of the Madrid meeting, a Friday, I flew back to find my Dad had been admitted to hospital with a heart problem. Nevertheless, that weekend I produced a lengthy report to send to Van Persie, containing full evidence obtained from Indonesia, proving beyond any doubt that I was not at fault. It was sent on the Sunday evening. It was copied to Mark Halliday. I demanded and expected an apology. It was defamatory.

I did not even get a reply let alone an apology. Halliday suggested I let sleeping dogs lie. I would have been happy to do that, had Halliday demonstrated strong leadership and his support for me. This did not happen.

Halliday's answer to the problem was to isolate me. I was excluded from regional meetings; the very forum that afforded me the opportunity to meet colleagues collectively, feel part of the team and keep 'in the loop'. He also withdrew from me the right to send 'grouped' emails to country Managers without first seeking his permission.

My name was deleted from circulation lists and a draft directory for customers. I was not invited to appear in the regional 'team photograph' that even included secretarial staff.

It became increasingly apparent to me that Halliday had taken sides; seeking to ally himself to the wishes of the Dutch MD, a long standing and recognised power base in the region. He was clearly a man that had no interest in people, and no interest in anything apart from his own career. He was not prepared to confront Van Persie. He was a weak man, and, it transpired, a coward and a bully.

With an increasing feeling of alienation, coupled with personal family problems, I decided in May 2004 to offer an ultimatum to Van Persie; 'apologise or I take action for defamation'. Mark Halliday was copied in on my ultimatum.

Within minutes the phone rang and Halliday attacked my actions. He threatened me. I had been prepared for him to criticize me, but not for him to start bullying. I had not expected him to be that stupid and brazen. I misjudged his response. The following day he decided, for the first time ever, to criticise my monthly expenses. A meagre £18 of expenses was un-receipted – never before a problem!

Van Persie refused to apologise and the stage was set for a step-down or a showdown. I decided to initiate grievance proceedings against Van Persie. I had been prepared to take this next step. But I now had to consider the verbal blasting I had received from Halliday and the intimidation in relation to my expenses.

I felt that I had little option but to counter attack. Things were never likely to get better, and if I capitulated Halliday would make mincemeat of me. The consequences were potentially catastrophic as far as my career was concerned, but as he had set out his stall, I had little option but to initiate proceedings against him also. The situation was clear; cower like a dog or fight. The best means of defence on this occasion was attack! If I had not I would have had no chance whatsoever. I followed the grievance procedure to the letter.

Halliday had overstepped the mark. He had attempted to intimidate me. I notified Biff Bowden in the US; the Company President and his line manager. I had the rule book, this was company procedure; complain to the next in line. It wasn't an easy decision to make but I had no choice. I didn't speak to Halliday ever again except during the two subsequent hearings months later.

Bowden did his best to protect Halliday. He handled me badly. His tactical mistake was to try to bring me to heel. He miscalculated my resolve, the position I was in, and my character. I was not for turning; I was not going to be humbled by shit heads! Halliday and Van Persie had to be flushed out, even if it cost me my career. Their true character had to be exposed.

Not surprisingly I suffered additional trauma. I saw my doctor, who treated me for stress and anxiety. I had seemingly no escape from stress. I took a mild antidepressant.

I had always thought that Mark Halliday had felt threatened by my popularity. He might have thought that I was being groomed as a future Managing Director. Certainly Van Persie thought so, because he told me. It was obviously a concern to him.

A couple of weird conversations with Halliday also gave me cause to draw this conclusion. I learnt of major new appointments and transfers in major companies like Munich Re before anyone else. His first question, 'How did you find that out?' When a company in Tanzania wanted to forge a strategic partnership with our company they contacted me – not Mark. His first question, 'Why did they approach you?'

Mark Halliday probably felt insecure. He was an accountant, yes, but he didn't know the business. He didn't even know how to adjust a profit insurance claim – he asked me! He didn't have an intimate knowledge of our business, and I did. He was just a former Arthur Anderson Director; a numbers man and a 'behind the scenes' hatchet man. Essentially a coward. Oh, and I've seen more personality in a pilchard!

There had been a number of incidents that led me to believe he was uncomfortable with my popularity and familiarity with people in the industry; customers and colleagues alike. During a meeting in our London office he quite casually called me a sycophant; a toady. He clearly didn't like a personality – he didn't have one.

To be honest I didn't even know what 'sycophant' meant; otherwise I'd not have left that office without words. I felt he was either provoking me or he was a poor judge of character. In fact it was both.

My decision to lodge a grievance against these guys was a bold, some would say suicidal move, I was now to be subjected to a long drawn out delay, a clear breach of the grievance procedure. Waiting for the wheels to turn, and the date for the grievance hearing, was stressful, and there was no attempt made by either man, to capitulate or offer reconciliation.

Bowden put the matter in the hands of Human Resources. There was a 'temporary' director heading the department at the time, but she could do nothing to help speed up the process. It was delayed and delayed. They were going to make sure it was drawn out. They had no intention of following the official grievance procedure, which was good enough for anyone else in the company. Meanwhile I did nothing. I was put out to dry!

The 'hearing' of the grievance against the Dutchman was held in London, and to the outrage of both men, it was handled fairly. The adjudicator, David Broadhurst, who had a difficult job, persuaded me to accept a negotiated settlement, essentially in my favour, and I agreed to move on. I received a written apology from Van Persie.

A significant concern was that Mark Halliday had sat in the hearing as a 'second' to Van Persie. This was hardly impartial and highly inappropriate, but I thought, in doing so he had shown his colours, and his true allegiance had been exposed. It was not the thing to do.

Halliday was criticised in the adjudicator's report for his failure to take action in relation to Van Persie; that must have been a humiliation for him. I subsequently heard that he had objected to this criticism. During the hearing he had been visibly shaken to hear support for my assertion that the allegations against him were quite separate from those made against Van Persie, and that therefore his case had to be heard separately. I think he was left in no doubt that he was wrong.

I was told that Halliday subsequently objected to Broadhurst's being the adjudicator in relation to the grievance I had lodged against him. He was too impartial for him.

There was a further unnecessarily long and uncomfortable wait for the grievance against Mark Halliday to be heard. I had to wait for him to return from holiday. The proceedings were chaired by Senior Vice President Willy (i.e. prick) Beacham (Human Resources, USA) during a trans-Atlantic conference call. I sat in our London Head Office, alongside Herma Prinson, the acting Human Resources Director. Halliday didn't have the bottle to attend; he spoke on the telephone from his home. I had of course objected to a conference call hearing.

Halliday's only response to my grievance was received by me in a written document presented no more than a day or two before the hearing. It was inflammatory and scathing. I was deeply angered. Under my aggressive questioning he was unable to give an explanation, or even an answer, to some points I had raised, and Beacham abruptly pulled him 'off the ropes' and bought the hearing to a close. I awaited the outcome.

The subsequent adjudication read rather like a grievance about me. It was heavily weighted in favour of Mark Halliday and most of it criticised me, and ignored my allegations. It did nothing more than suggest that Mark Halliday apologise for calling me 'stupid' (I felt embarrassed by this. It made my complaint appear trivial). Beacham then had the temerity to list a series of complaints against me and recommended that I be given a warning for failing to follow proper grievance procedure. The audacity of the man! It was a blatant and obvious whitewash; a metaphorical 'V' sign! It was an absolute disgrace.

I was so outraged by the 'white wash' that after considering resignation on the grounds of 'constructive dismissal' I appealed to Biff Bowden. I knew by now that my future career prospects were blown out of the water. I had no alternative but to continue to use the system properly to keep alive any hope of salvaging my job. I needed it at that time.

Bowden made me sweat, by ignoring my correspondence or delaying a response. This all had the effect of making me feel increasingly at threat. This I believe was by design. Throughout the entire ordeal I had been repeatedly asked by Herma Prinson, if I wanted to remain with the company and 'what I wanted'. She knew that I was being badly treated I'm sure.

Eventually on 1st October 2004, six months after I had raised my grievance, I had an hour long transatlantic telephone conversation with Bowden and I agreed to 'move on', having received his assurances as to my value and future with the company. The discussions appeared encouraging and conciliatory. But I didn't trust him 100%. In fact I explained to him why I was apprehensive about moving forward and he said he understood my apprehension. I had told him that I was concerned that I might be 'taken out' after the dust had settled. By this time there was no realistic prospect of succeeding in a case of 'constructive dismissal. You have to act immediately.

I asked him to drop me an email confirming our agreement so that I could be comfortable going forward. I knew there was a possibility that I would be stabbed in the back and something in writing would reassure me. He promised me he would do so.

He had assured me that I would be attending the forthcoming regional management meeting in Marbella and I did. We agreed that it would be sensible for me to have a new line manager, but I insisted that I should not be removed from my post, and that I should be able to continue with my work. There was a lot to do he had said and he assured me that I was to play an important part in 'the exciting future'. It all turned out to be bullshit and I should have taken the 'constructive dismissal' path that I so nearly trod.

I was feeling traumatised and thoroughly worn out by the entire matter, so it had not been difficult for me to accept the assurances given, and the undertaking that there would be none of the contrived disciplinary warnings given to me.

I never received the email that I had been promised. I rejected an offer to work on a catastrophe team working in Jamaica on the grounds that I had not received the promised closure letter.

I felt uncomfortable and vulnerable. I 'pestered' for the promised letter but he was 'too busy'. I drafted out a letter for him to sign based on our agreement. For this I received a wrap over the knuckles in an email. I prepared a resignation letter dated 2nd November 2004 and considered the 'constructive dismissal' route yet again, but after researching the subject thought I was probably too late.

I subsequently learnt, in 2007 when I was unfairly dismissed, that the 'wrap on the knuckle' email I refer to had been placed on my personal file together with other documents that gave the impression that I had been punished. There was no reference whatsoever to my grievance.

I had been conned. My chance of constructive dismissal had been lost. I decided to knuckle down, I was in no mental condition to seek another job and do it well; my confidence was rock bottom.

In January 2005 I met with Jonathan Coates, who was to be my new line manager, at a hotel near the NEC Birmingham to discuss the future. Bowden had said that I would find Jonathan a harder task master than Mark, and I thought this could only be a good thing. Jonathan had had a decent reputation and I expected some support, although I knew that I was taking a risk by opting for a future with the company, rather than following the 'constructive dismissal' route that I had been considering. I chose to trust him. He had a solid decent reputation.

I explained that I felt at risk of being ostracized in the future, that my confidence had been badly dented, and that I needed to feel valued and involved. We had a full and frank discussion and I felt much better about the future. I knew that I could do my job very efficiently if I was given the opportunity. I hoped that Jonathan had enough weight to enforce my involvement in the region, and support the agreed programme.

Unfortunately very little changed and I was unable to properly perform the role contained in the job description that he had prepared. I am not sure that this was Jonathan's fault. He was however self absorbed, and lacked either the bottle or influence to do anything meaningful. He wasn't a fighter.

In February 2005, just after our separation, my wife was compulsorily sectioned under the Mental Health Act and admitted to hospital, events that I will relate later.

As feared, despite reassurances and my agreement to work with Jonathan (responsible for the global quality assurance programme), rather than Mark, I continued to be alienated from 'team' activity. I continued to feel isolated, undervalued and meaningless. None of my work was given support and many of my proposals were rejected on the basis that 'someone else will do it'. I was not invited to group management meetings; 'I was not needed'. I felt for long periods as though I was on some form of 'gardening leave'. My name did not appear on circulation list or directories. In management circles I was a non-person. For a person that thrived on challenging work, engaging staff and customers, this was torture.

I was embarrassed when people asked 'where have you been?' or 'what are you doing?' or told me they thought I had left the company. People, Country Managers, expressed surprise that I was not present at Regional Management meetings given my role.

My attempts to do my work were hampered by a reluctance to promote it, and enforce agreements to deliver. I had been abandoned by Halliday, and Jonathan seemed powerless or uninterested in asserting any influence or pressure on him to change things; to heighten, or rather reinstate, my profile, authority, and thus the importance of my work.

Bowden's support for Mark can be explained. Bowden had owned a UK Loss Adjusting Company that had been sold to CCS. He had employed Mark, (who at that time worked for Arthur Anderson, accountants) to prepare the company for sale. He had been pleased with his work and when he became MD of CCS UK he recruited him as Finance Director. He was later further rewarded with the regional MD position.

In 2005 there was little working activity. In fact, when I recently trawled through my diaries I identified a few interesting statistics; the number of days worked outside my home/office. Obviously my inactivity didn't help, given the very serious problems that were present in my private life.

In 2003 I spent ninety days working out of my office (at home), with business trips to Rotterdam, Madrid, Copenhagen, Stockholm, Oslo, Paris, Düsseldorf, Milan, Athens, Antwerp, South Africa, Dubai and Bahrain included. In 2004 these out of office activities reduced to 53 days including visits to Munich, Oslo, Paris, Prague, Milan, Malaga, Grenoble, Dubai and Bahrain. In 2005 I spent a mere fifteen days out of office in Rotterdam, Munich and Lyon.

Things got even worse in the following year. In this dreadful year of 2006, just nine days were spent outside the office, with my colleagues in Munich, and my final trip, to Cologne in February 2006. Included in these nine days are my meetings with Jonathan. My diary show no activity whatsoever from September until the end of 2006, just before I was sacked.

In February 2006 Katy was committed to hospital having suffered a very serious trauma induced mental breakdown and spent two months in hospital. Events during the previous three years were undoubtedly the cause.

Nikki had, a year earlier, been committed to hospital with manic depression (bipolar). She had spent nearly eight months of the previous year in hospital. Around this time, Zoe, my other daughter, had a cervical cancer scare and needed an operation. My life, and that of my family, was a nightmare.

Although I had very little work to do anyway, I felt that I could no longer concentrate on anything. I was a devastated, broken man. I had been receiving treatment for trauma and the dreadful events surrounding my daughters' breakdown. I started to see Maureen Campbell, a counsellor, in August 2005, but BUPA could no longer finance my counselling. Maureen was good.

My confidence in the mental health service had been seriously damaged by events associated with my wife's treatment. I could not imagine ever feeling worse. My daughters' breakdown was the last straw. My doctor signed me off work. I paid for my own counselling through until May 2006.

262

In 2005 I had had nowhere to find any happiness or release from stress and anxiety. Both my private and professional life was in tatters. It is difficult to explain the depth of despair. Yet nothing work wise had changed. I didn't miss work because I didn't have any. I didn't miss business telephone conversation, because I hadn't had any calls anyway.

2006 was not any better. I send the company a doctor's note, stating 'stress related' illness. Surely this was enough information given all that they knew of my problems, but I then received a letter from 'Human Resources' requesting a medical report. My pay was cut and I needed to return to work. I did so after three months sick leave, plus a few days convalescing on a holiday in Cuba.

I was asked to attend a 'return to work' meeting in London. Jonathan and a Ms Clay of Human Resources were present. I was asked (again) if I wanted to stay with the company. I said 'Yes' and I asked Jonathan if the company wanted me. He said, 'there was a role for me'. I said 'that was a diplomatic answer'. I said that I needed some meaningful work. I needed to be active and involved. I needed to feel valued. The doctor's report had said as much, but he said he hadn't read it. Even the Human Resources representative admitted to not having seen it.

The report from Dr Singh, dated 3rd August 2006, read as follows:-

"In reply to your letter dated 27th July regarding Mr. David Wakefield, I am able to offer you the following information. Mr. Wakefield has been suffering with depression and stress since May 2004 and this was triggered off by problems at home but more so at work, where he was going through some grievance issues. He was commenced on treatment with Venlafaxine and this did initially help with his symptoms. I understand that it took a long while for things to be resolved at work, but once this happened Mr. Wakefield did feel a decrease in his stress levels.

Unfortunately at the time of the problems at work, Mr. Wakefield's wife also became unwell and was admitted to hospital.

This year Mr. Wakefield's daughter has unfortunately had to have a spell in hospital and he has also found this stressful.

From my conversations with Mr. Wakefield it also seems that he now feels undervalued at work and feels that he has not been given the same sort of work to do since the grievance issue as he was doing prior to it.

263

Mr. Wakefield has had some time off work this year from March up until late June. This has been because his mood deteriorated this year and he has had particular problems with concentration and motivation. However, these symptoms certainly have improved and I do not see any particular reason why they should not continue to do so. I would envisage Mr. Wakefield continuing on Venlafaxine for at least another six months and then this will eventually be tailed off as long as he continues to feel well. Hopefully things in his family life will now stabilize and therefore this will be one less stress for him to have to deal with.

I think Mr. Wakefield should be able to resume full duties in the future, although at present I think it would be helpful if work could try and keep any excess stress to a minimum. If it comes to a stage where Mr. Wakefield is unable to continue in his present post then it will be important to discuss any other role with him as I think he does need to feel valued in the work that he does.

I do not know whether Mr. Wakefield fulfils the criteria for a disabled person for the purposes of the Disabilities Discrimination Act.

I hope this information is of help to you."

I had hoped that this letter would not fall on deaf ears but it did and I was made redundant within six months and under the cruellest of circumstances. Here they are.

I needed work desperately. The trend had not been a good indicator. In fact my out of office activities, and remember I was a home worker, were statistically very revealing. .

In the August 2006 meeting, Jonathan outlined a schedule of work that needed urgent attention. That gave me heart and enthusiasm. I was asked to prepare to visit all the countries in the region to undertake audits. I had to have the audit reports completed in time for inclusion in the December report to the Board of Directors in the U.S. I felt excited about being back, and with something to do. I desperately needed substantive and meaningful work to help me get back on my feet.

I worked hard during August, and felt good. I had finished my preparation by the September and had prepared an itinerary. I was then asked to prepare a letter 'for circulation' to all country managers giving advanced notice of the visit and in contemplation of later telephone discussions to finalise arrangements and offer detail concerning the nature of the visit and requirements. I did so immediately.

264

I waited, and waited for the go-ahead. I sent a reminder by email and Jonathan eventually replied saying that he wanted to run the letter past Mark Halliday. There was a further delay. I again reminded him that I was waiting, and that the deadline was closing in. He then said that he wanted to run the letter past Ian Moore, the new CEO, 'as a courtesy'. Halliday had been sidelined from his role as MD and returned to a kind of 'Finance Directors' role which was, in my view, some admission of his incompetence. Weeks passed. It became too late to organise anything that would meet the deadline. Again I had nothing to do. No contact. I was again demoralized and depressed.

In 'The New Year' Human Resources sent a letter dated 9th January 2007 requesting a meeting because there was to be a 'reorganisation' that would affect my role. I never received the letter and only learnt about it on or around the 13th when I received a telephone call from Human Resources asking me if I was attending a meeting on 15th. I said that I didn't know of the meeting; I hadn't been informed about it. They said that they had sent the letter to my old address (I had moved to Berwick a year earlier).

Was it to be an uncanny coincidence? Richard Martinez, my MD in Asia Pacific region, had phoned me exactly four years earlier, on 9th January, my birthday, to give me 'notice of potential redundancy', because I had rejected the Shanghai move and there was no other vacancy. He said he had sent a letter, but I never got it!

Co-incidentally it was 9th January 2007 that I treated myself to my Honda S2000 – an iconic soft-top sports car - my 'penis extension' and something to cheer me up. The only 'bird' I was ever to pull in it was a pheasant, but more about that later!

I received a fresh (replacement) letter, requesting I attend a meeting at our London head office on 23rd January 2007. I turned up for the meeting early and waited downstairs in reception for Jonathan to arrive. He casually glided by, I said 'good morning Jonathan' and he replied without looking back at me. He went to his office and I helped myself to a coffee before following him through. Kelly, an H.R. junior was seated, with Jonathan to his side. She told me that I was on 'notice of potential redundancy'. I was shocked; stunned.

Jonathan answered my questions. Why was I being made redundant? He answered. The reason was that language skills were now required for regional roles and, that the role required residence in Continental Europe, have a better understanding of the regional operations, and he went on to say, 'other things'. I knew what he meant by other things. He checked himself and stopped saying anything more, but he did give me a nod. Deep down I knew that Jonathan was an OK guy, not a supporter, but not a force for evil. He was by this time facing difficulties of his own I think.

I said I was prepared to live on the continent, I always had been, and I asked "what languages? All of them?" He said 'yes'. He then backtracked and specifically stated a fluency in German and French, both written and oral. I said I was prepared to learn. Jonathan was clearly finding the whole meeting uncomfortable.

I was dismissed during a later meeting on 26th February 2007, by Sam Foot, a guy I hardly knew; a man of 'admin/IT' director status. Jonathan was unable to attend. I was told he had gone off sick. I was disgusted at the cruel way I had been treated and told Sam as much. I think Sam was disgusted too.

My subsequent appeal was turned down. My 'title role' in Europe was replaced with the 'title of 'Operations Manager', one I myself had advocated. I learnt that Sara of our Norwegian office had been earmarked for the job. Sara was someone who I had been heavily promoting myself as a 'top class' country MD, and someone who should be listened to a little more often. I had heard that she was ear-marked for the role back in 2006.

The job has not been advertised. Significantly Jonathan resigned. I feel sure that his reasons were associated with my redundancy. He had possibly been made redundant as well; but he was better placed to find other work.

Jonathan was the least likely of 'the cast' to have brought about my downfall, but I didn't know, and if I was to sue the company, I couldn't leave any gaps through which the company could 'crawl'. Jonathan had to be one of those in the firing line during my subsequent legal action.

I could have misjudged him, and it remains possible in my mind that he was party to my unfair dismissal, in trying to keep his own position. Deep down I have never really felt though that Jonathan had the stomach for the dirty dealings that Halliday, Van Persie, Beacham and Bowden were capable of. Jonathan was not indecent.

Sara was appointed Operations Manager for Europe. She deserved to be involved regionally no doubt. I was pleased for her but that job should have been mine! The company knew, or should have known from the skills matrix held by Human Resources, that I had language skills. Richard Martinez knew, Mark Halliday knew and my file contained reference to experience of speaking Cantonese, Indonesian and some Spanish.

266

Of course I had forgotten much of it through lack of use, but the aptitude to learn was evident.

With time, I could undoubtedly have leant German and French to a business standard, and I had learnt some French at school. I had repeatedly made clear, even when I returned from Asia, that I was prepared to live on the continent. My redundancy had been engineered, of that there was no doubt.

The company had spent some considerable amount of money producing my team management profile, but this was apparently ignored. Yet it was clearly a tool that they valued because I'd attended a 'Peoples Management' course in Birmingham in 2003 and in a classroom environment had taken a 'Belpin Test'. The results of that test corresponded with a later 'Rolls Royce' version commissioned for senior personnel.

My profile was that of a leader. I'm not sure that Halliday's was! During a regional meeting, one of course that I was absent from, a discussion was held concerning the profiles that had been obtained from consultants at some considerable expense. Mine was very impressive, I knew, because I'd had a copy, sent to me in July 2004.

The thirteen page report, framed according to the Margerison-McCann Team Management Wheel, had identified me as an 'explore promoter, an assessor developer, and a thruster organizer; it was an unusual combination. My major role was as a Thruster-Organiser. My major preferences are stated to be inclined toward extroverted, practical, analytical and structured.

The Thruster-Organisers, it stated, are outgoing people who make things happen by organizing people and materials so that ideas, discussions, and experiments are turned in to action They are important people to have on a team to ensure that attention is focused on results. they enjoy meeting with others and discussing issues, but will do so primarily on the basis of 'facts'........they concentrate on getting the job done in an efficient and effective way...they like to thrust forward........bla bla bla'

In the conclusion, I was pleased to see that I was the exactly what Halliday had criticised me for not being. As a Thruster–Organiser, the report concluded, I 'have the ability to see the 'big picture' and am the one person who can make dreams a reality'

It went on to say, many people with this pattern of scoring are quite influential. It is a combination of your ability to make things happen and your interest in implementing new approaches, products and services that can make you a force at work'

267

Interestingly the company had paid Khatiza, Joe Van Savages wife, to produce the reports. Joe, the Asia Pacific Claims Manager for AIG Asia, based in Singapore, had been one of the guys that had told me I might be in line to manage the region!

'A little bird' told me that Halliday had remarked during the regional meeting to discuss the reports, that 'there were some interesting ones' and mentioned my name, in a manner interpreted as being mocking. It was certainly a very strong report, that generally gave me immense pride, not least because I thought it was pretty much bang on. I would wouldn't I. Halliday had obviously felt threatened by me.

Jonathan had stated in our meeting of 23rd January 2007 that 'very serious consideration' had been given to my dismissal. I am absolutely convinced, and the evidence supported my view, that my dismissal was brutally and ruthlessly engineered. Ian Moore, the new CEO, was probably manoeuvred into sacking me, with probably little knowledge of what had gone on before.

There was no sound or logical reason to remove me from my job, except for ill health or past clashes with company titans. I had been aware of other injustices at the hand of Halliday, and I later used my evidence of that fact carefully, to preserve confidentiality of my information sources. As for cost, I had come cheaply, I had deliberately sold myself short - they had a bargain. I was certainly not kicked out on cost ground.

Two thousand and seven dealt me devastating blows that precipitated a new series of miserable and stressful battles. Two thousand and six had been a bad year, with Katy's painful breakdown and my continued alienation at work, but 2007 was no better, for different reasons.

Following my dismissal in February 2007 I was livid. I didn't miss my career, it was in any case in tatters, so I laid into the perpetrators of my demise like a man possessed. These bastards were going to pay a price, however small, for their treachery. I was (almost) merciless. I ran rings around them. They were a bunch of selfish guys at the top of the company who were so concerned with self interest (not the company) that they couldn't even coordinate an effective 'framing'.

I decided to go to tribunal, initially handling matters myself, gathering evidence and preparing my case. But I was under a great deal of stress, somewhat confused, losing my focus, perspective and concentration. I was in many ways a broken, bitter and tired man. I needed a solicitor. I got legal aid.

268

I started a smear campaign. I had earlier sent hundreds of letters to offices worldwide, and set up a website dedicated to an attack on those in the company that had wronged me. I exposed them. All that I set out was true, so when Ian Moore wrote to me suggesting that the site was defamatory, threatening legal action, I replied on 24th May 2007.

"Dear Ian,
Given the serious nature of the accusations made in yours of the 15th May I must insist that I receive the specifics of the alleged defamation so that I can investigate and respond.
If I do not receive a detailed response by the 4th June I shall assume that you have been misinformed as to the alleged defamation or that your letter was, as some people might see it, designed to frighten me into closing down my website. I shall then resume publishing information that I believe to be fact."

Ian never replied. The poor guy had probably never known the disgusting treatment that I had received. Indeed, he had, just months earlier told me that he had heard I was 'a quality guy'. I think his number 2 had told him that. I had introduced Nancy,Hamilton, the former Executive Director of Warwickshire Healthcare Trust, to his number 2 with a view to her taking over the Healthcare Division of the companies UK operation. She got the job. I had solved a big problem for the company.

After a protracted legal battle, I received a substantial, albeit on reflection inadequate, payment for Unfair Dismissal. There had been derisory, insulting, offers made by the company to settle, but just a couple of days before the tribunal date, the pressure I had been suffering, and the pressure I had been under from my own solicitors to settle, resulted in me agreeing an out of Court settlement. I was lacking clarity of thought and I was absolutely demoralised and broken; by events relating to work and to my personal life.

On the eve of the trial I tried to retract the agreement, but clearly annoyed, my solicitor informed me that the barrister had been stood down and it was too late. I was a fool; but I was weak. I could, and should have got considerably more had I been advised to take the matter to High Court rather than tribunal.

It is interesting to note that the company gave me a one line employer's reference that speaks volumes. Dated the 12th November 2007 the reference specifies my length of service, 6th May 1986 to 26th February 2007, and states, "We have no reason to doubt David's honesty." They could hardly contest the facts contained in this book then could they?

269

I did not receive any payment for the psychological damage caused to me. Tribunals don't deal with this aspect. So I then pulled an ace from under my sleeve and further claimed, and received, damages for the personal injury that the company had caused me; a kick in the teeth after they thought the matter was over.

I handled this case personally and, by winning, cleansed myself of much of the anger and bitterness inside of me. Again the money was not the issue. They settled for a small sum, out of Court.

What was important to me at the time was winning. Vindication was the most important issue and at the time nothing else seemed important. They got off scot-free. The only thing that really hurts this kind of lowlife is loss of money. They hadn't lost enough to be hurt. I regret not squeezing them more as a colleague of mine (with good legal representation) had done a few months earlier.

And while all the above was going on.........

My Marriage Hell

On reflection I probably realised that my marriage was in decline the early 1990's but soldiered on. I had hoped that the fresh start in Indonesia would have rejuvenated it. That wasn't to be.

From almost the day that I arrived back from the Far East it became apparent that Nikki was no better than when I had last seen her. She was, according to reports, drinking a lot, with Katy on her coat-tails. My first approach was to encourage her to find work. It was clear that she needed a constructive day and hadn't found the work that she needed to provide it. I'm not sure she had tried that hard, and her confidence was in any case low. In fact she had lacked confidence and self esteem all her life and later learnt that this was probably as a result of mental and physical abuse administered by her mother. She had sometimes blamed me.

The truth is she was capable of so much more. She was smart, intelligent and good looking. She had wasted her talents.

270

Drowning – My Analogy

I passed my bronze medal life saving award in my teens. I have never been a good swimmer but I was a strong and fit young lad and could swim a mile breaststroke no problem, and I could tread water for hours. I had stamina in abundance.

I ask you to image the time when I tried to rescue my wife from drowning. Put yourself in my place and imagine how terrible it feels to see your wife drowning and being unable to do anything to help.

I saw her in trouble; she had fallen in the river fully clothed and she couldn't swim. She was waving out to me and getting anxious and calling for me. She must have been doing it for sometime because she was getting angry with me. I swam toward her and she seemed to calm, but she was still in trouble. I talked to her as I approached. Her head was dipping under and I was trying to tell her how to help herself. She wasn't listening. I remembered what I had learnt and explained how I was going to help, but she kicked out when I tried to. I said she must trust me to help after all nobody knew her better that me - we had been together since 1974.

I tried another approach and made contact but she struggled and pushed me under, trying to keep her own head above the water. I tried again using another technique, but she wrapped her arms around me, and again, used my weight to keep her own head above the water, forcing my head under. I became weary and feared for us both. I made further attempts but repeatedly she climbed all over me in an effort to keep her own head above water. I pushed her away as I was taught. I was becoming very tired and anxious.

Whatever way I tried, I was failing, and what's more, I was struggling to keep my own head above the water. I tried one more time after begging her to let me help and reassuring her that she would be safe if she let me do so. I failed again, but this time, when I was pulled under the water; I swallowed some and felt I was drowning. It was a horrible feeling and I nearly passed out.

I knew I had to leave her; otherwise I would never be able to get back to the safety of the bank and save myself let alone save her. I grabbed some drift wood and left her with enough support to survive until I could find her help. I headed for the bank and called for help. Nobody heard. I shouted and shouted until I cried. I was exhausted. I was in no

271

shape to do anything. If I went back in the water and tried to help her, I knew I would drown. I shouted again. Nobody was listening and my wife was sinking.

I was no coward. I had correctly let my head rule my heart. The above analogy is that of the relationship with my wife over the years, culminating in our separation. With that separation came eventual recognition of her mental illness (bipolar) and sometimes secretive fondness for alcohol.

The Circumstances

By the time I had returned to the UK in 2003 Nikki had bought a big house with a bridging loan, and moved in. Our 'bolt hole' in Coventry had been unsold. We had the dreaded bridging loan! Nikki wanted her way on the matter and I reluctantly agreed.

I had trouble at work from the kick off, bad luck, bad finances and a wife that was suffering deterioration in mental health and simultaneously drinking increasingly heavily. She was also becoming awkward and assertive. She was attempting to change the balance of our relationship; to take control. To top it all off Katy was still living at home, having difficulty re acclimatising herself to the UK, and getting caught in her parents' crossfire.

Our social life continued to be fraught. Any chance of enjoying an evening out with friends was generally preceded by tension, misery and argument. Nikki would then skip into the company of our friends as if nothing had happened and proceed to either snipe at me, disagree with everything I had to say, and/or drink heavily. She seemed to be deliberately sabotaging our marriage. Nikki had been difficult in Indonesia but she had deteriorated even more dramatically. She was a different woman and as a family we were becoming dysfunctional.

I wasn't comfortable arranging evenings with mutual friends, and it wasn't easy to go out with my old mates; they were all married or otherwise engaged in a life that had not involved me for many years and I was desperate to find some refuge from the stresses and strains of the home life. I resorted to going out on my own and meeting new people . I was already accustomed to this in Indonesia, and felt very comfortable doing so.

The overseas business trips provided massive relief, and I felt productive making them, but even the value of these deteriorated as my authority and support was removed. I had an increasing amount of spare time as a result of my alienation at work. I found myself waiting around for emails and phone calls that never came. I began to feel that prompting,

272

or reminding Halliday that I was waiting for him to act, was becoming a nuisance to him and might be counter-productive.

I was spending more time dealing with an increasing number of domestic problems than working. I felt like I was on 'gardening leave' but nobody had told me or even suggested that this might be the case. It was torture.

I spent time bird watching, gardening, and spending time in the pub, meeting new people or reading. I was miserable and sad. I was becoming increasingly frustrated and low. I was also becoming angry.

I had tried every possible approach toward improving Nikki's confidence and mood. We had argument after argument, cool chat and discussion after cool chat and discussion. I had taken to writing letters to her because I never felt that what I was saying was being registered. With a letter I could be sure of getting my point across. It was a last resort.

I was desperate and in despair in just about every corner of my life, but especially in my relationship with my wife. I had returned to the UK for the benefit of my wife and family. They were the most important people in my life. If the wheels were failing off the marriage carriage, the family would inevitably suffer from the fallout. I had already decided that the family were my priority; that's why I asked for a sabbatical when in Indonesia, and was prepared to face redundancy. That's why I abandoned my career ambitions and dreams, cancelled my Shanghai posting, and took a regional role, basing myself back home in Blighty.

I had tried to explain to others the problems I had been having with Nikki, but to them Nikki was, OK. Low a bit lost and unhappy; but otherwise nothing to worry too much about. Nobody knew what was going on, so nobody understood. She was masking her ill health and emerging alcoholic tendencies. She was beginning to make me look paranoid and stupid.

On many occasions I would be talking, relating to people what Nikki and I had agreed, and she would stun me with statements that were entirely to the contrary! Sometimes it would be laughed off; sometimes it would provoke that uncomfortable argument that causes others to wish they weren't there. I would be quietly simmering if not boiling. Was she deliberately trying to destroy our relationship?

Nikki was developing her habit of wanting exactly the opposite to me, to a fine art, and now taking it public in a quite aggravating and antagonising way. She was not well. I encouraged her repeatedly to seek help. I encouraged her to find work. She ignored me.

I had come to the end of my tether and it was now time to discuss separation. It was all lost on Nikki. I started to send letters of desperation within just weeks of my return; such was the change in her. I kept one or two of the letters to evidence my efforts, to rebut denials by Nikki, and to preserve for my own sanity and peace of mind. To show them to Nikki to prove what I had said. On 12th April 2003 I wrote the first of my letters. 'I came back to the UK to make a further attempt at keeping our marriage alive, but have felt that I can do nothing that is right for you, and quite frankly feel that you will eventually be happier either on your own or with someone else. Our mutual unhappiness in each other's company has taken a very serious toll on our relationship, but more importantly on those around us that we love so dearly. I can see no justification for continuing to either make painful efforts to put smiles on our faces, or to be miserable in the company of others'.

I wrote four more letters in 2003 and a final letter in March 2004. Reading these letters again reminds me that my earlier hopes had been unrealistic and that I was clutching at straws. It also reminds me that I should have walked away a lot earlier.

I preferred being with friends and acquaintances rather than Nikki, our sexual relationship stopped, we weren't laughing together. Ironically Nikki was now interested in a sex life, but I was no longer interested in having one with her. I couldn't make love to my abuser. I had been saying I loved her without real conviction. In fact I did love her, but not on the same basis. I just felt the kind of closeness you do from knowing someone for so long; a fondness, but not the love for a wife.

I had been doing all 'the giving', throughout our relationship and making all the effort. I knew that if I gave in it would be all over. I had given in, and it was all over, but we spent the rest of the year under the same roof.

Nikki's strange behaviour was not recognised by anybody else until after she was committed to hospital. Before that I was alone. I had earlier enlisted the help of my daughter to convince Nikki of the need to see a psychiatrist. She eventually agreed, and Zoe went with her for the first appointment. On one occasion I asked to go along with Nikki. At first she refused, but then she agreed.

The female Psychiatrist clearly thought I was arch enemy number one! She gave me the impression that she thought that she was just dealing with a marriage under stress.

274

Granted, she was examining the deep rooted psychological reasons for Nikki's problems, whatever Nikki had told her they were, but she didn't get it! She was being duped.

I learnt from Katy that Nikki was drinking secretly. She told me where the drink was hidden. I knew that she had been drinking for some time, but I hadn't really noticed that she was being secretive about it.

She had found work as a nurse in the community, one she never thought she could get, but she was drinking after work. She spent evenings in another room in the house and was awake most of the night; we weren't sleeping in the same bed and I heard her walking around the house, and sometimes playing music loudly, but I never thought she was hiding her drink. Katy told me she was hiding it under the sink. We took turns in pouring it away.

I was still clinging; still hanging on to a thread of hope that Nikki was responding to help and that there would be a miraculous turnaround in her behaviour.

Things were not getting any better in reality they were getting gradually worse. The house went up for sale. It was costing us over 50% of our income, but it was what Nikki had wanted – a four bed roomed, triple garage detached house – just for the two of us! Not the direction I wanted to be going in any case.

The summer of 2004 was uncomfortable and unhappy and I waited for the house to be sold.

Nikki's' Breakdown: February 2005

Nikki had moved out of our house, in January 2005 I think, and moved in with my sister in Coventry. She had deteriorated significantly although nobody else seemed to recognize it. She was the 'master of masking' and very manipulative.

She eventually had a breakdown at my sister's house and was 'committed' under the Mental Health Act under the most distressful of circumstances. She was admitted to Solihull Hospital and then subjected to serious gross negligence that had a profound effect on the entire family. If I had had my own way, and had not respected the wishes of others, I would have sued the Birmingham and Solihull Mental Health Trust.

Re-visiting this subject is not easy, I was severely traumatized by the events of February 2005, and my recollections of events are 'foggy' and distressing to re-visit so I will use correspondence to help with clarity. I start with my letter to the Chief Executive of the Birmingham and Solihull Mental Health Trust dated 28th February 2005.

'On 7th February 2005 my wife was sectioned and admitted to Solihull Hospital where she spent a week on the acute ward then a week and a half on ward 21 before being discharged on the evening of 24th February despite the views of family that she was not yet well enough to leave. The discharge was in our view premature and indeed unnecessary.

Who are we? Just a well educated and respected family comprising teachers, social workers, mental health nurses and other professionals. We have known Nikki for years.

It is one thing to make a mistake and rectify it. It is another thing to make the mistake after being warned against making it, and yet another thing to compound the mistake by discharging my wife without any form of consultation or advice to family or patient, without any medication (that she had been taking on psychiatric advice for twelve months previous), and without any form of aftercare plan."

Nikki's doctor had refused to talk to me and had apparently diagnosed her as an alcoholic! The ward discharged my wife to the care of my cousin, Sue, who was able to pick her up (we were only aware of her discharge earlier that day). Sue said Nikki didn't want to leave, and insisted on stopping for a drink during the return journey. She caused a little trouble in the pub.

"It is a serious exacerbation of the error, when the authority ignore all efforts to bring to your attention the family view, reinforced by the view of the police and ambulance staff (who were in attendance today), offered on 25th that she would need to return to hospital as soon as possible). Our concerns of 25th went unheeded. I complained to your answer machine at 3.00pm on that Friday afternoon and eventually got to speak with the Director of Mental Health. Doctors would arrive the following afternoon"

We had been trying desperately to get help. Katy reported that Nikki had been talking to a boyfriend through the TV, and she was awake all through the night wandering around the house. Nikki stopped with my sister. Police were called by my sister I think, after she had driven off on the Friday morning (25th) and threatened to burn the house down 'with me in it'. Nikki arrived at the door. I answered. She came in and she was very weird indeed. Ambulance and police arrived at the house. They were wonderful, the police

276

woman sergeant, from Coventry, in particular, but they could do nothing without doctor's approval. The police promised to put names and addresses on high priority so that the control room would give 'top priority' to a 999 call.

"On Saturday 26th two doctors arrive (one from Coventry and the other from Solihull) .and complete the whitewash and postpone (any action) until the Monday morning when (unbeknown to us) they said that Nikki had an appointment to see her doctor (allegedly- there was no paperwork)"

Nikki was clearly a danger to herself and to others, but the two doctors decided that rather than readmit her to hospital immediately, they would expect me to leave the house, and my 21 year old daughter to stop with Nikki to care for her.

Solution? Move me out and turn the house into an asylum supervised by the 21 year old daughter, who herself is under severe threat of a breakdown. Exit husband in tears and close to breakdown himself. My brother in law volunteered to watch over Nikki and my daughter.

I moved out and Nikki moved in! I left the two doctors in my house having shaken their hands and warned them that if anything happened to my wife or family I would hold them personally responsible. The Coventry doctor was visibly shaking as he took my hand. The other doctor 'had taken the lead' he later admitted. He wasn't comfortable with the decision.

I went off walking for miles, in tears, from pub to pub having my own breakdown. I must have made a dozen 999 calls to police reporting gross negligence and demanding that my wife be re-admitted. I went out of my way to get myself arrested so that the matter could be highlighted in the newspapers and the TV. I asked everyone I met, to phone the police and complain about me, and tell them where I was. I put a 'window in' at a well known bank, crossed the road, told a gob-smacked shopkeeper who I was, and asked him to telephone the police and tell them that I was protesting against the behaviour of the Solihull Health Authority. I was on a mission!!!

As I walked I calmed myself; I flushed out my anger. A police surveillance van, complete with camera, slowly passed me. Nothing happened!!!!! I had made every effort to get arrested, without hurting anyone in the process. I had even dialled 999 to say my sister's house was on fire!! During the evening I had visited my good friend Steve Poole's pub and publicly cried. I believe that Steve contacted police and played a part in keeping me out of the 'fairy dell' (cell).

I wanted to draw attention to the family plight. It was only courtesy of the police, who I am sure ignored my attempts to get myself arrested, that I wasn't before the Court on the Monday morning. I have mixed feelings about that, but a thank you is warranted.

Following my eight hour walkabout I went to my sister's house, and then, before daybreak, on to Solihull Hospital and insisted that 'I was a danger to myself and others' and therefore I insisted I be admitted to the 'spare bed' (my cousin had heard a nurse state that Nikki had to leave because the bed was needed). I was threatened with the police – fabulous!

I played them like a good fisherman plays a trout. Eventually they called out a doctor with a view to agreeing to my request. I camped myself on the waiting room floor. I played the fool. When the doctor arrived he asked me who I was, my date of birth and address. I refused to tell him. I demanded I be admitted. He left the room. After four hours wasting their time I left, just at the point that I was to be admitted. I was tired, and frankly feared that I might become a classic victim, just like in 'One Flew Over The Cuckoo's Nest'.

I had annoyed the male nurse so much, countered his every move so skilfully, that he was angry and pissed off. In the end he resorted to what he knew best – the system. He had tried hard to convince me that I was not 'potty' but now his 'basic instincts' kicked in. His easiest course of action, even though he knew the truth to be to the contrary, was to take the line of least resistance. So he accepted my insistence that I was a danger to myself and others, even though he had spent hours insisting otherwise, and trying desperately to get me to leave the building and go home. He called the doctor to solve his problem.

"During the Sunday night my wife breaks down further. Damage caused. Monday morning she snaps. Police called again. Wife returns to hospital."

I stopped the Sunday night at my sister's I think. Sarah, Nikki's half-sister, stopped with her that night giving my brother in law a break. Sarah was going to take her to her appointment in Chelmsley Wood on the Monday morning.

At the last minute the appointment was cancelled!!!!!! Nikki cracked up. Police arrived and two police women took her to hospital! During the Sunday Nikki had driven off in her car. She received a ticket for driving at eighty five miles per hour in a sixty

278

limit but the police cancelled the ticket after my letter of explanation. She had caused significant damage to our house.

"Your staff has been untruthful, devious, arrogant and grossly incompetent, if not criminally negligent. They have destroyed our confidence in the service you provide.

Please accept this letter as a notice of the intention of every member of my family, including Nikki when she has recovered, to sue you personally, the Trust vicariously, and the doctors severally, for damage to health and property, pain and suffering caused".

Amazingly, the above is just a sample of the horrific nature of the experience we have suffered as a result of your actions and therefore a more detailed account of the facts, plus a fuller list of our grounds for complaint and summons, will follow, once we have appointed solicitors and taken further advice.

Meanwhile we would welcome a full investigation to provide an honest and transparent explanation as to how on earth my wife could have been released so early, and without a (care) plan, and why on earth, given the evidence available to the doctors on the Saturday, a decision to take my wife to a place of safety was rejected contrary to common sense, the pleas of the family and friends, warnings and obvious signs"

I wrote to 'Mind' for help. Rather like 'The Peoples Front for the Liberation of Palestine Suicide Squad' in the Monty Python Film, 'Life of Brian' they declared their 'support'. In the film, Brian was begging to be taken off the cross. The suicide squad praised him for the stand he was taking, and to show solidarity, they all committed suicide before his eyes! 'Mind' showed 'solidarity' with 'Brother Dave'. 'You're doing the right thing' they wrote. And that was that.

I educated myself on the legal position and the responsibilities of the authorities. I wrote to my Member of Parliament, Caroline Spellman who wrote a letter of outrage to the trust. The Chief Executive did not reply to my earlier letter and I wrote again on 2nd March 2005.

"I refer to the shameful events of the past week and in particular my letter. I would appreciate an explanation in response to the following key questions:-

1.Why my wife was discharged on grounds that she was not 'mentally ill'? Please consider S1 (2) of the Mental Health Act 1983 and the dictum of Lawton LJ in W v L (1974) when replying.

2.Why the living person who best knew my wife (me) has never been consulted at any time on any matter whatsoever about my wife? Try reading Planning Care in Mental Health Nursing by Robert Tummey. I did this morning.

3.Why no care plan of any kind was prepared by the hospital? Why there was no preparation before discharge? No research? No advice given to family? No aftercare arranged?

4.Why my wife was discharged without any form of medication, having been prescribed to her for over twelve months beforehand by her GP and her psychiatrist? I understand that this was dangerous?

5.Why doctors attending on Saturday decided not to readmit my wife, as they could easily have done(by their own admission) having been given ample evidence to clarify that there were genuine grounds and real concerns for the safety of my wife and others? Why was it necessary (to wait) for her doctor to make the decision on the Monday?

I am concerned primarily for my wife's good health and safety, and the mental health of my family in particular my daughters and my sister. I have lost confidence in the doctors and staff at your hospital and have serious doubts that they can provide my wife with impartial and correct treatment now that there is a potential conflict of interest vis a vis covering their own backs! Can you please therefore arrange for my wife to be transferred to another authority, preferably Walsgrave Hospital (Coventry) or a nearby BUPA hospital as previously requested?

cc: trustees
Mental Health Act Commission

I still received no reply so wrote again on 10th March. I got a written reply from Kate O, the Complaints Officer. It was disgusting: dismissive and cold. My response was short and simple.

"Ms O,

I find your response letter distasteful, insulting and distressing......my complaint has been swept aside.....there is no compassion or understanding in your approach. Your response is cowardly.

280

I regard you as being partial and incompetent and therefore quite unfit to fulfil the role of Complaints Officer".

I subsequently met with The Chief Executive, and she apologized for the letter and told me the Complaints Officer had been reprimanded. The CEO was understanding and fair, but stated that the decision of the doctors was not her responsibility (I knew that was true) but that the 'quality of the hospital' was, and assured me that Nikki had not been discharged because of lack of accommodation. She didn't tell me anything that I didn't already know, but she was conciliatory and did respond where she felt able.

She wrote to me on 6th April,

"Thank you for coming to see me just before Easter. I found our meeting most constructive, and I hope you found it helpful also. This letter attempts to summarise the main points of agreement...............I fully accepted and apologise for the bewildering situation you and other members of your family experienced following your wife's discharge from hospital in February.........we discussed some of the limitations of my ability to share with you information about your wife's ill-health and plan of treatment, due to her strong and consistent view that she does not consent to this......we agreed some important things;

........................'Nearest Relative' is Katy Wakefield.........this is the person we will consult with before making an application under the Mental Health Act, and inform of significant events subsequently, including discharge...........leave arrangements will be negotiated with full involvement of Katy, and, where possible, family members".

Poor Katy was 'the main man'. What a massive challenge for a sensitive girl of such tender years. No wonder she suffered a trauma related breakdown months later – although again the doctors got it all wrong again – they thought drug related!!!!! Another story not to be told; suffice to say Katy had some battle years afterwards trying to get the idiots to acknowledge the fact!

I never sued the Authority. How could I succeed without Nikki's agreement and help? The family had been through enough and only Katy supported my wish. But Katy was close to breakdown. I tried to tell her. I tried to get her to seek counselling. She wouldn't take my advice; she thought herself too strong, and later admitted that she buried her head in the sand. She tried to deal with the problem herself by trying to forget all about it. It cost her dearly!

281

The standard of mental health care in this country is abysmal. Solihull was responsible, in part, for destroying my family. They never had the decency to apologise, remedy or help. I was on my knees being attacked from all sides.

My own mini breakdown? It would be easy to put it solely down to my wife's predicament, but it wasn't. It was a combination of work and domestic issues that had made my life a living hell.

2003 – 2007 Disastrous Sideshows

During this period other problems occurred, any one of them enough to make the average guy stressed. But I was not the average guy. I was strong, resilient, determined and capable. Unfortunately I was also stubborn, and, I knew I was 'losing it'. I was unhappy, very unhappy. And misery upon misery seemed to be being heaped upon me. When would it all stop! When would my luck change?

So what of these other problems that plagued me during these four years (2003-2007)?

The UK was a different place to the one I'd left in 1997 and my experience has been that companies are operating less efficiently for the customer, but more efficiently for the 'fat cat' directors and their shareholders. Less staff, more systems, all promoted in the name of efficiency for the customer. Telephone systems represented the greatest of all my frustrations, and why there are not more reported cases of 'telephones' becoming embedded in lounge walls I will never know. Another cause for concern is poorly trained staff with 'limited' authority. It's the 'American Way'. WE, the people of this country are being stripped of our wealth. WE are witnessing corporate day-light robbery, and doing nothing!

I am excellent at dealing with difficult situations and awkward people. When dealing with incompetence and bullying I have a simple approach. Try to reason, resolve, help and show patience, if that doesn't work meet it head on slowly applying pressure. But be warned. I suggest a proven policy. Never to fight a battle that couldn't be won! And be prepared to face the consequences of defeat; and I did have my defeats!

My Jaguar was stolen off the driveway just a couple of weeks after I had purchased it, and only shortly after we had moved in to our new home. The story goes like this.

282

Nikki stayed up and 'walked the halls' as usual, like a restless ghost, and I went to bed. She woke me in the early hours and said she thought someone had broken in. I went downstairs. The toilet fanlight window to the side was open (I'd asked Nikki repeatedly not to leave it open). The rear conservatory door was open; drawers in the lounge were open. There was a knife on the lounge floor that had been removed from the drawer. Nikki said, 'your car's gone'. We had indeed been burgled!

I called 999 immediately and the police arrived twenty minutes later. A stolen car had been abandoned in the cul-de-sac at the side of the house.

It was so late by the time the police had left that I stayed up until 9.00am so that I could report the matter to the insurance company, and then sleep. The insurance was with Churchill through Nationwide. The claim was rejected during my phone call to report the matter! Astonishing. Why? Because of an endorsement on the policy that stated that if a downstairs window was left open or unlocked when you 'have retired for the night' the policy would not cover theft. The endorsement didn't exist as far as I was concerned. I would not have agreed to it. It was unsafe and in my view unfair.

The claims guy wouldn't give me any kind of reference number when I said that I did not accept the situation, but I demanded a claim form. He told me he couldn't send a claim form because the claim was not valid!! Was the industry going mad?

The claim was rejected after a formal letter and claim, so I wrote to the CEO of Nationwide.

...............My wife tells me we never received an insurance policy. The original schedule given to us indicated a sum insured of £35,000 on contents despite several instructions that it needed to be £70,000. From inception in early March it was £35,000, and as our written instructions to increase this sum were not being dealt with, I became involved in hours of telephone discussions to have this matter corrected, together with other amendments that had been requested, but that had not been made.

Frankly, your telephone systems leave a caller totally frustrated and at times enraged. Once I was asked to wait on the phone for fully fifteen minutes, then I was cut off. I then had to phone again and go through the same procedure.

.................you will note that between inception and mid April the sum insured on contents had been increased and as a consequence an endorsement was added to the schedule. We maintain that the wording of this endorsement was not notified to us.

A few hours after the burglary I telephoned your offices and I was politely told that the claim could not be paid because of the endorsement. The endorsement was read to me. I was promised a copy of the policy and the endorsement. I was not given a reference to quote for future calls or letters. This created massive communication difficulties in the several hours of telephone discussions that followed. I dealt with over a dozen people, two Loraine's, two departments, several teams, but no decision maker. The decision makers were in the Technical Services Department, and I was not allowed to talk to them.

I was not allowed to talk to Claims Department because they were not allowed to raise a claim until the policy dispute was resolved by Customer Services Department. I was not able to submit a formal claim in writing because your systems were not geared to such an approach. With no reference, and only Christian names to quote, the entire communication network within your Insurance Department became a confusing maze riddled with culs-de-sac.

After much stress, and nearly an hour on the telephone yesterday, I received confirmation that my claim was rejected by someone in Technical Services, who may, or may not, have the full facts. The reason given is that Nationwide conclude that the policy was issued with a mortgage pack when we purchased the house. Could I have that put into writing? I asked. "Yes, if you want".

Now aside from the significant reliance that is placed on your efficiency in 'packing' a policy document (presumably someone would stand before an arbitrator and state that your systems were faultless and there was no chance that Mrs Wakefield had not received the policy), the contrary assertion might be that my wife was not telling the truth.

We cannot accept that position, and will be seeking assurances from your Insurance Department that this is not the case. We maintain that the endorsement was not properly notified to us. Furthermore, had we known of its contents, we would not have accepted the terms of the Insurance because we regard them as unfair and quite frankly a shade ridiculous given our insurance position prior to my instruction for the sum insured to be increased being accepted. Why?

Consider this.

1.If my sum insured was £35,000 then the endorsement would not have been placed on the policy because we had no adverse claims record. We could have the claim paid to £35,000.

2.If the incident had happened during the day, when my wife was asleep upstairs, the claim would be payable.

3.If a car had backed into the front of the house and into the dining room, thieves had charged out of the back, stolen contents and driven off, my claim could not be paid because the toilet window was open.

4.If I had left my Mont Blanc sun glasses on the table in the garden, they would have been covered to a limit of £250.

5.If the thieves had climbed onto the garage roof and entered through my daughter's bedroom window, the loss would have been covered.

6.The endorsement is dangerous in cases of fire. To make it a condition that keys should be kept available in the event of an emergency is a sick attempt at sidestepping responsibility for someone dying of smoke inhalation.

7.If my family had not 'retired for the night', but had been playing monopoly upstairs, the loss would have been covered. If my daughter had not returned from her night out in town, then we would not have retired for the night and the house would not have been unattended.

8.If my wife was still in the bathroom then she would not yet have retired for the night.

The fact that my car keys were stolen from the house also affects the loss of personal belongings within the vehicle. ....I am very concerned that I have not been able to speak with the decision maker, or effectively communicate with him/her. I am very concerned that Nationwide appear to be confident that a policy was sent to us and that the endorsement was properly highlighted................. I am not satisfied, and I cannot accept the decision. .... the claims handling systems are flawed, but hasten to add that the staff have been professional in applying the system... exposing themselves to the......... customer backlash…….."

In a letter dated 9th June 2003, and after protracted correspondence and tiresome wriggling, my household insurance claim was accepted.

The motor insurers went on to pay enough for me to get a new replacement Jaguar. Katy wasted no time in reversing her car into it as she sped off to work!!

Kingston University – St George Medical School

In July 2003 Katy was 'apparently' accepted at Nursing School in Kingston Upon Thames. She was elated, celebrated, and subsequently humiliated and devastated at then being told there wasn't a place for her at all! There was nothing that could be done but I was appalled at the inhumane manner in which they casually treated the matter. I had to get it off my chest with a letter. How must it have felt for Katy to have been told she had a place, celebrated, told friends, only to be told there had been an administrative error, and she hadn't got it after all.

Universities are run like businesses and only one thing seems to count; making money! Katy never again applied for a nursing position; a loss to the vocation.

I return now to further tales of incompetence. I was to have further problems with Nationwide when Nikki and I parted, and other problems occurred following the sale of the matrimonial home in December 2005.

Estate Agents and the House

As a consequence of Nikki's breakdown in early 2005 I had to pull out of the house sale; Nikki was non compos mentis and I could not in all conscience allow a deal to proceed with my wife in hospital. The estate agent was aware of the remote possibility of complications associated with my wife's ill health at the outset. The story goes like this, and concerns an awkward, arrogant and proud estate agent who eventually sued me for payment of a fee after I had 'sacked' him for not properly and reasonably following my instructions.

In a nutshell we had a purchaser about one week before Nikki's first committal to hospital. When Nikki went in to hospital I contacted the agents the following day and withdrew the house from the market. I explained the reason to the prospective purchaser and she understood. I had no legal obligation, but I met her costs to date, a couple of hundred for the survey.

About a week later I told the estate agents that when Nikki was well enough I would like to re-advertise the property, but with a more accurate description of its location, as I had sought earlier. The property had been advertised as a Coventry address, but was in Berkswell, Solihull.

286

The agent, Mr Davis, refused. Why he needed to do so I don't know. I suspect that because of the complications that were involved, he thought he would just create confrontation, take the 50% of the fee that he felt he was contractually entitled to, and get out. Business was brisk at that time.

Because he would not follow my instructions I took the business to another agent that was prepared to do as I was asking. It was sold by that agent precisely according to the 'property description' I had asked for.

Nearly three years later, in 2008, Davis, by now retired, sued me for 50% of the fee; he was debt collecting! He was debt collecting under contract. I counter-claimed, alleging that he'd breached the contract and not me. I defended myself but I lost; I would suggest narrowly. I came up with good sound reasons why I shouldn't pay, and it was in the balance.

The judge said that Mr Davis was entitled to exercise his professional opinion! Personally I don't think that was relevant to the case, it was a contract issue, but I know that judges tend to support the establishment, and I couldn't afford the money to appeal.

The only crumb of comfort was that the judge agreed that Nikki (a joint signatory to the contract) should not be subject to the Court Order. The lawyers, who I had defeated in an earlier hearing, when they were seeking summary judgment, looked hurt. I hope the greedy old man enjoys his couple of grand!

Why he was so awkward? There was no logical reason for him to object to my instruction. The house was located about half a mile outside the City of Coventry boundary, in the Parish of Berkswell, in the Borough of Solihull. My Council tax was payable to Solihull Council. Schooling entitlement, medical entitlement, policing, ambulance, fire and refuse collection services were all supplied by the Borough of Solihull. The property was a rural property. It was not in Tile Hill, in the City of Coventry. At the end of the day I think it boils down to greed!

British Gas

The house was sold by 'good' agents, according to my wishes and description, on 20th December 2005, after Nikki had had a second spell at the Priory Hospital in Birmingham courtesy of my BUPA insurance, but I was still getting hassled for payment of household bills months, even years later. In May 2006 I wrote to British Gas.

"All bills pertaining to the said property have been settled. We moved out on the 20th December 2005 and on that date the meter readings were phoned through to your office because you would not come out and read them.........we subsequently received bills for(consumption) after that date. I phoned through and the bills were amended and then I settled payment. We continued to receive bills for the period after we left. I phoned through several times and told your offices but I have even received one dated 1st April for electricity consumed between 5th January and 30th March.......can you please get your records straight and please stop wasting your time and money chasing ghost debts."

In May 2007, I wrote to 1st Credit of Reigate (cc British Gas Correspondence Manager in Southampton). They were one of 3 agents that had been appointed by British Gas; Buchanan Clarke Wells, and Westcot Credit Services had preceded them.

"I refer to the above two accounts in respect of which you issued notices of intention to take legal proceedings against my wife...........I have explained a dozen times............I have had quite enough...please refer to your principals and either issue proceedings or get off my wife's back. She has had mental breakdowns, and does not need this senseless misdirected harassment from organisations that have no idea what they are doing. You are the third lot! The bills were paid. I have heard enough thank you"

Katy's Landlords

In October 2005 Katy was trying hard to carry on regardless. She was burying her head in the sand and wouldn't seek counselling as I'd suggested. Nobody at Solihull hospital had offered! Her mother was still receiving hospital treatment, and Katy was clearly under massive mental stress. I had noticed it from the day of my return to the UK.

I repeatedly suggested she move out, find her own feet; get away from the stress of her parents relationship. She was getting under our feet and getting caught up in our arguments; trying no doubt to stop them. She was doomed to fail of course, and moving out depended on so many other factors. She had nowhere, and no reason, in her own mind, to go. She had nobody to share with, and no university to attend.

She decided to start a course in Occupational Therapy at Coventry University. She took shared accommodation with 'new friends'. She asked for help with the deposit. I gave it and tried to guide her. She signed a contract for share of twelve months' rent. She fell apart during the first few weeks of the course, and was again disappointed with 'supposed friends'; they claimed that they couldn't find a replacement house mate, and so Katy was expected to continue to pay.

I tried to explain to the landlord's agents that there were significant family problems. Her college lecturer tried to help. They were insisting that she pay full rent for the full year. I knew her housemates (all girls) could find another girl from the university to take the room; they were trying it on - it was a con! I'd visited them and suspected someone was occupying Katy's room. The estate agents were of no help whatsoever – they just wanted money off Katy- period!

My letters to the agents fell on deaf ears. I had got a negative response and so decided to make a few investigations and call a bluff or two. I had visited the property, seen Katy's room and met someone at the door who gave her name and admitted that she lived there. A mate arrived at the door and I explained Katy's plight. She said the other girl didn't live there! This was a contradiction that had embarrassed the other girl. She wasn't interested in helping and said they needed Katy's contribution. I said that if that was the case I might use the room myself. I subsequently wrote this letter to the estate agents.

"I visited the address before Christmas as the tenants will confirm. I was shown the room allocated to Katy. It was full of furniture and miscellaneous contents that were identified as belonging to the last tenants. The room is uninhabitable and these items need to be removed if the room is to be usable.

I request confirmation as to the date these items will be removed, rendering the room usable. The room also needs security to the door. There is none. Please confirm when this has been done.

I have evidence that the house is occupied/sub-let by 'non tenants'. The tenants are believed to be receiving payment sufficient to cover Katy's share of the cancelled agreement. I need confirmation that this is the case within the next 72 hours. There is a possibility that the landlord is aware of the occupancy.

I wish to receive substantive clarification regarding the above, separately from each of the tenants within the next seven days. They can write to me at the above address. Please give each of them a copy of this letter. If there is denial, then I propose that I take up residence in Katy's room as soon as possible pending legal proceedings.

I have recently separated from my wife and could use the room. You have undertaken all the necessary credit checks, etc and so this should not create any difficulty. I would wish to have all keys in readiness for entry on 9th January.

If for any reason the above is unacceptable then I hope to arrange for a friend, Trisha Oatridge, to occupy the room.

Please confirm that either the action proposed by the tenants is abandoned or please surrender keys to access by the 6th January. Please post the keys to the above address.

A photograph of the room, an audio tape, statements and a video tape of comings and goings at the house will be released at the discovery stage of proceedings."

There were of course no audio or video tapes, and my good friend Trisha would only have moved in to help me. I never heard from the agents again. I had avoided twelve months' rent and wanted to press for the return of the deposit, but I decided to 'let sleeping dogs lie'; I had enough problems and I cut my losses.

Equifax (Credit Reference Agency) and Nationwide Building Society

After the sale of the house I set up my own bank account with Natwest. I had by now sold my Jaguar and brought a van because I knew I would need it for all the furniture removal work. I had also purchased a run-about classic Mini Mayfair through the Sunday Times (1990 immaculate 6,000 miles, showroom original, even the tyres), but I needed a loan to help Nikki.

It was January 2006. Nikki needed a 'top up' to buy the property that she wanted to buy for herself. I applied for a loan from my new bank. I had no mortgage and no debt, yet it was rejected on the grounds that I had a bad credit rating with Equifax. How come?

Nationwide, the building society we had been with as a couple for many years, had apparently reported missing payments on our mortgage account. This report was wrong. The records were incorrect. I needed the money urgently otherwise Nikki's property purchase might fall through. That would be a real blow. Weeks into 2006 and things did not seem to be getting any better!

After desperate efforts to have my Credit Score corrected I had little choice but to turn the screws..........I sued them both for defamation. Why? Equifax stated that once Nationwide had agreed, it would take twenty eight days to amend the incorrect record, Nikki might have lost the opportunity by then, and the false information was still being published.

Nationwide refused to recognise their mistake, even though it was an obvious one and I had highlighted it for them. My wife was in danger of losing the home that she wanted to buy. It would have devastated her at an already difficult time, and I didn't want that.

As it happened the purchase was not affected, but the behaviour of these companies was blinkered and uncooperative, and rather than thinking and probably considering my complaint they kept digging a hole for themselves, as many companies do.

In a letter to Equifax PLC I wrote,

"I note your view that responsibility devolves upon Nationwide (to change the record) because of the contract that you have with them. With respect, that contract is between yourselves and Nationwide and has no direct bearing on my allegation.......... I hold you jointly and severally liable.

The allegation against Equifax is one of defamation, and if you read the 'further and better particulars' (of the writ) more carefully you will note that Equifax, during telephone conversations I had with their staff, refused to accelerate the investigation and relied on the maximum twenty eight day allowance, despite being informed of the urgent nature of the matter and the very serious implications of delay.

You have a responsibility to those persons recorded on your system. A responsibility to take all reasonable care to avoid publication of defamatory material. You published that material despite being on notice that it was incorrect. You failed, despite being warned, to act to prevent this publication because of your rigid application of your systems.

...............Finally, please note that the summons has not been correctly examined by you. In future please write to the correct address."

And to Nationwide I wrote a demand that my records be changed, and also sent a letter to the CEO.

"I write to you personally because you are probably unaware that I am suing Nationwide for defamation of character; the consequences being very serious in the event that I win my case.

I am writing because of the disgraceful way in which your Northampton Centre have dealt with this matter and I feel that you should take a personal interest............ Your systems, your staff and your contract with Equifax have let you down.

I respectfully suggest that you contact your legal department at Pipers Way before things get much worse."

Nationwide later made the mistake of offering me money because I am 'a nuisance'. I write in reply in April 2006.

"Your offer is totally unacceptable and offensive. This is not a money issue and never was. You, and your colleagues, consistently overlook and disregard the conversational and written content of my communication, and, might I add, fail to understand the law of defamation/negligent misstatement.

I have demanded an apology from Nationwide for the factually incorrect data supplied to Equifax and I have demanded that the record be corrected. Whilst you have amended the Equifax record (which contradicts your assertion that the information was correct at the time it was recorded), it is still incorrect. Furthermore Nationwide stubbornly maintained that the information was correct when given an opportunity to investigate and correct the error before it was repeated. This caused serious distress to my wife and seriously threatened the purchase of a house.

You have repeatedly refused to apologise for the publication and the disgraceful manner in which you have handled my complaint. I must receive an unqualified apology or people will need to be exposed and brought to account.

I accept your offer to meet and receive, from well informed and responsible persons, an explanation for why you maintain, negligently at the very least, that I am incorrect in any material fact and also explain my 'misunderstanding'.

I have no interest whatsoever in your costs, these may or may not fall for consideration by the Court, and find it quite sickening that you insult me by offering me money because you find my complaint uneconomical to deal with!

292

If you have a reasonable explanation or mitigating circumstance concerning the libel then let's hear it in its entirety now. Protracted correspondence is not going to get us anywhere and your preoccupation with 'buying me off' is causing more damage to the chances of a successful resolution of this matter than you can possibly imagine.

I cannot accept the position you are taking in relation to Equifax. You cannot represent them, they take a different position to yourselves, and the facts substantiating the allegations against them are quite different to those upon which I base my case against Nationwide.

Equifax refused to fast track an amendment to the records and initiate an investigation on more than one occasion.   This refusal, despite the serious and exceptional circumstances, and implications that were explained to them, resulted in defamatory publication. Equifax will need to defend their corner and respond to my complaint in a like manner.

As the main perpetrator of the defamation is Nationwide I recognise the lead you have taken. In recognition of the relatively small role taken by Equifax in this case I will be prepared to simply accept from them an apology ....This offers them, in advance of any Court hearing, the benefit of any doubt."

I subsequently met Equifax Directors and Nationwide BS legal team in the London offices of Equifax. I kept the two parties apart. I insisted that I see Nationwide first, and alone, to the indignation of Equifax Operations Director, Neil Munroe, now the top man at Equifax.

A friend, Suzanne, played 'personal assistant' for the day, providing a professional touch to my presentation. Nationwide paid me £6,000 including my costs. They were extremely apologetic and reasonable. They had failed to understand the cock up and the manner in which it was handled. Nationwide were genuinely shocked.

Equifax, once they got off their high horse, also recognised their failings. I have to say that both these companies were, at the end of the day, fair, but it is so sad that there were so many occasions when staff simply failed to respond as they should have done by taking a complaint seriously, properly investigating it, and remedying a mistake immediately. Companies are simply too arrogant. Why did it come to this?

I was promised that Equifax systems would be reviewed in the light of the system failures exposed. Nationwide told me that 'lessons would be learnt'; the one casualty of this avoidable mess was the telephone girl that goaded and teased me on the phone and refused to do anything at all for me…she, I was told, 'was no longer with them'.

Particularly embarrassing for Nationwide was the fact that they had adopted a system whereby incoming post received at their mortgage department was being 'returned to the sender' if the post didn't bear a mortgage reference. As a result they returned the summons that I had taken out marked, 'please resubmit with a reference number'!!!!

December 2005: Breaking Away

Before the house was sold in late December I moved in to a rented house in Coventry on a six month rental while I waited for the conveyance of a home that I had purchased in Berwick upon Tweed to be completed. I had looked after Nikki financially and at the time I had a limited amount of cash. In November 2005, I had travelled to Berwick Upon Tweed for an overnight stay with the intention of buying a home and I found an affordable stone build cottage in an idyllic location. I had never been to Berwick before in my life, but within 24 hours of my arrival I had brought a new home!

I moved in to my new house after Christmas of 2005. I had earlier moved furniture and belongings up to Berwick to make it habitable. For several months I occupied a rented house in Coventry and a terraced cottage in Berwick (Upon Tweed) because I was in the process of completing a part time City and Guilds part 2 plumbing course in Leamington Spa. Such had been my level of inactivity and boredom at CCS that I needed to keep my mind active with creative learning and in any case skills in a trade might stand me in good stead for the future.

I had purchased my trusty friend, Jack, the Jack Russell Terrier in May 2005, and together we were relocating to somewhere 'far from the maddening crowd'.

Jack was born on 22nd April 2005. He was from working dog stock, and was born on a 'Darling Buds of May' type farm in Hampton in Arden. They supplied working dogs to the nearby Packington Estate. He was the runt of the litter and Steve, the owner, let me have him cheap. The first photo of him was taken with him sitting in a pint pot with his paws hanging over the rim.

Virtually from the day I got him, he got me in trouble He has become a friendly pub dog that big George, patron of the Barrels Ale House in Berwick, calls 'baguette' on account of his 'bite size'. Some think he is a corgi or Chihuahua cross, on account of his big pointy ears, but I point out that he is a 'fruit bat' cross and that he sleeps upside down in the cloakroom on a coat hanger, so he is also nicknamed, 'fruit-bat'. He is very well known in Berwick.

I didn't feel that much better in Berwick, but I am sure that I felt better than I would have done had I stayed living in or around Coventry. Indeed, loneliness was to become a substitute for some of the displaced stress. I am generally one to hide my emotions and I smile my way through life while having deep but short spells of despair. My troubles and frustrations back-up. I sometimes fester.

You may remember one of the early scenes in Bridget Jones Diary starring Rene Zelleger; the message answer machine 'you have no messages' and the song, 'All by myself', well I had arrived there! In moments, evening or a full day of despair, that is how I have felt. But then Berwick upon Tweed was in many ways one of the best places I could have settled down in under the circumstances.

I moved to Berwick upon Tweed, high up in the north eastern corner of England, just three miles from the border with Scotland, whilst still occupying the rented house in Coventry. I needed the rented house, at least for the time being, because I had unfinished business in the Midlands.

To keep my mind stimulated I had set myself challenges. In doing so I spent thousands of pounds. The plumbing was a two year part time City and Guilds evening course, Mondays and Tuesdays that I completed in spring of 2007. After vacating the rented house in Coventry I travelled weekly, from Berwick to Coventry, to complete the course at Warwickshire College in Leamington Spa.

To handle, understand, and cope with Nikki's mental illness, Katy's breakdown, and my own demise, I also obtained a Diploma in Hypnotherapy and Psychotherapy at Selly Oak Hospital in Birmingham. The ten weekend course involved the theory and practice of Hypno-psychotherapy, culminating in a written examination. I qualified in September 2006. I had also completed a two day foundation course in Solution Focused Therapy.

By October 2006 I was wholly Berwick based and, again to stimulate the mind, I completed a City and Guilds Level 3 Certificate in Delivering Learning.

I was demonstrating to myself my own capability, keeping myself occupied, and also providing myself with some therapy. Without these stimulations, and reasons for getting out of bed, I think I'd have gone under. CCS had abandoned me.

Business Link North East

After my redundancy in 2007 I signed on the dole. I received a bill for over £200 that the DHS tell me I should not have received from them. Despite reassurances that they would not seek return of the money, because they had made the mistake, they appointed debt collectors!

I was eager to get off the dole, and, although I had never received a genuine payment from them because I was drawing a pension, they were eager to have me off their books. Fair enough.

They referred me to Business Link because I was interested in self employment. Business Link promised to help me and, in return for 'signing off,' and on condition I set up a business bank account, they would pay 50% of an electrical testing course in York. I signed a contract.

I sat the course and paid by credit card on the last day of my completed course. I received a receipt. I submitted the receipt to Business Link within seven days. They refused to pay because I had not paid the bill out of my business account! My letter to them of the 18th January 2008 sums up the problem.

.

"I write with amazement and disappointment in relation to the above matter.

I entered into an agreement with Business Link and honoured that agreement in spirit and action. I did everything that was expected of me, or so it seemed.

My agreement was closed because my claim had lapsed due to missing evidence. I am still unsure what is meant by the missing evidence, but it would seem that because I had paid the course fee on my personal account (I am self employed) I was in breach of the agreement.

I regard this minor insignificant 'breach' as being immaterial to the spirit of the agreement and do not believe that it can be the honest intention of your organisation to not only demand such a ridiculous matter of detail, but to disallow payment as a result.

I do not feel in all consciousness that I can let this matter drop because I fear that others less fortunate may suffer as a result of such harsh application of an agreement designed to help people like me.

As previously stated I did not receive the second letter dated 28th November and I am surprised that you closed the matter so sharply and readily. I request that you re-open my file and try to explain to me what can be done to remedy this sad situation. A situation where I have acted in good faith, and somehow find myself in a position where, because I have paid out of my own account (I believe I did not have the money in the business account), I am refused a payment under the agreement.

I am sure that there is a mechanism within your organisation to remedy cases that result in injustices and I look forward to hearing from you with a favourable response."

An official appeal was rejected and, me being me, I gave them three written warnings of my intention to issue a writ for breach of contract unless they saw sense; these warnings went unheeded.

I issued a summons at a cost of £35 and outlined my case. Within a few days Mr Robert Cornell, the Corporate Services Director telephoned me to apologise.

He stated this should never have happened. He agreed with all I had said and asked me if I could stop the proceedings; he would be putting a cheque in the post! He did so.

Why couldn't I get the money I deserved in the first place? Why did it not succeed at appeal? For all the trouble and time and anxiety that had been caused I should have been more mercenary when he said, "How much do you want?"

Many people would have accepted the rejection bitterly, and not known what to do. Why should it have been necessary to issue a summons? These organisations are more interested in financing their own jobs than delivering help to those in need of help. They are all too often incompetent or cheats.

Chapter Nineteen
Banks and their Moral Bankruptcy: 2007 – 2009

I fell into debt. I would not have done so but for my dismissal in 2007, and I have to say my inability to curb my spending. But I wasn't in a good mental shape.

In late 2006 I was searching for anything that would raise my spirits and I decided to buy myself a car for my birthday on 9th January 2007. I did so, and took out a personal loan to pay for it. Sods law, I was made redundant weeks later.

At this point I also had had a loan with Natwest for the £25,000, extra money that I gave to Nikki, and I had taken out a mortgage of about £30,000 so that I could buy an office/apartment in a 250 year old warehouse building on the quay in Berwick; a great and un-missable investment opportunity. I owed about £80,000 in all, not an excessive sum given my level of income.

Suddenly, debts that would pose no difficulty for me at all whilst in employment became major problems. I didn't deal properly with these problems. I continued to live, and spend, as if I was still receiving an income. I also lived on the money from the unfair dismissal award. I put all this down to my mental state; my feelings of anger, betrayal, despondency and sadness.

To tell you the truth, although I was never any good with money, I was still suffering trauma related stress. I was in shock! In denial! Lost! I was mixed up and irresponsible. Financial trouble that I had resolved after my separation from Nikki was to return and plague me.

By the time of the onset of the economic crisis in 2008, the banks, as one of their staff put it, 'were closing in on me'. They were brutal. Natwest had lent me £25,000 that I had given Nikki, and Bank of Scotland was owed money that I had borrowed to buy my car. They took turns in beating me up with reams of letters and numerous unsolicited telephone calls and at the same time disregarding my own.

National Westminster Bank PLC (The Unhelpful Bank)

I wrote to Natwest in June 2008, because I realised that I couldn't continue to make monthly repayments on the loan. I felt that a proactive approach was the right approach and would be most appreciated by Natwest. I also appreciated how easy it can be for people to bury their heads in the sand. I had hoped that in return I would receive Natwest help and patience in carrying me through a difficult period. After all I knew that I had more than enough equity in property to comfortably fulfil all my financial obligations; eventually.

In fact my property was on the market and I was confident of getting myself back on my feet. I instructed Natwest to cancel all my direct debit instructions so that they would not bounce and incur costs. They refused to cancel all of them, and they were bounced for months. They also charged me for each bounce. They refused to cancel the direct debit relating to my loan, even though my loan was with Natwest. They charged me each time their own direct debit bounced!

The story starts when I received a letter dated 4th June indicating that I had a loan payment shortfall of £383. The letter also stated that I was £509 overdrawn on my current account. I had an overdraft facility of £2,000. The letter indicated that if I didn't respond within the next ten days my cash card would be withdrawn. The payment shortfall incurred a charge of £38.

I sent a letter dated 17th June in response to this communication. My health, my position, was explained and my CV was enclosed. I asked for the charge to be cancelled. I had had a long outstanding dispute with the bank about excessive and unreasonable charges.

On 23rd June I received notice, from Birmingham Collections, that a cheque for £87 had been returned incurring a charge. This crossed with mine of 22nd June advising them that in May I had asked that all payments (standing orders and direct debits) be cancelled. I instructed them to return money taken and stop drawing the monthly £383 loan repayment from the account. I also telephoned my branch in Kenilworth to tell them to stop the direct debits and the charges. I was told that there was nothing they could do and that the bank would continue to draw and bounce my loan sum.

On 30th June I wrote again. I solicited a call. I wrote again on 17th July expressing concern that I had had no reply. I asked that I be allowed to pay £50 per month on a temporary basis. I then received another notice of payment shortfall of £383 and another charge of £38.

On 28th July I received yet another letter advising me that my direct debit to pay Natwest had again bounced and notice of another charge. I was becoming frustrated and distressed. I was angry at the lack of response and the disregard shown toward me. I wrote on 31st July expressing my disgust. I repeated my instruction to cancel payments out of my account.

I received a letter dated 2nd August from Nottingham Collections, indicating the payment shortfall against my loan account, and my overdraft sum of £1,884.27 that had been inflated by charges. Please telephone was the message.

On the evening of 7th August I received a telephone call from Nottingham Collection Centre. He knew nothing of anything that I had written or explained. I wrote following that conversation. Because I had received letters from both Nottingham and Birmingham Collections about the same matter, I sent a copy to each! Telephone conversations had produced no progress, no result, and had been frustrating and futile.

On 11th August I received a threatening letter. A Formal Letter - Notice of Intention to File for Default and to Take Action to Recover the Debt. It went on to say that if they did not receive payment or satisfactory arrangements for payment within 28 days then credit reference agencies would be informed, and explained the ugly consequences. I happened to know that all missed payments are recorded in any case! It went on to say, 'all your standing orders and direct debits will be cancelled'!!!!!!! Responsibility for recovery will pass to Debt Recovery Area and only credits on my account will be accepted. My cheque guarantee card is cancelled, they told! There was no invitation to phone – just a number. The notices were for sums of £2,070.82 (current account) and £18,846.85 (loan account).

I was incensed, distressed and worried. I became very anxious. I remember feeling tightness in my chest. I could not concentrate and could not work. What made things worse was the frustration. I had tried desperately hard to communicate and make my point. To be heard. Yet I continued to receive repeated notices and threats that indicated to me that a 'machine' was operating a system designed to 'pound' me relentlessly, to worry me into 'doing something' I could not do. There seemed to be no human, and certainly no humane, input or consideration.

I wrote on 12th August reiterating my position in reply. On 20th August I received a letter from Barry Eldridge of Natwest Customer Relations in relation to a complaint that I had filed with their Financial Ombudsman's Service. I have no recollection or copy correspondence relating to it, and can only assume that I wrote at a particularly dispirited time. At any rate, Natwest acknowledged my complaint and I responded in mine of 31st August and enclosed mine of 12th August.

In a letter dated 3rd September my correspondence was acknowledged by Noreen King and I was promised an investigation and response by 22nd September.

On 5th September I wrote to Barry Eldridge at Customer Services and asked him to note that the Consumer Credit Counselling Service was acting on my behalf and I asked for suspension of charges.

I received a letter dated 13th September from Customer Services referring me to the Collections Team and giving me a telephone number. The letter indicated that the staff would be able to reach an agreement with me. I was hopeful that the hounding would now stop. I tried on a number of occasions to phone the number given but I could not get through.

I wrote on 21st September complaining of the bank's failure to listen and act upon my instructions and also regarding charges. On 29th September I received another repetitive standard letter advising me of a bounced direct debit of £383.

I immediately wrote and warned them of harassment practices. I received a letter from Ms Tsitsi G of Customer Services on 7th October acknowledging mine of 21st September. She reiterated the request that I phone the Collections Team and make proposals. I telephoned the number given as instructed. It was the same as the previous number given. I was assured that the matter would be dealt with.

I was given the wrong number. It was the Complaints Team, and after explanation they transferred me to another number…the Mortgage Collections Team…they transferred me, I spoke to Rachel, I was given some bank details but I can't remember what they pertained to, she transferred me to another number and there was no reply. I was being driven mad!

Was this just gross incompetence or was there an element of deliberate 'piss taking'. Was I deliberately being sent from 'pillar to post'.

In a letter dated 25th October Birmingham Collections Centre advised me of my loan shortfall and that my current account was now overdrawn to the tune of £2,182.13, in excess of the agreed overdraft by £182.13.

I wrote to Ms G of the Customer Relations Department on 25th and 28th October. I complained that direct debits were still being bounced and I was still being charged. One of the direct debits was for just £4!!!!. I asked for the direct intervention by Customer Services.

I received a further standard letter notifying me of a direct debit bouncing. The Natwest loan again! This really was becoming a worry and tremendous strain for me. Increasing costs, threats and refusal to deal with my correspondence and complaints. I was in despair. I dreaded the 'postman's knock' and the ring of the telephone. I was suffering stomach discomfort, acid stomach and sleeplessness. I was sometimes tearful, sometimes angry and sometimes even thinking suicidal thoughts.

I received a letter from Ms G dated 28th October. It was far from apologetic, in fact very matter of a fact. The £4 direct debit has been cancelled (at last), but I was told that the bank will continue to attempt to draw the £383 that they knew was not there. 'They have the contractual right to do so' I was told. Ms G wrote that colleagues had attempted to contact me on 28th October but because I would not reveal security information about myself they would not talk to me. I was being obstructive was the suggestion. I was given another (a different) number to contact the Collections Team on.

I wrote back to Ms G to explain my refusal to speak to the person on the phone. I don't give information about myself to incoming callers I did not know. I am happy to return a call and give my security information once I knew who I was talking to, and after I was assured that they had read my correspondence and knew the history of my case.

302

I was being bombarded by debt collection correspondence. I had other less significant debts. Natwest were well aware of these other debt as they contribute to the maintenance of the Credit Reference Agents together with other banks and financial institutions. It was clear to me that I was being deliberately harassed.

Between 2nd and 11th November I received 4 correspondences from Birmingham Collection Centre. In a letter dated 1st November I was notified of my loan shortfall and my overdraft running at £2,286.93 and asking me to note that if the position continues I shall receive formal default notices!!!! Hadn't I had them? I was given seven days for the accounts to be brought up to date. A letter dated 4th November demanded that I pay £21,880.02 by 12th November. I must write or phone with proposals if I could not pay in the allotted time.

In the correspondence dated 10th November I received 'formal notice of intention to file for a default and to take action to recover' the personal loan, threatening again to refer the matter to credit reference agencies and again notifying me that my cheque card had been cancelled. An Office of Fair Trading default information sheet, not the first I had received, was enclosed.

I received another letter dated 10th November, identical to the other, relating to my current account. The sum was now £2,346.95. A default charge notice of £30 was attached.

Natwest were tightening the screws. They were ignoring me, yet demanding of me. The lack of attention was intimidating as were the repeated demands. Even the silence was intimidating.

On 10th November I spoke with a Natwest employee on the telephone, and, following a very amicable and understanding conversation I formulated the opinion that my offer of £50 per month was acceptable, paid quarterly. This exceeded the sum suggested to me by the Consumer Credit Counselling Service but made me feel quite good. However, in a letter dated 21st November, Ms G of Customer Relations, explained that my offer of the10th was declined by the Collections Team and that they were transferring the matter to the Credit Management Services Team.

The letter gave the impression that this had been stated to me at the time of the telephone conversation. I was left in total despair, angry, and somewhat amazed. I was seriously distressed as it was now clear to me that the bank were giving me a very hard time and that nobody was prepared to take responsibility, help or progress matters. They were torturing me.

My letter of 24th November contained another allegation of harassment. A further letter from Birmingham collections notified me of an unpaid direct debit for £383, and of course an unpaid item fee. I then received a final letter from Ms G noting that my letter of 24th November crossed with hers of 21st. she made no reference to the content of my letter and, almost as if she was taking the final sarcastic swipe at me, she enclosed a 'Moneysense' brochure which, 'she hoped I would find helpful'. I was shaken to the core with rage.

Hot on the trail of the Customer Services letter came letters from the new boys; the Debt Collection Centre in Birmingham. Their letter dated 2nd December contained the usual notice under the Consumer Credit Act relating to the loan account. The letter was duplicated, so I could read it twice!

The letter did, of course, advise me that I would receive one at least every six months. The pressure machine moved relentlessly forward. I decided that I would not contact the bank again. Christmas was nearing, I had some work in the Midlands that would hopefully provide a short term, if not long term future income, and I was mentally exhausted. I would stop in Coventry at my Mum's for a few weeks. I'll explain about my move later.

In the New Year, I received two further correspondences. My mail had been re-directed. Firstly, a Termination Notice in relation to my current account from more new boys; the Credit Management Services in Telford. This letter was dated 31st December 2008.

Secondly, a letter for other new boys Triton Credit Services of Telford dated 24th December 2008. They identified themselves as 'a specialist Debt Collection organization appointed by their client 'Natwest Bank'. They demanded I contact them to make payment within seven days or, if I was in financial difficulties, contact them immediately to discuss alternative options. If I did so, they could protect my credit rating (ha ha).

Both letters were received as redirected post. The second letter was intimidating, but particularly annoying given that on 30th December, I had received a telephone call as I was leaving my home in Berwick to travel to my family in the Midlands for the New Year.

On the afternoon of 30th December I received a telephone call at my home from a company purporting to be agents of Natwest. It was Triton. I explained that I had not been notified of the involvement of any agent and that I would not speak with them. The male caller asked me who I was. He told me the call was being taped. He stated that he needed to ask security questions and I refused. He asked if I would take a number and call back. I said that I would but that it was not convenient that day because I was packing to travel to my family for the New Year. I would call in the New Year. He told me it would be too late and that Natwest 'were closing in on me'. He put the phone down.

The distress and misery created for me over the festive season, as a result of this call, was such that I wrote to Ms G without delay on 1st January 2009. I complained about the call.

It was outrageously blatant intimidation, and a County Court Judge was later to agree with me. I wrote advising her of my new postal address, my mothers in Coventry. I demanded an inquiry. I demanded that they listen to the tape of the call.

I advised (again) that, because of my employment prospects and the sale of my mini. I hoped shortly to be able to pay the arrears and then 'interest only' for the time being. I also had substantial equity that would pay the money owed, once sold.

My New Year was ruined. I was devastated and psychologically damaged by the events over the holiday period.

In a letter dated 8th January 2009, to my new address, Ms G dealt with my complaint. She explained that the call had been from Credit Management Services Team to discuss a repayment plan. Triton were actually Natwest 're-branded'.

They could not proceed with the call because of the security issue; emphasis on my refusal. It was claimed that correct call handling procedures were followed and she expressed her sorrow that I felt intimidated and apologized for any upset. She explained that her colleagues were keen to assist me and restated the bank's duty regarding security.

I was also advised that solicitors had been appointed to recover the debt. I was refused the standing order details that I had requested because her colleagues had requested that I contact them on the number given. She refused to accept my address change! I was told to go to a branch!

I then received a letter from Shakspear Putsman, solicitors acting for the bank, dated Tuesday 13th January 2009 and demanding £24,184.63p. The letter indicated that proceedings would commence if they had not heard from me by 10.30am on 20th January

2009. This letter was directed to my Berwick upon Tweed address and re-directed by the Post Office.

I wrote complaining to the Chief Executive Officer of Natwest on 19th January 2009 and copied the letter to H.M. Treasury and Mr. Ken Clarke the Shadow Business Secretary. Only Ken Clarke, belatedly, took a sympathetic interest.

The car had been sold. I enclosed two cheques, one for £1,700 to pay off my current account overdraft, and one for £800 in respect of my loan account. I wrote the loan account number on the rear of the cheque. I again complained about my treatment.

I received a letter from Ms G dated 23rd January 2009 acknowledging receipt of the cheques. She asked that I urgently contact the Credit Management Team to arrange a repayment plan. I was invited to either telephone on one of the two numbers given or in writing to the address given, not the Triton address or number. They appear to have been withdrawn. I was told that control was with Credit Management Services and that the only way to resolve the matter was to contact them directly to discuss a payment plan and my concerns.

I telephoned both numbers on 9th February 2009. Both numbers were incorrect. I was again given the run-around. I was eventually able to speak with the correct department and was told that the matter was now with solicitors. I was given a reference and telephone number to contact them on.

I telephoned solicitors, Shakspear Putsman. The reference number was not recognized. I spoke with a Mr James Morgan. I explained my problems to him in detail. He thought that the situation was unusual and irregular. He agreed to give me an email address to send all correspondence, to contact him on, and I sent the correspondence promised to him.

I wrote to the Chief Executive Officer of Natwest on 10th and 16th February 2009 and complained about the way I was being treated and requested a copy of the taped conversation of 30th December. I again sent copies to the Treasury, the Shadow Business Secretary and the solicitor, Mr James Morgan.

I received a letter from Ms G dated 23rd February in response to mine of 10th and 19th February. She indicated that where solicitors are instructed it is bank policy to refer the customer to the solicitors. Please contact James Morgan. The file had just been transferred to his firm when I contacted him (on 9th February). She went on to say that the banks litigation team had agreed that I could have until 6th March to lodge a defence to the Court or forward repayment proposals to them.

I was informed that the taped conversation had been destroyed following quality control review, and that this matter had in any case been dealt with in her letter of 8th January. I was reminded that it was my responsibility to ensure that my address was kept up to date.

On 2nd March I wrote my final letter to them although I knew the contents to represent a futile demand and inevitably a negative response.

A letter from the Customer Relations Manager, Miss Staveley, and dated 17th March confirmed my view. I was informed of my right to refer the matter to the Financial Ombudsman's Service who offer an independent arbitration service, but would not deal with the matter if I pursue the harassment issue through the Court.

What was happening to me was a mixture of incompetence, arrogant disregard, and downright harassment. I still feel I was subject of deliberate baiting.

There was subtlety in the approach taken by Natwest staff, and deliberate concealment of damning evidence.

The way they go about debt collecting is not helpful and it is not friendly. They demonstrate an arrogant disregard for any customer proactivity that does not meet with their own demands and requirements. Their systems are deliberately designed to pressure and intimidate.

A system that ignores correspondence and creates unwarranted and distressing results represents harassment and cannot be legitimized by hiding behind the system. They cannot hide behind their computer generated system. They cannot claim that they were 'stretched' by the volume of work. The telephone calls caused me anxiety and distress, in particular the wicked way in which I was treated on 30th December 2008 and the manner in which they treated me following my complaint of January 2009.

Not listening can in itself cause anxiety and distress. It did. I told the bank exactly what my financial position permitted me. I was led to believe, after an extensive and detailed explanation given during a telephone conversation in November that the offer I had been making from the outset was to be accepted only to be told by Customer Services that it had not.

And still they came at me. Like a machine rolling relentlessly forward. Like a steamroller. Threat after threat, veiled and brazen. All this, knowing full well of other creditors that were also chasing settlement of their debts.

Natwest, 'the helpful bank' is anything but. They have a wicked disregard for anything but money, as my experience demonstrates.

Such was my disgust at the banks reluctance to help me that I wrote to the Prime Minister in August 2008 and subsequently involved the Shadow Government. .

There is little hope for other weaker and less able citizens of this country, of defending themselves against corporate bullying. Natwest, and some others, create an illusion of helpfulness, because they must. The sinister reality is that they don't care 'a tinker's cuss' about the personal banker. People are mere commodities that are dealt with ruthlessly and with merciless savagery.

To this day I cannot accept bank behaviour. I had equity in two properties that even at a conservative estimate amounted to £150,000. Both these properties had been advertised for sale in order to meet my obligation to pay Natwest around £20,000. They knew this when they decided to take me to Court.

So why did they take me to Court? Well quite simply to punish me for having the audacity to complain about them on a range of debt collecting issues – in particular harassment.

There are others being bullied out there without the strength, know-all, the help, the time, the inclination, nor courage, nor the means to stand up for justice and human rights.

I counter-claimed against the bank for harassment. The task of preparing my case caused me stress and anger. I again represented myself.

Natwest inflated their claim with charges and interest. They failed to credit my loan account with the £800 cheque paid to them in the January. They used the £800 to pay disputed current account fees that were subject of a separate dispute.

In January 2009 Natwest proceeded at speed to appoint solicitors after my complaint concerning the harassment during the Christmas break, yet continued to pressure me to negotiate a settlement. They did so even after solicitors had been appointed.

I had been bombarded with letters, but complaints and issues were not fully addressed, and sometimes ignored completely. They were grossly unfair and unreasonable in their handling of the matter.

I had my Court hearing. The Judge stated that the telephone call that I had received between Christmas and New Year was definitely harassment and asked that this be brought to the attention of the bank. He was however unable to agree that the harassment was enough to satisfy the requirements of the 1997 legislation. The law requires there to be two separate and distinct instances, and there was only one that was recognised by the law.

I borrowed money from my sister and I agreed an out of Court settlement. I did of course pay her back. I have been waiting for Natwest to inform me of the outcome of the Judge's condemnation of the Natwest gift of a 'Christmas Kiss'. I'm not holding out any hope. They don't even reply.

2009 – Almost out of the fire?

Despite the above, in autumn 2008 there were signs that things were starting to look up. I was skint and I had debts, but I was starting to feel the blood flow a little faster, and felt a surge of confidence coming on! Was I on the up? Was it a false dawn?

I had been convalescing in Berwick upon Tweed, my retreat three miles south of the dark side – Scotland - on the East Coast (I jest). I had squandered money, ignoring the fact that I no longer had my usual income, and yet secured good investments; a cottage by the sea and an apartment paid for with cash drawn from the collateral on the cottage.

I had been drinking for three years in Berwick, socially in the main as I was lonely. I was now more relaxed and content than I had been for years. I hadn't worried. I was only drinking beer and wine, and not the hard stuff. I had suffered multiple traumas of such great intensity that I needed a diversion, and what better ways than after a fun time down the pub! I was off the happy pills. I needed the company of a crowd. Social interaction over a few pints is good for you-I don't care what anyone says-it works for me!.

However, these lost years had taken their toll: I would have difficulty finding employment. The Credit Crunch had arrived – several years later than I had predicted.

Berwick was, and is, a great place to get back on your feet. A beautiful Elizabethan walled town on the famous salmon river called the Tweed. The harbour, the sea, the sand, and the beautiful surrounding Border Country represented great therapy. My dog Jack was my close companion. However, Berwick was not giving me work and I needed to find some source of income; and fast.

In 2007 I had qualified as a Part P Electrician and an Electrical Tester. I also attended a week long course at the Centre of Alternative Technology in Wales to learn about solar water power and about how to install a domestic installation (BPEC certification). I had qualified as a Portable Appliance Tester.

I found, with some satisfaction, that I could be a practical chappy after all! And yet I was missing a couple of key ingredients that had never been missing before my career and marriage failure; confidence and a helping hand. I'd lost my mojo baby. I became fearful. I was still suffering anxiety and trauma. Anyhow, I wasn't an experienced enough worker for self-employment and nobody would be offering help to potential future competition in a small town. On reflection I should have left Berwick to run my own business selling services, and using 'real' tradesmen to do the work. Too much was going on. I missed the opportunity.

In autumn 2008 I saw the light; or rather a beacon of hope appeared. My debts, my life, would become manageable if I could find a modest income. An opportunity to return to my old stamping ground in Northamptonshire offered the chance.

An old friend asked me to house sit his bungalow and run his part time taxi service taking 40% of takings. Wow! Yes! It was from December till the end of February 2009.

The vision: rent out the cottage, and then down to my old stamping ground for Christmas, earn some money from the taxi, hopefully more from plumbing and electrical work and re- appraise the situation when Geoff returned from holiday at the end of February. Perfikt! Not!

In October 2008 I unexpectedly lost the Estate Agent case that I had been defending. I owed £2,400 to be paid by November's end. You will recall my earlier account of this. A nasty greedy estate agent sued me for half agency fees when I pulled out of house sale just days after it was agreed in principle, but just a day or two after my wife was committed to a mental institution! Could I really have proceeded with a sale?

310

It was the first time I had lost (outright) a legal battle, so, despite the fact that the action was immoral, and the judgement, in my view unjust. I accepted it. The Judge recognised that the basis for my defence was groundbreaking (there was no legal precedence) and think that he sidestepped it. I could not afford to appeal and in any case I was tired and fed up with the years of fighting. I accepted it with some 'grinding of teeth'. I think that if I had been properly represented I would have won!

I could not pay. I wanted time. They would not give it. I had to find the money quickly. Interest was accruing at the rate of 8%. Where do you get 8% interest these days? The courts!

I turned to the action that I was holding in abeyance; my other outstanding legal action – my case against CCS. They had settled out of Court for Unfair Dismissal but I had held some argument and action in reserve and immediately upon settlement, I had given them notice of my intention to sue for failing to provide a safe place of work under Health and Safety Legislation.

I took the £5,000 offered and closed the case before Xmas. I also sold my mini for £3,500 after months of waiting. It was a classic car in immaculate original condition.

I paid off money owed on a settee, a Natwest overdraft and part of a loan, and then paid off £2,000 of the judgement sum. Natwest were harassing me and in the words of their agent, 'closing in on me'.

The taxi business did not provide the income I had expected over 'The Season of Good Will' and then, after Geoff's departure, disaster struck!

I crashed the taxi in the snow. I lost the taxi phone; I damaged the rear light on my Honda S2000, the alternator on my van packed up, and then a leak developed in the power steering fluid supply. Oh yes, and this was when Natwest appointed solicitors and served a summons on me for recovery of debt.

The only wonderful thing that happened to me during my two months in Northamptonshire was meeting Jackie. Blond, beautiful Jackie – 44 but looking 34 – sexy intelligent and understanding. My first 'girlfriend' since being a teenager. The first woman in whose eyes I actually saw stars. No snowflakes. Love?

311

I burnt her saucepan when attempting to prepare her a Valentines' Day Dinner!! I couldn't cope with the angry response, I was still very vulnerable, and as a result I drifted away.

In January and February of 2009 I earned nothing and forked out £300 policy excess on Geoff's insurance, £80 for a new phone, £200 for a new alternator, £40 for the power steering problem, etc, etc. You've gotta laugh otherwise you cry.

Old Stamping Grounds

The great thing about getting back in my old stamping ground was catching up with old friends, being close to Katy, my parents, and meeting Jackie. I was swept off my feet.

I had the first meaningful sex in years, and with the first woman that I thought, "Yes. This might be the one". If not, I was going to enjoy every minute I could in her company. The sex was mind-blowing"!

I felt loved. My old friends and acquaintances were pleased to see me. They missed me. They remembered me.

It was like I had never left the village when I made that first appearance through the door at The Royal Oak (Weasel Central). The pub has always been my second home. I felt good again. I was amongst old friends. Nothing appeared to have changed. I loved it. It felt like home. I felt comfortable and welcome.

I took a six week gym membership at my old fitness centre and worked out four to five days a week, another positive to offset my catalogue of bad luck. At least I was getting myself fit again.

Reflection

By March 2009 I was back in Berwick. I asked myself, 'Where am I now?". I wrote down my thoughts of the day. I must have had a bad day! These thoughts, as I read them now, demonstrate to me how screwed up I could still get at this time. I'm embarrassed by them, but here they are-

"I am devastated; dead in the water! The word 'futility' comes to mind. The words 'frustrated' 'cheated' 'legally conned' 'labelled' 'misunderstood' 'let down by the system' come to mind.

Katy is sad and terribly traumatised, Zoe distant and quiet. My parents worried and probably traumatised; the misery I have brought to them is undeserving of their dedication and love to family.

I am asset solvent but my creditors are intent on stripping me of them despite my willingness and insistence that I will pay them back. I just need time. The creditors shamelessly and ruthlessly grind out a protracted pressure. Their position is simple; we want our money and we want it now!

I will probably need, within the next few days, to come to terms with the fact that I am not yet experienced enough to undertake full electrical testing; I have not been motivated enough to 'get on the bike' after initial training. I have forgotten what to do. Nor have I been motivated enough to take up Hypno- psychotherapy-something I was good at - or plumbing – something I was OK at. I am crap at electrical work..

I have my small pension; have a little electrical work, fifteen hours per week looking after an MS sufferer, but not enough to pay my bills. I must sell; but will I have time?

I feel tired, defeated and void of a great deal of my old determination. I hate the establishment and their entire 'old boy' network. My marriage is lost. I am reluctant to get involved with a woman. Is it worth getting involved? Frying pan into the fire?

I have long been angry at the inappropriate and almost obscene use of the word 'poverty' in the context of any form of living in the UK. People should experience first hand the life lived by the inhabitants of the shanties and on the rubbish tips in Manila and Jakarta. I saw it in Manila and in Jakarta this Century. You have to smell it, hear it, and touch its people; seeing it on television does not capture the depravity. And yet these people often seem more cheerful than the average frowning, miserable bad tempered moaning Brit! What have we become?

I am presently feeling ashamed. Ashamed at the fact that I can indulge myself in self pity while the enduring, suffering underprivileged billions in this World go about their daily business with dignity, and my respect. I can only take comfort in the fact that I know that too many people in the wealthy West are less sensitive than I am; either through ignorance or disregard.

313

I at least take 'the mirror test', taught to me by my beloved Mum. At least I have maintained a self appraisal and improvement programme throughout my life, even if I have transgressed my own rules and on a few occasions, the law. I have at least felt guilt and shame. Put into context I know that I am a good and essentially honest person, and, if there is a God, then he will allow me through the Pearly Gates.

I love, but fail to demonstrate it. I think that I am frightened to do so for fear of being hurt again. I am selfish and self centred in some respects, a hypocrite in some others, I can be cruel in condemnation and very hurtful to my loved ones; although not intentionally. I am a contradiction in my own mind let alone the minds of some others. I know that I can give the wrong signals; the wrong impression. I think that this occurs when I am trying to impress people. I should stop trying to do it.

I think I shall throw in the towel and try to live a penniless yet stress-free simple life with my dog Jack; a simple uncomplicated life."

But this dark account was not with me all the time; I was lifted out of the gloom by my own strength, the support of my family, and on occasions the shoulders of good friends. I had become withdrawn, and yes, I thought that I would be a nuisance to people; on the other hand I hoped that friends would recognise my despair and rally round me. I was being naive. Few people have the time or inclination to comfort others.

I received a telephone call from Captain Kirk (Austin), a good friend from my days in Indonesia. He had been trying to track me down. It reminded me of how withdrawn I had actually become, I wasn't keeping in contact myself. He directed me to the internet – Kaptain's Blog. On the 21st November 2008 he had posted this poem. It made me feel very emotional.

WITHOUT TRACE, By the Kaptain

For Dave Wakefield, wherever you are.......

Did you go to ground?
Harried by the hounds?
Did it seem, that day
Like the only way?

Vanish without trace....

314

To some quieter place....

Did they bite your heels-?
Agents of ill-will?
Was it never clear
That we shared your fears?

Vanish without trace...
To a better place...

Was it stubborn pride
Made you run and hide?
Don't you know your friends?
Would have helped you then?

Vanish without trace...
To an unknown place....

You're missed my friend
Please send a sign
To show us you're alive....
Return again
To make us smile....
We'll help you to survive...

I think you'll understand why it made me emotional. Cousin Sue, Steve and Chris Poole were always there for me. Paul Hough phoned me quite often; so did Jim Jameson (usually when he was pissed), Trisha was a comfort, and renewal of old friendships with Baz Bennett, Alan and Derek Blakemore an escape and a distraction, but that Kirk should have hit so many chords choked me.

Blog comments were typically mixed.

'Nice one Kaptain. Let's hope Wakefield is still out there somewhere, murmuring "You're nicked mate" and arguing the merits of Coventry FC. Still rcmember fondly the crazy Indian lunches with party hats and Bollywood's finest on the DVD. Ah precious memories.....'
And

'You spittin some sick beats man'.

More recently Jim Kirk and Brad Berg offered to pay my flight to Bahrain and Indonesia. I declined, but again I was choked. What good mates.

The Bank of Scotland (or are they Capital Bank? Or Black Horse?)

My creditors had not finished with me yet. Bank of Scotland (BoS) was on my case regarding my outstanding car loan. BoS, well I'm not sure, because I was getting harassed by their subsidiary Capital Bank as well!

I had been receiving messages on my home and mobile numbers. My letters were being ignored. I had repeatedly asked that they communicate concerning my debt by letter. I repeatedly indicated that a repayment agreement was in place.

In early September 2009 I received another series of such calls despite my repeated instruction concerning phone calls. I answered one such call inadvertently. I was at my sister's house in Coventry at the time. My father was dying.

I wrote angrily to Mr Richard Hawthorne, an Associate Director of Bank of Scotland on 16th September because of the anxiety, frustration, worry and anger he, and his colleagues were causing me. The letter was sent recorded delivery. The ultimatum letter is reproduced below.

"Further to my letter of the 31st August 2009 and all the previous correspondence that you have failed to reply to, I have no alternative but to give the bank a last and most serious warning.

It would seem that since mine of 31st the frequency of unsolicited calls from your office seem to have increased. I have indicated that I do not wish to be contacted by telephone. The conversations cause me anxiety and distress. I have an agreement in place. I would ask that you instruct Capital Bank and your own people to stop immediately.

If I receive one more telephone call from your office again I shall seek an injunction through the Courts to stop them.

316

Please note that this letter is recorded delivery and please note that I am happy to correspond by letter, and, if I feel well enough, I shall be prepared to phone an individual who is well acquainted with my case."

Upon return to Berwick I opened a letter from Central Collections Limited dated 31st October 2009 demanding an immediate payment and an immediate telephone call. The letter explained that as a consequence of the account being transferred to them, there was an additional £150 management fee.

This intimidation comprises deliberate disregard for written correspondence. Multiple and duplicated actions/ correspondence from Capital Bank and Bank of Scotland and the increasing pressure being applied by them, when they had been kept fully aware of my financial position and inability to pay more than the sum already being paid (£50 p.m.). The Consumer Credit Counselling Service recommended I just pay £1 p.m.

Furthermore they repeatedly asked me for information that had been sent several times over, and telephoned repeatedly to request that same information again!

It was driving me crazy! They were well aware that my inability to pay was temporary and that I would discharge my debt once assets had been sold. They now threatened me with Court action.

On the 4th November 2009, I received a telephone call on my mobile phone. The call was registered as 'No Number' so I could not have replied. I had received many of these calls over many months. A message had been left. I checked my message box. The message recorded was as follows, "This is a message for David Wakefield. Please call Central Collections on 0800 0157176 quoting reference number ..... ".

Listening to the message caused me great anxiety as had previous calls. It was received as I was just travelling back to Berwick upon Tweed from Coventry, where my father had been put to rest on Friday 30th October.

I was at Boroughbridge Service Station when I picked up the message. I felt tightness in my chest and stomach discomfort; nervous indigestion. I felt great anger and frustration. I spent the rest of the journey in a state of anxiety, anger and deep thought about how I was to stop the harassment being administered by the Bank of Scotland and Capital Bank. I was almost in tears and wanted to stop. I pulled over to compose myself.

317

I received another such call from an Andrew Finegan at 11.46pm on Saturday 7th November 2009. I decided to take action to prevent further harassment by applying for an injunction against these bastards. I took out an injunction to stop the bank, or their agents, telephoning me or visiting me.

They retaliated by seeking an inflated settlement of my debt. By this time the debt had been transferred to Black Horse, after a Lloyds Bank merger. There was a new loan account reference. I wondered if they had closed the account with BoS to make it look like they were clearing their own debts, and then opened an account with Black Horse to give the statistical appearance to Government that they were loaning money again. Despite a new reference being set up with Black Horse, BoS were taking control, and counter-claimed for retrieval of money under the old debt reference.

I thought the loan agreement was possibly illegal and flawed and stated my intention to defend their claim.

Luckily, by the time that the action reached Court I had sold my apartment and I was able to negotiate and settle all my debts. I was tired, very tired.

Believe it or not, there were other disputes too. Disputes with a credit card company, private car park companies, a pub bouncer, a nasty 'dog hating' woman, the council and retailers, but I'm tired of writing about all this shit, and you are probably tired of reading it!

I was heading toward 2011 debt free. I felt wonderfully at peace with myself and more relaxed than I could imagine.

Footnote

It's difficult to sift through the years 2003 to 2009 to find many good times; most good memories are shrouded by the bad. But there were some good times. I loved my travels, and, as ever, I enjoyed helping people and making them laugh.

I enjoyed telling my stories, and listening to others re-count theirs. I enjoyed my holiday in Cuba on the Ernest Hemingway trail. For the most part I enjoyed my trips to the Barrels Ale House and The Pilot Inn, my walks on the beaches and through the hills of 'the borders' with Jack.

318

Probably the greatest pick me up was the most valued of reunions; with Cousin Sue. My times with her and her work mates at the Tipperary pub near my home in Berkswell livened up many a lacklustre day during the period before my separation. We get on so well. She is a breath of fresh air.

That my sense of humour can be a little eccentric is demonstrated by the letter. I wrote to Colonel Gaddaffi seeking to secure financial backers for Coventry City Football Club, my beloved Sky Blues

21st January 2004

President,
Libya,
Africa

Dear Colonel Gaddaffi,

I am delighted that you have turned your back on weapons of mass destruction. Respect!

You must now be looking at new business opportunities, and my mate, Pierre Luigi (he knows your son, the one that plays for Perugia), tells me that Coventry City Football Club may be exactly the prestigious business investment opportunity that would suit you.

Coventry is a wonderful family football club and has a history of success – you will recall the 1987 Cup Final when they beat Tottenham Hotspurs in the FA Cup Final – my family were there! It was a great day.

Coventry City Football Club has a great tradition that dates back to the days before Jimmy Hill. Sadly, just a couple of years ago we were relegated to the First Division having held a Premier League position for over thirty threeyears. The people of Coventry are depressed about the Club's relegation and financial trouble. We need help!

Coming to the point - the Club is in debt to the tune of over $30,000,000 – they are broke! Realistically, we need to borrow about US$75,000,000.

We recognise that you have a family interest in football. And Steve, who sometimes works at the Railway Inn, and me, were wondering if you were prepared to loan the club the $75,000,000 required for us to help the club return to the Premier Division – where we belong! If you are, please contact "The Chairman', Coventry City Football Club,

Highfield Rd, Coventry, UK, mentioning 'Steve' at the Railway Inn, Berkswell, and me-an occasional customer. We are both passionate fans and would appreciate season tickets (for life) in return for successfully soliciting your support!

Sir, we know you have money, and would very much appreciate your support. You have become really quite popular here, and if you were in Coventry we would very much appreciate your attendance at the Railway Inn – even if you didn't provide the finance to the Club, as we would like. Tom will buy the beer!"

Bizarrely, not long afterwards, it was rumoured that he was interested in Crystal Palace!

My sense of humour has few bounds. Katy and her mates emptied my drinks cabinet. The morning casualties included my bottle of rare whiskey (raised from the SS Politician that was sunk during the war) and three bottles of House of Commons wine that I paid £120 for at a charity auction. Ha Ha Ha, it was so funny - not!

Then there was the pheasant that I hit approaching Jedburgh, in the Scottish borders. It travelled with me for sixty miles in the air intake of my car. Amazed to have found it, alive at that, on my arrival in Berwick, I took it in the pub for a pint while the assembled patrons decided what I should do with it. It was the only bird I ever picked up with that bloody sports car. Jack was the babe magnet!

During these difficult times I became much closer to my sister, without whose help my entire family would, at some time or another, have been helpless. Pete and Linda baled me out in more ways than one.

These last few words close a bleak chapter in my life; everyone has had, or will have one.

Chapter Twenty
Over My Shoulder

This might seem to be a surprising thing for you to read, particularly in the light of the last couple of chapters, but having thought long and hard about it, there is very little of my life that I would change if I had the opportunity. Every single moment has represented experience and character building; even the depths of despair can strengthen foundations of a character.

I have undoubtedly suffered wave after wave of post traumatic stress, and whether it amounts to a disorder is for shrinks to decide; but I won't allow them near me. The failures of unbridled capitalism and the social and mental health services of this country are responsible. How I have not topped myself is a mystery, but I am proud that I didn't have the courage. I have survived.

So where am I now; as of the beginning of 2012. Well. I still get myself into situations that I'd rather not be in. Here's an example.

Fight the Good Fight

On 22nd January 2012 I received a letter from Dr Peter Jefferys, an eminent geriatric psychiatrist, expressing his condolences on hearing of the death of Kathleen (Kath), an 85 year old friend of my family, in particular my Mum.

He wrote, "As someone who has been professionally committed to respecting the liberty of vulnerable individuals I welcome the initiative you took on Kathleen's behalf. Sadly very few people are prepared to take up the challenge as you did. I am sure she and her husband would be proud of you and your family".

He was referring to the Court action I had taken against Kathleen's niece, the closest of her surviving relatives. I received the letter with a feeling of sadness and a small amount of residual anger toward Kath's family.

Kath was a local girl and a friend of my Mum's for seventy three years; they were friends and confidantes since they were both aged thirteen.

Kath and Maurice were married in 1948, as were my parents, and they all remained united in friendship until my Dad died in October 2009 and Maurice died in May 2011.

Kath and Maurice were inseparable. They lost their only son through leukaemia when he was just seven years of age. They had no other family to speak of except their two nieces, one in Kent who they saw annually, the other in Lincolnshire whom they hadn't seen for several years.

They had lived their entire life in the same area, spent every Christmas at our family home and met or spoke with my Mum on a weekly basis. My Mum knew Kath for longer than anyone else still alive and 'their relationship possibly meant more to Kath than any single family member apart from Maurice' as Dr Jefferys put it.

Maurice was devoted to Kath and Kath depended upon Maurice for emotional support. When Maurice was admitted to hospital in April 2011, my Mum and my sister rallied around Kath and took her to Maurice's hospital bed side. They shopped for her; paid bills for her; entertained her (particularly on her birthday) and arranged for Social Services to support her at her home. Social Services kept her niece informed but she never turned up at Kath's side or lent a hand.

On the eve of Maurice's death one of his nieces arrived at the hospital and to the disgust of hospital staff and visiting friends, tried to persuade Maurice to sign a Power of Attorney document. Maurice died the next day and Kath was admitted to hospital for her own safety having been diagnosed with dementia.

Two days later a niece arrived and 'took control'. She prevented my family from contacting Kath and the hospital staff complied with this. Within a month Kath was placed in a care home near her niece which was over one hundred miles away. Her niece had concocted a story that Kath was under threat from my 'thieving family'. Social Services placed a safeguarding alert on Kath without question and not one of her friends or neighbours were permitted to contact her. The care home had enforced a 'deprivation of liberty'. Nobody affected was notified of alert, not even Kath!

During this period we did not know where Kath was and could not contact her. Another close friend of Kath's located her, discovered the ban and I immediately took action. Armed with contact details, I complained to Social Services and the care home. Within just a few days the safeguarding alert was removed and my family exonerated. There was not a shred of evidence, not even a hint of credible suspicion that my family were stealing from Kath or were otherwise behaving inappropriately. 'There are lessons to be learned' I was told.

Alarmed at the possible danger Kath was in, I decided to take the matter to The Court of Protection in London where I represented myself (as I have several times before) against barristers acting on behalf of Kath's niece, the County Council and the London Borough Council that initiated the ban. I insisted that Kath be returned to her 'homeland' where we all knew she wanted to be: close to the common grave of her son and husband, close to her friends and close to familiar surroundings.

Dr Jefferys had been belatedly appointed jointly by parties to the hearing to determine Kath's wishes and thoughts. I concurred with his findings. All parties at the hearing were quite clearly responsible for either illegally moving Kath and/or depriving her of her liberty; her human rights. The local authorities were slow producing their reports. Eventually, it was pretty much settled, by independent evidence and admissions made by the councils that Kath had been taken away by subterfuge, and had wanted to return home. She didn't want to be there so had been detained illegally; However, by November 2011 Kath had been taken into hospital for an operation. The prognosis was terminal cancer. She was in need of palliative care. She was dying. Kath's condition got the better of her and she was too unwell to return home. She died on 20th January 2012 blissfully unaware the selfish behaviour of her niece and gross negligence of the authorities.

I was executor to the last will and testimony of both Kath and Maurice and knew one of their nieces to be entitled to eighty six per cent of their estate. I knew because prior to his death, Maurice had consulted me on the subject of where he should leave their money.

I am currently carrying out the duties and responsibilities of executor, to the letter although suspect that if Kath had known of her niece's behaviour, she would have changed her will. Maurice would be rolling in his grave but I have chosen not to contest the will and to let sleeping dogs lie.

To their credit the County Council recognised their errors and promised that 'lessons had been learned' and that changes had been made as a result. The Borough Council have not responded. They initiated and enforced a 'deprivation of liberty' and didn't take any steps whatsoever to investigate if the niece was, as it turned out, making a malicious allegation. They have so far failed to respond to my insistence that this matter be communicated to other local authorities nationally so that this desperately sad ending of a life will never be repeated. It should be subject of a case study so that lessons will genuinely be learnt.

Kath's niece promised to return her ashes for internment with her son and husband. A week before the due date, as owner of the grave, she refused to allow internment before she was paid £380 of expenses. With my agreement, solicitors paid them. Forty eight hours before the internment, to the disgust of everyone from the priest to the solicitors, she telephoned the undertakers and refused to allow internment. We went ahead anyway.

Although like most people I am something of a contradiction at times, I am fundamentally honest. Money has, thankfully, never been a dominant reason for anything I have done in my life. Greed for money and power seem to me to be the foundation of all evil. Fending off 'the bad' and standing up for decency must have been my destiny. I've blundered like a fool and on occasions failed, but when I'm at my best I've prevailed. That alone I think makes my approach to life worthwhile.

Had my efforts to secure control of Kath's welfare succeeded before her death then she might have died a happier person. In my capacity as executor to the estate I visited Kath's bungalow and noticed a bible dated 1942. In it Maurice had written 'Fight the Good Fight'. Hence, 'Fight the Good Fight' had been on my list of possible titles for this book. I dedicate this book, in part, to Maurice and Kath.

Going Forward

I still find myself the butt of my own jokes. I like to make a fool of myself. There is one thing for sure; my future will not be without incident. It seems to be my destiny.

I have slowly but surely restored some of my old confidence. I am barmy again! I am playing the fool, joking around, and finding some sharp 'high risk' wit again. My slow recovery was apparent to me in 2010, my luck was still sporadic, but at least I was having some.

Clashes with authority will continue to arise I'm sure; mostly without any pre-emptive strike. By way of a short and comical anecdote, signs of my spluttering recovery, marked by setbacks, were apparent in 2010.

In 2010 things were apparently picking up, but I was still subject of bizarre incidents. In February 2010, when I was intending to start back in the gym again, I attended Sian's (Derek Blakemore's wife) Birthday Party at the Standard Triumph Club in Coventry.

I wasn't enthusiastic about going. I'd driven down from Berwick especially for that day. I was tired, and I was unhappy seeing Derek as an ill man. I was also still sore from a slip backwards on the stone slabs in the courtyard outside my apartment. To avoid hitting the back of my head I pulled it forward, pulling muscles in my neck, shoulders and stomach in the process. And, oh yes, the beer at the club was shit! But I didn't want to let Sian down, and so went.

I didn't complain about the beer, I didn't even mention it. I just drank a bad Guinness and then a pint of shandy. I felt tired and didn't feel very lively or sociable, but tried entertaining conversation and wit. But I wasn't going to last the evening.

Have you heard the one about the prawn that went to a dance and pulled a muscle? I didn't want to dance I told Sian several times. I was hurting, but each time she asked I felt guiltier because the dance floor was empty and she looked disappointed.

Madness struck up. It was 'Baggy Trousers'. "Come On" I said to Alan in a mad moment. I pranced out onto the dance floor like a dressage pony, suit jacket thrown back over my shoulders, and head bobbing back and forth like a chicken. The dance floor was soon full.

I bounced about on my toes like a twenty year old and then – like a sack of spuds – I dropped to the floor with excruciating pain in my calf muscle. 'Pop' it went, and 'down' I went. What a plonker!

I was on crutches and then a stick for weeks. My Achilles tendon had also 'pulled'. I couldn't work, but couldn't keep still. The nurses at the hospital were dancing in the corridor and singing 'baggy trousers'.

You will have spotted more than one of my 'Achilles heels' in the chapters that make up this book. I am working on healing all of them. I'm still on the road of self improvement.

Where I am now is not really an easy question to answer because I'm not sure I fully understand myself yet; which doesn't give others much of a chance does it? I'm an enigmatic character really, but I'll try to relate to you how I feel and where I think I am.

A couple of years ago I could have drawn some parallels with when I was sixteen years of age and a clueless Careers Officer asked me what I wanted to be. I was excited but apprehensive about what lay ahead of me, and concerned because I couldn't give a clear answer. Two careers have come and gone, and as I reflect, that is not a bad thing; not for me at any rate. Somewhere out there, there is a project, an opportunity that will provide me with the kind of stimulation that I need. The problem is finding it.

My marriage is over. Apart from Jackie, I have had two 'relationships' after my separation and in both cases they became far too intense for me. The ex-husband of the first girl was a 'nutter' who still thought he 'possessed' her, and that didn't help. I inexplicably walked away from the other. They were very tactile and affectionate, and yet I couldn't cope with it. It was exactly what I wanted and yet couldn't accept it. I was very fragile and I think I still am. I feel very vulnerable. I'm not sure that I understand women anyway.

I have female friends, Trisha, Cousin Sue, Suzanne, the barrels girls, Jaki (behind the bar at the Barrels) and Maddy Chandler (ex-Miss UK no less), to mention but a few, but romance is not in the air.

It is helpful to analyse my position in comparison to where I was in the early part of the new millennium. At that time I was at the peak of my career. Success breeds confidence and confidence breeds success. It's a fine line between success and failure, and confidence is a massive, massive ingredient in success. Determination and motivation is the driver. I'm not so determined these days; my batteries are low.

In 2004 the 'team profile' identified me as a person that is able to see the bigger picture, and the one person that can make dreams a reality. You could say that it is easy for me to agree with that analysis, and it is, but I also believe it to have been true at that time.

The report described me as a 'Thruster-Organiser' but I also scored highly as an 'Assessor-Developer' and as an 'Explorer-Promoter'. All very colourful gobble-de-gooch, but that's the modern world I suppose.

Thruster-Organisers are outgoing people who make things happen by organising people and materials so that ideas, discussions, and experiments are turned into action. They ensure that attention is focused on results. They enjoy meeting with others and discussing issues, but will do so primarily on the basis of facts. They will usually analyze in detail any information that they have at hand and then make their decision, based on what is necessary to ensure the satisfactory completion of the task. They concentrate on getting the job done in an efficient and effective way. They like to thrust forward into action by organising people and tasks.

My profile indicated that I can adopt the role of 'Assessor Developer' with ease. That I prefer a down to earth approach in my dealings with people and can at times be quite creative. That I don't always think up ideas for myself but, because of my extroversion, will interact with others working around me, and am quick to recognise the value of a new idea or approach, and will move on to implement it, provided it has a practical application, allowing me to achieve my goals more efficiently.

It is when I generate ideas that my belief in my ability to influence others is at its strongest. I can be quite lively and eloquent when supporting a new look at the way work is done. My ideas have usually been well thought out and I never let go of the practical aspects of what I am doing. I have an open mind and am quite receptive to change, but will usually want to assess new schemes in analytical fashion before pushing them in to action. I do not however want to leave things unfinished for too long and will want to push on to see how the new idea will turn out in practice.

I always try to put some structure to the way I work by setting deadlines and outputs, even if from time to time I miss them or have to rearrange them. However, it is my concern for having an efficient and effective team that can make me impatient with others when they do not fulfil my plans. At these times I speak my mind, but usually bear no grudges.

While my basic preference lies in the area of 'organising' the associated 'related roles' are an unusual configuration. Unlike some 'thruster-organisers' I have the ability to see the 'bigger picture' and the one person that can make dreams a reality.

In my 'explorer-promoter' role I enjoy the challenge of new projects and go out of my way to see that I am involved in them. If an idea captures my imagination I will be able to convince others to follow it, even if at times I have little hard evidence to support it. I usually have a network of colleagues and make it my business to find out what is going on in the organisation.

Now I repeat. I agree with all this, but I don't get carried away by it. The report drew attention to a number of weaknesses that I needed to work on; and I have. The one the family will love is that I can be impatient on occasions. I can also be impulsive. Given that you have just read my life history you can decide yourself how accurate the advice that the report gave me, is.

·At times, you need to analyse things more carefully before taking action. There is a tendency on occasions for you to want to push forward before all the planning has been done. Doing things and seeing the results are important to you, but success depends equally on listening to other people's ideas and careful planning. Be aware of the signs that your team members may not be following you and ask them how they can improve things rather than tell them yet again.

·Having people around to think through creative and innovative problems and provide ideas to positively challenge your own analysis is important. Your strength is making systems work. You can get things organized and translate ideas into practical output. You should make time to meet the 'Creator-Innovators', even though they may disturb the status quo. Either that or you may get left behind with an outmoded system. Provide your team with an opportunity to be constructively creative each year by having a one-or two-day workshop on 'new ideas' where 'thrusting and organising' takes second place to future options.

·It is useful to develop the skill of summarizing the views of others and reflecting their feelings before indicating your position if it differs from theirs. In this way, peoples' beliefs are acknowledged, even if they are not always accepted. You will also get a wider perspective on the problem, even though it may slow down the initial move to action. However the commitment of others can more than make up for this.

·You may need to spend more time gathering information where the problem is not a standard one. You may feel that time is being wasted and inefficiency is creeping in if too long is spent playing with ideas and collecting data. However, the higher you get in the organization, the more you will need accurate information. You will, therefore, need to build a team of people who can support you by supplying the data you need to come to a sensible decision.

I never got any real chance to apply this advice to my work, but I have applied myself and taken the advice into my private life. I am more patient and I listen more carefully. However, I recognize that at key moments in my life my weaknesses got the better of me, and when I was under sustained pressure in every facet of my life, I lost my discipline.

In the last few years I have ridden one hell of a storm. There have been false dawns, but slowly I have regained some of my strength. I believe I will find my exciting challenge and I may find the right girl, but I'm in no real rush. The qualities that I know I have will eventually reap reward.

I cannot say I'm happy; I'm sometimes contented and sometimes I'm unhappy. On the other hand there are occasions when I think I am more contented in life than I can ever remember. I still have the occasional brief short spell of depression, but at a normal level and less frequently. I need 'a break' of the kind that I've had before, but then my age is against me, and I have no money to launch my own business.

When I start to feel low, and that's not very often these days, I remind myself of the long good times and how lucky I have been in life. I remind myself of how much worse things could be, and how much worse things have been for others; those less fortunate. And I smile.

I make my usual point of saying good morning to almost everyone I pass in the street. I keep smiling. I am confident that once my batteries are fully recharged, my life will be back on track. I must however admit that I can no longer deal with stress in the way I have in the past. In fact I don't want to. I have less energy and I'm not as sharp as I once was.

I have done some care work, some portable appliance testing, a little electrical work and some plumbing, but I have never developed my new skills and don't think that I want to, or ever wanted to. I was keeping my brain exercised. I have stacked shelves at Argos and delivered pizzas at the local Holiday Park.

Last year I started a summertime business selling fresh fruit and ice cream on the historic Elizabethan Berwick town walls. Owning my own business is going to be the way forward. Selling ice cream gives me inter-action with the public, fresh air and a challenge. I am regarded as quite a novelty riding my tricycle along the street wearing a striped jacket and boater. I add some character and vibrancy to a town that has been neglected by its representatives and a handful of greedy selfish people that seem to control the place. I have a part time job at Currys as a 'senior trainee sales assistant' and appear to being fast-tracked towards the C.E.O.'s position - not!

I have become passionate about Berwick and it is where I expect to die- eventually but I'm not quite ready yet, I feel there is travelling to be done. I love the place, but I am becoming increasingly irritated by the dysfunctional nature of the local authorities and their leaders. Many public servants behave like little Hitler's, particularly the 'heads of local authority departments. Were these 'decision–makers' ever elected? The place needs innovative and imaginative input. Imagination is more important than knowledge! I have been encouraged to enter politics. I am certainly becoming a bit of an activist, but I don't think so.

Many of the wealthier people of the town are either "I'm alright Jack" or only interested in putting into the town what they can get out. The town needs to be driven in a progressive imaginative manner, but its not, and self interest seems to trump the general good. It's a bit of a plutocracy really.

"It's the way it's always been"; "You can't change anything"; "Oh you think it hasn't been tried"; "You're wasting your time".....all these are common answers to my view that the town is hamstrung by cronyism. Certain people in the town are suffocating it with their own self-interest. If they don't get a piece of the cake then nobody else does!

The wider interests of the people take back stage. I have observed this at local authority level in many places I've lived. Is Berwick Upon Tweed any different? To date my view is 'no'. Indeed it is perhaps worse than other places because Berwick is some isolated obscure town in a remote corner of England, and some distance from the heartbeat of Newcastle and Edinburgh. It is easy to get the impression that Northumberland County Council disregard Berwick. Maybe they would prefer it to be part of Scotland. Many of the towns' people are understandably apathetic.

The town needs to start with generating its tourism; so important to Berwick. The English Heritage informed me that visitor numbers to 'the barracks' have dropped from 24,000 in 2002 to 10,000 in 2011. Why? English Heritage have no idea how to promote tourism, neither it seems do the council. Quite simply - the town is neglected devoid of imaginative radical and inventive driving force.

Unsightly private and council property sit on the flagship attraction (the Berwick walls) and the lack of anywhere for tourist coaches to park and the failure to develope the quay and a marina are all as a result of successive councils failure to act and see the bigger longer term picture.

Enough about Berwick. I have two lovely grandchildren; both four years of age, and two daughters that I love dearly. Their happiness is paramount. Nikki has a decent guy, coincidentally named Dave. They have been together since our separation. We get together from time to time and things are pretty cool.

To be happy is to make others happy. I like to make others happy, laugh and smile. I will never stop trying whatever the cost.

330

The days of my life that have been squeezed into this book have, in general been magnificent. Baby boomers were born into an age that probably represents 'the best of British'. Today's teenager is highly unlikely to have the kind of opportunities that we, the baby boomers, have had. Some of my experiences are virtually impossible to duplicate today. I have been very lucky.

When I reflect on all the things I've seen and done I realise that I have already 'lived a life' and that I have been a very lucky man. And I again smile. I have learnt a lot from my mistakes, and tried not to make them again, but sometimes I do. Nevertheless, the journey from child to mature adult is an ever evolving one, and undoubtedly an older man is a wiser man. I can only get better!

I am reasonably content visiting the Pilot and Barrels pubs, attending the weekly 'Monday Club' and the annual 'Oliver Reed' and 'Dave Days'(6th June is D Day). I enjoy the banter and the contact that selling my ice cream on 'the walls' provides. I enjoy walks with Jack. I have some good friends and many friends-cum-acquaintances. I have an appetite for a stress-free challenge that will suit my general 'jack of all, master of none' talents. I am confident of finding that challenge.

I will never be the person I was, for obvious reasons, but as this last chapter of my life so far closes, a new one opens. It is likely to be eventful whatever happens. Maybe I'll get round to writing about it.